WITHDRA

9780802200990

REBIRTH AND DESTINY OF ISRAEL

DAVID BEN GURION
Prime Minister, State of Israel

Rebirth and Destiny of ISRAEL

Edited and translated from the Hebrew under the supervision of Mordekhai Nurock, *Minister of Israel in Australia*

PHILOSOPHICAL LIBRARY
NEW YORK

119877

COPYRIGHT, 1954
BY PHILOSOPHICAL LIBRARY, INC.
15 EAST 40TH STREET, NEW YORK 16 N. Y.
ALL RIGHTS RESERVED
DESIGNED AND COMPOSED
BY THE POLYGLOT PRESS, NEW YORK
PRINTED IN THE UNITED STATES OF AMERICA

TRANSLATOR'S NOTE

As editor and translator of this collection of Essays and Addresses by David Ben Gurion, now Prime Minister of the State of Israel, as they were delivered or written by him over the years from 1915 to 1952, I have felt a responsibility of almost historic moment.

For here, in power and sweep, in unbroken development, and constant enrichment, is the essence of the personal and public philosophy of one of the greatest of living Jews. Farm-worker and soldier, labor organizer and champion of Zionism, author and scholar with ancient Greek and Sanskrit at command, and now unchallenged for statecraft and statesmanship in a sovereign Israel which is so much his—that is the multifarious man. He uses a Biblical Hebrew grandly repetitive and of mounting parallelisms, iridescent, ringing and exact. In very truth, there is in his speech and writings, as in the bold imagination and faith of his leadership, not a little of the stuff of prophecy. So I have striven always towards an English akin to that of Bible versions, and if at times I have succeeded only in producing a condensed obscurity or too precious an archaism, or if I have indulged overmuch in alliterativeness, as a counterpart of the echoing Biblical phrases, the fault is not in the original. The Hebrew of Ben Gurion runs naturally, limpid, and at home.

The normal test of translation is that the translator present an expression that parallels the original utterance, that he convey faithfully the intention of the author, devise a matching linguistic rhythm and, of course, render with verbal precision, neither distorting nor clouding. But the heart of the matter is this: can you say: reading the translation, that if the author had himself written in the language of it, it would have read more or less as it now does? I think so, and hope others will. No doubt, recurrences will be found, but there are certain thoughts and pronouncements of Ben Gurion which do and must recur and I regard it as important that—by the indulgence of the editor—they should be reiterated also in the language of the translator. I record my very deep appreciation of the painstaking and comprehensive work of first translation that was done by Leah Ben-Dor, by Pinchas Rimon and Moshe Louvish in Israel, whereby my own labors were incalculably lightened.

CONTENTS

PRELUDE:

Earning a Homeland	3
In Judea and Galilee	7
Zionism—the Hard Way and the Easy	28
The Key to Immigration	41
Jewish Labor: the Origin of Settlement	45
Our Account with the British	84
On Three Fronts	89
A Nation in its Fight for Freedom	105
Test of Fulfillment	113
The Imperatives of the Jewish Revolution	133
Terrorism or Constructive Effort	142

Reply to Bevin	151
Unity and Independence	176
Address to the Anglo-American Committee of Enquiry	190
Preparing for the State	210

THE WAR OF INDEPENDENCE:

Introductory	223
With Strength and Understanding	227
The Four-Month Battle	234
A Review of the Military and Political Situation	240
The Cease-Fire	246
Peace and War	248
The 'Altalena'	251
Preparing to Meet the Future	261
Meeting the Future	265
Freedom and Independence	274
The Southern Front	281
In Lieu of a Summary	288
The Road of Valor	294

The Navy, Israel and the Sea 298

Mission and Dedication 314

PERFORMANCE:

Two Years On 359

Laws or a Constitution? 363

Civil Defense 381

Israel's Foreign Policy 391

The Call of Spirit in Israel 399

Israel Among the Nations 442

STATESIDE:

America and World Future 523

To America's Jewry 528

REBIRTH AND DESTINY OF ISRAEL

TO THE AMERICAN READER
Author's Preface

Thirty-seven years lie between the appearance of the first of these essays in 1915 and of the last in 1952. They have been years of such universal change, vicissitude and upheaval as in all its previous days humanity never knew. In that brief space two World Wars were fought, the empires of Austro-Hungary and Turkey, of Germany and Italy, were dissolved, the sun of imperial Britain began to set, the Asiatic peoples to awake to independence. On the continent of Asia arose the great Powers of China and India. All that Japan had won of domination at the end of the first World War was forfeited in surrender after Hiroshima. Nazi conquests in Europe were wiped out in the overthrow of the Third Reich. From Bolshevist revolution in Russia came the Union of Soviet Socialist Republics, to rank as the mightiest empire in the Eurasian hemisphere. North America mounted to world leadership. Conflict grew bitter between the free world and the Soviet bloc.

It is perhaps upon the life and fortunes of the Jewish people that these vagaries of history have left their deepest imprint, a people for two thousand years and more dispersed among the Gentiles, seldom regarded with favor by its master-neighbors, always and everywhere the first to suffer in whatever corner of the globe men were stirred to passion and violence. Yet never, in the long martyrdom of this banished and homeless race, was there a passage of time so dreadful for it as that of which I write.

Within the quarter of a century from 1918 to 1943 there descended upon the Jewish people a storm of savage blows more fearsome than any it had endured since the Roman legions laid waste its Land.

DAVID BEN GURION

First were smitten the Jews of Russia, then forming the largest single concentration of Jewry. Until the outbreak of the first World War, they numbered some five million souls, source and focus of Jewish survival. There, despite the restrictions and oppressions of Czarist Governments, an independent Jewish being was most securely preserved. There the new Hebrew literature flourished which gave us poets, novelists, thinkers, leaders—those who in the last century revived the cultural and intellectual life of the entire Diaspora. There, too, flourished the modern Yiddish writing which played no unimportant part in the lives of the Jewish masses in Europe and America up to the onset of the second World War. Thence sprang Haskalah and Chibbath Zion, Jewish Renaissance and the Love of Zion, which burst out of the confines of the Ghetto, to give the folk a modern philosophy and strengthen its immemorial hope of national revival. There the Jewish workers' movement blossomed, to open new horizons and cut new courses for the poor and youthful of a people athirst for freedom and redemption. To crown all, Russian Jewry was the dwelling-place of the strength and greatness of Zionism, which in a jubilee of years has magically altered the lineaments of the Jewish people and its status on earth.

That main body and chiefest core of Jewry the Bolshevist disfigured in furious haste. It was sundered from all other Jews; the Zionist Movement was outlawed, its leaders were thrown into jail or consigned to Siberian doom. The teaching of Hebrew was proscribed and Hebrew literature suppressed, and eventually even the Yiddish schools were disbanded. Thus was cruel discrimination visited upon the Jewish people, alone among the many races and tribes of Russia: forbidden to develop a national culture and, unkindest cut of all, denied all contact with the Land of Israel; for Russian Jews the way out to the National Home was impenetrably barred.

Surely there could be no greater calamity! But we were to know one infinitely more horrible in the second World War. The Nazi Fuehrer in his black mind resolved utterly to obliterate the

Jewish people from beneath God's skies. Shameless, he voiced his vile thought in harangue and in print, and none said him nay. Six million Jews, men and women alike, babes in arms and the old and helpless, were done to death with calculated and systematic barbarity. The main European centers of Jewry were destroyed and our people lost more than a third of its count.

Two further events in the kaleidoscopic period profoundly influenced the Jewish people. In November 1917, Great Britain declared that it viewed with favor the establishment of a National Home for the Jewish people in Palestine and recognized the historic association between that people and its ancient Homeland; in May 1939, Great Britain—and no other—told the world that the declaration was void and that Jewish immigration to the National Home must stop.

Is seemed as if these global tremors, and its own disasters, would at length shatter the foundations of this strange people after it had survived twenty amazing centuries of exile, amazing centuries, if indeed they were not miraculous. The dreadful tribulations which overtook it—severance of Russian Jewry, extermination of the Jews of Europe, slamming of the Homeland gates—would not these have been enough to break the will of far stronger nations? And in spite of all, out of all these monstrous buffetings of fate, there has come this incredibly fantastic renewal and recrudescence, this birth of the State of Israel, a new incarnation that is not only a tremendous and ultimate turn in the affairs of the Jewish people, but one of the most positive and astounding phenomena in the contemporary history of mankind.

The essays here assembled may help the reader to understand its inner springs and motivations, and what it means to the Jewish people and perhaps to the whole world.

D. B. G.

Jerusalem

PRELUDE

EARNING A HOMELAND
New York, September 1915

A ray of light pierces the abysmal darkness that shrouds our people at this critical hour; the urge for redemption is searing a path for itself in the heart of the nation. 'The dead has awakened and stirs.'

The calamity which has befallen, starkest in our records since Bar Kochba died, has aroused the people at last and from out the storm Messiah's trumpet-call reaches our ears.

The disaster is upon us, and the people sees and knows that it has no hope or hereafter, no redemption or amendment, save in a land of its own. The movement to regain the Land of Israel has burst the narrow bands of the Zionist Organization and become widespread and popular, and already it unites almost all sections and parties of Jewry. Out of sorrow and pain, the national consciousness is taking form; the thought of resurgence in Israel captivates all hearts and is bringing them near.

How can we win the Land and what must we do to win it?

Let the nation's forces be organized and integrated, let the parties each extend a hand to the other and consult together—and when the war is over, when spokesmen of the victors assemble to decide the fate of States and nations, then let representatives of the Jewish people be there too, to demand redress—redress for the greatest national grief in the story of mankind. In repayment and in retribution for our blood that flowed, as indemnity for our eternal sufferings, as solution of the Jewish problem which vexes the nations of the world no less, let them claim our share in the Land. The Peace Conference will heed our just plea and fulfill our entreaty; the verdict will be written down and sealed in charters of treaty and convenant between empires, and the Land will be restored to the estate of its people.

And so, it seems, our part is simple. It is for us only to ask for the Land. The rest depends not on us, but rather on the will of the Conference and the state of affairs existing after the war.

Let us assume that circumstances are benign, that the empires in debate take account of our needs and claims, and grant our petition. Will this alone ensure that the Land becomes *our* Land?

There are various ways in which a country may be had. It can be seized by force of arms or possessed by political devices and diplomatic pacts; it can be bought for cash. All such measures have but a single aim: rule to enslave and exploit. The English, for example, took India by devious stratagems and rule it by military force; and thus are dictators of its hundreds of millions of inhabitants. The British and other empires occupied territories in Asia and Africa to get markets for their wares.

Not so we. We do not ask for the Land of Israel for the sake of ruling over its Arabs, nor seek a market to sell Jewish goods produced in the Diaspora. It is a Homeland that we seek, where we may cast off the curse of exile, attach ourselves to the soil—that source of quickening, creativeness and health—and renew our native life.

A Homeland is not given or got as a gift; it is not acquired by privilege or political contracts; it is not bought with gold or held by force. No, it is made with the sweat of the brow. It is the historic creation and the collective enterprise of a people, the fruit of its labor, bodily, spiritual and moral, over a span of generations.

If a people has a right to say 'This is my own, my native land,' it can only be because it has *created* it. The soil is nature's guerdon and man cannot make matter out of nothing. Whatever serves for man's enjoyment is nature-made. All that man does is to work with hand and brain to adapt for his own use and benefit the materials which nature provides. Fitting the land by labor to a nation's needs: tilth and enrichment of the soil, paving of roads, setting up of means of communication, unearthing of hidden treasures and natural resources, building up of industry—these are the *making of a Homeland.*

The true right to a country—as to anything else—springs not from political or court authority, but from work. The real and lasting ownership is of the workers.

The Land of Israel will be ours not when the Turks, the English, or the coming Peace Conference so agree and set their signatures to a treaty to that effect, but rather when we Jews ourselves build it. Indefeasible title we shall never get from others, but by our own labor only. And a country is built up only by halutzim, by pioneers. Mass immigration recks not of history, but pours into the place where conditions for its absorption have been made ready in advance.

Preparing the Land and creating conditions are the job of pioneers, pioneers of labor, science and construction, armed with powerful wills and conscious of a mission, capable of merging their personal destinies in a sublime purpose and knowing how to yield their very lives for the fulfillment of their dreams.

No national or social end is achieved without the fervor and utter devotion of the first among its fighters and builders. It is not ineluctable fate that governs history; life is more than a game played by blind forces. The purposive and farsighted intervention of an active and creative will, aware of historical processes, is a cause and propellant of those same processes.

No nation is freed of itself, without an effort. And even more so, no land is automatically built and held with no exertion of will, with no dedication of its first founders. The history of American settlement shows how herculean were the tasks of the colonists who came to find a new Homeland in the New World, how many the sorrows and travails they had to bear, how many and how fierce the fights they fought with wild nature and wilder redskins, the sacrifices made before they unlocked the continent for mass influx and colonization. Had it not been for such, who quailed from no trial or privation, from no affliction or misadventure on their way, had it not been for their devotion and iron will, America would not today be the prodigally rich and populous country it is, vessel most capacious for absorption of the world's immigration.

Not with money, nor by privilege, but by our own acts will we win a Homeland. We will receive it, not from the Peace Conference or the nation that rules it, but from the hands of the Jewish worker who will come to take root in it, to bring it life and to dwell in it. The Land of Israel will be ours when, in best part, its workers and watchmen are from our own ranks. The real conquest of the Land through labor—that is the transcendent duty which faces the nation's pioneers, the builders and guardians of the Land.

IN JUDEA AND GALILEE
Written in 1917

As soon as I had disembarked and got through the Turkish customs, I hurried off to Petah Tiqvah. My friends pressed me to stay a few days in Jaffa, but I could not restrain an overmastering urge to see a Jewish village, and toward evening of the same day I reached the 'metropolis' of our colonies.

That night, my first night on Homeland soil, is engraved forever on my heart with its exultation of achievement. I lay awake—who could sleep through his first night in the Land? The spirit of my childhood and my dreams had triumphed and was joyous! I was in the Land of Israel, in a Jewish village there, and its name was Petah Tiqvah—Gate of Hope!

The howling of jackals in the vineyards; the braying of donkeys in the stables; the croaking of frogs in the ponds; the scent of blossoming acacia; the murmur of the distant sea; the darkening shadows of the groves: the enchantment of stars in the deep blue; the faraway skies, drowsily bright—everything intoxicated me. I was rapturously happy—yet all was strange and bewildering, as though I were errant in a legendary kingdom. Could it be?

My soul was in tumult, one emotion drowned my very being: 'Lo, I am in the Land of Israel!' And the Land of Israel was here, wherever I turned or trod . . . I trod its earth, above my head were skies and stars I had never before seen . . . All night long I sat and communed with my new heaven . . .

* * *

Beautiful are the days in our Land, days flushed with light

and full of luster, rich in vistas of sea and hill . . . But infinitely more splendid are the nights: nights deep with secrets and wrapt in mystery.

The drops of burning gold, twinkling in the soft blue dome of the sky, the dim-lit purity of moonlit nights, the lucid crystal of the transparent mountain air—all is steeped in yearning, in half-felt longings, secret undertones. You are moved by urgings not of this world . . . in the silence you listen to the echoes of childhood; legends of ancient days and visions of the last days take shape here quietly, flooding the soul and refreshing the anguished heart with the dew of hope and longing.

And if you are exiled from this Land, and stray far from its soil and skies, to wander beyond distant waters and dwell in alien places beneath a strange firmament, you will take with you the lingering memory of these nights—the birthright of your Land.

For a year I sweated in the Judean colonies, but for me there was more malaria and hunger than work. But all three—work, hunger and malaria—were new and full of interest. Was it not for this that I had come to the Land? The fever would grip me every fortnight with mathematical precision, harass for five or six days, and then disappear. Hunger, too, was a regular visitor. It would come to lodge with me for weeks at a time, sometimes for months on end. During the day I could dismiss it in all sorts of ways, or at least stop thinking of it. But in the nights—the long racked vigils—the pangs would grow fiercer, wringing the heart, darkening the mind, sucking the very marrow from my bones, demanding and torturing—and departing only with the dawn. Shattered and broken, I would drop off to sleep at last.

In this fashion, days of work alternated with days of fever and hunger, and then the recurring night. But the enthusiasm and the joy faded not at all. Who worried about malaria in those days? The few who did not suffer from it were a little shamefaced before the rest of us who did: imagine coming to the Land of Israel without savoring its fever!

REBIRTH AND DESTINY OF ISRAEL

* * *

That was ten years ago—at the time of the new Aliyah; every ship brought its quota of young people. Most of the new laborers settled in Petah Tiqvah, and for all that the farmers there had just started their 'boycott' of Jewish workers, our numbers grew from week to week.

Young men came from all corners of Russia, from towns and villages in Poland, Lithuania, Volhynia and Byelo-Russia; from the yeshivas, from primary and high schools. We had left behind our books and our theorizing, the hairsplitting and the argument, and come to the Land to redeem it by our labor. We were all still fresh; the dew of dreams was moist yet in our hearts; the blows of reality had still to sober our exalted spirits. We were gladsome, full of enthusiasm and free from care, like a caravan of travellers which finds a treasure at the oasis. Each of us felt that he had been born again. We had come from exile to redemption—our own. Far, far behind, we had left the narrow lanes and squalid streets, and were living in the midst of gardens and groves. Everything was new here: nature, life and labor. Even the trees were different, novel, unlike the trees there: olive and almond, palm and eucalyptus—and above all, the orange. And they were ours! We planted them and cared for them. We no longer sat on our class-room benches, wrestling with books and sharpening our wits on vain dialectics—we were at work. We planted saplings and picked oranges, we grafted trees, we wielded the hoe and we dug wells—we were delvers of the soil, and the soil we turned was Homeland. And we were not just working—we were conquering, conquering a land. We were a company of conquistadores—and in the Land of Israel—what more could we want?

We worked and we won, exuberant in victory. After a day of work, or maybe of fever, we would gather in the workers' kitchen, or in the sandy tracks between the vineyard and the groves, and sing and dance in a circle, sing and dance arm in arm and shoulder to shoulder.

* * *

In the first honeymoon months everything seemed new and 'Israeli.' But when the first bemusement of enthusiasm passed off, we began to perceive an old picture in the new frame—and it was a picture of the Galuth. The skies were new—the skies of Israel, the soil was new—it was our native soil; but the men and women, the folk of the Yishuv, were of the Galuth, and its ways were still their ways. Like us, they had come here in their youth with dreams of redemption and with the ambition of conquest—but their spiritual tint had long since faded, only a mundane soul survived and they had become speculators and shopkeepers, trafficking in the hopes of their people and selling their own youthful aspiration for base silver. They had brought the image of the Galuth into the temple of resurrection, and the remaking of the Homeland was sullied by idolatry . . .

We were bitter about this seeming desecration, we challenged the mercenary calculations which were destroying the very basis of reconstruction—and *they* could not bear the sight of us. In their eyes we were a living indictment, an inescapable reminder of their sins; they masked their dislike, but were flagrant in slander. A deep rift opened between the old-time farmers and the immigrant laborers.

Even the work itself, the interminable hoeing and spading, did not satisfy me fully. It was too mechanical and monotonous. The ceaseless clang seemed to echo the factory. I felt a thirst which was not quenched, a longing unrequited, as though there was an empty ache in my heart. I yearned for the wide fields, for the waving stands of corn, for the fragrance of grass, the plowman's song—and I made up my mind to go north—to Galilee.

Judea and Galilee have ever been poles apart. The sons of the valley and the lowland were always more cultured, more pampered, mercurial and soft-hearted; the mountain sons were hardier, simple, bold and daring, and set solid in their furrows. This distinction has not been blurred to this day, either among Arabs or Jews. Judea is richer, more civilized; Galilee stronger and more aggressive. The fellahin of Judea are weak and docile; there are few among them who bear arms. The fellahin of Galilee are audacious, skilled to spoil and fight and delighting in arms. It was the hills and crags of Galilee that threw a mountainy shield over its dwellers and breathed into them the spirit of stout warriors.

Likewise, the life of the Jews of Galilee is different from the life in Judea. There are no 'gentlemen' farmers in the moshavot of Galilee, no rich landowners employing many laborers. Here are no vineyards or groves, no wells or pumps for irrigation, and no plantation husbandry at all. But, instead, there are herds of sheep and cattle, poultry-coops and dovecotes, horses and plows, stretching fields and their grain. The holding of a Galilean farmer is not rich—but it is watered with the sweat of his brow.

* * *

Ten years ago Galilee looked not as it looks today. The network of farmsteads and settlements which has transformed the district of Tiberias into a little Jewish commonwealth was not yet built. The Beduin of Sheikh Issa camped where now is Kinnereth; at Majdal the Germans had only just gained a foothold; Sarona, ancient Sharon and modern Rama, was still in the domain of Said Bey. The tribesmen of Zawiah squatted on the site of Mescha; the hills of Mizpah and Poriah had stood gaunt these hundreds of years, and a plowman of Israel was yet to be seen in all the length and breadth of Jezreel. The Yishuv of Galilee was still in its earliest infancy—there were only four small, insecure moshavot, founded three or four years previously: Sejera, Mescha, Yavniel and Melchamia.

In those days Sejera was the hub of Lower Galilee. It was

the mother of our young settlement, and it was one of Jewish workers. Here began the new colonization of Jewish farmers who were workers, not employers: here was made the first experiment in cooperative labor—in those days we called the kvutza a 'collective': here developed the idea of a corps of Jewish watchmen and here, on one of the green hills, we dug the graves of the first to die.

* * *

From Judea I came to Sejera. After Judea, Sejera struck me almost as Petah Tiqvah did after Galuth. Here, at last, I found the Land of Israel. Nature, people, work—here everything was wholly different, more of Israel; here the perfume of Homeland rose from every sod.

Sejera almost monopolized the diverse lovelinesses of crested scenery with which the Land is clad. Mountains surround it and enclose it on every side. In the east, among the expanses of Trans-Jordan, are visible the mountains of Gilead and Bashan, veiled in blue mist like waves of the azure sea that surge upward and are frozen in mid-air; in the west, at the boundary, crouch the emerald heights of Nazareth; to the north soars the patriarch of mountains, standing head and shoulders above the lesser ridges—ancient Hermon, lifting his pale brow and his snowy hair, gazing out over all the land of Galilee; and to the south, in proud solitude rising, Tabor, eternal guardian of the Valley of Jezreel. The moshava itself is built on the slope of a hill— two rows of houses, one above the other, encircled by thickets of eucalyptus and pepper trees, and looking from afar like rungs of a ladder mounting to the peak. The farm itself stands there.

The people of the moshava were as diversified as its environment; they were a polyglot and variegated handful. Among the fifty-odd farmers and laborers were tall, broad-shouldered Kurdish Jews, as unlettered as their neighbors in Kurdistan; thin, bony Yemenites, highly learned in the Hebrew language and in traditional Judaism; young Russians, disciples of enlightenment and revolution; native-born Ashkenazi and Sephardi, who had left the yeshivas of Safad and Tiberias to take up the spade and the plow; converts, Russian farmers from the shores of the Caspian Sea, who had embraced Judaism and come to labor in the Homeland of their new faith; young Sephardis, educated in the schools of the Alliance Israélite. This motley community had Hebrew, Arabic, Aramaic—for the tongue of the Targum is still spoken by the Kurdish Jews—Yiddish, Russian, French and Spanish. But they were not like the generation that built the tower of Babel; this miniature ingathering of exiles was cemented and made one by a firm and powerful bond—the land and its cultivation. In Sejera—and in those days it was unique of its kind—there was nothing but Jewish labor, the labor of the farmers themselves and their children; even the farm, which belonged to the Jewish Colonization Association (ICA), employed only Jewish workers.

Sejera was divided into two parts: the staff of the farm, its officials and laborers, who lived on the hilltop, and the villagers, the farmers, who lived below, on the slope; but a covenant of peace and brotherhood joined the 'upper' and the 'lower' habitations. Almost all the farmers were young men who had formerly worked as laborers at the farm, and when they acquired land of their own, went on working it themselves. We, the workers, would meet them often, in the field and at home. There was no sign here of the rift that divided farmers from laborers in Judea. On Sabbath and festivals we would foregather and celebrate and make merry in unison, and on workdays we would meet in the fields, plow side by side and help out one another.

Here I found the environment that I had sought so long. No shopkeepers or speculators, no non-Jewish hirelings or idlers living on the labor of others. The men plowed and harrowed their fields and planted the seed; the women weeded the gardens and milked the cows; the children herded geese on the threshing-floor, and rode on horseback to meet their fathers in the fields. These were villagers, smelling wholesomely of midden and the ripening ear, and burnt by the sun.

The work, too, was more satisfying. There was none of the desiccation and monotony that attend the rigors of the hoe in Judea. You follow and guide the plow, turn the sods and open furrow after furrow; and soon the very soil you plowed and planted would clothe itself in green. Before your very eyes it would bring forth its crop. No sooner were the rains over than the grain would ripen, and out you would go to reap the harvest and carry the yield to the threshing-floor. You felt yourself a partner in the own act of creation.

* * *

But even here the purity of our aspirations was clouded. The fields were worked, it was true, by Jewish hands, but their watchmen were hired Arabs. In Judea we scarcely noticed that we were guarded by non-Jews. The moshavot were large and well-populated; the surroundings were quiet; arms were virtually unseen in the Arab villages; authority was greatly feared; public security was seldom disturbed. Not so here, in Galilee, amid the hills. The settlements were new and narrow. The surroundings were wild; our neighbors all expert and well-armed bandits. 'And the caves in the hills and the clefts of the crags are shelters for every seeker after revenge and every hero among his people.' Theft and assault were not uncommon, and the power of the Government was as nil and naught. The peace and security of the moshava in this vicinity depend entirely on its watchmen. In the moshavot of Judea the Arab watch was merged invisibly in the Arab labor and its nearness unknown. But here, in Sejera, Jewish labor—our labor—was the rule; the place was alive with Jewish youngsters—could we entrust all that to strange hands? Was it conceivable that here too we should be deep in Galuth, hiring strangers to guard our property and protect our lives?

We began to plead with the officials and the farmers to engage Jewish watchmen, but they looked upon us as babes. 'Jewish watchmen!—And what of the danger?' At first, they did not believe we meant what we demanded. Did we really intend to sacrifice young lives for the sake of some 'abstract principle'? Could enough men be found willing to hurl their lives into the breach? And would not a Jewish watch be a grave danger to the peace of the moshava? Why, the very Arab watchmen, familiar with every nook and cranny in the settlement, its every approach and egress, would be themselves the first to attack and plunder it! We were weak and few, ringed on all sides by strangers and enemies: the fellahin of Lubia, the largest village in Lower Galilee, famous for their fiery temper and aggressiveness; the Christian villagers of Kafr Kana, full of venom and hatred for the sons of Shem; the Zabiah tribesmen, their tents in the forest of Sejera, intimidating the entire neighborhood; the Circassians of Kafr Kama, renowned for their arrogance and daring. These Circassians, who had settled in the country at the invitation of the Turkish Government, enjoyed a privileged status in the Palestinian community. The Government favored and protected them more than the rest. Their sheikhs were appointed to high military office, and their families acquired great influence in official circles. But their privileges and hectoring ways were based not on political status alone, but on their own character. Could we afford to fall foul of them in such circumstances?

We stuck to our opinion. We wished to vindicate our national honor, the honor of our work of revival. But we pleaded and protested in vain.

We tried to win over the farm bailiff, who always treated us with respect and trust, and had slowly come closer to our philosophy concerning the value of Yishuv and of national effort in the Land of Israel. He admitted that we were right in theory, but he did not dare translate that theory into practise. The Circassians at that time were the guards of the farm. They were diligent in their work and outstanding for courage and spirit. No fellah nor Bedu would venture to provoke them. In Lower Galilee, between Sejera and Yama, they lived on friendly terms with the Jewish settlements. They had a virtual lien on guard duty in them, and they looked after the farm, wood and fields of Sejera. Our overseer would not hazard putting the moshava under Jewish watch, lest he arouse their wrath.

We grew convinced that we could not, by a single assault, storm this citadel of non-Jewish watch and ward—we would have to prepare for a long war, to fight our way step by step and guard-post by guard-post. We decided to start hostilities at once.

We stalked a new Circassian watchman for several nights, and discovered that he did not come at all to mount guard. He merely let his 'name' do the work in his stead. This was a common trick. The watchmen were generally appointed from among the most notorious thieves and robbers. They were sure that, once it was known they had taken over a post, no one else would have the audacity to come and steal. And even if 'something not quite correct' occurred, it was easy for them, in intimate relations with the underworld of brigands, to be able to track down the stolen property and return it to its owner—not, of course, without ample reward from him. Instead of pacing his beat around the stockade of the farm all night and spending the darkness in the company of the boulders and eucalyptus trees that envelop Sejera, the new man preferred to visit the neighboring Arab village and spend his time drinking with his friends.

Unavailingly we tried to open the bailiff's eyes to his guile and the loss this sort of watch entailed. So we decided to give him a practical demonstration. One dark night, we led his finest mule out of the farm, and immediately informed him of the theft. He ran to the stable—the mule was gone. He whistled frantically to summon the watchman—once, twice, a third time, but not an answering sound. He went outside, hurried the length of the stockade—the Circassian was not to be seen. Messengers were sent to seek him in the Arab village, and found him there—lying fast asleep. The bailiff dismissed him then and there, and gave the job to one of us. We had captured the first bastion.

We knew that the Circassian would not keep quiet. And indeed, not many days went by before the bailiff awoke one morning to find several window-panes broken and a number of Martini bullets embedded in his wall. Whoever fired had reckoned to frighten the Jewish watchman into relinquishing his post, but he miscalculated.

Immediately after that night, we resolved to organize and keep a good look-out. We set alternating watches of all the workers, two every two hours from dusk to dawn. We used to sleep in the big silo near the mill, our weapons close at hand; every pair, when their turn came, lay in wait in the cactus hedge or in the crevices of the rocks. It was the rainy season, and a fierce storm, such as had not been experienced for years, raged for a week all over the country. In Judea, it destroyed most of the oranges and caused enormous losses to the grove-owners. In Sejera, it was accompanied by pelting rain; darkness was stygian, and it was impossible to see a yard ahead. When I stood guard, my companion and I had to hold on to each other's hands. We could not even speak to one another. It seemed as though nature had joined forces with our foes to try our mettle.

Our ambush lasted a fortnight—until the assailants came to realize that their threats would not shift us; and they withdrew.

We had bested them in the first round.

* * *

And it was a lesson for the future. It taught us a Jewish watch was not enough. Unless the other workers were fit and willing to help, a Jewish watch would be useless and could not last. The Jewish watchman could not rely on his 'name' to be a deterrent of theft or attack. He would have to be on sentry-go all night long. To do this duty not only loyally but with success, a permanent 'reserve' was needed. This again required two things: the right human material and a sizable supply of arms.

Men there were—we were ready, but we lacked arms. Only a fortunate few owned pistols; and oh! how we envied them! We decided to ask the management for arms.

The bailiff granted our request unhesitatingly. A special wagon was sent to Haifa to bring rifles. Impatiently, we awaited its return; day and night we spoke of nothing but the arms, and when the wagon eventually came back, our joy knew no bounds. The rifles were of the most inferior type, cheap 'Jifts'—double-barreled shotguns. There were much better ones in the office—Martinis—but the management did not yet deign to entrust us with such dangerous weapons. Not a small thing, a Martini . . . but for us then, even the 'Jifts' were perfection itself. We played with them like little children; we never put them down for a moment. Reluctantly we went to work next morning—we had to say good-bye to them for a whole day. As soon as we got home and unharnessed our horses and mules, we dashed off to our beloved rifles, and they never left our hands till we fell asleep. Rifle in hand or on shoulder, we ate and washed, we moved and read or talked.

The big room in the khan where most of the workers lived was suddenly changed into an armory. Anyone entering of an evening was startled to see a score of young men, seated on their beds, each with rifle in hand! One would be cleaning the barrel; another testing the sights; one loading and unloading; another filling his pouches—comparing weapons, enumerating the virtues and vices of each, hanging them on the wall and taking them down again, slinging them over their shoulders and taking them off again—and so on until it was time for bed.

Now the farm—or rather its watch—was in our hands, we cast our eyes on the moshava. Here chance helped us. One night the horses of a farmer were stolen. When the farmer, who was a member of the village council, discovered the theft, he ran outside and met the Arab watchman returning from the fields. It was quickly proved that this Arab was the miscreant. At once we petitioned the council to appoint Jewish watchmen. This time they had not the temerity to put us off with their old objections. Our victory at the farm had silenced our few adversaries, and the guarding of the entire moshava fell to us. It was the first ever to employ Jewish watchmen.

* * *

From these vantage-points our way was open to clear the prickliest hurdle of the watch organization—the revia. This began during the second half of the rainy season, in the months of Shvat and Adar (February and March). At the end of Heshvan (November) the yoreh falls, which is the first rain, and the hard earth, which has cracked in the drought and scorching sun for the seven summer months, thirstily soaks up the drops. Then the farmer goes forth to his labor: he plows and sows, harrows and breaks up the loose soil. The bare furrows and pastures now are verdant; the grasses sprout. When the grass in the woods reached a certain height—in the month of Shvat—the night grazing, the revia, began. Horses and mules were not led to their stalls from work. The farmers drove all the livestock—oxen, mules, horses and donkeys—to the threshing-floor and thence led them to pasture. Night grazing was not like day grazing. A single herdsman or even two for the drove was not the fashion. There was no revia without armed guards. Here, in the hills, the stock could not be left alone in the darkness. A troop of horsemen and a posse on foot, armed cap-a-pie, spread out in the valley, their ears cocked to every rustle and quiver; eyes piercing the murk to detect the least shadow; sure hands on the butt ready at any moment to greet uninvited guests.

Guarding the herds was more difficult and dangerous than guarding the settlement. In the settlement the watchman had partners—iron padlocks on the stables and a stone wall round the houses. All was bolted and barred. A stranger would not venture in after nightfall. The place was strictly private; a suspicious noise had only to be heard for the watchman to whistle an alarm or fire a shot, and the entire village ran to his side. But the pasture was far from the village. The road was open to all; there was neither fence nor lock. All was open; the herds strayed freely in wood and valley, without bit or rein; there could be no hour more propitious for retrievers to reach out to the strays. There were many turns in the path and many hiding places in the hills—it was easy to lurk concealed, to baffle the herdsmen and guards and make away with the plunder, leaving not a track behind.

To secure the right to protect the revia was our third step that winter. Our conquest of farm and moshava watch had prepared the ground for it. When revia time came, we managed to place several of our group in the herdsmen's watch . . . the council and the bailiff thought it too risky to put the entire job in our hands at once. It was in this revia that Jewish watchmen received their first taste of blood-letting, but happily nothing fatal.

Dov Schweiger was one of the Jewish herdsmen-guards. He had only come to Sejera a few weeks before, yet had managed to win not only the affection of the workers, but also the hearty confidence of the bailiff. Hitherto the revia, like the other watches, had been the preserve of the Circassians, and this time they looked askance at their Jewish companions. Their pride and self-esteem had been hurt. Would these striplings fare forth with the mighty Circassians?

Hassan, the son of the Circassian sheikh, was particularly incensed that Dov, who was still only a youngster, should be taking part. At first he thought the tenderfoot Jew might tire and not muster strength enough. But several nights passed, and 'Berele' stuck to his guns, diligently, bravely—like an experienced herdsman. Hassan began to tease 'Berele'—to mock and insult him. But Dov could give as well as take. Every joke, every sneer, was met with sharp words and stinging retorts, till once Hassan could contain himself no longer and cried: 'Damn your religion!' Dov lifted his whip and swung it across the Circassian's face. Hassan was dumbfounded at such insolence from a 'puny' Jew. In violent anger he fell on Dov—but straightaway felt a grip of steel on his wrists. Dov seized and threw him, and while he measured his length, Dov lashed him until he lay still. Ali, Hassan's friend, hurried to the spot, and seeing him all bloodied, made to attack Dov in vengeful ire. Dov levelled his rifle, shouting: 'Stay where you are!' And all night Ali straddled his prostrate friend, not daring to move hand or foot. Opposite him stood Dov, blood-soaked no less, rifle sighted.

Toward dawn, as we prepared to go to work and were waiting in the courtyard for the return of the herd, Dov entered. We scarcely recognized him. The bailiff trembled with fear. 'What have you done? The Circassians will take revenge,' he whispered, and his face was pale as death.

We stood round Dov. No one uttered a word.

The bailiff threw a look at the small band of workers, and calmed down. The resolution and courage that showed in their glances gave him all the answer he needed.

The Circassians pursued no vendetta. After the incident, they began to seek out our company more than ever.

The Jewish watch at Sejera had entrenched itself and won a complete victory. After Sejera, Mescha and Yama followed suit and introduced one too.

* * *

Sejera, first in Jewish watch, was also the scene of its first casualty. It happened a year later, during Passover 1909. All through the previous winter the atmosphere had been explosive. Disputes had broken out between us and the villagers of Kfar Kana concerning the boundaries of the land of Umm Jebl. Several times they had tried to plow our fields and we had driven them off by force. The Zabiah tribe was also restless: Government troops had shot its sheikh. In Arab Sejera, there were quarrels between the Arabs and the Kurdish Jews who lived there. The fellahin from Lubiah had become particularly insolent, and had taken to molesting travelers on their way from Sejera to Tiberias. This was the first winter after the promulgation of the new Turkish Constitution, and the simple peasants understood it in their own way: henceforth there was to be neither judge nor justice. The Government was meddling no longer, a man might do as was right in his own eyes. And since the restraining hand was loosed, there was an appalling increase in theft and highway robbery.

A few night before Passover, several attacks ending in bloodshed were made on Sejera, but they did not prevent the workers from celebrating the festival. Many guests came from Judea, for the general meeting of the Galilee Poalei Zion was to be held in Sejera then.

The celebration was in the upper khan, the old Arab staging inn in the farm compound. The large hall, which had first served as a byre, and afterwards as workers' dormitory, was decked in Galilee style. The two long walls were draped with branches of eucalyptus and pepper, until they resembled an avenue of trees. On the inner wall, opposite the entrance, hung farm implements and rifles: plows, spades, harrows, and hoes wreathed in flowers at both sides of the window, and rifles, pistols, swords and daggers inter-locked above it. The faces of the young men who sat round the great table testified that this arsenal was more than just decoration.

The seder began with song and wine, as usual. The sadness that had oppressed us so long was gradually dispelled. All doubts and cares were forgotten. Joy grew with every new ditty and enthusiasm waxed from draught to draught. It was the blend of Hassidic ecstasy and wild Arab excitement that prevailed at every workers' feast in the Land. The songs were accompanied by dances—wild, formless and uncontrolled, to the sound of clapping hands, as the Arabs dance.

We were still singing and dancing when an agitated voice reached us from outdoors. The dance ceased abruptly and we fell silent. An unknown youth burst into the room, and in shaky, incoherent words, his face aflame, told of an assault just made on him. With an acquaintance, he had come from Haifa that day on foot. escorted by an Arab. In their baggage, loaded on the Arab's donkey, was a valuable camera. Toward evening they passed through Kfar Kana. As they left the village, three Arab robbers appeared from among the rocks. Only the narrator was armed—with a Browning pistol—and he defended himself and his companion until his ammunition ran out. The robbers then fell on the Arab, beat him mercilessly, and seized the donkey and all it carried. It seemed to him that one of the assailants had been wounded: when he and his friend continued on their way they saw bloodstains.

We grabbed our rifles at once and ran outside. Vainly we searched for tracks. On the scene of the incident we found only bloodstains—a long red line that crimsoned the length of the road, then suddenly disappeared. Angry and anxious, we returned home.

Next day, we heard that a wounded Arab had been brought from Kfar Kana to the Nazareth hospital, and several days later that he had died of his wound. His friends had said that his wound was self-inflicted—and the cause, the accidental discharge of his own rifle. Just before his death, however, he confessed that Jews of Sejera had shot him. We felt that something was brewing.

That was in the Passover week. None of us worked. We gathered in one of the farmhouses at the foot of the hill for the Poalei Zion meeting. The land question was on the agenda, but we were preoccupied with another question that was burked. We were all armed. I was in the chair, but my thoughts and feelings were taken up with the local situation more than with the course of discussion, and my hand never left the holster of my Browning. Before the meeting, we had posted watchers on the hilltop.

While we were still deliberating, one of them pushed his way into the room with the news that Arabs had attacked the herd and carried off several oxen and mules. The meeting was broken off. The members from other settlements were sent away immediately to defend their own homes should it be necessary. We of Sejera met in the khan to consider the position. The family of a murdered Arab must avenge his death, and the first seven days after the murder are the most dangerous. In that week the avengers may pillage and plunder; whoever resists takes his life in his hands. We decided in that period to do our utmost to avoid provoking the Arabs.

We decided not to send the herd out to graze in the distant forest; we would pasture it in nearby fields.

The following day, the Arabs descended on the fields between Sejera and Mescha, and harvested the near-ripe barley. No Arabs were to be seen in the moshava itself, but suspicious movements could be discerned close to the farm. From dawn to dusk armed men on foot and on horseback were viewed on the hilltops. Two of our number who went to Tiberias to buy unleavened bread stumbled on a band of Arabs, who attacked and beat them, and took their arms.

A black cloud lowered upon us—the shadow of death in ambush. No one spoke of it, but each of us sensed it in himself and read it in his neighbor's eyes; the sword of vengeance hung over us all—it must fall on the head of one among us . . . Fate was still to choose its victim. We were all ready, and waiting.

On the last day of Passover fate swooped, claiming not one, but two of our lives.

It was about two in the afternoon. We were at a small gathering of friends at the pharmacy, where we used to spend our free time. Israel Krongold, the watchman at the farm, came in fully armed, his Martini slung over his shoulder, a row of cartridges in his belt, his Browning at his hip. In normal times he carried his arms only at night, when on duty—but in days like these he went on guard immediately after his midday siesta.

As he entered, he told us that he had sighted two strange Arabs sitting on a hill opposite the graveyard. They had asked him something, but he had not understood—he had not been long in the country, and knew very little Arabic yet; and he had come to find someone who spoke Arabic well. 'Now,' he said to us, laughing, 'we will drag them in by the ears.'

A farmer, who had been born in the country, went out with him. We sat and waited. Half an hour went by, we heard a volley of shots. The alarm was sounded on the farm bell. We caught up our guns and ran. Behind the hill on the edge of the moshava we found Israel, dying. There was a small, dark-red hole in his breast. The rifle was no longer on his shoulder. Only the pouch and the pistol remained . . . .

Two of us stayed with him; the rest scattered in the hills to find the killers. We sought in vain and returned downhearted and consumed by impotent wrath. Israel had not taken the Arabs alive for us; we bore him home, dead.

But tragedy did not end there—a second was to die. We stood on the Nazareth Road, looking toward the scene of the murder—toward Kfar Kana. Suddenly we saw three Arabs in flight, pursued by two of our men.

Evening had already fallen. All the farm workers and the settlers were gathered near the khan. Among them was Shimon Melamed. He was a carpenter by trade, but had come to the Land to be a farmer, and had made his way to Sejera to learn how, when he heard that ICA had set up a farm there to instruct Jewish workers in husbandry. As he was a fine craftsman, the management employed him in his trade for several years, but he found no satisfaction in carpentry, although he earned three times as much at it as a farm laborer and even more than an independent farmer; his whole aim in life was to establish himself on the land. After five or six years of work at the farm, the management granted his petition and gave him a parcel of land on a share-cropping basis, in Sejera.

Shimon was the happiest man in the place. The dream he had carried in his heart for so many years had become a reality. His holding was one of the choicest and most fertile in the settlement. No one surpassed him in diligence and perseverance, and although he was a novice at the work, his granary even in the first year was no less full than those of the more experienced farmers. This was his second Passover as a farmer, and his splendid work during the winter and the plentiful rains promised him a fine harvest again. He was as brave as he was industrious and devoted to the earth. There was no raid or affray but he was among the first to defend the moshava.

He was in his house when the shooting took place at the farm. As soon as he heard the shots, he dashed out. In his haste, he forgot his hat and the gun that hung on the wall of his room. His young wife took down the gun, hurried after him, and put it in his hand. She returned home to look after their child and he went on up to the farm. The rest of the people followed.

When we saw the Arabs retreating with our men at their heels, we decided to send several men on to block the escape route. Three went: a Sejera farmer, Shimon, and myself. We raced towards the Arabs and fired at them. The Arabs were between the frying-pan and the fire; two of us at their heels, and we three in front of them. Arab Sejera village saw their plight, and the entire population of it rushed toward us three. When our people realized the danger we were in, they called us back, but in the whistling hail of bullets we could not hear their warning. The Arabs of Sejera closed in on us. In single file, at intervals of several meters, we returned to the farm. We were close to home when an Arab fired from the cactus-hedge, and the bullet got Shimon in the heart.

Mutely we bore our dead comrades from the seder room: mutely we bore them on our shoulders to Sejera's plot of eternal rest, mutely, without funeral oration, we lowered them into the wide single grave.

They had lived together and died together in a Jewish settlement; there they had dreamed their life's dream, dream of rebirth, and there they had fallen. Together now they lay in peace —the watchman and the farmer, in the soil which by their lives as in their death they consecrated.

ZIONISM—THE HARD WAY AND THE EASY
Opening Debate of the 17th Congress at Basle,
June-July, 1931

We are come not as a party's envoys but as couriers from a battlefront. In terms only of party, we might indeed rejoice. Though calamity has marked the recent years and our portion of it, as the workers of Palestine, was the bitterest, disappointed though we are and beleaguered within and without, unbridled though the instigation against us—yet we emerged from the elections to Congress with signal success. Among the Jewish masses, in Poland, Lithuania and Germany, the Labor list headed the polls; in our adored Zionist Palestine, two-thirds of the Yishuv were with us. For the first time our party is on top.

But there is no exulting in the victory. We appear from the battlefront of 'Zionism on the way,' sent to you by the Army of Fulfillment, linked in destiny, for life or death, with the realization of Zionism. For more than twenty-five years, first a tiny platoon, then in companies and battalions, and now in brigades and divisions, that Army stands guard, firm and fast, over our agricultural development, our educational advances, our political progress in the Land. It is as such that we face you here, swayed by a profound sense of responsibility and solicitude for the position of the Zionist Movement and all its works.

For good and obvious reasons, under spiritual and political duress, Dr. Weizmann rendered this once an account not of two but of thirteen years. Deliberately he abridged the chapter whereon particularly we must dwell, the chapter of the last two years.

They have meant a stern ordeal: we were murderously attacked, we are exposed to systematic and continuous incitement, to the libels and provocation of effendis, of the Comintern's agents, of Government officers. The essence of our right to be in Palestine is wantonly assailed, and not just by this officer or that but by a Great Britain governed today by the British Labor party. Even our civic status is disputed at every turn.

But I would be speaking less than the truth if I listed only external calamity. We have been afflicted also by stiff necks and stubborn hearts—I will not say 'treason.' We are afflicted by estrangement of an important part of the Yishuv. Even after the 1929 rioting and the embargo on pioneer Aliyah, with our share in Government works denied and unemployment rife, there are still far too many Jewish groves that excommunicate Jewish labor. Thousands of halutzim are workless, hungry and broken because Jewish colonies withhold employment. It is not the Mandatory that bars the way, it is no foreign enemy, but men over whose coming the flag of national resurgence waved, men who by national favor and at national cost took unto themselves of the beloved land we call Israel.

It is not doing full justice to the political situation to open the dismal chapter with August 1929. There was an earlier incident—at the Wailing Wall—which, understandably, I forbear to discuss with all the honest emotion I feel. One day Jewish history will lay down who was true to Zionism, who was clear-eyed always and concerned for our interests in those exacting days—whether he that counselled the Yishuv not to be drawn into a religious war or he that poured the oil of his rhetoric upon zealot flames.

You know of the riots enquiry, of the wicked Shaw Commission which on a sudden thrust us into the dock. You know of the stoppage of immigration in May, the Mandatory's first report to the Mandates Commission of the League of Nations, the factual survey and scientific expertise of Hope Simpson, and, in last and lowliest place, Lord Passfield's White Paper. I will only remark that even the MacDonald letter, well-intentioned beyond any doubt and of a political value not to be gainsaid, is still a dead letter in Palestine. It did remove the painfuller sting, and, in our desperate case, we cannot make light even of that. And there was a positive aspect to it, recognition of our right to work for Government, an authoritative and unequivocal declaration to that effect and, moreover, one prescribing a more or less acceptable yardstick for our share. That again, however, is still a dead letter and still the Administration apes certain of our colonists: except for a derisory quota in the port of Haifa, we are excluded from all Government works, even in wholly Jewish districts. And now something new—a Tenants' Protection Ordinance. We have long upheld the basic principle of guarding the Arab tenant against exploitation and oppressive interference, and we should welcome the Ordinance trustingly were it designed to do only that. To our sorrow, it is just a trick to subject all opportunity of acquiring land in Palestine to the caprice of the High Commissioner, and these last two years we have learnt what that can mean. So the untilled wastes are doomed to be everlastingly derelict, mortgaged to the grazing rights of the nomad.

What is the significance of these events? What is the lesson of this long chain of tribulation and catastrophe? There is a facile interpretation that goes with our 'easy' Zionism. It is all very simple, and every youngster in the Polish ghettos knows it by rote. 'There have been pogroms, do you know who is to blame? ... The Shaw Commission impugned us, and who was to blame? ... Immigration was stopped, the historic right of Aliyah challenged—whom shall we indict? The leader! ... You want our lives there to be safe. You do not want the Arabs to harm us. You want the lands of Palestine handed over to us for nothing. You want a Jewish State established on both banks of Jordan. Nothing could be easier! Just pick a new leader!'

On Congress Election day, a manifesto signed by the two

great Ministers of the party of 'easy' Zionism, Jabotinsky and Grossman, was published in Palestine. 'Give us a majority at Congress, and we give you a Jewish majority in Palestine.' I wonder if, considering the answer of the Yishuv, the signatories still believe in what they promised, but every schoolboy in Poland, as I say, maybe in other countries too, has it pat: 'Just dethrone the leader and everything will turn out fine.' I will not argue this profound thought except to remind you that the August riots are not the first we had in Palestine. It is not my desire to recount history from its proper beginnings of fifty years since. Enough to start with the post-war period. Riots in 1920, with many British in the country, and Jewish battalions too. Today's claimant to Zionist leadership was a leader of the Movement then and was in the country then, the same Jabotinsky who pledges us a majority in Palestine for the price of a majority in Congress; but he did not inveigh against the Zionist leader of the time as causing the riots by his blunders. No, he joined the Zionist Executive under Weizmann.

Riots in 1921, and much worse, though we had a Jewish High Commissioner. On that occasion every Zionist body in the world received a cable: 'Gather in your thousands and pass resolutions of confidence in the High Commissioner.' It was not sent by Dr. Weizmann but by Vladimir Jabotinsky of the Executive, the same who, with Weizmann, signed the White Paper in 1922.

We of the fighting-line, who defend the Land and labor in it, how do we view these disturbances? We were not altogether surprised—notwithstanding the tremendous political triumph which the Balfour Declaration signified and the dramatic achievement of 1922, when into the Mandate were written clauses dealing with the Jewish National Home—to find that still we were not masters of that Home, or of our right to build it. Not that, for all the saddening experience of the intervening years, we underrate either event—it is just that we never took as much stock of them as do the apostles of 'easy' Zionism. For us the annals of Zionism go back beyond the Balfour Declaration. We always knew that, with all its momentousness, it was at best an airy, colorful symbol, abstracted from hard reality. The ink was not dry on it, the Mandate and the first High Commissioner were yet to come, all were living in days of illusion and high hopes—and already ours was the clamant cry: 'Hasten—all of you —give the empty vessel its living content!' But you did not do it as you should, and our political gains are ineffectual yet. In part the fault is theirs who slackened the grip of Jewry and led it astray with vain imaginings: not by our own exertions, unrelenting, absolute and unconditional, was our place to be secured and our salvation wrought, but by fantastic diplomacy, by vociferous shaking of fists and especially by British aid.

We saw that international testimony and recognition did not dispel the universal unfriendliness, the atmosphere of hostility, suspicion and misunderstanding, which surround our eternal people. The Gentiles cannot yet stomach our strangeness, nor comprehend our longings and lament, cannot register consciously our basic, natural right to be independent again in our Homeland. In the global upset of a World War the foundations of all the earth are shaken, the great Powers fight for their lives and the least external succor is worthwhile. That succor our small nation gave, and, in return, a right was given it. But to the public opinion of Great Britain and the world it is not yet an ironclad, unappealable right. Unpleasant, perhaps, to say so, but we should be purblind, playing ostrich-politics, not to see exactly where we stand with the nations. The Balfour Declaration, the Mandate and fifty years of proudest construction in Palestine are behind us, and still it is gallingly necessary to tell an incredulous world of our rights and works, to make it see we come neither to extort nor exploit, but in equity to remodel our lives. It is the worst kind of self-deception to preach that if we possess a scrap of paper furbished with the seals of Britain and the League, a Jewish State on both banks of Jordan is safe in our hands and all we need do is elect a new leader and all will be well.

* * *

Nor was this our first collision with the Arab issue: we had long realized the danger there.

It is perception of the purpose and background of the riots in history and geography, perception of their character and of the real escape-route from their aftermath, that draws the line between us of 'Zionism the hard way' and you others. Fatefully, Congress must decide between the rival views.

If we prize political gains, it is—as I say—only on condition that life is breathed into them. Any fair account of the years must be honest regarding the means provided and the results attained. Here, too, we follow the unpopular path. I have heard 'easy' Zionists tell the folk: 'You did wonderfully, incomparably, for Palestine, no one could do more. You gave everything—but the Mandatory failed of its duty and an erring Zionist leadership landed you in this mess.'

We, however, are in solemn duty bound to speak less honied words: 'Only a few among you did your part, those that went to Palestine, pioneers of the labor and capital which in August saved the Yishuv and the Movement from annihilation. But you others in Galuth, you Zionists in your tens of thousands, you masses and myriads of Israel, did less than your part and so brought us to this pass!' Do you not blush to think that 200,000 Jews of Berlin spend on communal needs in a year more than Jewry entire has given for its own redemption and Homeland? We, at any rate, shall quarrel with any who, perhaps intending kindness, beguile Jewry, saying: 'You have not fallen short, someone else is at fault.' Without ceaseless work, without concentration of national resources, the glittering promises of Declaration and Mandate will not avail us. Rather will they be a blight upon us, angering and exciting Arabs already fearful of us and our fine phrases.

DAVID BEN GURION

If we are to be few amongst many in Palestine, as in every other land we are, trusting to the magic of superior intellect unsupported by moil and toil, or by husbandry and independent living, and if you think that the air of Israel and its ancient memories will then spare us an exilic fate, you will be tragically mistaken. If we are a minority, out of touch with creativity and labor, landless and denied all earthy livelihoods, in short—unless we become an autonomous nation, the Galuth malady, the plague of cultural assimilation and physical decline, will never quit us, not even in Palestine. For our future's sake, let us put forth the will, the faith and power to reconstruct the basis of our existence and establish a sovereign, self-governing Jewry in Israel. If we do not, we only make a second Galuth.

Achad Ha'am once dreamed of a new Jewish type in Palestine, a pattern to pilgrims who would enjoy the brilliance of this invention and tell the Diaspora of the marvels it did. Except we are a working people, that lovely dream will not come true.

What he saw in Palestine twenty years ago led him to conclude that the only invention was an upper-class of precocious Jewish landowners employing Arab labor. He did not then believe that the great proletariat that would do the rough chores of colonization would be Jews. He made two mistakes. First, a Jewish landowner without Jewish labor would be not a pattern but a pest. Second, lacking faith in the possibility of undiluted Jewish labor, Achad Ha'am could not grasp that, adrift in a great non-Jewish sea, we can create nothing, and that it will not take long in present circumstances of Palestine to turn a Jewish minority into what we were in Galuth: middlemen of foreign cultures and economies. On the fringes of our intelligentsia in Palestine signs of British coloring already emerge; if we continue a negligible minority, there will be Arab assimilation as well. Freedom and nationhood alone are the antidote.

As one who has lived and worked in Palestine many years, who came as a Zionist, I want to say that my faith in its promise was never so buoyant. Mine own eyes have seen the unfolding of infinite, hidden riches of dunes, of swamps and boulders. They saw the greater miracle, the creativeness of young workers aflame with vision and burning to resurrect Land and folk—in the Emek, in Sharon and Tel Aviv, in the trenches of Haganah, in industry and in organized labor. Labor and soul—if they bind the Jew in faith to his Land, then assuredly there is room in Palestine, there are prospect and capacity yet unrevealed. All we need is that the will of a few should grow into the will of a whole people.

In eastern Palestine, there are broader and emptier acres, and Jordan is not necessarily the perpetual limit to our immigration and settlement. I am not suggesting revision of the clauses of the Mandate which assign a special status to Trans-Jordan. We entered our protest at the time and the British Labor party endorsed it. No, I beg you not to criticize the Mandate: criticism, coming from us Jews, can only be irresponsible and politically dangerous. If there must be criticism, let others offer it as, and to whatever end, they choose. Just the same, without amending the Mandate, we are entitled to ask the right to enter and settle in Trans-Jordan; its closure in our faces neither accords with the Mandate as it stands, nor considers the crying economic needs of a fertile but underpopulated and impecunious region.

We are not blind, withal, to the fact that Palestine is no void. Some million Arabs inhabit both sides of Jordan, and not since yesterday. Their right to live in Palestine, develop it and win national autonomy is as incontrovertible as is ours to return and, by our own means and merit, uplift ourselves to independence. The two can be realized. We must, in our work in Palestine, respect Arab rights, and if our first contact was unhappy, we were not in the wrong. Nor, perhaps, were the Arabs, for there are historic imponderables. We knew we lived at the edge of the desert, that our neighbors still kept largely to its ways; so we quickly raised a posse for self-protection, and many of our finest men paid the price of insecurity with their lives. Before the World War, and after, we declared roundly that we should always be unsafe, till we were so numerous that we could defend ourselves.

This too we were taught: we have to do not only with local Arabs. We are encircled by Arab countries, and we must also reckon with Egypt and North Africa, all Moslems, all speaking Arabic. I implore you to draw the deadly conclusions. Ten years ago, with times normal and Jewish immigration at its peak, I spoke to Congress of global factors which Zionism should discern and which ought to determine its foreign policy. Strangely enough, those who are given, in season and out, to quoting Herzl's axiom that Zionism is an international world problem, are apparently the last to see what is going on in the world at large. In the eighteenth century, politically speaking, the world was virtually limited to the Continent of Europe. In the next, it embraced America as well. Now, in the second quarter of the twentieth century, it is taking in the whole of Asia. The East is awake, it counts decisively in world politics. Do not forget that. If you are serious about the realization of Zionism, then you must understand that we are becoming a people of the East again, in a new environment of politics and geography. How, then, can we possibly disregard the forces at work in that environment? Just look at what is happening in India today! Winston Churchill may not relish the thought of a half-naked fakir meeting the British viceroy on level terms. But responsible British statesmen —and not only in the Labor party but also dyed-in-the-wool Tories and rabid Imperialists like Baldwin, Chamberlain and even the former viceroy, Lord Reading—know well that this mighty empire must bargain with the spokesmen of India. Yet our pinchbeck Churchills go on believing we can afford to turn our backs on the Arabs and blandly rely on the military arm of Britain. It is they that embroil us with public opinion in Britain, and they that foster in so many Jews a hatred of Britain. Was it not the 'easy' Zionists, the very party that stormed in the Elected Assembly against negotiations with the Arabs, who simultaneously alleged that, as well as the officers of the Administration, every British Government, Conservative, Liberal or Labor, had with system and deliberation organized attacks upon the Jews in Palestine?

And you want this same Britain alone and for all time to shield us from the Arabs, the Britain which is exerting itself to come to terms with a vassal India? The moral and political assistance of European democracy, and above all of British, we must have. The tiresome business of justifying our case and cause we must conduct with greater energy. That is why we sense political risks in the trend which presents in a false light the aims of Zionism vis-a-vis the Arabs. The education imparted to our youth by 'easy' Zionism, that chauvinism steeped in racial animosity and a phobia of labor, darkens the moral values of Zionism and brands us as adversaries of the Arabs.

Congress must make up its mind: between the two philosophies there is a chasm none can bridge. We do not, as do the Revisionists, give the feckless pledge—'Elect us and a Jewish majority in Palestine is yours!' No, we warn you, and every Zionist in the world, that so long as we are few and weak, disaster stalks us. There is no easy diplomatic way—but only our own strength, only sacrifice and unceasing effort, only more and surer footholds through Aliyah and work and settlement, everywise and anyhow. That, to us, is the core of Zionist policy, and the essential concomitant is political activity in Britain and Europe and increasingly among the Arabs and in the East.

* * *

The moral content of Zionism and its necessary practical objects demand a policy of rapprochement and mutual understanding towards the Palestinian Arabs, in economics, enlightenment and politics.

DAVID BEN GURION

We endorse constitutional changes designed to give the inhabitants a share in administration, but uncompromisingly reject the Legislative Council which the White Paper proposes. Here, to Jewry, to Labor, and to the Arab nation, we vow that we shall never agree to one national group in Palestine dominating the other, now or evermore. If we do not accept the idea of a Jewish State wherein Jews rule over Arabs, neither do we accept bi-nationalism as in Switzerland or Canada. The political problem of Israel is sui generis. The rights to Palestine do not, as in those countries they do, belong to the existing settlers, whether it be Jews or Arabs. The crux is the Right of Return of Jewry dispersed, a prerogative of rebuilding and development, of freedom and sovereignty, yet not to infringe the prerogatives of others or hold sway over them. To be impervious to that conception, is to vitiate our title to Israel.

The suggested Legislative Council is based upon the status quo and planned to perpetuate it. In theory it means an Arab State, in practise it means arresting development, settlement and Aliyah. We dissent from dominion of present majority over present minority, for that minority is but the nucleus of a returning nation. So, too, shall we dissent from Jewish dominion over Arabs when the dynamism of Aliyah alters the balance of power in our favor. We scorn the plea that, while we are a minority, a British High Commissioner be empowered to prevent majority domination, but, as soon as we reverse the roles, he hand authority to us. It is playing with political fire to interpret messianic redemption and liberation as a lust to govern behind the bayonets of imperial Britain, condemning the right of those who are citizens of Palestine as much as we are.

In our view, the form of government should be so modified as to associate both national groups in it, together with Britain, on a basis of parity and without regard to numbers. But we shall never let ourselves become 'protected Jews' in Palestine, and never a ruling race. We shall be a free and self-sufficing nation, honoring Arab rights in an accord of equality, and living in peace with neighbor countries.

* * *

Grievous troubles await us, Gentlemen, within and without. We of Labor cannot, as others, take comfort in the strong hand of the Mandatory or in a tinsel democracy built on the status quo. Or in the Mandate itself, though for all its crippling blemishes we value it yet and will resist any plot that looks to rob us of our rights under it. Or in an Arab agreement, indefatigably though we shall work towards one, in and out of Palestine.

Our lever of Archimedes is now in ourselves, in the heart of the Jewish people. Painstaking and triumphant national endeavor on the land, careless of difficulty and distraction, a continuous flow of private and public investment, to enlarge and solidify our towns and villages with mass Aliyah of halutzim, and a growing agrarian and industrial economy—on such a pivot only can Zionism turn, only that lever can lift Jewry back from Galuth to new fortunes in Palestine.

Setbacks were many in recent years, but still we have done remarkably. Prosperous husbandry in Jezreel and Sharon. A Jewish city stands, an infant industry is expanding. Along the Jordan rise the great hydro-electric works of Rutenberg and Novomeysky's potash plant. The Jewish National Fund has acquired key-areas in Haifa Bay, which is being transformed instantly into the chief emporium of Palestine and of the vast hinterland stretching from the shores of the Mediterranean to the Indian Ocean.

We are nowhere near the end of the way or the worry. We shall be asked for more effort and perhaps more sacrifice. You cannot redeem a people or rebuild a Homeland overnight; it is hard to come by. But we who have seen the land respond to our obdurate strivings down the years, we take oath and say,

DAVID BEN GURION

that if Jewry rallies loyally and equips the pioneers of work and fulfillment with constant and copious aid, then the vision of redemption will be perfected and we shall not have suffered in vain.

THE KEY TO IMMIGRATION
1932

What Zionist propaganda for years and years could not do, disaster has done overnight. Palestine is today the fiery question for the Jews of East and West, and the New World as well. The 'certificate' is now the hope and salvation of thousands.

Can Palestine absorb them all? What manner of immigrant is most to be desired? What can the Zionist Movement do to enlarge the prospects? These are painful queries to answer.

In 1922, the British Government laid down, in the Churchill-Samuel White Paper, that immigration must be regulated by economic absorptive capacity. The Executive of the Jewish Agency, comprising Weizmann, Sokolow, Motzkin, Jabotinsky, Lichtheim and Soloveichik, subscribed to the principles of the White Paper and bound itself in writing to conduct Zionist affairs accordingly.

How are we to interpret the principle of absorptive capacity? In the eleven years since the White Paper appeared, the rate of admission has fluctuated considerably—in some years, over 10,000 Jews arrived, in others, only a few thousands; one year more than 30,000 immigrants; another year more emigrants than immigrants.

It is true that there were four changes of High Commissioner in that same period, but that was not the reason for the vagaries. During the term of Herbert Samuel, who was the real author of the White Paper, the rate varied from year to year; and so it did with his successors. The personal view of a High Commissioner has only a very restricted bearing on the progress of immigration. The main causes of fluctuation are to be sought not in a basically static policy but in internal pressures, in the economy of Palestine, in the speed of reconstruction and the tempo of development.

We must start by asking ourselves—is Palestine a land of absorption at all?

Before the first World War, it was a land of departures. Its structure and economic conditions could not support even the native-born. Thousands of people, especially Arabs, but also not a few Jews from Jerusalem, Safad and Tiberias, emigrated every year. They took up the wanderer's staff and sought new homes afar—in America, Brazil, the Argentine. We who came here over the past fifty years could not be absorbed in the economy existing, but were obliged to create new sources of livelihood. We did not settle in Arab villages or in the occupied towns, but founded new settlements and built new urban quarters and suburbs. We did not look for work in Arab vineyards and groves, nor in Arab shops and factories; we planted and erected our own. We came not as immigrants but as settlers, not to ancient Palestine but to a new land we made ourselves. Only this explains the miracle of a penurious land, a mere shelter from which its children fled, becoming suddenly a region to attract and digest an entirely new community.

The truth is that Palestine is a land of settlement, which alone makes it a land of immigration; but it must be an expanding settlement, born of Aliyah and with it, growing not out of the already existing but out of the constant new creation of imaginative and constructive enterprise. That is the only way to develop the power of absorption, and I mean not only agricultural settlement, whereon our future here will rest securely, but settlement in its wider sense, the production of new trades and vocations, new crafts and skill, more work, added economic elements in every walk of life.

It is most misleading to regard immigration as just a geographical transfer of individuals. Getting an entry permit and transport to Palestine are not the end of it. The ships that bring Jews here can also take them away. In the last decade, over 130,000 entered and 30,000 left; in 1926 alone there were 12,400 emigrants.

Immigration has real value only if it can take root in the nascent economy and play its own part in settlement, and the rate and pace of settlement in turn determine how large immigration shall be.

Government policy of course means something—if it is unfriendly it can restrict the flow artificially, or dam it altogether as in the days of Samuel and Chancellor it did. But it would be madness to think that a friendly policy is all that is necessary to swell immigration boundlessly: the Yishuv must expand as well. When Palestine was a part of Turkey, its doors open to Syria and other Ottoman provinces, it still was not a center for the absorption of neighboring surpluses. The 30,000 Jewish emigrants did not go because they had no right of settlement in Palestine. It is simply this. Throw wide the portals as you will, fling off every restraint, dislodge every political and external obstacle—and yet we should need great undertakings of settlement for the absorption and integration of newcomers in the mass: intensively developed irrigation on the coast, in the Jordan Valley and the Huleh; rehabilitation of the underpopulated areas of the Negev and Trans-Jordan; the setting up of sizeable and diversified factories to supply the hinterlands; the establishment of an ocean-going merchant navy, linking the ports of Israel with Jewish centers throughout the world; and the national and private capital, the trained man-power, which all this demands.

It is useless to survey only the country, as British 'experts' like Hope Simpson and French did—we must also take account of Jewish capacity and potential. Twenty-six years ago, what expert could have predicted that some thousands of dunams of sand-dunes near Jaffa would absorb the population of Tel

Aviv? What expert could have foreseen how varied in their intense production the new agricultural villages of Jezreel and the Jordan Valley would become, if he had seen only the wasteland and knew not at all the pioneer passion that came to fertilize it?

The key to immigration is the people, not the land, not the lifeless crust of earth but the dynamics and creation of farmer and factory-hand.

JEWISH LABOR: THE ORIGIN OF SETTLEMENT
An address before the Elected Assembly,
March 2, 1932

This year we celebrate the fiftieth anniversary of the founding of our first moshavot by the Shavei Zion: not counting Petah Tiqvah, settled four years earlier by Jerusalem Jews, the agricultural school at Mikveh Israel, set up by the Alliance Israélite Universelle in 1870, and Gan Montefiore near Jaffa, acquired in 1855.

In 1882, Rishon LeZion was founded in Judea, Zichron Ya'aqov in Samaria, and Rosh Pina in Galilee; yet in this jubilee year of 1932, we still cannot boast that we have solved a problem which involves the ultimate value and dignity, the hopes and security of colonization in Israel, and the whole Zionist Movement—the problem of Jewish labor.

It was not for want of recognizing its crucial importance. Many of the originators of Zionism, such as Rabbi Zvi Hirsch Kalischer, Zeev Yavitz, Mordecai Eliasberg and Pinsker, perceived clearly that cultivation of the soil, manual labor and a new incline of our economic life were indispensable to the renaissance of the nation.

Here are the words of Pinsker, opening the first conference of Chibbath Zion at Katowice in 1886: 'The frightful condition of Jewry will not change for the better unless we succeed in finding it a new place to live in, and a new kind of life; unless we pave a new way for it, a way based on skills and on handiwork. Every nation lives on its soil and among the sons of most nations are many farmers: their well-being flows from the sweat of their brow and the reward of their labors is solid and visible—they are busy with tasks of which the fruits can be seen and grasped, which bear fruit in the everyday meaning of the word. We have become a nation of pedlars and pedants, our physique is undermined and enfeebled. . . . We must gather up what is left of our vigor and trek to the open spaces. . . . Till now we have expended our energies as carriers of goods from place to place, from man to man. Let us now return to our ancient mother, to the land which in mercy awaits us, to partake of her fruits and to sate ourselves with her goodness. Let us change the merchant's yardstick and the Canaanitish scales for spade and plow. . . .'

In Israel, too, ahead of that Second Aliyah which unfurled so gallantly the banner of labor, men perceived the tremendous importance of rugged toil to our nation and society.

When further land was bought at Rishon in March, 1887, the purchasers bound themselves by the formula of the Baron— 'To hire the labor of our brothers only.' In his 'Diary of a Bilu,'* Dr. Hissin writes: 'In the beginning we doubted whether the Jewish worker was dependable and would stand up to the test; we were sure he would do an inferior job. Actually, the Jews did better than the Arabs.'

The number of Jewish workers in Rishon increased to between 20 and 30. In 1887 a 'Workers' Association' was organized so that its committee might constantly seek out openings and members not be out of jobs, that any unemployed might be helped and the workers lodge and eat together. This was the first of its kind in modern Palestine. On March 21, 1887, Hissin notes in his diary: 'With full consciousness of the Jewish worker's major task in settlement and full understanding of its exalted mission, the union went energetically about the ordering of its affairs.'

* The Bilu was a movement in Russia which, following the pogroms of 1881, brought the early settlers from Russia in 1882.

Taking his stand on strange assumptions as to Jewish labor, Achad Ha'am drew the remorseless conclusion that political Zionism was impractical, because you can construct no 'secure refuge'—today we would not see that the same assumptions clashed with his own spiritual Zionism. 'A national, spiritual center for Judaism, a center of Torah and learning, of language and literature, of physical labor and spiritual purity, a miniature of the Jewish people as the Jewish people should be'—how is this to be done in a 'superior' community dependent on foreign hirelings? How can a colony built by non-Jews 'bear a Jewish stamp and be animated by a national, Hebrew spirit?' And what is the moral, social and spiritual make-up of 'a supreme group of farmers' who live by the sweat of others? The repulsive sterility of a landlord, pitiable and foredoomed, who battens on alien toil—is that the image 'of the Jewish people as the Jewish people should be?'

Many another question of like bearing we might put to the begetter of this concept of a 'spiritual center,' who yet lacked faith in the emergence of a Jewish working class because the clever and cultivated Jews he knew were unable to visualize labor as their own basis of living, because to them the plowman is serf to the soil. He philosophized from Jewish ethic and absolute morality, but was blind to the inner conflict in the man of culture who drinks long and deep at the fount of contemporary civilization, but himself adds nothing.

Happily, after twenty years, we can say with certainty that this gloomy prediction was to be disproved. We are today met in a city where all labor, the heaviest as the lightest, is done by only Jewish hands. Tel Aviv is a household word not because of its Jewish shops or Jewish banks or Jewish mayor—you will find such in many other places—but because, as no second city is, it is a metropolis of Jewish labor. Immigrants accept the phenomenon calmly, as a matter of course, as something that was always so. But Tel Aviv was not born full-fledged: even after the first World War there were citizens to champion the 'national' ideal, forsooth, the ideal of 'mixed' labor which is still the passionate cause of a few colonists. It took the bloody riots of May 1921 to install Jewish labor unchallengeably in Tel Aviv.

In the moshavot, too, confounding the incredulity of Achad Ha'am, there are thousands of Jewish workers of every sort. When he wrote 'Summing Up' in 1912 there were about 600, the following year the Palestine Office counted 650 men and 151 women. Toward the end of the first World War, our moshavot in Judea employed 607 all told, Samaria 145 and Lower Galilee 125, making, with half a dozen in Upper Galilee, a total of 883. (I do not include clerks, technicians, or members of the professions.) At that time there were, in addition, 410 workers in the labor settlements.

The first post-war census recorded 1,968 laborers in the moshavot. The second—a Histadruth-census, taken in September 1927, recorded 3,745 men and 937 women, plus 631 workers' wives. Fifty-three percent actually worked on the land, the rest were builders, factory-hands, artisans, clerks and employees in public works and services.

In March 1930, the figure had risen to 7,748, excluding wives—4,982 on the land itself, mostly in the orange groves, 280 on building and public works, 678 in industry and trades, 346 in offices.

Now we have over 8,000 Jewish workers in the moshavot—with wives, over 10,000;—and many more in urban employment. A Jewish working class has come into country-wide existence, and to the credit of its constructive efforts we claim many a town and village, macadam-paved roads and tarred highways, quarries and hewn stone, ditches and bore-holes, swamps drained and cleared, transport and porterage—every kind of agricultural and industrial job, bar none.

It is not just successful placement of Jewish labor—there is the present wonder which our visionaries, even, glimpsed only on the far horizon: rolling acres broken to the plow by Jewish labor and no other, in labor villages established on national demesne according to the principle of self-labor, and by hired Jewish labor as well, on privately-owned land. We have travelled a long way since a Jew was not to be had to drill a well in a moshav, and a Jewish school was built by non-Jewish workmen, and the foundations of a Jewish city were laid with hardly a Jewish trowel. These are almost fairy-tales by now, one listens, but it is difficult to believe that such was once the somber truth, when we see Jewish workers in their thousands today at lathe and bench, with coulter and hoe.

But it is not only a wonder of land transfigured and ruins restored. Our settlers performed prodigies when, upon empty sand-dunes, they set up a flourishing city, endowed with civic institutions and cultural organizations; when they planted grapes and citrus and grain in slough and desert, on soil damned to aridity and soaked in malarial blight; when they probed the natural riches of the Dead Sea, and harnessed rivers to dynamos of power and light. All this, however, can be done, with dollars and scientific aids, in the jungles of Darkest Africa or at the North Pole. Everywhere Jewish capital, intelligence and resources have helped to develop revolutionary industrial and technological undertakings. No, the real miracle of Palestine is the Jew who masters the labor of orchard and garden, field and vineyard, quarry and harbor, water and power, factory and craft, highway and byway. That sort of Jew the Diaspora never made—and to many, only a few years ago, he still seemed a will-o-the-wisp even in Palestine. Not without reason were they skeptical.

If circumstances are anywhere unfavorable to the growth of a Jewish working class, it is in Palestine. The Jewish worker, wherever he be, has two enemies: estrangement of the Jewish employer from him, and pressure of environment in that he is a Jew, regardless of class. The economic anti-semitism of Gentile worker and employer alike usually shuts him out of openings in basic industry, and a large proportion of Jewish employers are no better in this respect: the farmers of Petah Tiqvah were not the first to boycott Jewish labor.

In Palestine, there is a third and over-riding factor: an enormous reserve of cheap, unorganized labor without class-consciousness and with infinitesimal demands, insured to constraint, acquiescent and easy to exploit. A contributor to 'Hamagid' fifty years ago, enumerating the virtues of Palestine, cited among its chiefest boons that which in truth is the very bane of Jewish labor—the supply of Arab workers, plentiful on ridiculously low wages. Cheap and numerous—the mesmeric adjectives have thinned our labor's life-blood to this day.

How, despite this treble threat—estrangement, boycott and the competing Arab—was the Jewish worker made?

Bear with me a while, I will give you the answer.

* * *

As immigration swelled in 1890 and 1891 and the colonies of Rehoboth and Hedera were founded, the enrollment of Jewish labor grew, and in the summer of 1891 the Rehoboth workers endeavored to unite all their local like into a 'Land and Labor' association. This time the aims were two: to watch the interests of the members and their material and spiritual welfare and thereby improve their lot as laborers and their demeanor as Jews and as decent men; and to contemplate, as an end-aspiration, that every Jewish worker, after serving a fair term as such and on certain conditions, might gain tranquillity and a plot of his own. The rules give clear, precise and profound expression, classic almost, to the ideal of labor, and the phrasing of 1892 is not outworn in this year of grace 1932. In a preamble, the philanthropic and the businesslike brands of colonization are analyzed, the defects pointed out, and a new blueprint of working settlement is attempted. Here is what was said:

'Of the first settlers some came with means, some with empty hands, but all came to do physical labor, and we must in fairness say they did their job faithfully. As is natural, things did not go well for them at the start, their funds gave out dismayingly and their labor went for nothing. They had to depend on charity, and friends abroad came generously to their aid and went on giving and giving again to help them reach their goal. The givers had their hearts' desire in some degree perhaps but not in full, and counting the heavy payments against the gains we must be dejected. How much was thus squandered in benevolence from which no slightest blessing came! Nay, this philanthropy was a chronic malediction, demoralizing the recipients and teaching them to beg.

'Last year was something entirely new in our settlement world. Propertied men from abroad bestirred themselves to buy land here for plough and plantation, to be tilled or tended not by their own lusty toil but by means of their money. They combined in a society, which appointed certain of its members to be supervisors of work that others did. This odious innovation degraded settlement into a kind of business. Where the muscles strain and sweat beads the brow, product and producer are blent in a fabric of sinew and nerves which is indestructible. But money and business are linked only by a knot easily undone. Money takes on and puts off shape without trouble. Today's dinar is land tomorrow, and the next day it is a dinar again. We cannot, therefore, regard these monied men as permanent colonists, as real settlers. They are only accountants, trafficking in settlement whenever it happens to be profitable. Worse still, they can never bring us to the end we seek and swell the rural numbers of Jews in the Holy Land.

'We know to our cost that without Jewish labor the colonies are doomed. Arab labor is a broken reed, whether you consider its numbers or its capacity. To our colonization Jewish workers are what blood is to a man: they will give it health and keep it from rottenness and death.'

These brave words, of a timeliness that abides forty years on, were penned by one of the finest and most distinguished writers of Chibbath Zion, friend and tutor of the Bilu pioneers, one whose merits have yet to be recognized—Yechiel Michael Pines.

The association's motto was 'For Land and Hand.' Its rules were signed by Arye Leib Gordon, Meir Dizengoff, Moshe Rattner and Aaron Eisenberg, members of the provisional committee. Bitterly they criticized the earlier labor Aliyah:

'The storm that of late blew from the north heaped upon us hordes of shopkeepers and middlemen, hucksters and beadles, scribes and butchers. All became laborers overnight. One after another they gathered up their bundles and went off to the colonies. The patrons of our settlement rejoiced but the rejoicing was shortlived. Soon, all too soon, the newcomers vanished as though they had never been. Only a handful stayed. Many of the recreants could never have adjusted themselves, they had been irresponsibly precipitate; but a fair number were fit to work on the land and very much wanted to stay, only that the labor conditions prevailing compelled them to go back to the towns or emigrate altogther.

If we wish to bring in Jewish workers, we must revolutionize conditions. We must make the work pleasant and hold out incentives of hope and ambition which will draw workers to us—sentiment is not enough, there must be inducements of advantage as well. We must found a tribe of settlers, faithful and wedded to the soil, the very pillars of the field, apt to multiply and fill the whole land, not as spendthrifts reaching their goal, but by robust toil.

To accomplish that end, the Jewish workers that labor in the furrows and vineyards of the colonies in the Land of Israel for daily wage and, with them, all others to whom settlement is precious are met together to form this association, whereof the standard proclaims 'For Land and Hand.' That is the name and that the purpose, to enable the many Jews with a pair of hands and craftsmanship as their only capital to settle on the land and live from it. The association will protect them, body and soul, and confer upon them an ultimate end and expectation in reward for their labor—that they shall come to possess something of their own here, a footing for ever and ever!'

But this high-flown program was not realized: there was a crisis in Palestine, and internal friction. The whole structure came apart, and, at the beginning of the summer of 1892, the association was dissolved.

So the Jewish workers scattered, each to his own point of the compass. Of the two hundred who till then had been at work in Rishon, only a few remained. The work was not too hard but most left because they could not bear the regime of fines and discrimination, and deadly illness also took its toll. In 1898, there were 97 Jewish workers, but only three did farm work, the rest were in the wine-cellars and in local workshops. 'The greater part were married and had children, yet their daily pay was only 1.5 to 1.7 francs, so you can understand they led a wretched existence. Novices, who did not earn as much, got one and a half piasters a day from the Aid Committee in Jaffa' (Lunz's Palestine Calendar for 1898). Agricultural work was done almost entirely by hired Arabs.

It was no different at Zichron. 'That great colony, where for the last ten years two thousand Arab workers have been employed and by dint of mixing constantly with Jews have, little by little, acquired a smattering of culture . . . many will ask, and rightly, how can there be work there for two thousand Arabs and none for our poor and miserable brethren in Jerusalem, who would be glad of a morsel' (Chaim Dov, of Shfeya, ibid.).

When the Baron came in 1899 he asked the farmers to employ Jews in their vineyards: 'You must succor each a brother, remembering that you yourselves once were poor, therefore do not forsake your kinsmen, nor give only to strangers.' But his words went unheeded. The percentage of Jewish workers in the colonies was negligible and they could barely keep body and soul together. When the Baron transferred his colonies to the Jewish Colonization Association (ICA) in 1900, there were in them five hundred and thirty-two workers' families. Fifty-seven families had emigrated only that summer. 'Most of the workers had been in the country these twelve years; fifty came eighteen years ago among our original colonizers. A hundred and seventy were employed in the cellars, at from 8 to 24 piasters a day, the others as farm laborers with pay varying from place to place—in Galilee 4 to 6 piasters, in Judea 6.2 to 9—and also according to domestic circumstances and seniority. With the new system, which means an end to the Baron's subsidies, there will be practically no work in the colonies for them, and what is to happen to them? Peradventure they must take up the wanderer's staff and flee the beloved country' (ibid., 1900).

And indeed many had to go, staked by the ICA bureaucracy so that they should not linger. The writer A. S. Hirschberg, visiting the country in 1901, has this to say: 'The attitude of the colonists to the Jewish workers does not redound to their credit. They almost all prefer the Arab to the Jew at any job the Arab can do, for a Jew is uppish towards an employer of his own kind and a Jewish farmer cannot impose tough and avoidable usages upon his worker-brother. At first the colonists were constrained to put Jews to special tasks, like pruning and grafting, which demand previous aptitude and knowledge, but the Arabs gradually familiarized themselves with those too and so the Jew is out of work again. Besides, the Arab, on a low subsistence level, is content with a smaller wage and is ready to give his master grace until the harvest before he gets it, which the Jewish worker cannot possibly do. Jewish workers complain that the colonists browbeat them, allow them no voice in communal affairs, and even use the community chest for their own purposes. Protests are loud against the ICA's staff, and Chovevei Zion: the officials are forever plotting mischief for the workers, . . . and, for instance, in Nes Ziona, the Chovevei Zion have a well, which the workers used to approach through the farmstead of one of the colonists, but the way has now been blocked by a high wall and the workers must make a long detour to get water.'

We have the first census of colony workers, made that same year by A. Komarov, of the association that was established before the Second Aliyah: there were four hundred and seventy-three in twelve colonies—161 in Zichron, 103 in Rishon, 52 in Petah Tiqvah, 40 in Rosh Pina, 25 in Ekron, 22 in Metullah, 4 in Mahanayim and 4 in Mishmar Hayarden.

Zichron, Yesod Hamaaleh, Metullah, Petah Tiqvah, Ekron, Rishon and Rosh Pina were lavishly subsidized by the Baron. In his essay 'Settlement and its Guardians,' Achad Ha'am calculates how much they had cost him up to the beginning of 1900, when they were handed over to ICA's care: 'He has about 360 colonists all told. According to the last budget of his managers in 1899, he spent 1,500,000 francs a year on them, or 4,000 francs for each family, over and above the expenses of the Rishon and Zichron cellars, amounting to 1,200,000 francs, of which only a fraction is recouped from sales. And if we recall, further, that outgoings fell off in recent years, we may guess that the budget used to be more. So local experts are apparently conservative when they reckon the up-to-date cost as not less than forty million francs. The fact is that all the gainful sources put together— plowland, vineyards, fruit trees and so on—are in the best of circumstances only enough to sustain a hundred families naturally, without charity or specious revenues. If, then, the Baron were willing and able to give the colonies a normal character by evicting the redundant families, the balance sheet today would be truly remarkable: for forty million francs and after eighteen years of strenuous effort, he has lived to see a hundred families support themselves by their own earnings, which is 400,000 francs a family.'

By 1900, Zichron, which at that time, with its offshoots Shfeya and Bath Shlomo, housed about 100 farmers, cost the Baron—all to no profit—more than ten million francs; the annual expenditure, aside from the cellars, was at the rate of 750,000 francs. And how much has it entailed for ICA during the last 32 years? It has probably cost Jewry more than our whole labor colonization, yet, when it celebrates its jubilee this year, hardly one Jewish laborer will be found within it.

Over 25 years ago, between 1904 and 1906, came the pioneers of the Second Aliyah. There were no Zionist funds, the Jewish National Fund had yet to begin work and no one dreamt of labor colonization. The ideas of self-labor and national ownership of the soil had still to gain currency, even among the workers themselves. The existing colonies, all twenty-five without exception, stood for unadulterated private enterprise, for private property and hired labor, though most of their capital came not from individual colonists but from Jewry in general or from Jews who gave magnificently for the common good, as did the Baron, and though the hired labor was virtually all non-Jewish.

The following passage, dated 1928, gives a brief but comprehensive survey of how things were at the onset of the Second Aliyah: 'The Jewish settlements have swallowed up ninety million francs, and almost the whole of this gigantic sum, except for cash left with the managers, has filled Arab pockets. Part of it, the payment for land and building materials, was of course bound to feed other people's incomes—we had not come here to grab. But the lion's share went to enrich others, not perforce but voluntarily. It is not overstating the case to say that forty-five million francs passed to Arabs in wages alone! Today we have about a thousand farmers, and each furnishes a livelihood for an average of three Arab families, so that Arabs are getting close on a million francs year after year from us for their work. Out of all this colossal disbursement nothing comes back to us, for the Arab has no need to buy from the town Jew and everything he gets in the colony he takes home. Every Jewish farmer added to our number means sustenance and livelihood for three extra Arab families. . . . Let Israel clearly know that Jewish landlords will never restore the land to Israel unless there be Jewish workers.' It was no worker, no socialist, no sworn foe of colonists that wrote thus, but a veteran of the Yishuv, himself a farmer, an early settler, with a Zionist conscience, uncorrupted by class-doctrines—Moshe Smilansky.

Ninety million francs—a thousand farmers—three thousand Arab laborers—there you have the results of the first quarter-century of our colonization under private enterprise. Every farmer, with three alien workmen in his employ, cost 90,000 gold francs more or less, better than 5,600 current Palestine pounds—disregarding price differentials.

It is not my business here to discuss the subsequent course and cares of the Second Aliyah, its desperate struggles, its great suffering and greater courage, its plethora of disappointments and, withal, its vindication of the Jewish laborer's right to work. But for an understanding of the changes in that direction over the years—which is important in relation to our work hereafter—I would like to cite a few striking excerpts from contemporary letters which reveal how we fared at the start, and what so far we have gained.

Petah Tiqvah—1907: 'It is vintage time and the hullabaloo is terrific . . . labor is not to be had, not Jewish of course, it is just that there are no Arab workers. Couriers have rushed out in panic to distant villages, pleading with the fellahin to save the situation, to lend their youngsters for a few days. . . . What a glorious sight to see some thirty boys and girls go forth from Arab Kfar Saba, their recruiting-sergeant in the van!'

Haifa—1908: 'There are forty Ashkenazi workers here. It is principally the soap factory 'Atid' and Miller's mechanical workshop that find the jobs.'

Nes Ziona: 'Wadi Hunein is very good for citrus. Our growers employ a good deal of labor—more than 200 Arabs, but only nine Jews, of whom five are farmers or farmers' sons and four new immigrants.'

Jerusalem: 'When Herzl was in Jerusalem eight years ago he planted a cedar in Motza. It is only natural that his admirers think to establish a memorial to him there: a writers' home of rest and sanatorium. The Anglo-Palestine Bank lent the money, a wall has been put up and a cistern dug. But is it not a disgrace that it is non-Jews who are actually building this monument to our leader! The bank—our national bank—stipulated that Jews were to be employed, but the contractor protested that he had searched and searched for Jewish laborers and masons and could discover only one.'

Herzl Forest, Ben Shemen: 'Two years ago, Arabs dug the wells and erected the boundary fence on this land, which belongs to the Jewish National Fund! And now Arabs have begun to plant the nursery forest. How lordly a privilege for our nation that its work, even such a work at this, should be performed by stranger hands!'

Lower Galilee: 'The tally of Jewish workers is higher than last year but most have jobs with the management. Every farmer in the colonies here employs an Arab who lives, with his family, in the colony. In Yama and Sejera, several employ two or three Arabs. In most colonies, therefore, the Arab families outnumber the Jewish.'

Petah Tiqvah: 'It is true that all the other colonies have fewer Jewish laborers than we, but considering that from a thousand to fifteen hundred Arabs are usually at work here, the half-a-dozen or so score of Jewish workers is nothing to boast of.'

Ein Ganim: 'The local settlers invited a Jewish contractor of

Petah Tiqvah to build them a well with Jewish artisans. He answered that there were none and so he could not take on the job. They sent a special messenger to Wadi Hunein and Rishon, where there were other Jewish contractors, but the reply always was—no Arabs, no well!'

Samaria and Galilee: 'Throughout Galilee, including Hedera and Zichron, there are now 82 Jewish workers, without those in the cellars: 7 in Hedera, 3 in Zichron, 1 in Shfeya, 1 in Bath Shlomo, 45 in Sejera, 6 in Mescha, 4 in Yama, 7 in Milhamia and 8 in Metullah.'

Jaffa: 'In Tammuz, the Odessa committee of the Chovevei Zion began to put up a girls' school. The building sub-committee demanded construction by Jewish workmen wholly, but was ignored. The contract then provided for fifty percent of Jews, if possible, but the contractor invented all sorts of pretexts for cutting the wages of the Jews until they could stand his extortion no more and left in a body.'

Petah Tiqvah: 'Everybody here is wildly indignant about a rumor, which the Palestine Committee confirms, that certain of our farmers intend to bring Egyptians to work for them.'

1909. Again Petah Tiqvah. 'Four years ago a few young Jewish workers started here. Two years ago there were 250, but that peak quickly fell away. Last year, 100 remained. Now there are not more than 25 or 30, half of them steadily employed by the one and only orange-grower who takes on Jews exclusively. And there are at least 1,200 Arabs.'

Tel Aviv: 'As you know, Ahuzath Bayit—which was the first name of Tel Aviv—got a loan of about a quarter of a million francs from the Jewish National Fund. We had every reason to be confident that all the work would be done by Jews. But the sorry facts are now public property. . . . The foundation stone of this first Jewish suburb of Jaffa was set by non-Jewish labor. Last week Jewish carpenters asked to be given the joinery jobs, but the only answer was that it made no difference to the committee who got the work and please not to be a nuisance!'

1910. Jaffa: 'Tel Aviv is nearing completion. From dawn to dusk the great area is full of bustle and movement. The hammers clang, but within the rising walls of the Jewish quarter you rarely hear a Hebrew phrase or melody: Arab contractors have taken over all but one or two buildings.'

The ICA groves: 'All the principal jobs in Petah Tiqvah and Wadi Hunein, in Mikveh Israel and Gan Montefiore, are in Arab hands. After trees had been uprooted in Wadi Hunein, we implored the management to take on additional Jews, but were turned away.'

* * *

Of course, even then ideologists tried to justify boycott of Jewish labor on political grounds. Except that the catchwords 'government by the workers' and 'dictatorship' were not in vogue among the landowning class at that time, there has been no real change of front. 'I have talked with the best of the colonists,' writes Eliezer Ben Yehuda, 'and I am persuaded that before many years go by not a single Jewish worker will be left. It is not that the Jew is a bad or an expensive worker: the reason is his ways and methods—his demands, and the Jewish farmer-employer simply cannot lay his neck beneath the yoke, however much the "organization" sanctifies them.'

There was still no Labor Federation or even a farm-laborers' union. Labor exchanges were unknown, the workers had no social or contracting institutions: the sole urge of our young people, who had left their parents, their schools, their ordinary lives, and come to the Land of Israel, was drudgery for hire in a private colony for a franc and a half or two francs a day, to help regain Jewish labor on Israel's soil for Jews. Nowadays we often hear that 'once upon a time' relations were excellent, it was almost an idyll of farmers and workers. In the Second Elected

Assembly, six years ago before the Farmers' Federation broke away from the organism of the Yishuv, Smilansky did his best to convince us that 'in the good old days,' when Joseph Aaronovitch lived in Rehoboth, farmers and workers were wonderful friends, but it had changed for the worse because, forsooth, Aaronovitch and Berl Katzenelson lost their influence over the workers and 'the guileless farmers were terrified by the Jewish worker and by aims so unsuited to the Yishuv and its needs.'

But what are we of the Second Aliyah to do, who recollect those 'good old days' so well, when the farmers of Petah Tiqvah boycotted us and the colony committee forbade not only employment of a Jewish worker but even his tenancy of a room to sleep or his receiving medical aid? It was not one of us, but Smilansky, who wrote in 1908: 'We know about the Petah Tiqvah boycott. It is no secret that, apart from the open boycott, there are hidden embargos. Who has not heard the whispers breathed into the ear of every landlord that these laborers have come to wreck our world, to pound its walls and to fight all we hold sacred—just because of an isolated incident or the canard of some foolish or naughty young man?'

So things stood, such were relations, in the days of the Second Aliyah.

Twenty years ago, in an essay from 'The Parting of the Ways,' Achad Ha'am penned these devastating words:

'Thirty years' experience demonstrates once and for all that Jewish colonies can maintain themselves in the Land of Israel and can go on multiplying. . . . A Jew can be a diligent farmer, a rural landowner like Boaz in his day, subsisting by cultivation of the soil, expert in that calling and entirely absorbed in it. Morning after morning he goes forth to his field or vineyard, he overlooks his workers as they plough or sow his land, as they plant or graft his grapes, and unhesitatingly works by their side with his own two hands when he must. But what profits this for the building of 'the safe refuge?' A superior farmer-class, dependent on the labor of others, cannot be its basis. The heart-beat of every country is its rural population, the workers and impecunious peasants who earn a bare livelihood with their bare hands on their own small plot or in the wider acres of the superior class. The rural population in Israel is not yet ours, and it is not easy to see how we shall create one of our own, even if our colonies proliferate in every corner of the Land. It is an open secret that, at present, the work is mostly done by fellahin from neighboring villages, some of them daily hirelings who arrive in the morning and return at night, others in regular employ and living in the colony with their wives and children—and all together doing what we should be doing ourselves—building 'the safe refuge.' Our only hope is these young workers from the Diaspora. For they are to yield up their lives upon the altar of a national ideal—Jewish labor, and none other, for the Land of Israel. They are vowed to bring into our colonies, whether existing or yet to be, the agrarian mass that is absent now. It is not for nothing that this question has latterly begun to focus the Yishuv's concerns. Everybody feels that in truth it is the germ of a much greater issue—the whole purpose of Zionism. If these workers too should fail to fill the gap, it is proof that our national idealism is powerless to engender the spiritual qualities that are demanded, and that we must reconcile ourselves to the idea that our rural population in the Land of Israel, even if in the course of time it expands to the very limit of possibility, will always be an upper-class population, a highly-developed and cultural minority and strong only in intellect and wealth. There will be no population of countryfolk, mighty of muscle. By this the character and purpose of Zionism are altered out of recognition . . . In the colonies you could doubtless make men of the soil, the superior type which has others to do its work, and perhaps, as well, an exiguous class of workers for the finer, lighter and better-paid jobs. But not a rural population, not a real proletariat that will take hold of the hard and rough work, the work that requires much and that rewards little, but which alone can support such a population in its tens of thousands. In Petah Tiqvah for example, 300 or 400 workers at most could earn a living on light jobs, while there is ordinary work there that keeps thousands busy.'

And today? The Jordan Valley and Jezreel, the Sharon and Tel Aviv, Jewish workers in their thousands in Judea, in Samaria and Galilee belie the Cassandras who ranted against Jewish labor and made little of the nation's revival that it seeded.

How, then, the miracle? I have told you once. I tell you a second time. Not from the altered aspect of the Land, not from the rebuilding of its wreckage, splendid though that was. Daringly, upon barren and abandoned sands, to lay out a flourishing city, to plant groves and vineyards and cornfields on desert and swamp plagued by famine and fever, to scoop natural wealth out of the dead waters, to turn torrents into light and power—all that, with knowledge and capital, men can do anywhere, and Jews have done. The particular and peculiar wonder of today is the Jewish worker ubiquitous as a husbandman and factoryhand, in railway and on turnpike, pumping water or generating electricity, stevedore and stonecutter.

And, if for decades he sought in vain a sure support in our young but thriving Jewish economy, let us not blame overmuch the Jewish employer, scurmudgeon and antagonist as he was. The convenient abundance of underpaid and tractable Arabs was too tempting.

By what magic were the hurdles cleared and the wonders worked?

Jews employ Jews after all. Patriotic conscience—the Zionist outlook? What we heard from Tuchovitsky this evening was the expression of that attitude. How far he spoke for the farmers, I do not know, but he spoke as a farmer and only a nationalistically conscientious man could have said what he did. There are others like him, and not only men risen from the working ranks, scores of farmers loyally observing the commandment 'Ye shall have Jewish labor,' veterans of manifold experiences, men who have been through the mill, alive to the vexation and travail which observance means. Perhaps the finest type is that same man whom I cited, already managing his groves with entirely Jewish labor twenty-four years ago—Kroll of Petah Tiqvah. Nowadays, with labor colonization solid in the Emek as a living testimony to Jewish agricultural skill, with the colonies conquered and Tel Aviv and the Sharon fully 'Hebraized,' it is rather easy to take Jewish labor for granted as Tuchovitsky does, and to follow his suit. But there was a time, I tell you, when Jewish labor was tabu, when Zionism in practise, as in textbook, kept the principle of it at arm's length, when the most eminent thinker of Chibbath Zion disavowed flatly as impractical what he should have heralded as indispensable to Jewry's rebirth and his own spiritual center. Then, believe me, it needed a discerning and devoted conscience as a Jew to breast the current, to observe the principle with unremitting and unequivocating zeal, careless of the taunts and execration of your fellow-farmers. The historian of the Yishuv will surely count Kroll a hero of colonization. Risking one's imperiled life in a moment of exaltation is unremarkable, but it takes moral courage to keep on performing, day after day, a prosaic Zionist duty that still lacks the official cachet of the Movement and all your class revile. Arrant folly—they jeer. Are there not still farmers aplenty, come as 'idealists' and owing their farms to the bounty of the Movement, yet stilling their Zionist conscience to ban Jewish labor? In Zichron and Rosh Pina it has scarcely a foothold. Dozens of groves in Nes Ziona, Rishon, Hedera and Rehoboth are marked 'keep out!,' and Petah Tiqvah, last April, could 'boast' more than a hundred groves where no Jewish worker ever trod. At the beginning of 1930, the five colonies gave agricultural work to 2,733 Jews and 3,078 Arabs; last February, 4,230 Jews were employed, some on building and public works, and 4,000 Arabs. That is not the Zionism, nor such the conscience, to bear our burdens.

For others, the secret of success is labor organization. I, of all people, will not be suspected of discounting the positive importance of that factor. The slightest knowledge of conditions shows that Jewish workers could not possibly hold out here unorganized. To be a worker is a penance anywhere. It is ten times as hard for a Jew to be one, and to be one in the Land of Israel is a hundred times as difficult. The reasons are several: the work is strange—this is a country of immigration at the dawn of reconstruction—its economic basis is shaky—the market is restricted, uncertain and indeterminate but always liable to be flooded by cheap labor—the employer class, though multiplying, is unfriendly and is not beholden to Jewish labor at all. Never before has the Jewish worker been so awkwardly placed. Without a powerful class-organization, the trusted aid of his comrades, mutual responsibility, collective trial and centralized training, his own vocational, managerial and cultural institutions, and cooperative media of achievement, he must forfeit opportunity, must lose character, must blunt his creativeness, and fail as a Zionist. It is double-dealing to accept Jewish labor but not its organization.

I do not say organization did it all, but how else explain the upthrust, from a sea of cheap and unorganized Arab labor, of islets of costly, organized Jewish labor—both in the lighter branches requiring wits or expertness and in plain, tough jobs that cheap labor can do as easily and as well? Supposing German or British workmen had found their way here by accident—do you think they would have contrived to establish themselves in thousands in lowly jobs and yet maintain a high standard of living in competition with local helots in myriads? Would organization by itself have helped? No labor movement in the world has matched ours. Elsewhere, if there are two standards of living, the superior class must limit itself to work privileged by law or skill, but in Palestine dear union labor captures the cheap market in the teeth of non-union labor, without lowering its own standards or halting its social advances.

Gentlemen, I hold that the overmastering strength of Jewish labor lies in the dynamic strength of Aliyah, in the impact and growing urgency of an historic need, the need of our masses in Galuth, bereft of all provision now and of every hope to come, their only salvation a life of labor deep in Homeland soil. A mighty and resistless power is this, though the eye perceives it not, the will-power of Jewry to survive, thirsty for earth and effort, for freedom and resurgence. This galvanic momentum, which nothing could stay or weaken, coursed through pioneer veins. In the name of national existence it took the labor market of Palestine and opened a highway for the homecoming of Israel. That is how the miracle came about, Zionism's glory and fount of our hereafter.

As the Jewish worker is product, messenger and voice of Aliyah, so is Aliyah dependent upon his fate. It is significant, and hardly fortuitous, that splenetic opponents of Jewish labor fight Aliyah as well. The political spokesman of the Jewish Agency, discussing the causes of the stoppage of immigration last year, told us what harm was done our case by the attitude of 'Bustenai' (a publication of the Jewish citriculturists). It is just disingenuous window-dressing to talk loudly about mass immigration, mass colonization and large-scale Zionism and not also take honest and truthful thought in everyday practise, in every single thing you do, for the well-being of Jewish labor, for its consolidation and expansion to the economic utmost. The issue was never so acute, never so desperately tragic, in all the fifty years of our modern colonization; not because of incidents last winter, but because Jewish plantation has reached a decisive stage of development. Soon the future of Jewish labor must be settled, for better or worse, and that means the future of plantation and of Aliyah in coming years.

REBIRTH AND DESTINY OF ISRAEL
* * *

At the first session of the Second Elected Assembly six years ago, we were debating the economy of the Yishuv and the question naturally arose of augmenting the Jewish labor force in the colonies. Smilansky, as chairman of the Farmers' Federation, then produced figures to show that absorptive capacity had reached saturation point and for years there could be no addition: indeed he went so far as to claim a surplus of some hundreds who ought to be taken away. But events proved him wrong—absorptive capacity has risen steadily. I have dependable information that in 1936 Jews owned 10,500 dunams of bearing citrus compared with 900 dunams in 1901 and 9,200 dunams in 1914. With 1926 the ownership began to increase progressively: in that year by 5,000 new dunams, in 1927 by 5,500, in 1928 by 8,000, in 1929 by 15,000, in 1930 by 14,500 and last year by 6,000. In all, 54,000 dunams and, counting the 1926 area, a grand total of 64,500. The Federation puts new planting this year at 11,000 dunams but other trustworthy sources put it as high as 17,000, whence an over-all of nearly 80,000 dunams may soon be realized. By contrast, Arab ownership is in the region of 55,000 dunams.

How many workers for the Jewish area? I once worked in the groves myself but am not a citriculturist, still, I have been given certain figures, carefully checked and expertly clarified.

The area under citrus before 1926 was all in bearing but densely planted in the old style, and required one regular laborer through the year for every ten dunams, as well as seasonal hands. The new groves are mostly not yet in bearing but cultivation is much improved and one regular laborer can look after every 15 dunams right up to the tenth year; after that, at a rough average, again one can look after every ten. Therefore, when all groves already planted or planned are in bearing, they will absorb the following labor, regular and seasonal:

For the pre-1926 dunams—1,050 regulars.

For the 70,000 new dunams—4,670 regulars in the first ten years and after that from 6,000 to 7,000.

For picking and packing, four months a year, one seasonal for every 500 dunams, or 16,000 altogether.

So, not reckoning what may come later, our citriculture alone already calls for up to 8,000 regulars and 16,000 seasonals. And what of vines, almonds, olives and field crops? What of industry, public works and building, office jobs and services that are bound to keep pace with growth of plantation and population? We may miss mathematical exactitude, but considering how rapidly the Jewish agricultural population has risen in recent years, we can be sanguine that employment will be much more forthcoming. For example, in 1901, we had 18 colonies with a total area of 225,000 dunams and a population of 4,750; in 1914, there were 43 colonies, 408,742 dunams and a population of 11,990; in 1922, 70 colonies, 649,000 dunams and a population of 15,000 or thereabouts; last November, 110 colonies, 1,200,000 dunams and 46,465 souls. Hired labor only affects settlements founded by private enterprise—which gives particular interest to statistics for 1930 published in this year's 'Bustenai': 'Of the acreage in the colonies within the citrus belt, 74% belongs to private landowners; in general terms of plantations, about 88%; in terms of citrus only, 91.7%.' 'Bustenai' mentions 37 colonies in the category of private enterprise, with an area of 232,891 dunams whereof 104,213 is plantation, including 59,864 dunams under citrus. Much additional land was broken since and work has increased.

We will not be far out in figuring that all this should absorb at least 20,000 laborers, more or less regularly. At the moment there are only 8,000 Jews at work. So we put the crucial question: the extra 12,000—is Aliyah to find them or will cheap labor oust Jewishness from our colonies?

Already, one branch—building—has been taken over entirely

by Jewish labor. Even where mixed labor is still used for other purposes, this is so. It is a fairly recent victory, won not without many a sharp fight. Only six years ago in Rehoboth, which, with some justice, prides itself on a positive approach in this respect, there was a serious incident because a central building was being put up and no single Jew employed. It is worth remembering as marking the end of the local war for 100% Jewish employment on building, and as high-lighting the methods to which colonists resorted to prevent that victorious end. It brought vividly into focus the political hazards which this question of labor involves. The owner and two of his friends sent a memorandum to the District Commissioner in the name of 90 residents of the colony, describing the cordial relations that had prevailed for years between them and their Arab laborers, the gainful employment the Arabs always found and so on, until Jewish workers appeared on the scene, who were driving the Arabs away by all manner of violence and vilification, and so forth and so forth, and by so doing were like to excite enmity between the Arabs and Jews and endanger the peace of the country—the Histadruth and its leaders were to blame for it all—and, please, would the District Commissioner take steps against the Jewish workers and their union and safeguard Arab lives and welfare. This calumny got no response even from British officialdom, which cannot be said to be lovingly disposed towards the victims of it.

In December 1927, the trial took place of 11 Jews arrested for picketing groves in Petah Tiqvah—where women and men in the line were shamefully beaten up by policemen. The District Officer who ordered the beatings and arrests admitted on oath that there had never been a dispute between Jewish and Arab workers in Petah Tiqvah, and that no such case had come to his knowledge during a long service in charge of Rehoboth and the southern colonies.

Too often peaceful picketing, which the law allows, ended with the colony committee summoning the police. Scuffles and arrests followed, and the farmers' Press would bemoan the fisticuffs of the workers! Hedera was typical a little while ago: an Arab broker had bought the fruit in a certain grove, and was using Arabs from Jaffa to pick it. A Jewish picket appeared. The owner protested: 'What do you want of me? I am not a Zionist!' The police were called in, and again the second day and again the third day, when the inspector threatened to beat up the picket if it did not scatter after he had blown his whistle thrice. But the beating started after a single blast, and at the end the colony was full of bleeding and bandaged workers. At the trial, the Haifa magistrate described the picketers as intent only on demonstrating to get local labor taken on: it was evident to him that criminal purpose was lacking, and that picketers had been needlessly assaulted, for, he remarked, they could have been dispersed by other means much pleasanter to both sides. A circular of the Federation is my source for the following account of a subsequent interview with the acting District Commissioner by a deputation from that body: 'Smilansky expressed alarm lest trouble start in other places . . . and sought to explain how the Histadruth had latterly seized the labor market. . . . He distinguished between this and the picketing, say, of a factory on strike, and suggested this be made unlawful, which would do much to preserve quiet in the colonies. . . . The orange-growers were entitled to ask the Administration, by use of the civil arm, to uphold the farmers' liberty of self-management. . . . The Administration tended to post-factum mediation and compromise. . . . It was its timely duty to prevent violence and in particular the pickets which invariably led to it.' A few days later the Hedera committee advertised in 'Bustenai': 'If the police had its orders and obeyed them, neither the owner of the grove, nor any other of us, can be reprehended. . . . From now on, if there is assault, if force is used or picketing, we will call in the police.'

I must, in fairness, add that on occasion angry workers aggravated matters: their cause was righteous but they were sometimes less than restrained or tactful.

So long as incidents recurred within the four walls of the Yishuv and impinged on inter-Jewish relations only, the danger was not great. Now, however, as our plantation economy expands, portending the integral admission of masses of Arab labor into the realm of Jewish settlement, there is grave political peril. In the National Council, four years ago, I sounded a warning: 'This little enclave of planted acreage is likely to be soon the hub of our colonization. We shall not wait until grasping capital assembles cheap multitudes on it from all parts of Palestine, from the Hauran, from Syria and Egypt. The Jewish effendis of Petah Tiqvah are smuggling fellahin into new colonies now. It is no good our coming afterwards and shrieking to high heaven. We do not want to war on Arab labor, nor shall we stand by and watch Jewish colonization turned into a cockpit of Jew versus Arab. But if the Yishuv and the Zionists everywhere are not vigilant at this hour of crisis, we shall be too late.'

The Jewish people is trekking back homeward, but no one in his senses dreams of evicting the people that settled here when we were driven forth. We accept the Arab population as a fact and base our future on new means and sources of livelihood, not replacing what exists but over and above it, so that we may plant our myriads deep-rooted on the land, side by side with the Arabs. If, creating these fresh possibilities, we do not find prior room for Aliyah, if all we do is congest them with Arab labor, our purpose here and our future are sabotaged: we should never shift the Arabs from our economy, once they were given sanctuary within it.

The Yishuv endures only as the nation's herald, with no right or hope of survival except in the Aliyah that will make it a people: the Zionist Movement speaks for the people and its determination to be reborn. If neither grasps the crucial meaning of this labor problem, if both fail to solve it surely, they will answer for it at the bar of Jewish history.

* * *

The new plantings are still young and few are in bearing. Jewish groves were reckoned to give 1,400,000 cases fit for export last year, the current estimate is 1,270,000, and in each of the next four seasons the rising figures are: 2,250,000, 3,220,000, 4,470,000 and 5,570,000. Two men go to every thousand cases. When all groves are in bearing, 10,000 to 16,000 seasonal workers will be required. Some packing jobs are well-paid by comparison, but we cannot expect a Jewish worker to keep himself for a year on four months' pay. It is imperative, and with good will it is feasible, to find him work in the colonies during the other eight months on those jobs which can be done conveniently while the groves are idle.

What prevents full satisfaction of our demand? Smilansky mentions three obstacles: economic, psychological and physical. 'The extra shilling a case is a heavy burden and will ruin us altogether when prices fall, as inevitably they will. The margin would be even greater if we agreed to employ only Jews. That we cannot and must not do. We must not build a Great Wall of China between the Arabs and ourselves, saying: "So far shall ye come and no further." Agricultural labor is creation, and creation cannot be without congenial liaison between farmer and farmhand, without mutual trust. None ought to take on agricultural labor save the man fitted for it, devoted to it and so fashioned as to live it' ('Bustenai').

How far congenial liaison and mutual trust link the Jew and his Arab employee today, Smilansky knows as well as the next. When representatives of the Histadruth conferred with an important colony committee a couple of years since, the chairman explained why he had to prefer the Arab worker: 'If I employ a Jew and the work is finished on Thursday, I have not the heart to send him away jobless on the Sabbath eve, but I can send an Arab packing at a moment's notice.' Yet Smilansky once wrote: 'I dare proclaim I love the Arab, much in him reaches my heart. But I can still frankly see the risks wherewith he is fraught for our colonization. I love him in his own village, but in our midst I see him as a dangerous enemy, who may yet rob us of our last comfort and hopes. . . . I know him pretty well, the way he speaks and how he regards what we are doing here. That is why I say, that so long as colony work is not done with our own hands, we and all our expectations teeter at the crater's brink. That is why I place Jewish labor in the forefront of colonization, and cannot put my mind to any other issue.' That was in 1908. It seems as if, in the years between, Mescha and Sejera in mourning, stricken Tel Hai and Yajur, the outbreaks of 1920 and 1921 and 1929, had convinced Smilansky that the peril was no more.

The main overt argument, of course, is economic, the wage-differential that may crush the farmers entirely. Jewish labor is certainly dearer, although experimental tendering for contracts on the basis of Arab wages shows that it can be so efficiently organized as both to step up production and earn more. Almost all groves, however, pay by the day, which explains the differential, and it will undoubtedly go on until the Arab worker attains to Jewish standards of living and organization.

Experts say that, for the first five years, planting and maintenance amount to 58 Palestine pounds a dunam, less land and well: this covers 75 working days, so that Jewish labor at twenty piasters a day would cost fifteen pounds. But fifteen days are for skilled work, for which even some Arab orange-growers employ Jews, and, for 60 working days, the Jewish wage bill is not quite five pounds costlier than the Arab. In the sixth year the trees begin to bear and dunam-income is about three pounds. By the tenth year the average dunam-yield is set at 120 cases, and then Jewish labor represents two piasters extra a case.

Jewish picking costs 20 to 22 mils a case, Arab picking 12 to

14 mils, and packing costs, respectively, 38 to 40 mils, and 33 to 35 mils; it is only unskilled Arabs, however, that get the lower tariff.

In short, the whole discrepancy is 33 mils a case. Since the war, the average price, on the tree, was 300 mils a case, and the average dunam-income 36 pounds. If we deduct maintenance, which with Jewish labor might be as much as 16 pounds, the net is 20 pounds; with Arab it is slightly over twenty-two. If we adopt Smilansky's scheme, employing, say, two-thirds Jews, the gap is narrowed to below a pound. And that is the sum and substance of the argument! It is for this petty profit, not a twentieth of net income, that he would foist upon the colonies the evil of mixed labor, which can only provoke trouble on national and social fronts alike.

But the economics is really secondary. The social objection is uppermost—class-hatred of intelligent Jewish labor. Arab labor is the scourge our 'nationalist' employer wields to humble the presumptuous Jew. Smilansky does not bother to conceal it. He writes: 'The moment we bind ourselves to employ only Jewish labor, its wages will rise to disastrous levels. One grove using mixed labor, the bulk of it Jewish, will be going smoothly. The one next door, with only Jewish workers, will be harassed by interminable pourparlers.'

How wonderfully the Lord provided for Jewish workers when He banished us and settled a million strangers in our Land! If, Heaven forbid, the Land were intact and our people never exiled, the Federation would have had to bow to the edict. . . . Because he fears the Jewish worker, Smilansky would handcuff Jewish settlement to non-Jewish labor for ever. But he is not content with that. The ratio of Jewish workers in his mixture— he now agrees it should be a preponderant majority—must nevertheless be made up of types you can trust, not members of the Histadruth bold enough to stand up for their right to work and even demand civic rights in the colony their toil creates. 'The farmers ought to select from groups not organized in the Histadruth—men from Brith Trumpeldor, Yemenites and the like'—that was his secret instruction this winter to his faithful henchmen. Others go further: a young farmer from Binyamina, truant from the Halutz movement, demands that Histadruth types not only be banned from work but kept out of Palestine. 'It is clear to us now,' he writes in 'Bustenai,' 'that the Jewish worker is not interested only in work and food as he avers, but aspires to power, to economic and social dictatorship over the agricultural domain and those who own it. For us farmers it is therefore a matter of life and death. We must fight back, but the tactics of the past will not bring success. The neutral labor exchange is no answer. The bane is in the conduct and orientation of Aliyah, and only by rooting out that bane can we alter the make-up of our labor community. Thousands in the Diaspora today, famished and unemployed, would be glad to supply their wants in our Jewish milieu and conditions. Certificates should be given to the able amongst them, and not to young labor ideologists.' At a recent farmers' conference in Tel Aviv, the same gentleman enlarged on his theme—converting the Jewish masses into a helotry. 'Fear not!' his message ran, 'lots of Jews will come to work here, we can dispense with the 'peculiar' kind: the plain, ordinary worker will adjust himself to the rigid law of husbandry and abate his standards: the main thing is to prepare the kind of worker overseas in advance, and fight the Histadruth to a standstill.'

History repeats itself. Forty-five years ago, with the Baron's bureaucrats governing, a 'revolt' against the management broke out in Rishon that united most of the farmers and workers. The manager, Ossovitsky, brought in Turkish gendarmes to quell the 'insurgents.' Whereupon, to the intense displeasure of the Baron, the farmers threw him out. Leadership of Chibbath Zion, fearful lest subventions be cut off, was divided in opinion: the sycophants sided with Ossovitsky, and one, a very celebrated writer who shall be nameless, so far lowered himself to say: 'You cannot make farmers out of an intelligentsia which cultivates ideas, not the soil. That sort is unfit for the task. There are in Jewry thousands of wretched paupers, rough and ready, knowing naught except slave-labor—and they cannot always get that—to buy a crust for their children. These serfs will be our cultivators. We cannot build up colonies save with men who will submit to bureaucrat and behest, men that have lived only the raw and rugged way.'

Little did he know that his noble ideal of colonization by slave-labor was to be realized by that self-same farmer-intelligentsia! He erred, too, in seeking his serfs where none are—in the people of Israel. Our skillful farmers were quick to get their bondsmen from the Arab market, cheap and easy.

But there is a market the adversaries of Jewish labor overlook: it is the Jewish people, under compulsion of will and history, returning home, not to slavery but to freedom and creation on its native soil. That gives us our only chance. Where would the colonies be without the millions of Rothschild and the Chovevei Zion, the political struggles of Jewry to win our right to colonize, the economic, agricultural and political reinvigoration which Aliyah injects? The one and only aim of these endeavors is to multiply the numbers that wish to build and be reborn by labor. That alone, morally and politically, justifies colonization. Private investment, making so many openings for Jews, has done great things, and the Jewish worker must not decry its importance and advantage for the Yishuv. But, however private his capital, a settler can only possess his land by grace of Zionism and its works. Take away the resources of Jewry, its help and protection which buttress the Yishuv, and no Jew here can enjoy peace or property.

The pioneers of work, defense and fulfillment will not resign themselves to the barring of Jewish labor from an economy the people's grace has built. Filch opportunity from them by whatever pretext, and they will counter-attack undismayed, no ordinary jobless but envoys of a nation. Not if every man here now were working six days in the week every week in the year, not even then would they pause or would a single opening be surrendered: for there are thousands yet to come.

* * *

But you ask me: 'What about cooperation?' Yes, we favor it, but still we champion full Jewish labor, still with utter faith in the sure prospect and morality of Jewish labor—and just because our twin principles are those. We want it for the Jewish worker in the Jewish economy and for the Arab in his, and for all Government employees, urban and country-wide.

The Revisionists and Communists affect to see a contradiction: either full Jewish labor or cooperation, they say—not both. If the only duty of the Jewish worker here is to be an instrument of social revolution among the Arabs, why indeed should he exert himself so? Will not the 'imperial budget' for the global overthrow of Governments satisfy his needs most generously? But that duty is abhorrent to him, he yearns to live by his labor, not in isolation, not only now and again, but integrally and always, with a working class that is fit and fated to become a working nation. He has no revolutionary mission more vital or more fruitful than persevering to multiply the working guarantees of a strong and stable future.

You politicians of 'expansionist' Zionism, so competent, in verbal vanity at least, to set up a Jewish State on both sides of Jordan—without pioneering or colonizing, with no effort of reconstruction, no armies of volunteers—why should you trouble your heads about little things like Jewish labor or better working conditions? You have unswerving trust in a system of Government, not socialist of course but colonial, which the Mandatory will install and straighten out the affairs of the Jewish State beautifully. It will merely intone 'abracadabra', forthwith ridding itself of all issues and problems, even of how to handle the Arabs. We are not quite as sanguine. Above all else, our Zionism has taught us to rely on our own exertions, to unravel our perplexities ourselves. That is how we shall seek adjustment of neighborliness, by forging comradely links and finding common interests. It is our privilege to launch the organization of Arab labor, our duty to go through with it to the end. Not that we are missionaries with a gospel. We are here to make a life of our own, and by self-labor to pattern our nation. That is why we deem it right and rewarding to extend a helping hand to our Arab fellows. International class-solidarity, our consciences as Zionists and as of the Yishuv, make us want for the Arab worker conditions as good as our own. That equality concerns more than labor. It is no less necessary that the fellah should not undercut the Jewish farmer, or the Arab industrialist his Jewish competitor.

Who except a few intransigent colonists really wants the terms of work and wage in Arab groves to be depressed everlastingly? Cooperation complements the policy of Jewish labor, which—in organization or individuals—makes it possible, not impairs it; but in time, in urgency and in importance, it is work that comes first.

Jewish labor never scored by offering to work for less, or less decently. Its successes came in the wake of higher wages and better conditions. If Arab labor encroaches on Jewish employment, it always means reducing wages; if it is the other way round, wages go up, and expulsion of Arab labor is nohow caused. The Jew only fills the job which is his by rights, the job newly made by Yishuv and by Aliyah, and for their sake.

In the last analysis, so far from losing jobs, the Arabs get added work from our colonization, wholly 'Hebraized' though it may be. Some of those whom an archaic industry sustains are likely to suffer when there is modern development of it. Railroad and automobiles will take custom from cameleer and donkeyman, Jew or Arab. But the new sources of livelihood, the new branches of economy, are not in general apt to lessen the chances of indigenous labor, for all that immigration pours in. Citriculture is an excellent example. Thirty years ago, there were 30,000 dunams, but only 9,000 belonged to Jews. There are now 115,000 and 65,000 belong to Jews, who thus expanded seven-fold, while the Arabs own nearly three times as much as before. So the new Jewish groves could not have thrown a single Arab out of work; the truth is they mean extra work for Arab stevedores, cameleers and clerks, and that without considering the new Arab groves.

You ask how all this fits in with the dual policy of Jewish labor and cooperation. Well, the 7,000 men at work in the Jewish area for 20 piasters a day would like the 5,000 Arabs in the Arab area to get the same. Hence the organization of a union of citrus-workers, Jew and Arab, for the whole of Palestine, in an effort, by pooling resources, to secure fair and, if possible, equal conditions of labor throughout. Everybody in the country, not only Arab and Jewish workers, will benefit. Growers may grumble at the loss of cheap labor, and politicians with a flair for racial feuds may grieve: but their lament is not ours.

* * *

A renegade squirearchy and its retainers, apostates of the Labor movement trading pen and conscience for cash, false prophets of 'emotional' Zionism, such were ready to vilify the working class, its Histadruth, undertakings and ambitions. They churned up the murkiest class-instincts of the man of means who neither understands nor esteems the power of labor, new and national, that is cleansing our economy and society.

Nothing is further from the mind of Jewish labor than to engineer disputes, with all the material and political loss in their train. For it, the supreme charter of our generation is reconstruction and Aliyah, to it all impairment or hindrance, every contradiction of the charter, is anathema. It is a charter meaningless without Jewish labor, and until Jewish labor has become immovably the boundary cairn of our colonization, marking securely the length and breadth of our economy, until it is no longer a suppliant for alms but natural, necessary and self-evident, the Jewish worker will fight on.

This we would rather do by peace and pacts, but if there is no option, we will fight, and not by picketing alone. 'Bustenai' upbraids the pickets as hooligans and sluggers, and proclaims a 'holy war' upon them. Yes, these are the very men that 'picketed' long since, to defend our villages with their lives against Arab onslaught, and those that did not die have gone forward without flinching! If they could keep fearless watch then over Jewish chattels, will they not now protect Jewish labor? They are not angelic or infallible. Of some the Zionist allegiance is worn threadbare, and they try to patch it with jejune revolutionary slogans. Some, in spirit and intellect, are unequal to complexities and hide their heads in the sand of barren, vapid diction. And there are the irresolute and faint-hearted, fleeing the battlefield and even joining the enemy. Even the faithful ones—and they are far and away the most—are only flesh and blood, and not each remembers his historic errand every hour of the day, not every act of his is informed with a sense of Zionist and socialist duty. No one knows better than I the weaknesses, defects and shortcomings of us workers, but this I say with undiminished faith: the generality of workers, the working community as an organized whole, comprising not members of the Histadruth only, but Hapoel Hamizrahi and Yemenites as well and all groups true to Jewish labor and upbuilding, is second to none in Jewry for vigilance and loyalty. None outdoes it in responsibility, in concern or preparedness for fulfillment. And it sincerely seeks regular and normal relations with employers, knowing well the damage and dangers else.

The Histadruth is one of the few Trade Unions to expand massive means and energy in establishing agricultural settlements, and sustain them with such care and affection. But it is not only working settlement that exercises us but private settlement also, which can absorb Jewish labor no less. Like all his fraternity, the Jewish worker dreams of social freedom, and believes that in time Labor will come into its own all over the world. The Arab worker, too, whom unthinking employers regard as a robot, will throw off his torpor and enter the ranks of combatant labor, he too will behold the vision of its freedom. The rights Jewish labor seeks are those of man, worker and citizen. Tomorrow or the next day Arab labor will echo the demand, for who is so short-sighted as to think that the Arab will meekly consent to be robbed forever of his right, to be exploited mercilessly, and never once claim a plot and patrimony of his own? Built on Jewish labor, a Jewish economy will stay Jewish, be regimes the world over what they may. Of one that is not, all Jewish memory will perish when Labor governs.

We live in a capitalist era and in it must reconstruct our Land. Therefore, I see the need, and for all our differences I hold it possible, amicably to safeguard our economy and labor, both, on the following basis:

Guarantee of Jewish work in the Jewish economy, not as charity but as unchallengeable obligation.

Fair conditions of work within the economic capacity of agriculture, and against an undertaking of quality of performance, and output, according to norms.

Each party to recognize the other's rights and interests. The farmer wants to be king of his own castle, but his castle needs hired labor, which means the human beings called workers. The worker has his own castle, too—his capacity to work: that is his sole capital and livelihood, and you must not subject it to an employer's arbitrary whim. It is not so much that we appeal to the employer's sense of justice. He too ought to be concerned to prevent disputes and disturbances. Perhaps not eliminated altogether, but they can at least be minimized. In every big factory we have come to agreement, written or oral, with the owners, and labor procedures and connexions now exist which ensure a desirable minimum for both sides. Before the last Congress, we had talks with the Manufacturers' Association, and be it said to its credit that it never for a moment questions the policy of Jewish labor. Cardinal questions were discussed and an understanding was reached: the Histadruth is more than willing to resume the talks now and carry them to a conclusion.

But mark well! Jewish labor will not forget or fritter away the greater entitlement of the first-comers. If any truly merit the honored name of halutzim, a name blurred by surfeit of use, but destined to shine again, to be revered and loved again, they merit it who half a century ago hammered the first tent-pegs gallantly in the Judean desert and after 1800 years renewed our covenant with Israel and its Land. No subsequent delinquency can dim the radiance of that new Genesis, or lessen its worth. The precious name of Bilu, that lit up the way of the Second and Third Aliyah, will eternally glow in our eyes, and we shall not allow its works to be desecrated by pursuit of gain which makes slave-camps of our first-born colonies, marts to buy and sell the proceeds of others' labor. The Jewish worker, true heir of Bilu, has saved our colonization from moral and political bankruptcy and set our right to soil and Homeland on the only path that gives a nation that right—the path of labor.

The contest, protracted and exhausting, continues. We recall that the heartless and avaricious sponsors of a concern that was, with unconscious irony, styled 'Repose and Reward,' greeted the labor pioneers with insult and mockery when few: now that we are many, they are craven but vindictive. Boycott and procrastination, constabulary batons and false charges—these are their weapons. They still don a praying-shawl of Zionism and bewail the 'Zionist' sin, the 'national' menace which, to them, full Jewish labor is. Their strictures grow more strident because the sturdy Jewish worker will not seek quarter but battles on for his right to work, for the Yishuv's duty to absorb Jewish immigrants to the maximum and accord them full and equal rights of citizenship.

This is not a class war. The real class war is between the disciples of 'Zionism on the way' and its adversaries. The strength the Jewish worker has shown in this long, hard struggle he draws not only from class organization and social vision, but from national duty, willingly and wittingly self-imposed, because he knows that in the background a whole people is fighting for existence, yearning for redemption. He is imbued with a deep Zionist faith, unshaken and undimmed, he believes implicitly in the justice and necessity of his pleas. Thus trebly armed, he will fortify Jewish labor and expand it until it triumphs fully at last.

OUR ACCOUNT WITH THE BRITISH
*At a Meeting of the Zionist Executive Council,
Jerusalem, November 14, 1936*

This harsh indictment of Britain is neither the fair truth nor in our own interest.

I have much to charge the British Government with, but not so much. I am not quite so innocent as to believe that all it does here is in heaven's name. No nation does things that way, and many things Britain does run counter to our advantage. We do not let them pass unprotesting; all our political activity is a continuing struggle with her. But I cannot associate myself with exaggerations—to put it mildly—which travesty the truth and imperil our politics.

One will not have it that there is a 'revolt'. There was absolutely no reason, he says, for the Arabs to rebel, since the regime is Arab, and one does not rebel against one's own. And why is this an Arab regime? Because Musa el Alami is District Attorney, and such-and-such are District Commissioners. That is enough for him. But he is not an Arab, and it is not for him to decide whether or not to rebel. The Arabs have a totally different idea. What they say is that the regime brings in 30,000 Jews one year, 42,000 the next, and 62,000 the year after. What does it matter if Musa el Alami is District Attorney? 'If it goes on only a few more years, we Arabs,' they cry, 'are lost! We must arise and overthrow it.'

It has been argued that there was no real rebellion, because the Government could easily have put it down. Even so, does that mean the Arabs did not rebel? If Britain had despatched a large expeditionary force to South Africa at the outbreak of the Boer War, the Boers would have been overpowered at once—would the Boer rebellion in that event have ceased to be one? Would anyone say that Britain arranged for the war to last two years, and that the Boers did no fighting at all? If you have the courage to look facts in the face you must admit that the Arabs did rebel against the so-called Arab regime. If the speaker were an Arab himself, he would, I suspect, join in too and not be satisfied with Musa el Alami's appointment or the District Commissioner's. No, immigration is the crux for Arabs as for Jews, and the Arabs are not prepared to swallow large-scale immigration at his price.

I am not defending the Government, but blindness to the complexities and difficulties is unlikely to add conviction to our protests and complaints. We will go on protesting and complaining against the Government for not showing enough vigor at the right time. Hyperbole and sweeping generalization, however, can do us no good.

We will not take the counsel of the hot-heads who preach that everything that Government has done over the past twelve years has been a succession of malignancies and plot and discrimination aimed against the Jewish National Home and for an Arab State. I am not suggesting that we pass over the errors and evils of the Government—on the contrary, let us submit our grievances to the Royal Commission and the British public. But no wholesale charges, please! Not all of Britain's work in Palestine is bad, or was prompted by conspiratorial ill-will. She admitted 350,000 Jews; built Haifa Port, and Haifa has now a Jewish majority; linked our settlements with roads, and—if inadequately—supported Jewish industry. Such facts I cannot ignore. I do not pine for the Turks again, although I know we could do things then we cannot today. We live now within a political set-up and must consider political realities. We need the helpful sympathy of the British people; we must reinforce, not wreck it.

Wild, baseless denunciations will earn us neither British affection nor respect. If we would have them fair to us, we must be fair to them. How bitter our resentment when we are all blamed for the sin of a single Jew! Are we then to reproach the British people, or the British bureaucracy, for the sin or blunder of one Civil Servant? The British are not a nation of angels, and I know of their shocking behavior in Ireland and elsewhere; but they have a great deal to their positive credit too. They are a great and cultured people, not extortioners and thieves. Do you call it doing us harm to have been the first to recognize our historical right to Palestine, to have given Hebrew official status, to have permitted large-scale immigration? If we balance accounts, let us be honest about it.

Take, for example, adverse differentiation in the giving out of public works, very real and easily demonstrable. But it is not so simple as all that. Is it only the British who discriminate against Jewish labor? What is going on in our colonies? When the subject is raised, certain persons are expert in vindicating the boycott of Jewish labor. There is cheaper labor, and a man must think of his pocket. So do the British prefer cheap Government labor, and it is our business to explain that there are such things here as the National Home and immigration, and higher standards of living, and that economy alone cannot be the deciding factor. It takes some time for the British to grasp it—many Jews, including self-styled Zionists, have not grasped it yet.

Another instance: arming the Jews. When I was in England, one of our consistent sympathizers, who always backs us in Parliament, told me it was risky to arm the Jews, it would be better for the British to protect us. He was wrong; we knew it, and we insisted that the Yishuv must be armed—and we got our way. But there are pros and cons, and you can err in assessing them. You cannot ascribe everything to dislike, to sinister motives or antagonism. Understanding should be mutual. Our interest in Palestine is unique, our needs and conditions are unusual, and there are British traditions and habits which do not go with them. It is all very hard for the British to comprehend. Balfour could, and Lloyd George, but not every Englishman has their spiritual greatness and insight. Much of the discrimination which irks us is the consequence of our exceptional postulates. Gentlemen, the conclusion is self-evident—British officials are not all our enemies, but to carry out the Mandate requires a Civil Service imbued with the spirit of the Mandate, and pre-conditioned to its special problems and specific needs. That we have not, but we do have the valued friendship of the British people, and we must treasure it. Always Jewry was fenced by hatred, in Israel and in exile. Hatred endures and grows no weaker. It rages in Germany, it smoulders in Poland, in Rumania, throughout eastern Europe, in Asia. It is not wholly extinguished in France or Britain or America. Nearly everybody wants to get rid of us, gently or by force, and such, of course, are likely to let us pass through the gates to Palestine. But Jabotinsky's latest escapade* only whets the appetite of our enemies to expel their Jews, and prejudices the few rights left to the great Jewries of Europe; it is stupid too, because Poland is neither anxious nor able to send Jews to Palestine of all places. Aggravating Poland's eagerness to be shut of her Jews will probably prompt her to seek colonies or to consign Jews to Madagascar or some other island; she is interested not in the Jews going to Palestine but in driving them out of Poland, that is all. How can she move hundreds of thousands of us here, having neither the keys to Palestine nor the power to bend Britain to her will?

All that Jabotinsky is likely to achieve by his irresponsible foolhardiness is to sour the Poles' stomach for Zionism when they see that Palestine is not absorbing their Jews quickly enough. The same will happen elsewhere. Is any of you really so crazy as to imagine that Poland or any other country will quarrel with

* In 1936 Jabotinsky proposed to Poland that 75,000 Jews be taken out of Poland each year in return for pressure by that country on Britain to permit Jews to enter Palestine freely and arm themselves.

Britain over Palestine? With the possible exception of the United States, the whole world is intent on winning Britain's favor. Britain alone agreed to accept Jews into a country she rules. We are dependent on her goodwill and friendship, her understanding and sympathy. And miraculously we have won them, somewhat. They were not easy to come by, but they can easily be lost, and we can make ourselves detested. The British are a good deal better than others as regards anti-semitism, but fundamentally no different. Not even in their own country do they invariably act according to the principles of absolute justice. I do not know if Jews always do but I am sure the British will not, so far as we are concerned. If we have the least spark of statesmanship and statecraft, we shall so school our policy toward Britain as to maintain our friendship with her and even strengthen it. We need not bow our heads meekly to arbitrary decrees, or tolerate every injury, but we must know our limits of protestation. The British are used to criticism—their own literature delivers the severest censure of British policy. But our criticism must rest on fact not assumption, our demands and our plaints must take stock of the feasible and the practical, we must be candid and admit objective hindrances and hardships.

ON THREE FRONTS
August 3, 1938

We are fighting on three fronts at once. Our own ranks are divided, our quarrel with the Arabs has taken a violent turn, the political conflict with the British is of the gravest. We must go back to the days of Bar Kochba to find the like troubles. Arab murder and savagery have gone on now for over two years, and there is no sign of an end. No wonder the Yishuv is confused and feels itself now helpless, now despairing. This state of mind is possibly worse for us and our prospects than are the outbreaks. Inaction and complacency are anathema, but neither must we let hysteria drive us to insensate, hopeless acts. We must face facts and perceive their historical causes, we must be wise and staunch and strong. Only that way lies victory.

The murder and atrocity we witness so often are not simply the doing of bandits, rioters or robbers. Do not fall into that fatal error. This is political terrorism, with a definite political aim to a careful plan, and of widespread popular appeal.

Trouble began on April 19, 1936, but months before there were rumors of political changes concocted—the setting-up of a Legislative Council, restrictions on immigration, schemes to curtail Jewish settlement by limiting our right to acquire land. The Arabs, internally at odds, but fairly united in opposing Zionism and all its doings, demanded the complete stoppage of Jewish immigration, a ban on all sales of land to Jews, and, in lieu of the Mandate, an Arab national government.

We should neither underrate nor magnify the present disorders. This is no national uprising. The Arab people is not involved, not even the bulk of it: it lacks the will, the capacity and the strength to revolt. Equally, these are not just highwaymen and thugs. A small minority is fighting to the death, using any and every means, perpetrating the foulest crimes. But a large part of the Arab world encourages it and supports its political ambitions. The gangs get help in and out of Palestine — money and arms, concealment and shelter and, most important, political aid. We must not judge the terrorists by the political importance of the Palestinian Arabs alone. For us, looking back on a Land of Israel in existence two thousand years, its link with Arabia, Iraq or Syria is no stronger than with Cyprus or anywhere else. For the Arabs this is Southern Syria. The Syrian Arab senses himself cut off from it not because he wills or feels so, but because a foreign Power says so; the older Arabs still remember when Palestine was one, politically and geographically, with surrounding provinces, and so do we who were here before the World War. For the Arabs the link is unbroken, and the national and political aspirations of the Palestinian Arabs are largely those cherished by the Arabs of Syria, Iraq and the rest. It is no secret that, at the commencement, terrorism drew most of its strength from Syria and Iraq. Apart from certain resources out of Europe, those two provided the men, the commanders, the cash and the weapons. Now we are in the stage of mainly local participants, but external supplies, and not only of sympathy, still arrive.

Three principles have guided our resistance—to avoid follies tending to aggravate terrorism and add to the number of terrorists; to build up a Jewish militia to guard the Yishuv and wage a war of extermination on terror and its agents; and to enlist the aid of the British Army and nation for the protection of our status and the fulfillment of our ends.

The first principle is not mere negation. It means we reject the infamy of assailing an Arab just because he is one. It means we reject revenge wreaked upon Arabs that had no hand in terrorism. We will not play the terrorists' beastly game.

Here the collision of views in the Yishuv, and perhaps abroad as well, is sharp. We cannot know, and it is not our business to discover, what Jew has dealt in reprisal. For it does not matter who—the whole of Jewry, not the guilty man, must bear the responsibility and suffer the consequences. We are galled by pain and disappointment, we are impatient and bitter, Arab terrorism is unchecked and the Government ineffectual against it, and some of us think it just as well to repay the Arabs in their own coin. There can be no compromise about our answer.

First there is a question of conscience: it is a sin to spill innocent blood. Unhappily the world we live in is not moved by the voice of conscience. We shall not prevail over the spirit of vendetta by an appeal to conscience. When we explain that the Bible commands us not to kill, nobody listens, not even observant Jews, for the commandment can be rebutted by a contrary verse. But what are the political and practical considerations?

Terrorism benefits the Arabs, it may lay waste the Yishuv and shake Zionism. But to follow in the Arabs' footsteps and ape their deeds is to be blind to the gulf between us. Our aims and theirs run counter: methods calculated to further theirs, are ruinous to us.

Already the Arabs have had political dividends, if not economic: the disturbed conditions checked immigration before official stringency was applied. The wider terrorism spreads, the worse the paralysis of constructive work, the less absorptive capacity, for capital holds aloof and new enterprises shy away.

The Government has not yet altogether capitulated to terror, but patently it makes political concessions to it from time to time. The Royal Commission was one: we had not asked for it. The contraction of Aliyah was a second, to announce that the Mandate was unworkable was a third. Doubtless there will be others. Some will say: 'This is a wicked Government.' But I defy anyone to show me a better: Hitler's perhaps, or Poland or Rumania? Terrorist pressure could hardly fail to tell upon the

British Government. England has yielded to terror in matters of her nearest concern—in Ireland, in India, in Egypt. How much more likely, then, she is to yield when only Jews are concerned!

Terrorism has closed the Arab ranks. Split and divided the Arabs may be but terrorism frightens, and the Mufti's power is growing steadily. But reports from Arab sources hint that nothing has united the Arab camp so much as Jewish reprisals of the last few weeks.

Terrorism has aroused the sympathy of Arab and Moslem world for the Arabs of Palestine. Some Arab peoples scarcely knew that the country existed and took no interest in its fate. Now it has become an Arab citadel. In Europe, too, sympathy is awakened, for when men are ready, as the terrorists, to kill and be killed, their cause must be near to their hearts and in these disorders ten times as many Arabs have died as Jews. Their plan is not without political logic and practical justification; to the ethics of the Koran which also says 'Thou shalt not kill,' they pay no heed. What we have to remember now is the national movement behind the plans, its discipline and leadership.

But what good can Jewish terrorism do for us? It will only lead to more Jewish blood being shed. It will not intimidate the Arab gangs or their captains. What cares the Mufti if an Arab boy is murdered in Rechavia, or a wretched fellah in Tel Aviv? What does he care if a thousand Arabs are killed, or ten thousand? Are we scared because Jews are murdered every day? Jews have been killed ever since resettlement began sixty years ago: did that frighten us away? The Arabs are fighting to keep this country Arab: why should our ambush and killing of Arabs stampede the Arab terrorists, when the Army's many killings and hangings failed to? The Arab gangs murder without distinction any Jew they can lay hands on. Are we to be as vile? Is not that exactly what the Mufti would have us do—kill every Arab that crosses our path, innocent or guilty? Those who protest against the policy of 'self-restraint' are really not asking for self-defense or an organized campaign against the gangs, but for retaliation on any chance Arab, which is no earthly good to us, let alone being morally wrong. Clearly it will not enlarge immigration. If it influences immigration at all, it can only be to limit or stop it altogether. When we ask indignantly why the Government does not end Arab terrorism, we sometimes forget that it could—and quite easily, without an army, without firing a shot, simply by stopping immigration. Terrorism is only one of the ways in which the Arabs fight immigration. Immigration was held up after the disturbances of 1921 and again in 1929. The present troubles have already lasted thirty months but it has not yet been halted. But what Arab terrorism has not done, Jewish may.

Their terrorism has brought the Arabs closer, the Jewish counterpart is certain to bring about a dangerous and shattering cleavage in our ranks. There are still Jews who obey the sixth commandment, be the pretext for breaking it as falsely 'patriotic' as it may. The Arabs too have their 'patriotic' excuses, they do not murder for fun, but we call them murderers all the same and implore the Government to fight them boldly and relentlessly, without pity or pact. We cannot all subscribe to this inverted morality. What is wrong for Arabs is wrong for Jews; if we insist on Government suppressing Arab terrorism, how can we not insist on it suppressing Jewish terrorism? If no Jew is to be hanged without the testimony of two witnesses and a previous warning, as the code of the Sanhedrin requires, no Arab must either. So far our legal luminaries have made no outcry against the hanging of Arabs, but the Yishuv has a conscience, and will never agree to whitewash murderers, Jews or not, or justify their crimes. Those of us who dread the internal disruption that Jewish terrorism may create, who are not to be provoked into dereliction or beguiled by 'patriotic' clamor, believe the commandment to be binding on Jew and Arab alike, that if an Arab 'patriot' who kills a Jew is a murderer, so is the Jewish 'patriot' who kills harmless Arabs.

DAVID BEN GURION

As we read each morning of further Arab evildoing, we know that we at least can look the world in the face, and carry on our task with a clear conscience. This satisfaction we must not relinquish. We must cast out any that would spill innocent blood in the name of the 'kingdom of Israel.'

One other thing: terrorism which starts abroad, inevitably ends at home. The Arab gangs do not restrict themselves to the 'enemy without,' and probably more Arabs than Jews have been killed by Arabs. From Jewish terrorism against Arabs it is a short step to Jewish terrorism against Jews.

Self-restraint does not describe the course we have chosen and must pursue. We are not holding back at all; we are defending ourselves under arms, we are actively searching out the murdering gangs and destroying them. It is an independent course unconditioned by the actions of the Government. Our abhorrence of reprisals is not to please the Government, it is a moral and political requirement in our own best interests.

The Arab war against us will be a long one: the Arabs have nothing to lose in it, they can only profit. They are not dependent on Britain, they do not need to buy land and bring in Arabs from abroad. Everything is theirs but government, and it is government they are fighting for. We have much to lose—our domestic strength, our hopes, our relations with Britain, the chance of coming to an understanding with the Arabs. We need immigration and, for that, British help. Are we likely to achieve immigration by trying to scare the British?

And another example. Our specialists know that never since 1918 have opportunities of buying land been so plentiful. The country is impoverished. It is not only the Yishuv that has suffered from the disturbances—the Arab masses have fared far worse. The Arab landowners, too, are not as affluent as they were, and would like to sell their surplus acres. Yet it was never as hard to redeem the land as it now is, for terrorism strikes at the vendors, and their lives are in danger. Can we buy land by terrorism? No, terrorism can only prevent, not acquire.

So with immigration, terrorism can prevent but not further it. It is all very well to cite parallels, but some are harmful, both morally and in practice. The Arabs murder Jews and Englishmen indiscriminately, say some, and still the Government truckles to them; why should we not do likewise? The fallacy is that no Government is so stupid as to give entry to the people it fears. The Arabs already possess the land, they need neither laws nor administration to transfer it: only we do.

The Arabs do not worry how the British feel about them, because they would like to be rid of them—their main purpose is to drive the British out and end their authority here. So what do they care? But the Jews cannot afford to be indifferent. Were we concentrated in Palestine, and not scattered through Poland and Austria, through Galicia and America, perhaps it would not matter to us either. But with only a handful, and the rest, for whom that handful is fighting, still far away and kept out by Arab bombs, we must mind what Britain will think of us. So we go our way, which is not the Arab way, and in the bitterest days, though anger seared our hearts and indignation shook us to the depths, we still said: These things we will not do, we will uphold our cause.

But we could not be content with just sitting back. We declared that we should form a Jewish militia to defend itself and the Yishuv, and go out as well to destroy the Arab terrorists. It was not easy without British accord and help; we needed a legal militia which could carry arms openly and, wherever protection was sought or raiders had to be fallen upon and pursued, go forth not under cover but in full view of British soldiers and policemen. But all that was scarcely in line with British tradition generally or with it in Palestine in particular.

Many of you will remember 1929, when all British Civil Servants were armed—except the Jews. An English Jew was Attorney-General, they took his rifle away. Another was the son of the first High Commissioner, and his was taken away too. In 1936, after the outbreak of disturbances, I met in London one of the noblest figures in British politics, one of our best friends. To him I spoke of the need to arm the Jews. His answer was that it could not be done while Palestine was ablaze with racial war, it was inconceivable that Britain should arm one section of the population against the other. Yet he was no enemy of ours, he just expressed British tradition. And you cannot easily get the British to break a tradition for others. We have, however, achieved something sensational—for the first time in 1800 years a Defense Force has been established which is Jewish, for a Jewish reason, to protect the Jewish population. And when I say that, I am not forgetting the war-time Jewish Legion. But even those two battalions of volunteers from the United States and Palestine were not a Jewish Army; only a Jewish detachment within the British Army, and not allowed to defend the Yishuv. When rioting started in Jerusalem in 1920, I was still in uniform, but my fellow-soldiers and I could not go to its defense. In 1921, when rioting started in Jaffa, and only a rump of the Legion was left, its men did go to Tel Aviv. As a result, it was disbanded and its Jewish commanding officer faced court-martial. We have gone a long way since then: our Defense Force is not yet adequate, but it is far from contemptible and it has shown its quality.

It is mainly the rural sector of the Yishuv that has been caught up in this struggle, that has had to make the biggest sacrifices and shoulder the heaviest burden, that, in the Bible phrase, 'with one of his hands wrought in the work, and with the other hand held a weapon.' In the towns, and especially in Tel Aviv, we live more or less tranquilly. But if ever there were dangerous incomprehension, weakness, confusion and pessimism, then it is in Tel Aviv. Perhaps the reason is that they do not know what is happening in the villages; the black-bordered announcements in the papers every morning tell nothing of the heroism in defense and attack which our settlers have shown.

5,000 Jews have been sworn in by the Government to defend Jewish settlements; we have 4,500 Army rifles, 1,000 'Greener' guns and many revolvers. There is a special Railway company of 300 men, and from Lydda to Haifa every station has its Jewish protectors under British command. Another special unit guards the northern frontier and boundary fence, a plan which many of us, and more British, ridiculed three months ago. They argued that you could not possibly erect a wall a hundred kilometers long in the wildest region, on the Lebanese marches, where the gangs were active; that it would not be done in the time, that those working on it would be an easy mark for the terrorists; that it would be pulled down as fast as it was built. How could barbed wire keep out men who had the whole countryside behind them?

But wonders will never cease. The job was finished ahead of schedule, and from the first step to the last it was a Jewish effort —in initiative and organization, in labor and defense. A second foreboding was proved empty—that we should pay dearly in lives. We paid a price, two priceless lives, but Jewish guards killed a score terrorists and more, and others who tried to blow up the fence met their undoing in a minefield. When I traversed the frontier from Ras el Nakura to Rosh Pina and Tiberias ten days ago, I realized how right were the workers and constables who assured me that this was now the safest part of the country. The eastern frontier is open yet, but across the gap in the north a stout barrier now stands.

At first, we were permitted only stationary detachments of auxiliary policemen, each posted in a village to defend it: they could not operate outside. We demanded freedom of movement; it was intolerable that we should have to sit and wait for the terrorists to attack. Again difficulties! If we let you leave the villages, the British said, how do we know what you will do with your arms? But we got a mobile unit in the end, that goes from village to village in Jewish areas; and you can imagine how much it means. The Government provides the arms and the authority, the Jewish Agency the armored cars and their upkeep. It is not a large unit, and we are pressing, with some hope of success, for a considerable reinforcement.

We were still not satisfied, we wanted to go over to the offensive. Let us be fair—the British Army has been attacking the gangs, there have been British casualties too. Day and night, British soldiers risk their lives patrolling roads infested with terrorists, entering villages where murder waits, trying to stamp out the plague. Our claim to help encountered the familiar objection. No, they said, leave that to us, it is the most difficult, dangerous and thankless part of the job. And we answered: we know you are not doing this solely for our protection—British prestige is also involved, but it is after all mainly to safeguard the Yishuv and its rights. Why should British soldiers take the whole strain? It is our wish and duty to share.

We made some headway, as witness the modestly-named 'night squads,' composite groups of Jews and British soldiers, under British officers, which stealthily seek out the villages where terrorists gather or the hills whence they descend, ambush them, carry the war into their territory, destroy them.

We have not yet had all we are entitled to, or all we need. But we could not win alone, even were we to get everything we ask for. The aid of the British army and the British people would still be necessary. For the struggle is not only physical, it is political as well, and not only against a few gangs but a far-reaching Arab movement. We have known to our cost, in the British, vacillation, divergency and hesitation; we have known an international crisis of unprecedented gravity. We have striven to defend ourselves and to strike as well but we are not defiled by vindictiveness nor at war with every Arab as such. Always, however, we have held it to be a cardinal aim to keep and strengthen friendship with Britain. Not that it is easy for us to explain our point of view. For too many of us think in our innocence that, because one fine or rainy day—for it usually rains in England in November—a British Cabinet Minister made a Declaration to the Jewish people, then Palestine is already in our pocket, the steady goodwill of the British people is guaranteed, and all we have to do is taste the fruits. How very naive! The most formal promise in the world, no matter how many countries back it, will never fulfill itself. Since Balfour declared as he did, quite a few international treaties and pledges have been torn up or repudiated, promises and pronouncements forgotten. The Treaty of Versailles has been ripped to pieces. Where is the guarantee of Austria's independence? Where is the demilitarization of the Rhineland? Where are the restrictions upon the Reichswehr, and on traffic through the Dardanelles? Null and void—every single one. Whoever engaged in Zionist politics knows that with every new day we have had to regain the help of the British people for what we do in Palestine and shall be doing for many long years. It may be that in Britain, too, a 'new king' will arise. Ministers come and Ministers go; a Pharaoh may come that knows not Joseph, that may want to forget the promises of his predecessors. Just as the war-debt to the United States was left unpaid. It is not enough to tell our story—our aims, our works and our merits—to a Cabinet Minister, Britain is a democracy where the Ministers are dependent on the House of Commons, and Parliament is dependent on a free people which maps its own course from one day to the next. It is, therefore, to British public opinion that we must finally appeal. But how?

You can meet Ministers, or Members of Parliament, or journalists. But what of the millions in Britain who, in the last analysis, decide? And the thousands all over Palestine for the first time since the war? They wear khaki now, but before that they worked in factories and on farms, in offices and on newspapers. They are the British masses, and their officers are Britain's intelligentsia. And it is just now that the Arab-Jewish quarrel has come to a head, the gravity of the problem is once more manifest, and every Englishman asks himself in bewilderment: Who is right? One side says: 'We have been living here, not for a matter of days or months, but for 1,400 years. Our fathers and forefathers are buried here. Grant us liberty to live as we please, give us a democratic government, let us be ruled by elected representatives, as you are. Why should you strangers govern us from afar?' These arguments he will understand because they are straightforward, because of their elementary appeal. The other side is the Jewish people, with a genealogy of 3,500 years, the Bible as its sacrosanct title-deed to Palestine, and a promise from the British Government. It can point to immense achievements here and unspeakable torment in the Diaspora. It claims the Right of Return.

It is all very confusing. British soldiers are hazarding their lives in Palestine, for the honor of King and Empire, but all the same they know they need not be here if only Britain did one little thing—stop Jewish immigration. Then they could cease their wandering in the hills of Nablus, Tulkarm and Jenin; they would not be killed; they would escape the hatred of the Arabs and of Islam; they would not be making Hitler a gift of the telling propaganda that 'the English are always preaching to us, but look what they are doing in Palestine, look at *their* hangings.' All those consequences might be averted if only the British would do that little thing which a Jewish High Commissioner, a Zionist himself, once did. But the British have not done it, and so terrorism goes on. They want to know whether it is all justified. Who are these Jews, they ask, whom we must bring into Palestine and for whose sake we must die? Do they deserve it? Are they worth the trouble?

At this moment of their severest testing, the impression we make on these British is of vital importance. Luckily, they saw us too at our finest. They saw us under siege, brutally attacked and resisting bravely, standing our ground and hitting back. They know what Tel Aviv does not, they can testify to the courage of our boys in many a village. They differ from the arm-chair critics who think that if we do not launch reprisals we must be supine or run away like rats. In the turmoil and tragedy, they saw us working and producing, building and creating, loving the Land, with steadfast gallantry of body and spirit. All our printed words, all our silver-tongued spokesmen, are of less effect than what scores of thousands of British soldiers here have seen with their own eyes.

More than once immigration was gravely threatened, more than once it seemed the axe must fall. If, this time, it did not crash upon our heads, we do not owe salvation to the vigilance and resolution of our delegates—and I will not be suspect of wishing to cry down their efforts, for I was of their number both here and in London. We owe it principally to the courage, prudence and dignity of the Yishuv. We could turn to the British and say: 'See how loyal and devoted is the Yishuv to the Land, how deeply rooted these Jews are, that came perhaps only yesterday from Germany or Poland, how they carry on throughout this deadly storm of terrorist bullets, how they work and defend themselves, and their hands are clean. They are enlightened, stable and creative; they have moral courage and civic discipline. They will smash the terrorists in fair fight but, under the worst of provocations, never raise a hand against an unoffending Arab. Is it on this Yishuv that you would inflict the most unkindest cut of all and stop immigration? It is unthinkable.' It was the magnificent stand of the Yishuv that drove the thought from Britain's mind.

If immigration is continuing after two years of blood and fire, no British Government will ever dare balk it. It is more than asserting a theoretical right—35,000 Jews entered Palestine in that time. They do not comprise the nation, there are more than that number in Germany or Poland, but they are almost as many as returned from Babylon. A Jewish port has been built, and twenty-six new settlements have been founded. In our peak years,

DAVID BEN GURION

1934 and 1935, only sixteen settlements in all were established.

Intrinsically these achievements mean a great deal; politically, they have shown the world, and, above all, the Mandatory, what Palestine signifies for us, our attachment to it, and that no blow can cripple our work, no stranglehold choke our vitality. No speech or book or propaganda could show it as impressively: this is the deep engraving of the Zionist idea upon the British consciousness. The choice is still for us to make: shall the world see us in our heroism, physical and moral, in our creative power —or shall it see us in ignominy, as the worst and most debased among the nations? Shall we then be heroes still, or disgraced and degraded by ways that bring shame to us and comfort to the Mufti?

There is no disguising it: we have few friends. And we need friends. Of course Zionism has its internal resources—Jewish will and national strength, talent and faith. But we have the Arabs arrayed against us, here and on our borders. Whence are we to get help? From Hitler's Germany? Stalin's Russia? Or Mussolini's Italy?

The Americans made a splendid gesture at Evian.* We are grateful even for good intentions, but these were not translated into acts, and we left Evian with empty hands, while the United States took up an isolationist stand in world politics. In China vital American interests are at stake—but they do not intervene. They see what is happening in Spain; all their sympathies are with the Republicans, with Spanish democracy, they have nothing but contempt and dislike for Franco—but they do not intervene. Who is so bemused as to think that these same United States will fall out with Britain for our sake? Send good wishes to a Zionist Conference—that they will do; but pick a quarrel with another Government certainly not. Ask our friends there

---

* In 1938, an international conference, sponsored by President Roosevelt, sought, unsuccessfully, to solve the European refugee problem.

who are close to the Government, and they will tell you. The times are distracted—anti-semitism is raising its ugly head so high, powerful States seek to destroy not only their own but all Jewries and all over the globe their mischief-makers are provoking hatred of us. Hitler's emissaries are in Egypt and Iraq, in Syria and Palestine itself, disseminating the poison of Nazism. In this desperate need, there is still a nation by which we were helped a little: a great nation, though not compact of ministering angels; it is selfish, as are all people, including ours; it has interests in every quarter, and they often conflict, so that it is prey to doubt and hesitation, and not only toward us. It was in 1914, with Germany on the eve of declaring war on Britain's ally, France; it is so now over Spain, and over China. Every interest gives rise to all kinds of considerations. Intervention in one place may harm interests in another. To meddle here may hurt there. It is concerned as to Arab and Moslem reactions. But with all its shortcomings and all its wavering, it alone stretched out a hand and was the first to affirm our right to a Homeland. If it did not grant us all we hoped for, nor keep its promises as we interpret, at least it interprets itself from time to time, in the light of its own requirements. We have no power to give it 'orders.' Whatever a Revisionist meeting may draft, as between nations there is no giving of orders. No State, large or small, can give Britain orders. Czechoslovakia is stronger than we, living in its own territory, fortified by an international treaty, member of the League of Nations, its frontiers fixed in keeping with the decisions of—among others—British delegates; the very Minister who signed the Balfour Declaration also agreed to those frontiers. Still Czechoslovakia cannot issue instructions to Britain. No more can France, larger yet and menaced now by the same adversary. No, France is trying to win the friendship of the British as they are, because it realizes that they cannot be turned into something else. We must do likewise, not wait idly for them to start living to suit our comprehension, our concepts, and our interpretations. Not for eternity but now, at this moment of time, Britain's help or abstention may decide our destiny. Here is the crux; not the Arabs' bloody onslaught, but the political war on the British front. In that, we are fighting not for the lives of 400,000 Jews in Palestine but for the hopes and the rights of the nation; our actions and our policy must be designed to bring victory.

Courage, understanding and clean hands are called for. Courage to hold our own, moral strength to preserve our way of life and all the progress achieved, to expand and extend against the toughest opposition, courage in self-defense and assault. Understanding that will find a way to win us more helpful friends and lessen the count of our foes. And clean hands. Hitler may occupy Austria by brute force, destroy Jews and threaten France and Czechoslovakia. We are a small folk, no army, no State, no power to compel—we cannot over-awe the world. Our strength lies in the one great asset we possess—the moral asset, the moral purity of our lives and works, our aspirations and our philosophy.

Given these three—courage, understanding and clean hands—we shall win.

A NATION IN ITS FIGHT FOR FREEDOM
*A Speech to the General Zionist Council,
Jerusalem, April 18, 1940*

It is superfluous to say that all members of this Council are good Zionists. Every Zionist is a good Zionist. I do not question anyone's Zionism. But we are not now examining conscience; we are seeking a way—and not every way a Zionist follows is a Zionist way. I fear that I cannot choose the path of most speakers.

At our previous session I said that it is not easy to be a Zionist, because it means living—and, if need be, dying—as one. There is another difficulty: thinking as one. Thinking is a strenuous art—few practise it: and then only at rare times. Man often regrets the truisms of his environment and generation. Surely great thinkers do, and your intellectual giant throws off convention of thought in almost every respect and strikes out on an uncharted sea. But the average being is content to repeat the standard view and avoid mental effort. Nevertheless, the plain, ordinary citizen thinks for himself sometimes, when faced suddenly with exceeding peril, with a matter of life and death. Then patterns and conventions disappear: his senses become taut, more acute; he sees reality undimmed, just as it is, not in the semblance of popular belief; and he looks for a way out.

Zionism, I feel, has reached its crucial moment; it must think afresh, and afresh search for escape—if indeed it still perceives the danger.

For Zionist thinking, too, is cluttered with a mass of useless and misleading forms, heritage of a non-Zionist past we all share, of the long years through which Jews had not Zionist eyes to survey their national and human lot. Zionist theory was not made in a day round and perfect, with solutions in advance for every imaginable problem. Zionist enterprise began with modest undertakings and now it grows and expands, it branches out and broadens, brick upon brick and tier upon tier. The same is true of Zionist thinking. From time to time, Zionism encounters new obstacles, new circumstances and a call for new exertions, which its founders and first planners could not foresee. Basic assumptions will not do. When we meet a new pitfall on the road to fulfillment, an issue to which Zionist thinking has found no answer yet, the non-Zionist intellectual tradition of the Diaspora frequently prompts a reply which is not Zionist, although the speaker is. It is hard, even among our best, to find minds and hearts freed from the spell of non-Zionist axioms that have bound us for centuries.

The outlook of the ghetto divided the universe into two: this world for the Gentiles—the hereafter for the Jews. Power and sovereignty in this world had been given to the Gentiles; the Jews were condemned to impotence and servitude until the Day of Judgment when the last should be first and the first should be last. In the ghetto it was natural that the Jew should be downtrodden, helpless and ostracized; that he should wield no influence, and be without means to tackle the powers that be of this world. He did not altogether despair of happiness, his redemption would come about by supernatural agency and till then he was resigned to be different. State and Government, power, justice and independence, war and peace, were for the Gentile, not for him.

Zionism rejected this philosophy, which, moreover, was never that of Judaism, nor was it known to our religious leaders of old. Zionism, political and secular, held that Israel must be redeemed by its own efforts and by natural agency, that the Jewish people must itself create foundations of a new life, geopolitical foundations such as sustain every free people living in its own land

and autonomous. Thus, far, maybe, all Zionists are agreed. But this cardinal principle has varied aspects and interpretations, and whenever Zionism is in stormy waters, when old-fashioned formulae are not enough, and solutions must be devised more apt to a novel and complex difficulty—the ghetto mentality regains its ascendancy over even the elect.

The assimilationist approach is but one facet of this mentality. Contemplating the Gentile world, assimilationists, not like the faithful of the ghetto, distinguish between the nations., They know there is no 'Gentile': there are English and French, Russians and Germans, large nations and small, weak and strong, good and bad, cultured and barbarian. Theirs is a realistic view of the non-Jewish world, with full understanding of all its contradictions and interplay of forces. But when they quit that great arena and come to deal with Jewish affairs, their sense of reality fails them, and they see the Jew through ghetto lenses, oblivious that the laws of nature and history by which all nations are ruled do not except Jews, that Jews conversely can do what others can. Jews live under different conditions but in needs and capacities they do not differ, they too represent an innate force for good and bad.

Let me exemplify. This very Council once arranged a committee of leading Jewish financiers to survey the prospects of a loan to the Jewish Agency. In the chair was a member of the British Cabinet, who could handle a loan for Great Britain itself with the greatest of ease. But when it came to a Jewish loan, his worldly wisdom vanished, he changed from financier to Ghetto Jew, and concluded that it could not possibly be done, a pusillanimous verdict with which his Anglo-Jewish fellow-members agreed. And so the idea was shelved until a young Jew from Russia was appointed Treasurer of the Agency, and revived it from a Zionist viewpoint with the common-sense that makes no distinction between Jew and Gentile. He it was who persuaded the City of London to make the loan.

DAVID BEN GURION

Again, during the debate in Parliament on the Palestine Land Law which virtually strangled all hopes of progressive colonization, a Jewish member spoke in vehement denunciation of what he stigmatized as an unjust and unfair law, not befitting the dignity of the British people. For all that, he said, he would vote in the Government lobby, because the House was not voting for or against the law, but for or against a vote of non-confidence moved by the Labor party. In this speech all the tragedy of the Ghetto Jew is enacted. Member of the Mother of Parliaments he may be, but his assimilation is still darkened by the shadow of the Ghetto: as one of God's creatures, he knows the legislation to be wicked; being a Jew, he votes for the Government that is all-powerful.

This Council is not discussing a vote of confidence in a Government; but many of the speakers bring that pathetic Jew to mind: True, they say, the law is bad, but we cannot resist it, for the Gentiles are strong and we are weak. Theirs, however, is not a Zionist premise, nor a sound one anyhow, but child of ghetto philosophy and assimilation.

Zionism originates in the simple truth that there are not only individual Jews, there is a Jewish nation. The nation may vary in status and way of life, in power and capacity, from numerous other nations as they do among themselves. But like them, and within similar limitations, it is the arbiter of its own fate and it has resource and potentiality to contract its limitations, if only it be willing to exploit resource and potentiality for the common weal. Whatever means of self-defense other nations employ, *we* can, possibly with less success, but then not all nations succeed in all they undertake. Thus far our success has not been negligible either in constructive work or in the political sphere. Whenever we used the methods of normal human beings, we have had success. Why should we not also succeed in fighting the Land Law and the White Paper?

It has been pleaded that the Gentiles do not like being

thwarted. Neither, I say, do we, yet the Gentiles thwart us. Why should we not thwart in return?

I call for action, action as our strength dictates. Enough of this ghetto concept of might. What do you mean by 'Gentiles'? Is the whole non-Jewish world—are all the British Gentiles—backing this Land Law? Was it not debated in Parliament? Did not responsible statesmen ask that MacDonald and Chamberlain be dismissed because of it? Yes, a majority voted for the Government, but do they favor it? Did not the Colonial Secretary beguile his supporters with the promise that it would bring peace to Palestine? Does this dreadful, crushing complex of fear of the 'Gentiles' not reflect utter ignorance of their nature? Will not the 'Gentiles' honor the riposte of a minority, that is no longer only hollow words?

Some say that this is the eventide of small nations, and that we are setting with the rest. It is the modern vogue to allow only great nations the right to exist. Who started the fashion? Was it not Hitler? And is Zionism to be led by his decrees? Have England and France announced that there is no room for small nations? Are not the western democracies fighting for the freedom of Norway, Denmark and Poland? Are they not ready to defend Belgium and Holland against Nazi attack? Why this Jewish haste to swallow Hitler's new dogma as though it were holy writ?

Others say that we must try to 'preserve our assets.' That, in my opinion, is not Zionism. In any case, I am sure we cannot preserve our assets that way. And what are they? Two months ago equal rights for Jews in Palestine were one such 'asset.' We have, as it is, the asset of a slight degree of autonomy in education. Are you convinced that by giving in again and again, out of alarm lest you provoke the 'strong,' you will retain it? Doubtless our education techniques are flawed. Can an alien Civil Servant put things right, however friendly to us he be? Do not I, does not every Jewish father, know more than any such about the kind of teaching our children should have? There is much we can learn from the English but does the Yishuv need a colonial bureaucracy to superintend our schools in their curricula and morals? How will you safeguard your 'asset' if resistance to the 'Gentile' is everlastingly tabu?

We have an urban and a rural economy—are you certain you can secure them? Frankly, I am not. An economy is more than house or machine, land or plantations, it means the human operatives as well. The economy you wish to secure means Jewish labor. Are you confident you can hold on to that 'asset,' or will you fall out with the 'Gentiles' again?

By and large, it is all very meager, this inventory you are so anxious to keep. It omits immigration—the Gentiles put an end to that when they issued the White Paper. It omits the waste lands, wherefrom the Land Law has cut us off. It omits free speech: there is a censorship, not a war measure—of which we should not complain—but an instrument of the policy of the White Paper.

For many of us, for the sabra generation, there has been till now the precious sense of dwelling in our own Homeland, of walking with heads held high, not miserable underlings. Will it be ours henceforth?

I ask myself if we can preserve our 'assets,' yet yield up our Zionist spirit. We cannot be thinking only of material possessions. Not for their sake ought we bow to each behest and tamely accept confinement in a Pale! Nor will submissiveness save our material things.

Many instanced Finland, which defied a great Power, only to fail. As though the rest of the Baltic States, less defiant, were more fortunate! But analogies are misleading. No two political cases are alike. Finland and Russia are not Palestine and Great Britain. The Russians wanted Viborg not for a third party, but for themselves. The twenty-five million dunams now banned to us are not needed by the British Government as a zone of British settlement. If it needed them as badly as it needs, let us say, the Royal Navy, I am afraid all our arguing would be useless. Every schoolboy knows that England is the stronger, and that in a duel for any of her vital interests, even one most harmful to us, we should lose. But the Negev and mountainous Galilee, the Valleys of Jezreel and Jordan, Samaria and the hills of Jerusalem and the Shephelah, all under the ban, are not indispensable to the British for colonization or as military or naval bases, as Viborg was to the Russians. On the contrary, the wastelands are a military liability, for where a Jewish settlement stands, the British feel safer, aware that in us they have a faithful ally. But the Land Law was passed because they wished to placate the Mufti and his gunmen as they once tried to placate Hitler. All the same outstanding and influential Englishmen regarded it as a political blunder, a moral crime, a breach of contract: to fight against a blunder and a crime is surely not to fight against Britain and British interests?

Proud Finland's case, I say, is not as ours, but we can praise her gallantry in the face of aggression, and see in her agony and defeat a finer episode than the capitulation and 'salvation' of her neighbors. This was not her first revolt against Russian despots. She struck back at the tyranny of the Czars, and the whole of liberal and socialist Russia, the whole enlightened world, respected her for it. The account may not yet be closed. In these darkling days, Finland's heroic struggle is a brilliant expression of man's greatness and spirit, to be reverenced and admired.

The Norwegians, too, are resisting: who can tell if they will be luckier? But, whatever the end, they also have our undisputed admiration and respect.

You will ask: What are our own chances of success? There is no guarantee. Who but ourselves stood guarantor for our lives during four years of Arab terrorism? You do not know England if you do not realize that, more than any other nation, she honors honorable defense. She is not Germany, and the British Government, even Chamberlain's, is not a Nazi one. But let us assume the worst, that we fail. Is not the fight worthy for its own sake? Will we not forfeit more by humbling ourselves in compliance and surrender? Is there not a spiritual, educational and humanitarian balance-sheet, besides that of material gain and loss? Shall we forget what we still owe to young souls in Palestine and the Diaspora, to the nation's spirit, to posterity?

We must be custodians of our Zionist 'assets' in the Diaspora. Millions of Jews this very day are in their death agony in that vast concentration camp which is Nazi Germany. But there are millions who are free Jews, and love the Land of Israel. To this affection the gravest danger is that the Yishuv should submit to the White Paper, playing false to its stand against Arab rioters and rebels, a stand that exalted its dignity in the sight of Jewry, and ennobled its own self-respect.

Zionism is the greatest venture in Jewish history since the destruction of the Temple. The worldly-wise and practical of the Diaspora foresaw hazards, and they were not wholly wrong. When Jews emerged from the Old City of Jerusalem to found the first Jewish colony in the Yarkon swamps, that was an adventure. The establishment of 'Hashomer,' the watchmen's association, was another; 'realistic' men of affairs were against it, and so many of our finest pioneers paid with their lives. The defense of Tel Hai was an adventure—a military 'realist' like Jabotinsky opposed it. 'Illegal' immigration was a great adventure. It seems that Zionism is unfulfillable otherwise. And now our latest and greatest adventure: we go forth to smite the policy of the White Paper, and let us not be found wanting.

TEST OF FULFILLMENT
*From an Address delivered at an Extraordinary
Zionist Conference in New York, May 1942*

Come, let us take the measure of Zionism's capacity to achieve its purpose. This universal war, in which the whole human race is plunged, puts all peoples and civilizations, all political institutions and purposes, to a merciless test of survival. Our own people was brutally singled out by the Nazis for extermination, but we believe that we will emerge victorious and, as a people, survive. Zionism will then face its hardest test: that of fulfillment.

In two vital aspects its position then will be quite different from what it was after the last war. The situation of both Jewish people and Jewish territory has changed. After the last war, England and America, with France and Italy—other free democracies of the time—resolved to undo the historic wrong to our people and recognize its right to be restored to its Homeland. The plight of the Jews, even in countries where they had suffered most, was not yet as hopeless as it will be now, and it seemed that our task of rebuilding Palestine to absorb new settlers could proceed at a leisurely pace.

This time we will find quite a different state of things. The size and urgency of Jewish migration will be unparalleled. The old debate, whether Zionism is spiritual or political, is dead. Either Zionism provides a radical and speedy satisfaction of the consuming need of thousands of uprooted Jews and, through mass immigration and settlement, lays the sure foundations of a free, self-governing, Jewish Palestine, or it is meaningless.

In the last war Palestine did not exist as a political unit nor did Syria or Iraq. All three, as well as most of Arabia, were parts of the Ottoman Empire. Under Turkish rule for 400 years, Palestine had still no Turkish population or Turkish culture. It was a country to all intents and purposes unclaimed, except by the Jewish people, which never, for all this stretch of centuries, ceased to regard it as the Land of Israel.

Meanwhile, some of the neighboring territories became independent Arab kingdoms and Palestine is now claimed as part of an Arab empire. The post-war settlement will have to include a decision about Palestine one way or the other.

Since the last war, Palestine has taken in more Jewish refugees than any other country, and in certain periods, when artificial limitations were relaxed, more than all other countries together. But in view of the magnitude of the coming refugee problem, the question is legitimately asked: How many more Jews can settle in Palestine on a sound economic basis?

No one can profess to give a clear-cut answer. Science has not yet discovered a sure method for predicting how many people can be settled on a given area anywhere. All this speculation about absorptive capacity is a peculiarly Zionist, or perhaps an anti-Zionist, invention. Absorptive capacity is no fixed and static measurement, but a fluctuating, dynamic quantum, which depends as much on human factors as on nature and area, if not more. No human factor is more decisive than need, and our desperate need creates immense absorptive capacity. Then there are our creativity, enterprise and halutziuth, and the deep love and devotion we bear our Homeland. Paramount, however, is the regime: the political, legal and administrative conditions under which we shall enter and colonize.

The potentiality of agricultural development is certainly determined largely by the size of the country and the amount of land available for additional settlers. But even land is not a rigid datum, for although its length and breadth cannot be made more, it also has a third dimension—fertility or productivity—which can, as Palestine has shown.

At the London Conference in 1939, the Arab delegation made public a statement that, in the whole of western Palestine, there are only seven million dunams of cultivable land. The whole area is twenty-six and a half million dunams, so that, according to the Arabs, some nineteen million dunams are uncultivable and are certainly not cultivated by them. Practice has shown that what is uncultivated, and considered uncultivable, by the Arabs is cultivable and has been cultivated by Jews. In fact a large part of the area settled by Jews is land up to now considered uncultivable: the sands of Rishon, the swamps of Hedera, the rocks of Motza, the stony hills of Hanita. The most striking example is the Huleh Basin, the largest malarial zone in Palestine: classified not only by the Arabs but also by the Government as uncultivable, it is now being turned by our halutzim into the most prosperous and productive area of the country.

Jews had not merely to acquire land, but to reclaim, drain, reforest, fertilize, and irrigate it. In this way, and by the introduction of modern and intensive methods of cultivation, modern machinery, new breeds of cattle and poultry, new plants and seeds, rotation of crops, and by utilizing surface and sub-soil water to the best advantage, they made new acres available for settlement. And they so increased their yield that they were able steadily to raise the standard of living, while gradually reducing the subsistence area from the 250 dunams per family necessary in the earlier stages of colonization to 100 dunams in unirrigated plain land, 50 dunams in the mountains where fruit trees were planted, and 20-25 dunams under irrigation.

In purely Arab districts, the Arab population remained almost stationary, in areas of Jewish settlement it greatly increased, and there the economic standard of the Arabs was raised and they made use of the improved methods of their Jewish neighbors.

DAVID BEN GURION

For the purpose of agricultural settlement western Palestine can conveniently be divided into four areas: the plains, comprising 4,602,900 dunams; the hill country, 8,088,000 dunams; the Negev (southern Palestine), 12,577,000 dunams; the wilderness of Judea, 1,050,900 dunams.

In the plains some 3,500,000 dunams are irrigable; at present only 350,000 are irrigated. One irrigated dunam yields at least as much as ten unirrigated. Each million of the three million dunams, when fully irrigated, makes room for from twenty-five to thirty thousand new settlers, leaving enough still for the former occupants, whether Jews or Arabs.

In the hill country some 4,500,000 dunams are at present uncultivated, and officially considered uncultivable. So far Jews have acquired some 350,000 dunams and, the Government definition notwithstanding, established flourishing villages in the hills of Jerusalem, Samaria and Galilee. At least another 2,500,000 dunams of so-called waste hill-country can be brought under Jewish cultivation, making room for another 50,000 families.

With regard to the Negev, Hope Simpson reported thus: 'Given the possibility of irrigation there is practically an inexhaustible supply of cultivable land in the Beersheba area . . . Up to the present time there has been no organized attempt to ascertain whether there is or is not an artesian supply of water.' The Peel Royal Commission in 1937 pointed out that 'since the date of this report, it appears that very little has been done by Government to discover water in Palestine.' But it has been discovered by Jews in many parts where it had not been believed to exist, and it is the view of our experts that water for the Negev can be made available either by boring artesian wells, or building dams, or bringing water from the rivers of the north. Given the necessary authority and means to provide the water, it will be possible for hundreds of thousands of new immigrants to settle on the land in the Negev alone, which, making up half of western

Palestine, is unoccupied at present except for a few roving Beduin.

Our experience is that for each family settled in agriculture at least another three families can be settled in industry, trade and the liberal professions.

Though deficient in certain important raw materials, Palestine has the advantage of favorable geography as the bridge between the three continents of the Old World. It has easy access to the sea in two directions: through the Mediterranean and the Red Sea; it has the infinite mineral riches of the Dead Sea and its own electric power. It has an extensive hinterland, the whole of the Near and Middle East as far as India, as a market for its wares. And with their proved ability to develop industry in many countries, there is no reason why Jews should not make Palestine the industrial center of the Middle East.

The Peel Commission stated: 'Twelve years ago the National Home was an experiment, today it is a going concern. The number of inhabitants has increased fourfold. . . . The process of agricultural colonization has steadily continued . . . yet more impressive has been the urban development. Tel Aviv, still a wholly Jewish town, has leaped to the first place among the towns of Palestine. Its population now probably exceeds 150,000 . . . rising so quickly from a barren strip of sand it is quite startling . . . There is the same effect at Jerusalem. The population of Jerusalem has grown to 125,000 and of that some 75,000 are Jews. The growth of Haifa, too, which now has a population of over 100,000, is only less remarkable than that of Tel Aviv . . . about one-half of its inhabitants are now Jews and much of the business of its port is Jewish business . . . Broadly speaking, the remarkable urban development in Palestine has been Jewish. The relation between rural and urban areas, between industrialists and agriculturalists, has remained fairly constant from the start . . . From 1918 to the present day over £14 million has been invested in Palestine through 'national funds' and roughly

£63 million by private industrialists. The total investment therefore amounts to £77 million and of this at least one-fifth has been contributed by the Jews in the United States. Lastly the amount of Jewish deposits in Palestine banks reaches £16½ million. These . . . figures . . . bear witness to quite an extraordinary measure of economic expansion.'

Since then there has been further expansion. New industries have been started, textile, chemical, wood, metal, electrical, food, building and clothing, which supply the home market and the Near and Middle East. In 1941 alone over 200 new Jewish industrial undertakings were established.

The youngest Jewish adventure in Palestine is the sea. Jews as a seafaring people may seem fantastic to those who know them only in Europe and America. Forty years ago the idea of their becoming farmers also seemed fantastic. But it happened. Six years ago there was not a single Jewish sailor on the seas of Palestine, although the main sea trade and transport were Jewish. On May 15, 1936, the High Commissioner personally telephoned the Jewish Agency to announce that he recognized the justice of our claim, since the Mufti had closed the port of Jaffa, to be allowed to unload in Tel Aviv. And, literally almost overnight, the beginnings of a Jewish port took shape. Thousands of Jews became marine workers in Haifa and Tel Aviv. And Jewish ships manned by Jewish skippers and seamen crossed the seas.

It was a Hebrew-speaking tribe that gave the world seaborne trade and navigation: the people of Tyre and Sidon, who founded the great empire of Carthage. Jewish privateers fought the Romans in a bloody sea-battle off Jaffa before the fall of Jerusalem. The people of Tyre and Sidon perished, but the scions of the privateers are very much alive. Many of them are back in Palestine and more are to come. They went back to the land. They are going back to the sea as well. There is no reason why the Italians should keep their monopoly of passengers and cargoes on the Mediterranean. Palestine merchandise and passengers to Palestine can be carried in Jewish ships. Palestine is a small country, but its two seas, the Mediterranean and the Red Sea, are big. Jewish sailors and fishermen will call the seas to Palestine and our people take its place among the sea-faring nations.

* * *

I come now to the political aspect: and, first, the Arab problem. In few of the complicated problems of Zionism is there so much confusion and misunderstanding as in this. The first thing to make clear is that there is no Arab problem in the sense that there is a Jewish. There is no homeless Arab people; no Arab migration. Just the contrary. The Arabs are among the rare races which are almost entirely, with insignificant exceptions, concentrated in their own territories. They are in possession of vast lands, and if they suffer at all it is from a paucity, rather than a surplus, of population.

In a paper prepared in 1926 for the Royal Central Asian Society, Ja'far Pasha al Askari, then Prime Minister of Iraq, said: 'The size of the country is 150 thousand square miles, about three times that of England and Wales, while the population is only three million . . . What Iraq wants above everything else is more population.'

The same applies to Syria. All Syrian economists are agreed that the small numbers and inadequate means of the present population prevent the development of the country's productive assets to the full. Trans-Jordan, almost four times as large as western Palestine, has only one-fifth of its population. This under-population constitutes not only an economic impediment, but a grave political danger, as the case of Alexandretta proves.

A second point must be made clear: the immigration and settlement of Jews in Palestine have not been at Arab expense. In industrial and maritime development, this is self-evident as there is practically no Arab industry and the sea is entirely vacant. But even in agriculture, either we occupied so-called uncultivable land, or, in the case of cultivated land, so heightened the yield that the same area not merely provides for additional settlers, but makes it possible for the old ones to enjoy a higher standard of living. Mass immigration and colonization on the largest possible scale, such as we must expect after this war, can be effected without the slightest need to displace the present population.

In some quarters the idea of transfer is advanced as the perfect solving of the problem. Let us understand once and for all that to enable Palestine to absorb all the Jews who may be expected to want a new home in the post-war period, there is no economic necessity for any transfer whatsoever. In post-war Europe, resettlement of populations may become urgent, even inevitable. In the period between the last war and this, we saw a remarkable transfer of population between Greece and Turkey, from Asia Minor to Europe. Syria and Iraq may also have an interest, economically as well as politically, in strengthening their position vis-a-vis their Turkish and Persian neighbors by transferring new Arab settlers to their country, and the only source of such settlers is Palestine. But this is a purely internal Arab problem, in which we may help if asked by the Arabs, but neither can nor ought take any initiative. It is not a prerequisite of large-scale Jewish settlement; and it is necessary and wise that we should base our future plans for the rebuilding of Palestine on the assumption that we have to reckon with the presence of something like a million Arabs, their rights and claims.

There is no conflict of economic interests between Jews and Arabs in Palestine, none between present population and new arrivals. The very fact that the Mufti and his friends, and the Chamberlain-MacDonald Government which tried to appease them, insisted on abolishing the principle of economic absorptive capacity as the only yardstick of Jewish immigration implies that the Arabs as well as the authors of the White Paper realized that on purely economic grounds there is room for a very large influx, which may turn Palestine into a Jewish country.

The Arab problem really means political opposition by the Arabs to Jewish immigration. Many people, ignoring this simple but unpleasant truth, try to solve the problem where it does not exist. One solution offered is a bi-national State. If this means simply that all the inhabitants of Palestine, Jews and Arabs alike, must enjoy complete equality of rights not merely as individuals but also as national entities, which means the right freely to develop their language, culture, religion and so forth, then certainly no Jew, much less a Zionist, will hesitate to support it. But I am not altogether convinced that the Arabs will agree to that equality, if they have the power to determine the constitution. When the Mufti was asked by the Royal Commission on January 12, 1937, how the Arabs would treat the Jews already in the country, if they had control of it, he said: "That will be left to the discretion of the Government which will be set up under the treaty and will be decided by that Government on the considerations most equitable and most beneficial to the country.'

When asked whether the country could assimilate and digest the 400,000 Jews then in it, he replied: 'No.'

The chairman then remarked: 'Some of them would have to be removed by a process kindly or painful as the case may be?'

The Mufti answered: 'We must leave all this to the future.'

Thus far no other Arab leader has publicly differed from him. We must also remember the bitter experience of the Assyrians in Iraq, to whom protection was guaranteed under the Anglo-Iraq treaty as well as by the League of Nations. The Anglo-Iraq treaty is still in existence and so, at the critical time, was the League of Nations. But the Assyrians were massacred.

Others offer parity as a solution, or interpret a bi-national State to mean parity, so that, irrespective of their numerical strength Jews and Arabs should, in all main departments of Government, legislative and executive, be represented on a fifty-fifty basis. I was one of those who strongly advocated parity under the British Mandate. But I doubt whether a regime of parity without a Mandatory is practicable, or whether a self-governing State can carry on at all under what may mean a permanent deadlock. Again, no Arab leader has been found to agree to the principle, with or without the Mandate.

But assuming that parity in a bi-national State is workable, assuming that not only Jews but Arabs also will agree to it, it does not in the least solve the only problem that matters: Jewish immigration. The example of Switzerland, where the divergence of several nationalities was satisfactorily resolved, is not applicable to Palestine, because the crucial issue, the root of all friction, is not so much the problem of Jews and Arabs already in Palestine, but almost exclusively, the problem of further Jewish arrivals.

Should there be Jewish immigration or should there not? That is the question. No solution, real or illusory, for all the other problems of Palestine, actual or imaginary, means anything, if it does not give a clear and simple answer to this simple but vital question.

Can the Arabs be expected to agree to Jewish immigration and under what conditions? There is no deception worse than self-deception. We must face facts: if it depends on Arab consent, there will hardly be any Jewish immigration at all. It is critically important, politically as well as morally, that our position be unequivocal. Jewish immigration to Palestine needs no consent. We are returning as of right. History, international law and the irresistible life-need of a people nothing can destroy, these have ordained Palestine as the rightful home of the Jewish people.

A Jew is no stranger, no intruder, no immigrant in Palestine. He is at home. History and the links of history, an attachment unbroken for thousands of years in spite of all vicissitudes, in spite of expulsion on expulsion, have made Palestine our inalienable Homeland. It is an historical fact that there are a million Arabs in Palestine, who legitimately regard themselves as its children, whether we like it or not. So is it an historical fact, disagreeable as it may be to the Arabs, that Palestine for more than 3,000 years was and has stayed Eretz Israel for us. And so international law solemnly confirmed, for the Mandate explicitly pronounced a recognition of the historical connection of the Jewish people with Palestine and of the grounds for reconstituting in it their National Home. But there is something stronger even than international law, and that is the living, desperate want of a folk for which return to Palestine is the only way of salvation and survival.

No political opposition or obstruction by Arabs, no terrorist intimidation, no restrictions of a White Paper that morally and legally is invalid, will prevent Jews from getting back to the Land of Israel. For any who still doubt it, the story of the *Patria*, the *Struma*, and their many sister-ships should be final proof. Their plain meaning was: Palestine or death. As soon as this war is over, hundreds like them will sail to Palestine.

Ours is a realistic generation. After the many disappointments of the last war and peace, men fear idealistic illusions and want to be sober and practical. And he must be a visionary, a dreamer, who cannot see how grim and bitter will be the reality of Jewish migration after this war, of Jewish urge for Palestine. No other reality of Palestine can be as vehement and impelling as that unstoppable Jewish tide setting toward Palestine where are the deepest biological and psychological origins of our very existence.

The Arabs will acquiesce in Jewish immigration and adjust themselves to the new reality when it becomes an established fact. You will recall that, after the last war, the Arab representatives at the Peace Conference agreed with and accepted the decision of the Powers to fulfill the 'Jewish Palestine' part of their scheme for the future of the Arab countries. Feisal (later

King Feisal), son and representative of that King Hussein with whom England negotiated, during the war, signed an agreement with Dr. Weizmann on January 3, 1919, wherein the following is laid down:

'In the establishment of the constitution and administration of Palestine all such measures shall be adopted as will afford the fullest guarantees for carrying into effect the British Government's Declaration of the 2nd of November, 1917.

'All necessary measures shall be taken to encourage and stimulate immigration of Jews into Palestine on a large scale, and as quickly as possible to settle Jewish immigrants upon the land through closer settlement and intensive cultivation of the soil.'

In a letter written on March 3, 1919, to Felix Frankfurter on behalf of the Hejaz Delegation, Feisal said this:

'We Arabs, especially the educated among us, look with the deepest sympathy on the Zionist movement. Our deputation here in Paris is fully acquainted with the proposals submitted yesterday by the Zionist Organization to the Peace Conference, and we regard them as moderate and proper. We will do our best, in so far as we are concerned, to help them through; we will wish the Jews a hearty welcome home. . . . The Jewish movement is national and not imperialist. Our movement is national and not imperialist, and there is room in Syria* for us both. Indeed I think that neither can be a real success without the other.'

There was also a delegation of Syrian Arabs, representing all communities: Moslems, Christians, Jews; one member was Jamil Mardam, later Prime Minister of Syria. In the concluding part of his statement before the Supreme Council of the Allies, on February 13, 1919, M. Checkri Ganem, chief representative of the Central Syrian Committee, said:

'May we say one word as regards Palestine, although the subject is said to be a thorny one. Palestine is incontestably the southern portion of our country. The Zionists claim it. We have

* Syria is here meant to include Palestine.

suffered too much from sufferings resembling theirs, not to throw open wide to them the doors of Palestine. All those among them who are oppressed in certain retrograde countries are welcome. Let them settle in Palestine, but in an autonomous Palestine, connected with Syria by the sole bond of federation. Will not a Palestine enjoying wide internal autonomy be for them a sufficient guarantee?'

It is then on historical record that, when the decision was taken, there was no Arab opposition. Indeed, there was explicit Arab consent. When and why this opposition then? When implementation of the decision was handed over to agents who cared little for its success: the Mandatory Administration of colonial traditions and staff had neither the understanding, the vision and sympathy, nor the ability to carry out what is admittedly a complex and difficult task of ingathering and resettlement. And because some of the Arab leaders in Palestine were not slow to perceive the—to put it mildly—rather reluctant mode of implementation. Naturally they took immediate advantage of this hesitancy and half-heartedness, believing that, after all, the decision was perhaps not very seriously meant and could be easily reversed.

It was the Royal Commission itself which condemned the instrument designed to fulfill the international pledge and coined the phrase 'the unworkability of the Mandate.' Whether we agree with all the reasoning of the Commission or not, one thing can hardly be disputed: the system set up to work the Mandate did prove to be unworkable.

Though we have had, and still have, frequent differences with the Mandatory, some of them very bitter, some even tragic, especially since the policy of the White Paper began, and culminating in the controversy over a Jewish army in Palestine and the *Struma*, we cannot say that the Administration's failure to carry out the Mandate for the last twenty years is due to the fact that it is British.

The unworkability was inherent in a unique situation: the incongruity between the nature of the task and of the instrument. The Administration was composed of an officialdom trained to administer backward peoples, used to dealing with primitive tribes, where its main duty was to preserve the existing order as far as possible.

In Palestine it encountered an advanced and progressive Jewish community, and a dynamic situation requiring constant initiative, unrelenting effort and creative energy. It was only human nature that the officials should feel themselves much more at ease dealing with Arabs and ministering to their needs, where they could indulge their ingrained habit of maintaining the status quo.

Mass colonization on a large scale will be necessary to meet post-war needs of Jewish migration, and require a large outlay of capital from inter-governmental sources. The principal and indispensable readjustment for a task of such magnitude, however, is a new regime—political, legal and administrative, especially designed for the maximum development of the resources of Palestine and the absorption of the maximum number of immigrants in the shortest possible time. The fundamental laws of the country, land and water regulations, labor legislation, fiscal and commercial statutes, must be entirely altered to match intensive settlement, the speedy building up of industries, the growth of town and village. And not only the laws, but their daily administration, must be guided and inspired by this steadfast and unwavering purpose. Only a Jewish Administration can be equal to it, one completely identified with the needs and aims of Jewish settlers and whole-heartedly devoted to the upbuilding of the country. Jewish immigration in great volume is bound to result, in the not distant future, in a growing Jewish majority and the establishment of a self-governing Jewish Commonwealth.

Reviewing the events of the past score years, taking into account our requirements in the period following immediately after this war, our first conclusion is that the Mandate must be entrusted to the Jewish people and no other.

I do not mean the formal Mandate as of 1922. The whole system of Mandates may go. I mean the responsibility and necessary governmental authority to rebuild the country and secure the restoration of the Jews to it. To start with, immigration and colonization should be made the charge of an agency of the whole Jewish people.

It is too soon to plan in detail for the constitution of Palestine after the war and attempt 'crystal-gazing' now. It is, however, possible and expedient to lay down the most essential principles for our own guidance and for the instant political job of Zionism, to educate Jewish and generally public opinion toward a Zionist solution of the Jewish and the Palestine problem.

These principles are three:

1. An unequivocal reaffirmation of the original intention of the Balfour Declaration and the Mandate to re-establish Palestine as a Jewish Commonwealth, as was made clear by the President of the United States on March 3, 1919.

2. The Jewish Agency for Palestine, as the trustee for prospective immigrants and settlers, should have full control over Jewish immigration and be vested with all due authority for development and upbuilding, not least of unoccupied and uncultivated lands.

3. Complete equality, civil, political and religious, of all inhabitants of Palestine; self-government in all municipal affairs; autonomy for the different Jewish and Arab communities in the management of all their internal affairs, educational, religious and so forth.

Whether Palestine should remain a separate unit or be associated with a larger and more comprehensive political entity—a Near Eastern Federation, the British Commonwealth of Nations, an Anglo-American Union or the like, will depend on circumstances and developments we can neither determine nor predict and does not constitute a special Jewish or Palestinian problem. We will be part of the new world and of the new pattern which, we believe, will come out of this war, with victory on our side. But whatever proves to be the constitutional relation of Jewish Palestine to other countries, there must be a continued willingness and readiness to cooperate closely with the Arabs in Palestine as well as in neighboring countries. Once the bone of contention of Jewish immigration is removed by a clear-cut international decision on the one hand, and on the other, by assurance that the Jews are to control their own immigration, there is no serious reason to abandon hope of Jews and Arabs working together.

Zionism in action means building nation and State. Many have conceded the justice and beauty of the Zionist ideal and the Jewish people's right to a free existence of its own, as an equal of all other nations. But they found it hard seriously to believe that Jews, who for centuries had become more and more denationalized, uprooted from their native heath, set apart in cities, and confined to a very few occupations and trades, who had forgotten their national language and loosened their national ties, who remained Jews largely because they could not become something else—that these could again become a nation, rebuild a country and recreate an independent economy and culture.

There was, indeed, much more in this viewpoint than they knew who advanced it. The idea and vision looked simple, natural and necessary, but translated into action they were at once involved in countless obstacles and almost insurmountable difficulties. They meant not merely the transfer of a people, but its total transformation, not merely the return to a country, but its upbuilding. And what a people! And what a country! The Jews had to remake themselves and remake Palestine. We must remember that Zionist colonization is possibly the only example, or certainly one of the very few examples, of successful colonization not undertaken and not supported by a State.

We are still very far from our goal, the most difficult test of fulfillment is still before us. But past performance gives us confidence that it can be done, and that we can do it.

Defying economic dogma, Jews in Palestine went from town to country; urbanized for centuries, they became husbandmen. Over 30% of them live in rural settlements. Even more remarkable is their reversion to manual work. Of 500,000 souls, 125,000 adults are members of the Labor Federation. As nowhere else, they are active in every kind of work: in fields, factories and quarries, in mines on buildings, roads and railways, in harbors, fishing and aviation.

Coming from all ends of the earth with diverse languages and cultural traditions, they are being welded into a new uniformity, Hebrew their common language, the rebuilding of Zion their common purpose.

Living in their own villages and towns, providing for their own defense, education and social services, they have developed a comprehensive system of local and national self-government rising firmly from an independent economy and culture, and thus, for all practical purposes, have laid the foundations of a Jewish Commonwealth.

What 500,000 Jews could do, six, eight or ten times their number can. What was done on an area of one and a half million dunams can be done on six, eight or ten times as much. There is no truer, more abiding and convincing test of fulfillment than fulfillment. Zionism has stood that test, and not once only.

A test of nationhood faced the Yishuv four years before the outbreak of this war, when the Mufti, on instructions of Mussolini and Hitler, tried to destroy it by starvation, interrupting its communications, stopping its work and the arrival of newcomers by terror, by indiscriminate murder. Never before did the economic self-sufficiency and strength of the Yishuv, its great valor, its deep attachment to its ancient soil, its creative energy in face of the most deadly and constant danger, manifest itself more strongly. Not only was there no retreat or abandonment of the least position, but there were continuous and manifold development and expansion in agricultural settlements, absorption of new immigration, industrial advances and conquest of the sea, and the creation of a defense force such as Palestine had not seen since the seventh century, when Benjamin of Tiberias led a contingent of his fellow-Jews to help the Persians fight the tyrants of Byzantium.

The outbreak of this war brought a sterner test. I can best tell you how the Yishuv fares by quoting a recent message from Moshe Shertok, who now conducts our political front in Palestine:

'Amid this sea of pain and horror, Palestine today stands out as a rock of refuge, a beacon of hope to an agonized Jewry. Steeled in adversity in the four pre-war years, the Yishuv is now called upon to act in this war as vanguard of the entire Jewish people, shouldering on its behalf three major responsibilities. The first and the foremost is fullest cooperation in the defense of the country and in the Middle Eastern campaign by mobilizing all available resources for a distinctive Jewish war effort, in the military, industrial and agricultural spheres.

'The second is the utmost exertion to save Jewish victims of the war.

'The third is preparation and bold efforts for post-war construction.

'Here are the landmarks of our progress:

'In the military services 12,500 men and women[*] are enlisted.

'Thousands of Jewish technicians and skilled artisans are engaged in essential war work in Palestine and in the Middle East. Jewish industry employs 35,000 workers, who are increasingly harnessed to war production. Its output for war has increased eightfold since 1940. Many plants are working day and night.

'The Jewish National Fund has acquired 133,000 dunams of

[*] By the end of the war, the number had reached 33,000.

land during the war period. Eighteen settlements were founded, breaking new ground for agricultural production and increasing space in the old and new settlements, whose manpower and resources are strained to the highest pitch. Despite the veering fortunes of war, tens of thousands of refugees have entered Palestine since September of 1939. The Yishuv is bracing itself for a fresh, a supreme, effort in defense and production. Thousands of youngsters from the towns are on their way to work on the farms. Large numbers are being trained for defense duties. New contingents of recruits are being raised for the Army.'

* * *

In our re-building of Palestine we could not altogether escape the conflicts, contradictions and evils of the present economic system. But it is not vainly that we fought for all the centuries to maintain our identity and our Jewishness, molded in the Homeland whence our Prophets bequeathed to humanity the still unrealized vision of human brotherhood and justice, love of neighbor, peace among nations. Without bloodshed, without coercion, by a voluntary moral effort, assisted by the goodwill and sympathetic help of the whole Zionist Movement, our halutzim set up a new type of communal and cooperative settlement—kvutza and moshav—embodying an original human kinship of free creative work, mutual help, common interests and complete equality, and combining an ideal social structure with a sound economic foundation, so far not elsewhere known. And it has stood the test of time—the first kvutza was set up in 1910—and proved its economic and social superiority to other types. It is a message of living faith for all Jews, and for the world at large, that a better society is not just a myth.

This is the second World War in our generation. Never before was all humanity threatened with such danger of complete and total slavery. Never before was our own people threatened with such complete and total annihilation. While the war goes on we must devote every ounce of our energy to complete and total victory. But we must beware of the perilous fallacy that the smashing of Hitlerism alone will free the world of all its ills and the Jewish people of its misery. There is something fundamentally wrong in civilization, if a Hitler can bring the whole of mankind to such a pass, and something fundamentally wrong in the Jewish set-up if, whenever there is any trouble, Jews are singled out as its first and most catastrophic victims. Victory over Hitler will not be an end, but the beginning of a new set-up for the world and for ourselves.

Our past work and achievements in Palestine have a double contribution to make to the reshaping of human society and the remaking of Jewish history. They will serve as the pedestal upon which to build the Jewish Commonwealth, and a Jewish Commonwealth means a Commonwealth of Justice. To build it will need maximal effort by the entire Jewish people, in the Diaspora and in Palestine. As part of the great human cause, America, England, Russia and other nations that champion humanity, may be expected to help us. But we must do the job ourselves. Palestine will be as Jewish as the Jews will make it.

THE IMPERATIVES OF THE JEWISH REVOLUTION
*An Address to the Youth Section of Mapai,
September 1944*

Right at the beginning, I want to say that not only you, who are here assembled, but every boy and girl in this land of Israel are called to the most painful task in our or any history, are summoned to pledge outright allegiance to the Jewish revolution, allegiance in sentiment and will, in thought and deed, in your lives and, if it must be, with your lives.

Ours is not the only, or the first, of man's revolutions, and it will not be the last. You recall the British revolution in the seventeenth century, the American and French revolutions in the eighteenth, and the Russian in this. But there is one basic difference and difficulty—all such were or will be uprisings against a form of government, a political, social and economic form; ours is pointed not only at that target, but at destiny, the unique destiny of a unique people.

The singularity is earlier than Galuth; it was manifested when a small people still dwelt in its own small parish, which in itself is not exceptional. But this was a small people with a great spirit, a people of genius with faith in its pioneering mission to mankind, a mission preached by the Prophets of Israel, and a people that gave the world everlasting moral truths and tenets. It foretold the unity of the Creator and His creation, the supreme worth of man created in the image of God and thereby precious. It foretold social justice and universal peace in the great principle: 'And thou shalt love thy neighbor as thyself.' It was the first to behold the millennial vision of a new human society.

DAVID BEN GURION

The uniqueness of the Land is in its geology and topography and in the geographical placing which vest it with a special, world-wide importance. With its folk, it has lain from the dawn of its days betwixt two rich and spreading lands—or, in modern parlance, two mighty empires—Egypt and Babylon, great in their cultures, founders of civilization, inventors of science and mathematics, of geometry, and astronomy, and of intensive husbandry, for both were lands of fertile plains, irrigated by great rivers—the Nile, the Tigris and the Euphrates. Each gave birth to a famous and many-sided literature, in history, poetry and science, of which fragmentary relics still astound us. Perhaps you may have read part of Tchernichovsky's brilliant translation of the Gilgamesh epic, and that is only a tiny crumb of the splendid feast.

And so we Jews shuttled perpetually between these cultured and wealthy kingdoms and our seeming dearth of material things and outward show. But the treasures of our human values and moral concepts, our universal vision for mankind which all the progress and reforms of civilization have not yet brought true—these we never let go, and by these we were saved. We could withstand surrounding pressures, we could cling to independence and, unique always, stamp our character of fruitfulness upon history. But to win through, we had to show ourselves more than mortal in struggle and sacrifice.

* * *

In the period of the Second Temple, one by one the suns set—of Egypt and Babylon and Persia, and the star of Greece climbed in the heavens. Then, in the days of the Hasmonaeans came the climax: no mere political tussle but a spiritual combat between what were, perhaps, the deepest cultures known to mankind—the cultures of Judea and Greece. Greek culture was, indeed, declining by that time, some hundred years after the close of the classical era, coinciding with the emergence of Alexander the

Great. But his supremacy transformed Hellenism into a global force in culture as in politics, and spread its language and learning from the Mediterranean as far as India.

Palestine was encircled by Hellenistic lands. Athens was still the seat of two great universities—Plato's Academy and Aristotle's Lyceum; and disciples still taught the lessons of the great mentors. In Alexandria, at the very threshold of Palestine, a new center of Hellenism arose.

Reinforced as it was by the political influence of the Hellenists in Egypt and Syria, Greek culture drew the Jews strongly, and a dual conflict was provoked—political between the Jews and their Greek overlords, internal between the guardians of Jewish tradition and autonomy and Hellenistic assimilationists among the Jews. That inner quarrel only ended when Jewish independence was destroyed with the doom of Bar Kochba.

Saul of Tarsus, afterward Paul, was perhaps the outstanding Jewish assimilationist. He transfigured the career and teachings of a modest and simple Jew from Nazareth, who had lived and died a Jew, wrenched him from his Jewish environment and past, and made of him a divine symbol. Thus did Saul found the Christian religion, and it swiftly overran Europe. He affirmed the universal human values of the Jews, but tore them out of their Jewish setting, and in the place of national and historical Judaism established a creed professedly universal but in fact anti-Jewish.

To his disciples he bequeathed a magnificent hymn on the love of man (Chapter 13 in the First Epistle to the Corinthians), one of the noblest ever written, but those who followed his creed of love sent Jews to the gallows century after century, and Europe was our valley of the shadow of death. Not for nothing was that epoch known as the 'Dark Ages'.

Bar Kochba made a last valiant effort to win back our freedom with the sword. Rabbi Akiva supported him loyally and at his bidding thousands of his pupils joined the ranks of revolt. Akiva died a hero, his flesh scourged by Roman rods, his breath departing with the cry—'Hear O Israel . . . the Lord is One.'

There a new chapter begins for Israel—exiled but unyielding, homeless, helpless and vagrant, enveloped in misunderstandings and contempt, in hatred and prejudice, disfranchised, expelled, harried and slain. In Babylon and Persia, in Spain and Italy and medieval England, in France and Germany, in Russia, Poland and Rumania—everywhere, always, Israel was prey of malignant persecution because of its Jewishness, its difference from other peoples—and through all that torment and tragedy, unbowed and unblemished it guarded its distinctiveness.

Many Jews did, of course, give in. Extermination and conversion took a heavy toll, and are not yet outworn. Some could not bear the hourly peril of ignominy or violence. Some lacked stamina to repel the magnetism of an all-embracing and dominant civilization and creed, which seemed to bring peace and happiness to all but the Jews, and they laid down their arms and left the battlefield. But not the Jewish people as an entity; magnificently it held out over the centuries. Every nation can point proudly to heroic episodes in its annals, for heroism is a universal quality, and in the second World War millions displayed it amazingly. But with us it was not an episode, but a determined and unflinching stand for thousands of years. Other nations, displaced and banished like ours, soon faded from the world's scene. We alone, in that dread plight, stood fast—from Hadrian's persecution to the uprising of the ghettos in Warsaw, Lublin and Bialystok. No surrender to what the fates assign—such is the meaning and essence of our history in exile.

How then did they differ in their heroism, these who in Galuth were not affrighted by stake or scaffold or living tomb, from us here, outriders of a pioneer revolution now three generations old? This is the difference—we have said we must conquer the fates, we must take our destiny in our own hands, not just resisting banishment but ending it for ever!

Exile is one with utter dependence—in material things, in politics and culture, in ethics and intellect, and they must be dependent who are an alien minority, who have no Homeland and are separated from their origins, from the soil and labor, from economic creativity. So we must become the captains of our fortunes, we must become independent—not only in politics and economy but in spirit, feeling and will. From that inward self-determination stem the outward forms of way of life and government, foreign relations and economy, which are shaped by achievements in labor and farming, in speech and erudition, by means of organization and defense, by the opportunity freely to live and create, and, at the last, by attainment of national sovereignty.

That is the message our revolution brings, a revolution that is not a laboratory experiment, but something real that is happening to a Yishuv and a Diaspora set in a complex pattern of international conditions beyond our control and ruthlessly in action whatever we may do.

It is well that I should speak to you of the dangers—within and without—which those conditions threaten, bearing directly on the tasks that confront the younger generation.

Throughout the world the times are revolutionary, and we must suffer the profound and potent impact on our meager resources of seismic forces revolutionizing mankind's affairs. We are least, though not negligibly, in peril from men who with deliberation and without concealment spurn our aims and needs. There is peril from the Jewish agents of foreign governments, middlemen for alien cultures and nations, once known as 'they who sin against the Covenant,' and now as the Yevsektzia or, here, the Fraktzia,* but their very dependence on a foreign master lessens their influence among us.

* *Yevsektzia*: Jewish section of the Communist party in the early days of the Russian Revolution. *Fraktzia*: (Fraction): one of the names of the Jewish Communists in Palestine.

But the real risk is lest the capacity be dulled, in the protagonists of our revolution, to assess sturdily the forces that will shape our future, lest confidence be shaken in our own potentialities as the focal and final authors of the morrow of our own small universe within the larger, lest we may belittle ourselves and our creations, being few and infirm beside the proud catalogue of great nations that rule continents and oceans. We must beware not to pin our hopes on the forces of tomorrow, of the future, of other peoples. Our orientation must point toward the inner strength.

This is not the first time that we Jews have been perplexed by this issue of 'orientation'. Open the Book of Books and consider the words of Jeremiah in Chapters 42 and 43. They describe the argument between the Prophet and Johanan and Jezaniah, itself, in all likelihood, not the first of its kind. Tell us, they ask, 'the way wherein we may walk, and the thing that we may do.' He answered: 'If ye will still abide in this land, then will I build you and not pull you down, and I will plant you, and not pluck you up . . . Be not afraid of the King of Babylon.' And to those who said: 'No, but we will go into the land of Egypt, where we shall see no war . . . nor have hunger of bread; and there will we abide,' he answered: 'If ye wholly set your faces to enter into Egypt, and go to sojourn there; then it shall come to pass that the sword, which ye fear, shall overtake you there in the land of Egypt, and the famine, whereof ye are afraid, shall follow hard after you there in Egypt; and there ye shall die . . . and ye shall be an execration, and an astonishment, and a curse, and a reproach; and ye shall see this place no more.' This was an original, bold and vigorous statement of the principle of 'orientation towards ourselves'.

The argument has gone on, forever befogged by cloudy thinking on the forces of yesterday and of today. 'Yesterday' and 'tomorrow' are, historically, only relative—what was, three dawns ago, a 'force of tomorrow' is today become the 'force of yesterday', and a seeming 'force of yesterday' is galvanized overnight into irresistibility.

In our littleness today, is it strange then that the great ones of the earth should dazzle us with the blinding radiance of their overpowering strength and numbers? It demands superhuman effort to have faith in ourselves.

In the days of the Prophets, likewise, we were—we always will be—few, and nations of vast pomp and panoply ringed us about, so that even the cultured citizen, who met the great seers face to face, needed tremendous trust in the destiny of his nation to stay loyal to it. The neighboring peoples were not drawn to Hebrew as to the Egyptian and Babylonian tongues. Yet Micah and Hosea wrote in Hebrew, a provincial speech comprehended only by a small sect, and still are their works deathless and universal.

Those who believed in the potency of Egypt and Assyria, of Greece and Rome, are forgotten, their footprints buried in the sands of time. But all civilization bears the impress of the men that kept faith with frail Jewry, of their works and vision. This is the 'orientation' to a puny but independent authority, this the belief in an independent and unique purpose, that has sustained us and brought us thus far. No following after strangers, or courting the derision that is heaped upon the wisdom of the subservient. Over thirty years ago, a score of young men and women founded the first kvutza on the Jordan: they did more for Jewish and world affairs, for the Jewish and international labor movement, than schools of Jewish socialists and reformers who swam in the wake of the 'great' revolutions and mocked at the 'slight and eccentric' doings of Jewish pioneers in Palestine. Yet the modest achievement of those self-reliant pioneers is today the sole anchor and beacon for the remnants of Israel, an object-lesson to hundreds of thousands of Jewish girls and boys everywhere, and I am sure it will be one day a model to the world.

* * *

DAVID BEN GURION

We must let nothing, nothing, impair the independence of our Movement, its inner freedom, moral and intellectual. By all means, let us always be cognizant of the nature and importance of all that goes on in the world at large, the mighty forces that control it, the revolutionary phenomena that are now so ubiquitous—but remember also, with deepest clarity, that the Jewish revolution is ours alone to carry through, faithful to our own desires and ideals, within the bounds of our own capacity and resource and ever broadening those bounds, to make ours the 'force of tomorrow'.

The second imperative of the Jewish revolution is the unity of its executants. Unity alone will develop fully our internal forces. Unity our mission and our destiny enjoin, but unity it is that we the most accept in principle and neglect in fact. The separatism that has filtered into our midst defends itself by the cheap catchword of 'proletarian origin', so repugnant to the essence and spirit of our movement. Not the origin but the end, not the 'Whence?' but the 'Whither?' decides the issue, for our end is to make of Jewry a working people. Not our beginnings and our past must guide us—but our destiny and our hereafter, and the turning-point is halutziuth, the transition to a life of labor and personal service.

The workers of the Yishuv need something more than self-unity. They must be at one with the nation, in a mutual allegiance of epic import, and they must as well attain to solidarity with the international workers' movement. For ours is part and parcel of the world revolution, to free mankind from bondage, exploitation and all manner of restraints and prejudices. Upholding our moral and intellectual liberty, we must yet strengthen our ties with the workers of all other nations. It may be that great glory awaits a Judea rejuvenescent, but only by devotion to the Jewish revolution and its independence will that glory be won. That is why I would sooner have a kvutza like Degania than all the Yevsektzias and assimilationists in the world.

The third imperative—perhaps the mightiest—is halutziuth.

We are nearing the end of the war. City after city, country after country, is being ransomed—but for us there is no joy. For them, liberation—for our Jewries, almost obliteration. The wellsprings of the Jewish revolution are destroyed, Polish, Lithuanian, Galician Jewry is no more.

Yet never did we need so many loyal pioneers. The desolation of the land, the wastage of the people, cry out. The call is for halutziuth—to revitalize the desert hills of Galilee and the Negev plains, to bring plenty to the Jordan Valley, the sand-dunes of our shores, the Judean ranges; to clear the way for newcomers from the Yemen and Persia, from Turkey and Egypt, from Syria and Iraq, from Rumania and Greece, from France and Belgium, from wherever a handful or a host survives—England and America, North and South Africa, yes, and Soviet Russia too, one day.

For the measure of success in our revolution is the full ingathering of the exiles in a socialist Jewish State. But in history no goal can be the last, and this ingathering is itself only a stepping-stone to fulfillment of our people's destiny. Only when we throw off the fetters by which, as society and nation, we are constricted, and are free men again on the soil of a free Homeland, nationally independent and equal as men, only then will we be fit to perform man's great mission on earth and harness to man's advancement the secrets of the elements and the inventions of our own genius in all its originality and strength.

Knowledge I cannot claim, but invincibly I believe that not only you, the younger generation, but all of us present here and all our comrades, wherever they may be, will be vouchsafed to behold that wondrous consummation.

TERRORISM OR CONSTRUCTIVE EFFORT
Address delivered at the first session of the Annual Conference of the Histadruth, November 20, 1944

Two problems face us, or, more accurately, two inescapable alternatives. The first is between terrorism and political, Zionist, resistance, for in no circumstances can these co-exist. The second is between terrorist organizations and an organized Yishuv, an organized people, an organized movement of workers. One or the other we must choose; both we cannot have.

Things are being done in this country today which, without using the glosses of politics, we may flatly call murder and robbery, blackmail and theft. Even were they done with no quasi-political purpose, for no self-styled cause, they are not to be borne within its borders by any civilized community. When a community is self-governing, it has its own police force and governmental authority to repress them; when it is not, it must rely upon agencies of control set up by others.

Plain murder and robbery might be less perilous. But the crimes I speak of are committed in the name of Zionism. The peril, therefore, does not affect merely the life, the property and well-being of individuals. It is infinitely worse: it threatens that which ranks above our very lives—it hazards our mission and our vision. For this murder and robbery, this terrorism so-called, that profess an idea as their author and end, supplant it at the last; they are done for the sake of political warfare, but it is that idea they displace.

We must convince ourselves that only one is possible of the two—terrorism or political, which is Zionist, resistance. What does such resistance mean? It means immigration continued under any and every condition. It means applying all our energy and strength to colonization. It means educating the nation and mobilizing it for its redemption, gaining public opinion for Zionist policy, winning the favor of princes and the sympathy of labor leaders, of political parties, of religious bodies and of all manner of societies. It means publishing newspapers, challenging discrimination in law, fighting against any curtailment of our rights, organizing our stand against foes and persecutors, as any nation would that has will, mission and ability, that can think, poise and appraise, that is responsible and resolved to protect and defend itself.

Murderers there may be in a community where most citizens are righteous; robbers there may be where most are respectable; thieves too, where most are law-abiding. Not that this unhappy leaven, as it were, is an ideal to be prayed for, as one among us foolishly prayed to see the day when we should have thieves and robbers of our own in our own State! It will always be time enough for that! By malefactors such as these, no community that is sound will ever be placed in dire jeopardy. But here they wrap their wrongdoing in a cloak of nationalism, they claim to offend in the name of the community or for its sake, in its behalf, for its freedom's sake, its future and emancipation, forsooth, while the community seems resigned and inarticulate. It is the duty and the will of every citizen with might and main to extirpate the lone criminal, and he therefore pays taxes for the upkeep of a constabulary. But if I, the citizen, am silent and unmoving when murder and robbery do their dreadful work in my name, in my behalf, if the whole public is dumb and palsied when men kill and steal in its name, in its behalf, then do we all admit these criminals to be somehow our spokesmen. Then only the way of terrorism remains, no other way, to the achieving of our political aims.

Regard now the second alternative. Look first on this picture.

A Jewish people sensible of past tragedy but seeing now the way to freedom; a people united in construction, politically untiring, telling its story to the world, if need be waging war; a people of national unity, responsibility and judgment, backed by public opinion and authority. An organized Yishuv united in more than speech, every member of it free to air his every view, so that only fair debate and counsel can lead to operative decision. An organized movement of workers—not regimented serfs, but free men conscious of a great mission, of a tremendous life's work, knowing the virtue of unity, collective effort and productivity, building and creating, striving and struggling when they must.

Now look on this. A gang which buys an automatic gun, or a stick of dynamite, and with it makes bold to decide our problems neither by our leave nor heeding our opinion nor indeed seeking it, to determine how we shall react, what stand we shall take, who shall represent us and in what mood.

There is no compromise, no equivocation. The way of terror or the way of Zionism, gangsterism or an organized Yishuv; murder from ambush and banditry in darkness or the voluntary self-discipline of youth movements, of farmers and industrialists, a union of freedom and cooperation in argument, decision and act.

Whenever and wherever there is a self-governing community of free men, gangsters find no place. If gangsters rule—free men are homeless. Take your choice—violence and repression, or constitutional liberties.

If, then, we yearn still to be a responsible, efficient and organized Yishuv, let us rise up against terror and its agencies, and smite them. The time for words is past.

It is salutary to explain the origins, in history, ideology and society, of this virulent and criminal phenomenon. It is important to spread the information among all sectors of the Yishuv and of the Histadruth. The true state of affairs must be made known by every means, so that every one may understand the harm and risk involved. I sought the privilege of addressing you, because I wished to sound a warning. Explanations, indictments, fine or lambent phrases are pointless now: deeds must follow them.

Terrorism that is mere ideology we might counter with ideological retaliation; but we have to deal with terrorist acts—and acts are the only answer. Gangsters comprehend no language—be it of justice, of Zionism, of socialism, or any known medium of reason. All they understand is the language of force, the show of strength. It is no longer enough to clarify in talk: their operations must be stopped and their organization broken up. I do not mean that the men themselves be liquidated; I want no bloodshed and pray they do not provoke it, I want no single life lost. And I believe, if we enlighten them soberly, we can yet save some, the younger ones especially, who were misled and crazed by distortion and misrepresentation of Jewry's disasters, anguish and wrath.

Today, gangsterism serves these heady draughts to its new recruits, but it was not itself born of the happenings of recent years, and argument alone will not exterminate it: let there be no mistake on that score.

Gangs seem to be working against some external enemy, but in fact it is always an internal enemy they fight, and that is anyone who disobeys them. I divide their members into two kinds; maniacs and charlatans. There are simpleton maniacs, persuaded that this or that assassination will bring redemption to Israel. They murder Englishmen and Jews with the same fanatic zeal. But the trouble is that terrorism neither needs nor depends upon a large following, so even if we retrieve a few of their youthful adherents by effective propaganda, terror will go on.

We shall persist in this propaganda, and simplify it, in the youth movements and for the many more young people not yet organized. But what counts now is not taking a stand, whether it be taken by the Histadruth, the Yishuv, the Zionist Organization, or united Jewry. The gangs will only scoff, only action can pierce their defenses. Make every announcement imaginable, couched in the sternest or most captivating terms, brand them fascists, genocides of Israel, what you will, it will all rattle harmlessly, emptily, against their armor. In vain, for six months past, we have used that weapon: fulminating in every newspaper, from every institution. And the result? The terrorists were heartened, their insolence and, I fear, their power have grown.

So act we must, and for the moment four courses of action have been resolved on, which I wish to discuss simply and clearly.

The Zionist Executive and the National Council demand a purge of terrorists from our ranks. Therefore, I solemnly invoke the workers in any factory, the clerks in any office, in which a member or supporter of the gangs is employed to drive him out of his job. I can say this much more easily here than in any other place. I would find it hard to say at a meeting where the right of every man to work might lack moral and organizational sanction. Here, it is redundant to preach the sanctity of that right.

Thus, deliberately, I choose the draconic step. Whosoever traffics with the gangs or aids in any way, handing out their prints and billposting their placards, though he press no trigger and throw no bomb, must incontinently be dismissed from his place of work, his desk or bench or plough, and struck off the rolls of the labor exchange.

And not otherwise at school or college. If any student be known to take part in murder or marauding, or only distributes the poisonous effusions of the terrorists among his fellows—tear the wretched leaflets from his grasp and burn them! Expel him, so that he may feel, and his parents and companions, how we abhor his traitorous felony.

Thus far I have laid my charge on the workers. The Yishuv as a whole, and the Zionist Movement everywhere, must lay as binding a charge on the Associations of Farmers and Manufacturers, on the guilds of traders and merchants, to cast forth any in their midst who gives money or comfort to the gangs. Protection or not, landlords should evict contaminated tenants. Every organized group in the country must spew such out.

It would be tragic to repeat the error of Lansbury, that splendid and beloved figure of British Labor. For he foresaw the Nazi danger, yet in his simplicity believed it could be held at bay not by a powerful army that would abruptly shatter Hitler's dream of world domination, but by soft words; and so journeyed to Berlin to plead with him, citing to an unmoved infidel from the Sermon on the Mount. If we speechify and are inert, we fortify terror, not hinder it. To be sure, the gangs are watching and waiting for the upshot of this very Conference. Will it be declamation or deeds? I would rather a grain of action than a mountain of revolutionary rhetoric.

Refuge and shelter must be stringently denied these wild men. We all know each other, I think. We are all of us filled with Jewish pity, I am no less a Jew than the rest, I have no personal hatred of these people. But I see the awful calamity they are bringing on themselves and us all. Like every Jew who is needed to defend the hopes of his people and his Land in this grievous and critical moment of our fight for life, I must try to suppress my normal emotions touching individual lives. We have sent thirty thousand of our finest sons to the Army. We are now calling up new recruits. The men and women in the front-line, they too ask of us that we set personal feelings aside. If we would be Zionists now, we dare not be merciful, lest we suffer destruction. No refuge, no shelter: it means, I know, that we repress a lofty and noble instinct, one especially Jewish. But if we are not to be unpitying of Jewry that is nigh to drowning in the deeps of torment, we must not lend ourselves to the hypocrisy of compassion for the agents of terror.

And we must blunt the gangster's weapon of intimidation. Threats and blackmail are his favorite stratagem, and so serious now are his menaces that citizens entirely out of sympathy with the gangs, fiercely opposed to their methods, are yet constrained to implore that no counter-action be taken, lest it provoke civil war. To such we say: already a state of war between citizen and citizen exists in the Yishuv, and it is the gangs that caused it, but for them it has to be one-sided, so that unappealably and at will they can extort money, punish 'traitors,' pass sentences of death or murder the recalcitrant. That must never be!

A few days since, a terrorist, telephoning to Ada Golomb, pronounced her husband a traitor. We know what that signifies; tomorrow some member of the Jewish Agency Executive or National Council will get the same call. Neither Golomb nor the others will panic, but in our half-million many are newcomers, many are not in the tradition of the founders of Petah Tiqvah, of our first watchmen, of Tel Hai's defenders, and when armed youngsters enter the home of a meek Jew of that kind and demand money, he yields in fright.

To teach the Yishuv wholesome contempt for this browbeating, we must create conditions that will make fear impossible by making intimidation so.

This effrontery and license has got to be stopped. We can no longer permit these rascals to parade our streets, vaunting their terrorism almost openly. 'Make way,' they cry, 'for we are come to rob'—and the citizens fall nervelessly back! This is our worst disgrace since the beginning of the modern Yishuv. The founders of that Yishuv were no cowards in Rishon or Tel Aviv, nor were the standard-bearers of Jewish labor and those who built the labor settlements. How then—to take one glaring instance—can a few hooligans walk into a warehouse, in the heart of a town with 200,000 inhabitants, in the middle of the day, and send everybody scurrying out of it frantically at the sound of the words: 'The Irgun is going into action!'?

We cannot afford to let this vicious arrogance plague us and our children. The gallantry of the first protectors of our villages, great names like Abraham Shapiro, Israel Giladi and Joseph Trumpeldor, taught us much that is good. Unless we act in time, the lawless ways of the terrorists may teach us too, but lessons only in negation and destruction.

We have blundered in overdoing the healthy Jewish instinct not to appeal to alien governors for help. It is an instinct that our history in dispersion proved right; it has not yet been proved wrong here. Not for nothing did the early pioneers set up local councils to be a form of domestic self-government, an autonomy, jealously guarded, that developed and grew: and out of it, in the end, grew the Jewish State.

But it is a strange paradox that those in rebellion against our civic responsibility, who are undermining our autonomous existence, should be shielded because of Jewish reluctance to accept aid from the constituted forces of law and order.

It is no exaggeration to claim that terrorism harms us, imperils us, far more than it does authority.

Churchill spoke bitterly of the murder of Lord Moyne, his personal friend and Great Britain's emissary in the Middle East, yet not with the bitterness of Weizmann. For the murder hurt England less than we Jews felt the blow. No British cause was jeopardized. It was no more than merely twitching a hair of the British lion's tail; for us, it was a knife-thrust in the Jewish back, and we must bring the assassin to book.

As yet we wield no official power. The Jewish State is still to come. Some power we do have, and it is as false to lament that we are a helpless nonentity as to argue that terrorism alone pays. But there is not the normal apparatus of a Jewish Government.

DAVID BEN GURION

In the measure of the Mandatory's anxiety to uproot terrorism, we will cooperate: it would be foolish, suicidal, to withhold cooperation or reject aid where our interests are the same, just because we have much, nor unmerited, to charge Britain with in other respects.

It is our hearts—not the heart of Britain—that the terrorist iron has entered. Our hands then, no others, must pluck it out.

REPLY TO BEVIN
*An Address delivered at an extraordinary session
of the Elected Assembly, held at the
Hebrew University on Mount Scopus,
November 28, 1945*

I have just come back from the internment camps of Europe where I looked on the survivors of the Nazi charnel-houses. I was in Dachau and Belsen. I saw chambers where hundreds of Jews were throttled every day. They were brought naked, as if to bathe, and the Nazis would peer through peep-holes and watch them writhing in their death agonies. I saw crematoria in which millions of Jews were burnt alive. I saw the gallows in Belsen where Jews were hanged each Jewish holy day, while the rest were paraded to witness the ghastly punishments of men who had perhaps come a few minutes late to their daily grind. I saw kennels where ferocious dogs were bred and trained to attack any straggler as the Jews were driven to work or led to their graves. I saw racks whereon Jewish men and women were stretched out naked to be shot at by warders.

I saw the pitiful relic of European Jewry, what is left of six million, butchered before the gaze of a world frigid, aloof and indifferent to the fate of a people that has been hounded and tormented for two thousand years of exile.

From the tragic few miraculously saved, I bring two prayers. One, for the unity of Israel. The hangmen made no distinctions. Jews resisted and died together, torture and murder took no account of origin, class or party, and a people united in calamity must face its future four-square. The second, for a Jewish State, a call that goes out from the dead millions to surviving Jewry and the conscience of the world. Their dying hope was that the generations coming after would be free and happy in Zion; that hope inspired and upheld those spared from the horrors. And that hope, the new British policy of Mr. Bevin sets out to destroy.

The true purpose of his statement is unmistakable to us who will have to suffer its consequences. But it has been couched in such ambiguous terms that public opinion in England and America may be led astray. To analyze it is not easy—evidently the Foreign Office thought it well not to be too precise or explicit about a policy which reflects little credit on its authors.

First, people may be misled into thinking the entire statement a joint Anglo-American affair. In fact it consists of two parts, of which only one has been agreed between the United States and Great Britain, namely the one referring to the setting up of the Committee of Enquiry and its terms of reference. But as the President made clear immediately after publication, the United States Government accepts no responsibility for the second part. The two countries disagree on one of the main issues. The United States Government stands by its request for the admission at once into Palestine of one hundred thousand Jewish refugees from Europe; the British Government has turned it down. Secondly, and generally, the statement has been so adroitly drafted that it can be cited to various listeners in proof of different and conflicting conclusions. A Foreign Office spokesman could found any argument he pleases on it and give chapter and verse in evidence to all concerned—the British Labor party, the Jews, the Arabs—that they can find all they wish in it.

There is no denying that the Labor party is pledged to a specific policy in Palestine in support of the Jewish National Home. Disturbed by reports about the Government's intentions, the party Executive appointed a committee to discuss them with Mr. Attlee, the Prime Minister, Mr. Bevin, the Foreign Secretary, and Mr. Hall, the Colonial Secretary. All three abstained from divulging the terms of the forthcoming statement, but, according to Press reports, gave definite assurances on three points: that their new policy aimed at the repeal of the White Paper; that it would comply with all the Mandatory obligations; that it would implement the traditional policy of the Labor party on Palestine, re-affirmed on the eve of the General Election.

If the Labor party critics were now to challenge it on these grounds, a Government spokesman could argue that all three promises were duly written in. The abrogation of the White Paper, he might point out, is implied in Clause 18 where Mr. Bevin speaks of 'a new approach.' Again, Clause 16 declares that 'any violent departure without adequate consultation would probably cause serious reactions': that wording itself implies that such a departure, namely, the cancellation of the White Paper, is contemplated, if need be with adequate consultation. Moreover, the spokesman might go on to say, that was the reason for appointing a Committee of Enquiry into Palestine's absorptive capacity and the migration needs of European Jewry. Finally, in Clause 15(1) the Government declares its wish to avoid an interruption of Jewish immigration, showing that it does not intend to maintain the White Paper.

As for the promise to fulfill the Mandate, Clause 15 could be quoted as saying that 'it will be clear that His Majesty's Government cannot divest themselves of the duties and responsibilities under the Mandate while the Mandate continues.'

There remains the little matter of the Labor party's own undertakings and pledges on Palestine, which require an immigration policy that will allow the Jews 'to enter this tiny land in such numbers as to become a majority,' leading, in the words of Mr. Hugh Dalton's declaration on behalf of the Executive, 'to a free, happy and prosperous Jewish State in Palestine.' Criticism on this score could be countered by the rejoinder that such a decision falls within the permanent solution which the Committee of Enquiry is expected to recommend. The Government might claim that it has done all that could be expected of it at the moment by giving an undertaking in Clause 15(3) that it 'will prepare a permanent solution for submission to the United Nations.'

Called upon to rebut Jewish objections, the spokesman might say that the statement shows much concern for the Jews. It opens by affirming that His Majesty's Government are taking every possible step to try 'to improve the lot of these unfortunate people.' The Foreign Office could go further and as testimony of its high sentiments recite the sentence 'the Jewish problem is a great human one' and as testimony of its kindly feelings toward the Jews the words 'we cannot accept the view that the Jews should be driven out of Europe and should not be permitted to live in these countries without discrimination.' Jews naturally resent Mr. Bevin's remark that 'they should not push themselves to the head of the queue,' but it was only made at a Press conference and does not appear in the statement, so it is not the responsibility of His Majesty's Government. On the contrary, it might be claimed, the statement pays high tribute to the Jews. For example, it wants them to be able to contribute 'their ability and talent' toward rebuilding the prosperity of Europe, while Palestine is given its due prominence since it is clearly mentioned that 'the whole problem of Nazi victims in Europe cannot be solved in Europe alone even after everything possible has been done in this respect to suppress racial discrimination and to improve the conditions of the displaced Jews.' Further, does the statement not declare that 'even after all has been done in this respect in Europe it does not provide a solution of the whole problem,' (Clause 2) and that His Majesty's Government 'are anxious to explore every possibility which will result in giving the Jews a proper opportunity for revival' (Clause 3)?

So far as concerns the White Paper, so execrated by the Jews, well, it is not even mentioned once, and of course it is well known that the Labor party and the members of the present

Cabinet have proclaimed time and again that the White Paper is a breach of faith and a betrayal of international obligations. On the crucial issue of immigration, it could be indicated that, for the first of the three stages in which the Government proposes to deal with the Palestine problem, a promise is given in Clause 15 that there will be no immediate interruption (although the rider is added that 'they will consult the Arabs with a view to arrangement'). For the second stage, it is true, nothing is said about what will actually happen, but it may be urged that an extension of immigration is not excluded. As for the third stage, this, once more, falls within the permanent solution to be recommended to the United Nations, among whom, as the Jews are reminded in Clause 7, 'the Zionist cause has strong supporters.'

To mollify the Arabs, our Whitehall interpreter could fairly assert that the statement ensures everything, or almost everything, they want. The White Paper is perpetuated, in fact if not by name; Clause 16 states explicitly that the Government feels itself bound to honor all the undertakings given at various times to various parties, which obviously includes the White Paper. Granted, that only a few years ago Mr. Herbert Morrison on behalf of the Labor party in the House of Commons thundered: 'The White Paper and the policy in it is a cynical breach of pledges given to the Jews and the world, including America.' But the Arabs might be reassured, the events of the last four months have demonstrated that, since Labor has come to power, there has been a change of attitude and that the provisions of the White Paper are being faithfully complied with. The White Paper land transfer restrictions which were denounced by the party four years ago as inconsistent with the terms of the Mandate, as discriminating unjustly against one section of the inhabitants of Palestine, are still in force. The White Paper bar against Jewish immigration is being enforced by warships and airborne divisions, tanks and armored cars, and R.A.F. patrols.

The statement, confessedly, says that there should be no hold-up of Jewish immigration in the first stage, but the Government 'will consult the Arabs.' The continuation of Aliyah in the first stage, always within the current monthly limits of 1,500, thus depends on Arab consent. In the second stage, no undertaking has been given to allow one Jew to enter. As for the third stage, the stage of permanent solution, the Arabs have been comforted by Mr. Bevin's assurance in his Press conference that they need feel no alarm, as a Jewish State was never promised.

So the Arabs have no qualms as to Mr. Bevin's benevolence, but might still demur to the Committee of Enquiry, which may find in favor of the Jews. Unlike Mr. Bevin, the Arabs may suspect that Jewish survivors will be disinclined to remain in Europe at his invitation and contribute their 'ability and talent' to the reconstruction of Europe by way of reciprocity for the slaughter of their brethren. They may foresee that those Jews will insist on coming back to Palestine, and that the Enquiry will show there is room in Palestine for all of them. To set their minds at rest, it would be pointed out to them that; although the Committee is naturally expected to make an impartial investigation, its conclusions have been prejudged in the statement, which lays down that Palestine is not capable of solving the problem of Jewish refugees from Europe. ('Palestine, while it may be able to make a contribution, does not by itself provide sufficient opportunity for grappling with the whole problem.') In fact the statement ends on that note, reiterated in the concluding clause: 'the problem is not one which can be dealt with only in relation to Palestine.' If Arab critics were still not content and questioned the Government's dictum that 'the Jews should be able to live without discrimination,' it might be explained to them that this refers only to Europe, that it is nowhere said that in Palestine it is equally wrong to discriminate against the Jews or introduce differential immigration and settlement laws, as under the White Paper. The apologies might be rounded off by adding that the underlying conception of the statement reduces a gigantic problem of national homelessness to the 'disposal' of a comparative handful of Jewish survivors in Europe. To make assurance doubly sure, the Arabs might be reminded that, according to the statement, a part of that handful will have to stay where it is to 'contribute to Europe's rebuilding,' and another part will be dispersed outside Europe, so that only the barest fraction may be lucky enough to get to Palestine in the end.

I have tried to illustrate hypothetically how different things might be established to different parties by playing up one or other clause of the statement. I wonder if it was in fact thus variously construed in an effort to make it palatable to the several interests involved or salve the conscience of the Labor party and mystify public opinion in the United States. That party and public are beset by many concerns of their own, nearer home, and only a few may find the time to study the statement closely, to pry into its esoteric meaning, or analyze its contradictory possibilities. Whatever may be said of it, it was certainly not drafted in haste or by men incapable of logical thinking or lucid expression. If it abounds in ambiguity, evasiveness and equivocation, it is because it reflects a political design which seemingly could best be served by puzzling and misguiding public opinion in Great Britain and America.

But all this verbal camouflage cannot altogether veil the overriding purpose. Study the Government's new policy, not only as set forth in the statement but also in the light of what was added in explanation by the Foreign Secretary at his Press conference, view it against the background of the Government's behavior since it took office four months ago, and you will discern that purpose.

First, it is relevant to consider not only what the statement contains but what it omits. The omissions, which cannot be accidental, are illuminating and significant. The principles and ideals to which the British Labor party has been pledged for so long are passed over in silence. This is a Labor Government commanding an overwhelming majority in Parliament, sent there with a clear mandate to implement the party's program which the electorate endorsed—a great party which prepared seriously for power and brought with it long-excogitated plans and ideas, its pledges framed not as an electoral stunt but as responsible policies which it undertook to carry out. Its program no doubt represented the advice and had full concurrence of its leaders, and some of them, like Attlee, Bevin and Morrison, had been members of the War Cabinet for five years. The Labor Ministers cannot plead that they were suddenly staggered by unforeseen problems of statesmanship and had to improvise solutions, or that four months ago they were unaware of Britain's responsibilities or of international issues bearing on Palestine. The clear commitments in the program are, to say the least, at variance with the principles of Mr. Bevin's expounding. The resolution to which Labor stands committed is this:

Palestine: Here we have halted half-way irresolute between conflicting policies. But there is surely neither hope nor meaning in a 'Jewish National Home' unless we are prepared to let the Jews, if they wish, enter this tiny land in such numbers as to become a majority. There was a strong case for this before the war. There is an irresistible case now, after the unspeakable atrocities of the cold and calculated German Nazi plan to kill all the Jews in Europe . . . The Arabs have many wide territories of their own; they must not claim to exclude the Jews from this small area of Palestine, less than the size of Wales . . . Moreover, we should seek to win the full sympathy and support of both the American and Russian Governments for the execution of this policy.

Speaking on behalf of the party Executive, Mr. Dalton, the present Chancellor of the Exchequer, declared that, remembering 'the unspeakable horrors which the Jewish people have suffered, it was morally wrong and politically indefensible to restrict the entry into Palestine of Jews desiring to go there.' Facilities must be given, he added and I repeat, 'for the creation of a free, happy and prosperous Jewish State in Palestine.' Two months before the General Election, the Executive unanimously adopted a resolution reaffirming the policy on Palestine adopted at the annual conference of the party in December 1944, and calling upon the Government to remove the unjustifiable barriers to Jewish immigration and to announce without delay proposals for the future of the country in which it would have the full sympathy and support of the American and British peoples.

There are other essential and revealing omissions. The statement speaks of 'Jewish community,' of Jews, but the term 'Jewish people' which was used in the Balfour Declaration, in the Mandate, even in the White Paper, is studiously avoided. It observes that, while the Mandate lasts, His Majesty's Government cannot divest themselves of their duties and responsibilities under it. But the first principle of the Mandate is recognition of the existence and rights of the Jewish people as such, always referred to as such and not as a community of anonymous Jews. The phrasing of the statement is not merely a matter of designation; it is symptomatic of an entire policy. Instead of a people entitled to national rights and a will of its own, there are only individual Jews who become, as it were, an object of Mr. Bevin's philanthropy. The 'Jewish National Home' disappears as well. Even the White Paper invariably alluded to it: the statement only mentions a 'home' for Jews, not a National Home for the Jewish people.

At his Press conference Mr. Bevin said he had gone through all the documents on Palestine, among them the Bible and the Koran, but, search as he might, he could not find anywhere the promise of a Jewish State. Evidently he had not read the whole of the Bible, or all the documents, not even so authoritative a paper as the report of the Royal Commission which prepared a most searching survey of the Palestine problem and British obligations. Its principal finding was that a Jewish State was envisaged by the authors of the Balfour Declaration, and its principal recommendation, accepted by the British Government, was for the establishment of a Jewish State!

Mr. Bevin seems no less unfamiliar with what President Wilson said in March 1919: 'I have expressed my personal approval of the declaration of the British Government regarding the aspirations and historic claims of the Jewish people in regard to Palestine . . . The Allied Nations, wth the fullest concurrence of our Government and people, are agreed that in Palestine shall be laid the foundations of the Jewish Commonwealth.'

Mr. Bevin not only refers to Great Britain's responsibilities and declarations but he also comments on America's undertakings, which are scarcely his concern. The only one he can unearth is that the United States would take no decision on Palestine without full consultation with both Arabs and Jews. He seems to have overlooked the more positive and fundamental obligations flowing from unanimous endorsement by Congress of the Mandate and the Balfour Declaration, and the preamble, spontaneously added by Congress, saying 'the Jewish people are to be enabled to recreate and reorganize a National Home in the land of their fathers which will give the Jewish people its long-denied opportunity of re-establishing a fruitful Jewish life in the ancient Jewish land.' He seems never to have heard of the undertaking more recently given by the great American parties, and by the President, in favor of a free and democratic Jewish Commonwealth 'in accord with traditional American policy and in keeping with the spirit of the four freedoms.' But can it also be possible that he has never even read the texts of the Mandate and of the Declaration of his illustrious predecessor, which pledged Great Britain's best endeavors, not for a home for a few Jewish refugees, but for the establishment of 'a National Home for the Jewish people'?

There is another remarkable lacuna in his statement. In Clause 5, he sums up in one brief sentence 'the whole history of Palestine since the Mandate was granted,' and according to him it has been one of 'continual friction between the two races.' Is that really all? What of the transformation of Palestine, the reclamation of many of its wastes, this great feat of reconstruction by a poor little people in a neglected land, a feat seldom equalled in world history, and, between the two Wars, perhaps unique? It was a feat made possible by the urge of a great vision, the compulsion of a nation in distress, love for an ancestral Homeland, the toil of thousands coming home—with or without permission—to be pioneers. These immigrants have transformed Palestine, magnified its capacity to furnish new sources of livelihood for hundreds of thousands, built towns and villages and power-stations, drained marshes and planted forests. Thanks to them commerce has improved, a progressive industry exists, trades and professions multiply, cooperative and communal settlements are established, and the standard of living for everybody, for the Arab worker and fellah as well, is higher. Yet Mr. Bevin dismisses it all!

He has long been a leading member of the trade union and labor movement, playing a conspicuous part in the struggle of the British working class for its rights, its unity, and better social conditions. But the like achievements of Jewish immigrants in Palestine are apparently a sealed book to him. They have developed a great trade union and labor organization which is by far the strongest and the most advanced in the Middle East. The Histadruth has enlarged its membership in this time from 5,000 to 150,000. The labor settlements it sponsors are setting a unique example of cooperative and communal farming, in number now grown from 22 to 200. It has promoted a cooperative movement which has ramified into a vast network of producers', contractors', transport, credit, and consumers' societies. Few labor movements in the world can boast of so much. We have won the admiration of labor visitors from all over the world, from Mr. Morrison to Mr. Maisky. But Mr. Bevin is blissfully ignorant, and for him there is no chronicling of this remarkable democratic and socialist success, in particular none of the rise in the standards of living of the Arabs, the wages of the Arab worker, the welfare of the Arab peasantry, all to higher levels than in any Arab country. Jewish development in Palestine is responsible, though Mr. Bevin knows nothing of it, for the striking disparity between the condition of the Arab working classes in Palestine and in lands neighboring, where misery, ignorance and disease are just as bad, almost, as a quarter of a century ago. A maximum daily wage of 1s. 6d. in independent and progressive Egypt against 10s. for an Arab worker in Palestine!

In the wake of the prosperity that Jewish immigration brings, the Palestinian Arabs have changed into one of the healthiest, most prosperous and rapidly growing Arab communities in the Middle East. Natural increase has reached a record figure, so that our Arab population has doubled in the last two decades, whereas next door, in Trans-Jordan, where there was no racial friction, and where, contrary to the intention of the Balfour Declaration, Jews were not allowed to settle, the population remains static.

I take it that the Foreign Office officials who advised Mr. Bevin in the past few months, and the representatives of the Arab League with whom he tells us he had a meeting that went on for twelve weeks, did not enlighten him. But is it conceivable that he heard absolutely nothing from his colleagues in the Cabinet who visited Palestine and put on record what they saw? Mr. Morrison, for instance, had this to say in the House of Commons in 1936: 'I have seen these Jewish agricultural settlements. They are one of the most wonderful moral demonstrations of the human race in the whole of the civilized world . . . Here are colonies in which people are working on a voluntary cooperative basis with no element of dictatorship or compulsion behind them, actually reclaiming soil hitherto unfertilized and untillable and making it productive. It is being done not as a mere capitalist exploiting business but directly in association with and under the control of the great Jewish trade union organization, the Federation of Jewish Labor, which is one of the finest trade union organizations. One of the most elevating moral efforts in voluntary communism that I have ever seen is among these agricultural communities in Palestine. I have seen these fine young people coming from various countries . . . I came back with a humble feeling that I should like to give up this game of House of Commons and politics and join them in the clean, healthy life that they are living. It is one of the most wonderful manifestations in the world. When I think of these splendid young people happily working in a cooperative and communal spirit for the building up of a National Home, subject to murders and shootings, I feel indignant about it, as if there is some crude and bloody butting into one of the finest moral efforts in the history of mankind.' These fine words have a topical ring today. The same year, Mr. George Isaacs was as lyrical in describing Jewish accomplishment in Palestine to the British Trade Union Congress in Plymouth: 'I have recently paid a visit to Palestine, where I saw the new miracle of modern times taking place under our very eyes. In Palestine you can see today an experiment in socialism on the highest possible scale, a complete cooperation between trade unionism, the Labor political movement, and the cooperative movement . . . In agriculture miracles have taken place. I saw land which a few years ago was sandy desert, now transformed into groves. If you could see these men and women you would realize the truth of those words that you sing in one of our Labor hymns about 'the flame of freedom in their souls and the light of knowledge in their minds . . .' We must see to it that the door of Palestine is kept open and give these people the opportunity of developing socialism as it is being developed there, extending to them our blessing, and helping them to build a new Jerusalem in Palestine.'

Three years later, even the White Paper could not withhold a tribute: 'The growth of the Jewish National Home and its achievements in many fields are a remarkable constructive effort which must command the admiration of the world and must be, in particular, a source of pride to the Jewish people.' But all that Mr. Bevin could see in Palestine was unbridled racial friction.

And there is one cardinal, one pivotal, omission. The statement professes great pity for the Jews and for the plight of Nazi victims. But we saw no sign of it when the Nazis were putting myriads to death who could have been saved if the gates of Palestine had not been barred against them. I saw little evidence of sympathy for the survivors in Belsen in the British Zone. At the Kramer trial much public solicitude was shown for the Nazis. But none is being shown their victims at Belsen. They live on a hunger diet, seven or eight to a narrow room, several sleeping in one bed, while unused rooms are to spare. The statement is full of humanitarian protestations but ignores completely the root cause of our age-long anguish, our homelessness. For its authors the Jewish problem seems to have begun with the Nazi tyranny twelve years ago. They appear to think that before 1933 Jews throughout the world were peaceful and happy, that they were not persecuted, that there were no pogroms, that communities were not attacked in almost every European country. Mr. Bevin knows only of Nazi excesses in Europe. Outside Europe he is wholly uninformed of anti-Jewish outbreaks: to take one example, the other day in Tripoli, which is under British military control. But perhaps Mr. Bevin's charity does not extend so far.

Jewish suffering is not confined to Europe. It did not begin with the Nazis, it has not ended with their fall, and it will not end until the Jewish people owns a Homeland and, at least in that one land, is no longer a minority. It was this fundamental compulsion which drove the Jews to start their Return long before the Nazis were ever heard of, this was the mainspring of their great effort of creation in Palestine, the source of the international recognition of Jewish national hopes that the Balfour Declaration and the Mandate embody.

Not only is Mr. Bevin deaf to this central motif of our tragedy, he vilifies those who see the truth in it. Here, as throughout his policy, Mr. Bevin repudiates the concept which underlies the traditional attitude of Labor. Mr. Arthur Greenwood, acting as Leader of the Parliamentary Labor party, thus defined it: 'Since the first World War we of the British Labor party have come to see the truth of the concept that the root of the problem lies in the homelessness of the Jewish people, and in order to remedy it, that people must be given its chance to rebuild its national home in the Land of Israel. Of course Jews everywhere must enjoy full equality of rights and opportunities as citizens of the countries in which they live; Jewish communities must have the right to maintain their identity and tradition and to develop their group life in the sphere of culture, religion and historical inheritance. But all this cannot replace the necessity for allowing, and indeed helping, the Jewish people to reestablish its status of full equality among the nations of the world by reconstituting Palestine as a Jewish Commonwealth. Only thus can the position of Jews in the world become normal again.'

But Mr. Bevin is uninterested in a real remedy. He declares war on Zionists, while paying compliments to the Jews, as if they were different breeds. Not content with mobilizing the Arab League and Islam to his side, he tries to muster against Zionism the few Jewish dissidents and renegades, the Quislings of our nation. He makes out the problem to be a matter of charity for some odd refugees, for whom, out of sheer kindness, he is even ready to seek homes outside Palestine. That is why he draws a distinction between Jews generally, who he thinks would show proper gratitude for his generosity, and Zionists who are obstinate enough to demand a national status for the Jewish people with Homeland, freedom and nationhood. There is nothing new in attempts to exploit the existence of small and unrepresentative factions. We know that there are Jews who are not merely non-Zionists but anti-Zionists. If Mr. Bevin had really read all the documents on Palestine he would have learned that the only Minister in 1917 who actively fought the granting of the Balfour Declaration was a Jew, Mr. Edwin Montagu. But the Government of that day paid no heed to him, because it did not regard him as representative of the Jewish people. Mr. Bevin would also have learnt that the then Secretary of State for Foreign Affairs, in his official letter, termed the Declaration a 'declaration of sympathy with Jewish Zionist aspirations.'

Mr. Bevin draws a second distinction: 'not all Jewish survivors wish to come to Palestine'. Have British flotillas, planes and paratroopers been sent to Palestine to prevent the immigration of Jews who do not wish to come? And when the hundred thousand certificates for which President Truman asks are denied, is it from Jews who wish to stay forever in Europe they are withheld?

So much for omissions and distortions. But the statement introduces new and insidious arguments never previously advanced against the Jewish case in any Government document in the past twenty-five years, not even excepting the White Paper. For the first time the 90,000,000 Moslems of India are brought into the picture. Mr. Bevin has yet to know the number of Jews in Europe who wish to come to Palestine, although there is a very simple and speedy way of finding out: he has only to broadcast an announcement that all Jews so wishing may present themselves at British consulates. He would soon get the answer. But he is taking a great deal of trouble and making very elaborate arrangements to ascertain the statistics, to the extent of appealing to the United States to establish a joint Committee of Enquiry which will visit Europe and count how many of the hundred thousand Jews still alive in concentration camps want to enter Palestine. But he needs no such apparatus to ascertain whether 90,000,000 Moslems in India do genuinely take a deep interest in Palestine. It does not occur to him that they may take a deeper interest in their own wretched and servile state, or perhaps in the affairs of the Moslems in Java, on their doorstep.

Another of Mr. Bevin's innovations is the idea of a new Galuth for remnants of Israel. He expatiated on British undertakings and commitments, but who gave him authority for this new dispersion of decimated European Jewry in new exiles where it can only cause or aggravate a minority issue and where the same doom may await it that befell the Jews in Tripolitania and the Assyrians in Iraq?

He has set out, it would seem, not only to discredit the Balfour Declaration and the Mandate but to scrap them altogether, and with them all British pledges and promises to the Jewish people. One thing he told the Press was that the authors of the Declaration were not aware of the existence of the Arab population in Palestine, a claim, be it noted, that hardly jibes with his simultaneous pronouncement that the Declaration held a dual obligation—to Jews and Arabs. In 1939 Mr. Malcolm MacDonald had voiced the same theory, only to see it refuted in Parliament by Mr. L. S. Amery, the veteran statesman who had served both as Secretary of State for India and Secretary of State for the Colonies, and was Secretary to the War Cabinet in 1917. Mr. Amery said: 'I had the privilege, as Secretary to the War Cabinet, of being very closely associated with the long discussions which preceded the Balfour Declaration. My Right Honorable friend told us that the authors . . . were not aware of the existence of a population of 600,000 Arabs in Palestine. Believe me, that is entirely remote from the situation. On the contrary, all the relevant facts, all the difficulties that might arise, and were indeed bound to arise . . . were canvassed for many months and were fully understood. But the statesmen of that day viewed their problems from a wider perspective.'

Mr. Bevin went further. He averred that the undertakings given to the Jews were unilateral and the Arabs did not consent to them. But the fact of the matter is that Arab representatives accepted the principles of the Balfour Declaration and expressed concurrence with its policy. Again a strange oversight on his part—he failed to scan the affirmations of the official spokesman of the Arabs at the Peace Conference in Paris or of the leader, then, of the Syria-Palestine committee.*

What is the essence of the new policy in its stark nakedness? It is, paradoxically, double repudiation: to jettison at once both the White Paper and Zionism. From the Jewish point of view, it goes far beyond the White Paper in assailing Jewish rights and violating pledges given to the Jews and the nations. It not only demolishes the National Home, it ostracizes the very idea of Zionism. It endeavors to dissolve our unity by driving a wedge between 'Jews' and 'Zionists.' It is heedless of our homelessness, and where we would have a nation's regathering in a Homeland, it seeks to perpetuate its scattering in exile, and keep the Jewish people forever vassals living everywhere on sufferance.

To the Arabs, the statement signifies a retreat from the White Paper. It withdraws the promise that at the end of ten years Palestine would become an independent State, which for all practical purposes means an Arab one, as a permanent two-thirds majority was to be safeguarded by law. It reserves for Palestine the new role, not of Jewish State, nor of Arab, but of a permanent British possession to be a military base for British troops who are not wanted in Egypt, Iraq and Syria. It aims at transforming Palestine into a Crown Colony, under the new-fangled

---

* See "Test of Fulfillment," page 113.

style of international trusteeship, a second Malta on the eastern shore of the Mediterranean. Jewry, as a people, is to be liquidated; the solemn assurances of the Labor party, of the great American parties and Presidents, of the League of Nations itself are to be brushed aside, the Balfour Declaration and the Mandate laughed out of court.

To justify this monstrous backsliding, Mr. Bevin and his aides magnify the allegedly irreconcilable discord between Jews and Arabs. They bring into play against Zionism the millions of Indian Moslems, they whip up the Arab League, which they themselves spawned, and try to divide the Jews among themselves. At the same time, to fool public opinion in the United States, to bring the English Labor party into acquiescence, to soothe the 'moderate' Jews, crumbs of comfort are held out to Jewish refugees in the form of vague prospects of migration. To delay the need for action, lengthy investigations into the absorptive capacity of Palestine and the position of the Jews in Europe are set on foot. But it is carefully announced in advance that Palestine is incapable of solving the problem, and that in the third and final stage of permanent solution 'the trusteeship agreement . . . will supersede the existing Mandate and will therefore control ultimately policy in regard to Palestine.' This in effect is continuing British rule without any of the irksome Mandatory pledges and duties.

In the circumstances, why is there any need to fix the Jewish population rigidly at one-third, as in the White Paper? The percentage may conceivably be allowed to rise to, say, forty percent, which incidentally might be useful to the new policy, because it would make a permanent British occupation more plausible and easier, and weaken Arab political claims. But the Jews would never be permitted to attain a majority, or independent national status. Any such ambitions must be wrecked at all costs, and to discredit and undo them by anticipation Mr. Bevin is reticent about the crux of our sorrows, and the mention of a

Jewish National Home or of the Jewish people strikes him dumb. That is why the history of Palestine is misrepresented as conflict and friction unending, so that a third party must govern, why the Labor party and public opinion in Britain are to be scared by the bogey of the Arab League and an Arab revolt, and why, to offset the sympathy and support of the United States, the imaginary perturbation of 90,000,000 Moslems is produced out of the bag of tricks of Foreign Office propagandists.

But this travesty of policy, we trust, is not Britain's last word. We believe it is the outcome of the temporary ascendancy of a narrow and reactionary view of British interests in the Middle East. There have always been two conflicting trends of opinion on Palestine—the anti-Zionist view championed by such reactionary politicians as Lord Winterton, Brigadier Spears, and most of the British bureaucracy in Whitehall and the Middle East, with which Mr. Bevin has now saddled the Labor party; and the view deriving inspiration from a broader grasp of history, from a far-sighted understanding of British interest and human needs, the view of statesmen like Lord Balfour, Lloyd George and Winston Churchill, and until a few months ago the unchallenged official policy of that great instrument of progress—the British Labor party.

It is this statesmanship that the Balfour Declaration translates out of three fundamental motives, still relevant and compelling today. The first, as Mr. Amery disclosed in the debate on the White Paper, was the unique opportunity given of contributing 'to the solution of the baffling and tragic problem of the fate of a people which is yet not a people, which is a minority everywhere, with no home to call its own, whether as actual refuge from oppression, or merely as a focus for its pride and affection.' The British statesmen knew that 'that problem might become acute again at any moment.' And that was twenty-five years ago, long before the Nazi advent from which Mr. Bevin dates his history.

The second was that these same statesmen, convinced it was a British mission to restore prosperity and civilization to the old lands of the Middle East, recognized nevertheless that while Britain 'might give the indispensable framework of law and order and of modern administration, real regeneration could only come from some more intimate and directly quickening influence. It seemed to us that the Jews alone could bring western civilization to the East with an instinctive understanding of its outlook. Above all, they would come, not as transient administrators, not even as colonists, looking back to a mother-land elsewhere, but as a people coming back to their own homeland, prepared unreservedly and wholeheartedly to identify themselves with its fortunes. That was a view which appealed not only to the Zionist leaders but to the best among the Arab leaders at that time. Some day it may appeal to them again, but that will require a very different approach, a very different attitude on our part from that revealed in the White Paper.'

Lastly, Mr. Amery pointed out, there was a more narrowly British view. It was based on the fact that Palestine occupies a position of unique strategic importance in relation both to the Suez Canal and to the junction of the air routes between the three continents of the Old World. 'In our view it was a vital British interest that Palestine should be a prosperous, progressive State, bound to us by ties of goodwill and gratitude, able in the hour of need to furnish resources both of personnel and of material which only a densely populated, developed, modern community could furnish'.

The events of the past twenty-five years, the second World War and its aftermath, have proved that the reasons whence the far-seeing and beneficent policy of the Declaration was inspired are more compulsive today than ever they were.

The anti-Zionist conception in British politics assumes that British interests in the Middle East can best be secured not through cooperation with a liberal and modernizing element but by alliance with aristocratic feudal classes in the Arab countries, who, being unsure of their hold over their own peoples and suspicious of their neighbors' designs, must always depend on the goodwill of Britain, and might be relied upon to remain loyal to the British cause—or so it is thought.

Who are these whom Mr. Bevin chooses to partner a British Labor Socialist Government? From a mass of evidence I take an article published only a few weeks ago in the London 'Times'. The picture it paints of realities in Egypt is typical of conditions prevailing in the Arab East. On the one hand there are the people, the fellahin, 'poor, under-nourished, wretchedly housed, and often little better than serfs.' At the other end of the scale, at the apex of the social structure, is 'a small group of men of great wealth, owning a large part of the cultivable land. They pay lip service to the principles of democracy but with few exceptions have little understanding and less desire for practical democracy. For many years they have ruled Egypt in their own interests, with little regard for the well-being of the people. The Egyptian Parliament is largely recruited from this group and from their clients. Landowners pay scanty wages, barely enough to keep the fellahin above starvation level, and have been reluctant to raise the standard of living, especially educational standards. Most of them fear what they call 'communism,' that is, any movement that might give the lower classes a greater share in the government and income of the country . . . Autocratic governments in Egypt have barely troubled to garb their procedure in constitutional form. Popular governments have proved equally scornful of constitutional rights and just as indifferent to the needs of the people and no less venal.'

The 'Times' cannot be suspected of anti-Arab bias or radical partisanry.

It is with such autocratic rulers and rapacious politicians, then, that a deal has been made, a conspiracy between exploiters and oppressors of the masses in the Middle East and reactionary influences in the Foreign Office—anti-American, anti-French, anti-Russian, that have imposed their prejudices and their will on Mr. Bevin.

I will not dwell on the curious discrepancy between the domestic policy of the new Government—progressive socialist, implemented by Hugh Dalton, Aneurin Bevan, Shinwell, and others —and the reactionary foreign policy directed by Attlee and Bevin. At home Mr. Bevin and his colleagues know that what the worker, the farmer and the common man want are a better standard of living, freedom and independence, a decent home, food, education for their children. But for the millions of Moslems in India the best that Mr. Bevin can offer is that he will shut the gates of Palestine against the victims of Hitler, and sterilize all that has been done by the Yishuv to reclaim the wastes of Palestine and make the lives of its people happier.

We challenge the starting premise that Jewish development in Palestine and the interests of the Arab commonalty in the Middle East are irreconcilable. We assert that our work answers the timeless needs of that enormous backward area, that it is part and parcel of the destined process of rehabilitation, from which all its peoples and all mankind stand to gain. Jewish pioneers are toiling to solve the basic problems which prevent the Middle East from taking a rightful place in democratic society. Jewish achievements in economic progress, higher standards of living all round, agricultural reclamation and irrigation, schemes of public health and popular education, set it an example of reconstruction and democratic culture. Primarily concerned, as they are, with the salvation of their own people, the Jews are also missionaries for the revival of these forlorn lands, where, in one little corner, they are rebuilding their ancient hearth. The differences between Jew and Arab are transient, just as the momentary clash of the Jews and Bevin's policy is no perennial feud between Great Britain and the Jewish people.

We are a people with a long history; we look far back into the centuries and far ahead into the future. Our bond with Palestine is thousands of years old. No fleeting event, be it never so hurtful, can weaken it. No temporary deviation of policy can hinder the Jewish people from discharging its destiny in the end and returning to its Homeland. A Jewish State in Palestine will not erect a barrier between Britain and the Arab world, rather will it be a connecting link in constructive cooperation between the West and the East. We are linking our fate and future to Palestine and to our neighbors, building up a progressive and prosperous Palestine and in it a better society and a new culture; we are helping along the Arab lands and peoples in their march to a finer life, human dignity and democratic freedom. Prosperous, progressive, free and forward-looking Syria, Egypt, Iraq and Lebanon are to the vital advantage of the Jewish Palestine we plan, just as regeneration of Palestine is to theirs, if side by side with the peoples of Europe we are all of us to go forward to a new and better age.

As a European nation, although of Oriental and Semitic origin, the Jews have pinned their faith on a covenant of friendship with democratic Britain. But they must passionately resist any policy, from whatever quarter it comes, that seeks to deny their nationhood, to multiply dispersion, to filch their hopes and rights to independence and Homeland. In spite of cruel disappointment, they believe that the conscience of mankind, the conscience of the British citizen and worker, will not countenance a policy so unjust, barren and backward, that can foster neither stability nor peace in Palestine or in the Middle East or anywhere in the world.

The tombs of Jewish millions are still open in Europe, and already Jewish blood is being spilled again on the soil of the Homeland. Jewish farmers and workers in the Plain of Sharon, defending their national cause, have been shot down, and it may be the beginning of a reign of terror. But our halutzim will not falter, they will face any danger and the mightiest armaments with faith in the justice of their plea and the purity of their ideals. It is not for me to say whether the British citizen and worker empowered Mr. Bevin to treat the Jewish people as he does. But I can give him this reply on its behalf. We have no desire to be killed. We want to live. We believe, despite the teachings of Hitler and his disciples, that the Jews too are entitled to live as individuals and as a people, just as much as the British and the rest. But again, like the British, there are things we value above life itself, things for which we are ready to die rather than surrender: freedom to enter Palestine, the prerogative to remake the wastes of our Land, and a sovereign Jewish nation in its own Israel.

UNITY AND INDEPENDENCE
*A Letter from the United States to the
Sixth Convention of Mapai, August, 1946*

I will not try to find words just now for all the heartache and mental anguish inflicted by the events of June 29 and after. In a dangerous crisis such as this, we must be calm and smother our emotions. We must with steady fortitude search out the causes of our present situation, never relinquishing the pursuit of our ultimate end.

But one thing I cannot keep from you—the personal sorrow, the agony, the sense of painful loss that has haunted me since David Hacohen brought me the tidings, one blackest night, that Berl Katzenelson is with us no more. The burden of this grief will bear me down until my dying day.

For the first time Mapai meets without its great leader, that prince among men, mentor of this generation and a shining light to posterity; the mind, the heart and the voice of the Movement; faithful counsellor of youth, worker and Yishuv, of all the people. Deep was his thinking, a prophetic sage he was, blessed with creative ideas and a revolutionary outlook. Fearless in vision, he was yet a man of parts, versed in all the intellectual treasures of Jewry and mankind, applying his talents to the redemption of his fellow-worker and of his nation, a pioneer of thought and action. In his life's span he wielded spade and sword and scroll alike—he made himself a toiler and tiller of the earth, he stood staunch in our fighting front-line as writer and editor, he was a worker of miracles. Faithful to the end, he gave the best of his heaven-sent and many-sided genius to all he did, stinting neither bodily strength nor spiritual gifts nor his great soul, so that his tongue, his pen and his way of life bespoke with steadfast courage the fortunes of his own generation and were an example for all who came after. He was a loyal and cherished comrade and friend, an aristocrat in spirit yet walking humbly among great and small. He knew how to love and hearten, to chastise and pity, to understand and forgive, yet could he be wrathful and wrestle as truth's champion.

'How dear you were to me, Berl, dearer than brother and friend! Since I first met you in khaki in our bivouac in the Egyptian desert, and together we dreamed a dream of perfect unity among the workers of Israel that they might fulfill their tremendous destiny: to build the Homeland and establish in it a Jewish State, to make a living socialism and exalt man upon earth ... since that day I have loved you with love everlasting. Unto yours my soul was bound, and now, all too suddenly, you are gone, and there is no returning. You are gone from us and are no more.

'Orphaned and bereft your friends gather, and the hour is dark indeed. Your face is seen no longer, your voice unheard. Ours no longer are you criticism and correction, the guiding survey and illuminating analysis that glowed with kindness, encouragement and trust, but in our hearts, so long they beat, we will be true to the summons of the great mission to which you gave up a life rich in achievement, so tragically brief.'

* * *

But I must turn from my own heartbreak and go on now to a study of the issues before you.

It seems to me that there are two vital, central factors which will determine the strength of the Yishuv and of the Zionist

Movement, and their independence in the making and planning of policy.

Neither the antagonism of the outside world with all its perils nor the fear of aggression thence constitutes the major threat or need dismay us, although it would be folly to minimize the risks or delude ourselves as to the intentions of foreign Powers. What may destroy us utterly is a rift in the Yishuv itself or in Zionism or in both, and schism in one leads inevitably to schism in the other. We may be weakened and even undone no less by bending from our policy of independence and letting outsiders appoint our aims and our spokesmen.

Disunity is likely to spring from ideological or domestic differences, which are natural and necessary in an autonomous Yishuv and an unfettered Movement. So long as they come from within and are resolved after free discussion among ourselves, we have nothing to apprehend. But when one party seems to impose its will and policy on the whole by employing external forces and giving them the opportunity they want to pit one Jewish faction against another, we are heading for complete disaster. Zealous guardianship of our unity and independence, inseparable twain, must be our clarion-call: that must precede any plan of action.

Secondly, there must be neither despair nor self-delusion.

We have been battered from without and undermined from within, the bloodstained hand of evil and heresy bruises us yet, but our strength is not harmed. The Yishuv has its fibers deep in its native soil: no fiercest storm will shake us, none ever uproot us thence. Jewry is united around Palestine as never before, and watches developments with anxious affection. I saw this for myself in France, in England and in the United States. And in many of the Diaspora's youth, in Europe and in America too, I discern a heartening and significant change. They are ready now for pioneering, for the heroism of their counterparts in Palestine resounds throughout the world and has captured their imagination.

But our basic conditions are relentless. The troubles of the Jews grow worse; resettlement of European Jewry elsewhere is virtually out of the question, yet it is unthinkable that they should remain, and to the extent that any emigration is feasible it will aggravate, not solve, the problem. The Yishuv is the only community in the world that awaits the newcomers with open arms and can absorb them; its capacity for expansion and growth is no longer challenged even by our sworn enemies, and the capacity of the Land itself to respond to our devoted and loving labor stands proven beyond the shadow of a doubt. And when we can command airborne divisions and set mighty naval forces in motion to speed the transfer of 'illegal immigrants' if we must, rest assured, my friends, that behind immigration, behind the pull of the Land, there will thrust onward an incalculable historical impetus which cannot easily be withstood or vanquished. So why bewilderment and hopelessness? But no complacency either; the long trail away from dependence, dispersion and exile to Homeland sovereignty, freedom and statehood is not rose-strewn. There will be misfortune, adversity and suffering before we reach the end. If old friends have left us, let us not fondly imagine others will help, just for the asking. As we did one, five, forty years ago, we must rely upon ourselves first and last. Let us but act, let us but be resolute and fortify ourselves, and the 'old friends' will return and new ones join us when they see it is worth their while, even those who have vowed us enmity and eternal hatred. But flaming words and eloquent resolutions are so much fustian.

Even if toilsome days lie ahead, never forget that we do not gird up our loins for a last despairing battle, we do not seek, like Samson, to perish with the Philistines; self-annihilation is not our intent. We go forward without panic, unwearying, our constant purpose to keep those merits that are the wellspring of our life, our energy and creativeness, and, come what may, to broaden the basis of our existence. The political backdrop shifts and flickers, now light, now shadow, and the curtain is risen still upon our acts. But once we compromise and the will is relaxed to defend our own in Palestine and in the Diaspora, the moment we drug ourselves with hollow, foolish phrases and ask 'What are we and what can we do?,' slowly but surely we shall begin the black-out.

Were it not for the gallant fight of the Yishuv during the past year, had we not quickened the world's awareness of a wide-awake and self-reliant community of pioneers in Israel, who knows but that our existence would long since have been forgotten, and the world have moved on to an agenda whereon the sole item was our political liquidation?

* * *

Like all human activity, like the grandest impulses of man's emotions, struggle can be distorted and perverted. Hitler prostituted socialism and nationalism and poisoned them, but neither socialism nor nationalism was thereby damned. No more do the mad adventures of gangs lost to moral and political discretion render null Jewry's defiance of the policy of the White Paper, or any policy which aims to overthrow Zionism.

The move of June 29 was planned as far back as March or April by the advisers on British policy in the Middle East, the most reactionary among the diplomatic, military and colonial staffs now centered in Egypt, and it was forced by the Foreign Office on the Cabinet. There is reason to doubt whether all the members of the Government, even those most nearly concerned with Palestine affairs, had foreknowledge.

It had a dual purpose. First, to cancel the independent representation of the Jewish people. Not representation altogether, for something of that kind is necessary to carry out the White

Paper policy; even if Zionism is negated, a Jewish representation of sorts will still be wanted, one chosen by the Foreign Office or the Palestine Administration. The old London trick of gradualness in reform—you do not replace an elected leadership by appointed officials at one fell swoop: first you eliminate one section, and befriend another. When you have had your way and the 'moderate' element has done its task, you discover that it, too, is 'extremist' and still champions Jewish immigration to Palestine, White Paper or no. But by then there is no difficulty in appointing a completely 'kasher' representation which will write letters to 'The Times' and castigate 'law-breaking immigrants.'

Second, shatter the Yishuv's resourcefulness and make it more dependent on the Mandatory for security and for very life. This, too, has to be done by degrees, both because of inherent difficulties, and because of the political and ethical imbroglios of the present British Government. Here, too, Jewish aid will be needed in the successive stages, not necessarily active aid. Submission is enough, to prepare and reconcile public opinion in England and in the rest of the world.

To submit is to be a second Vichy. I do not speak of traitors and informers—I cannot conceive of anyone in the Yishuv so depraved—but of submissiveness under the urge of principles seemingly patriotic and earnest, as they were with the elect in the original Vichy, of fatal compromise that would devour the soul of our Movement just as a stand against impossible odds, at another Massada, would consume its body. Either way is downfall.

I was in America straight after the events, and saw how Jewry and Government and public opinion there reacted. I was convinced that the harm the British Government had done itself was infinitely graver than the hurt it caused us. The debate in Parliament on July 2 did not mend matters. I felt that our condition was no worse than before June 29, despite internment of members of the Executive, occupation of the Agency building, arrest of thousands of farmers, and punitive rapine and violence by the 'guardians of the peace.' If only it had not been for the internal shocks that followed. I do not mean only the insane crime of July 22.* The authors of the White Paper could have hoped for no finer aid from Jews than that outrage affords. But I will not stop to analyze the phenomena or origins of terrorism, we do not control the terrorists, we wield no influence over them, and we need bear no sort of responsibility, direct or indirect, for their actions. They have flouted every form of national and communal discipline, they mark the awful danger of every split in our ranks, every irresponsible breach of group authority.

No, the ailment we contracted after June 29 was the plague of inaction, that nemesis of all politics. For several weeks the Yishuv was confused, at its wit's end, worn out and undirected. It seemed as though all prospect of a militant Zionist comeback was vanished, and in our gravest crisis we cringed. The meeting of the Executive in Paris at the beginning of August, not without avoidable delay and interference within our own midst, at least was the first step towards shaking the Movement out of its calamitous stupor.

All divergencies of view in the Yishuv and in Zionism were freely aired. We were conscious that, in this feverish and fated hour, it rested with us to safeguard the unity and autonomy of Zionism. Unanimity marked our resolutions.

I will treat here of only one of the matters discussed—the program to federalize the country. As you know, the general principles are these:

>Annulment, in 80 percent of Western Palestine, of all the rights assured the Jews under the Mandate, including, of course, the rights of immigration and settlement.

>Ostensible self-government for Jews and Arabs in two

* On July 22, the wing of the King David Hotel in Jerusalem housing the Palestine Secretariat was blown up by the Irgun Zvai Leumi, and over eighty persons—Jewish, Arabs and British—lost their lives.

separate 'provinces'—for the Jews in an area amounting to only 15 percent of the whole, and, in effect, a complete and perpetual British government of all Palestine, just as now; with one small difference—the positive obligations of the Mandate would disappear.

Jewish Ministers for the Jewish province appointed by the British High Commissioner, and Arab Ministers likewise for the Arab.

Immigration restricted according to the dictates of the British High Commissioner within the limits of the absorptive capacity of the province measured by its economic opportunities.

The sorry program is calculated endlessly to prolong the two current disputes: the Arab-Jewish and the Anglo-Jewish. Even as the Arabs persisted in fighting Zionism when Trans-Jordan had been carved out of the original area of the Mandate, only concentrating their fire thereafter on immigration and settlement in Western Palestine, so they will go on aiming their guns at those targets in a British-dominated Jewish province.

The Anglo-Jewish conflict will be as little resolved even within the bounds of its own narrow province, the Yishuv will be up against an alien and hostile officialdom, apt in the usages of suppression and force.

So the Paris meeting would have been well worth while even had it done no more than inform the British Government, and world opinion, that the Zionist Movement is not prepared so much as to discuss a plan of that character.

Are there really politicians still among us who believe it possible to revert to the pre-1937 Mandate, before immigration was again restricted, or that England, or any other Power, would be agreeable to help us immigrate and settle exactly as we need and wish to, while responsibility for governing rested on the Mandatory for an unspecified period of years, in effect until we were ready to assume it? If there are still in the Yishuv and the

Movement any so simple, they will never learn, and I will waste no breath arguing with them.

It is time we drew conclusions from the political facts, not sporadic and evanescent but basic, which underlie the political situation—British and international—as it was before, during and after the second World War. These facts constitute a reality we cannot control: it is only a reality we *can* control that we need not accept and, if it be unacceptable, must not compromise with. In my opinion, these are the assumptions we must make:

England neither desires to perpetuate the Mandate, nor now can she, even to the degree she discharged it from the setting up of a civil authority in 1920 until 1937, when a monthly quota of immigrants was fixed.

Without Mandatory commitments to the Jews, any Administration in Palestine will lack legal and moral warrant.

The weak may have to yield to the strong—even when the strong has not law and right behind him, but he yields under compulsion and only as far as he is compelled; yielding thus is not acquiescence, nor betokens it the philosophy of 'offering the other cheek.'

We are the first nucleus of an independent people in the Homeland, the vanguard of militant Zionism, and no proffered solution of the Palestine problem will command our support that is not based on a Jewish State where Zionism may fulfill itself.

Unless the end in view is a transitional stage that leads surely to a Jewish State, we must reject any attempt by whatever Power to gain control over the country under a new international charter granted by the United Nations.

The over-riding conclusion is, that the fight to establish the Jewish State has become more fierce and more actual than in the war years, when we might still have hoped that the end of the war or a change of Government would restore the Mandate to its early shape. But now, no talks on a final settlement are conceivable with any Power, save on the premise that a Jewish State is to be set up. No adjustment of our relations with England is possible—and sooner or later she will have to ask our opinion—so long as they are the relations of ruler and ruled. We shall treat only on the basis of a political pact between two independent parties, equal in rights if not in power. We must also be prepared to enter into conversations with our Arab neighbors to bring about a settlement that will affirm a Jewish State existing in cooperation with the Arab States. In the welter of recent afflictions, we are likely to forget that our valorous stand has lifted us in their regard. They know now that, besides our economic achievements and our advances in agriculture, industry and communications, in education, culture and science, we are established as no mean force in the world. Never were we as close as we now are to the possibility of an understanding.

Of course, while the British Foreign Office pursues its sterile policy of the White Paper, there is no chance of a realistic agreement between Arabs and Jews. Nonetheless, the year's events have bettered, not damaged, the prospects—the breach is not healed, there are still Arabs and non-Arabs deliberately seeking to widen it, but the gloom, though it persists, is not entirely unrelieved.

But politics alone is not the answer, neither diplomatic talks nor negotiations with foreign Powers will figure in the ultimate accounting. What will, is consistent and persistent gathering of energy and resources for expansion and entrenchment. For the moment we must reorganize our means to suit our needs under changing conditions, and to withstand familiar trials which we may be forced soon to face again.

Further, we must verily secure what we hold in every sector of our life. All this is evident. What may be less so is the need to improve vocational and technical education, as well as our scientific capacity in general. In all we essay we shall meet troubles, and not least the competition of cheap Arab labor in one direction and of rich and well-equipped countries in another. In the long run we cannot hope to meet it either by lowering our standard of living or by superior natural resources and greater wealth. We can meet it only by enhancing the quality of our products, by our talent for work, by the exceeding skill of our workers. For one significant and valuable asset we do have that others lack—we have the Jewish mind. The quintessence of this mind must be injected into our every enterprise and effort, so that we attain the limit of human capacity. The requisites are two: firstrate vocational training for our young people and for those already employed; the perfection of our scientific establishments and the application of our finest brains to scientific work and research. Science and technology are the key to our future, and at any rate we possess the quality that can turn the key.

Finally, we must evince a spirit of halutziuth toward the survivors of Jewry in Europe, where immense potentials stand within immense dangers—as all will agree who, like myself, saw the Jewish camps in Germany or Polish immigrant camps in Hungary. The Yishuv apart, there is no body in world Jewry which will affect the destiny of Zionism, for better or for worse, as decisively as will these Jews: we shall have to be united in purpose, and in action unsparing of ourselves, to rescue them and bring out the good—or bad—in them.

Devastated by harsh and harrowing trials, they will not blend with the Yishuv unaided or with ease. They will not be persuaded by 'philanthropists' or pedagogues who attempt to impose doctrines and ways upon them by preaching, be it never so inspired. They will admit none save comrades who come and live among them, with them, as they live, who will share their every experience devotedly, in simple love and true friendship, whose very existence and way of life will be example and precept. No others can endow them with their own spirit and vitality. And none will win them over that do not come, not split and splintered but in unison, wedded to the fundamental values of halutziuth, not decked out with the trumpery titles of dissidence which wreck our internal unity and cohesion. Amid party rivalries and wavering dogmas Palestine is unique in harboring those fundamental values, which are now the everyday expression of a common destiny; yet there, of all places, the deadly sin of fission is draining away our nation's life-blood. It is dreadful to envisage the spiritual shambles into which our dissenters have hurled the few who escaped sword or conversion in Poland, in Germany and other exiles. In what hideous depths of havoc may they not drown us, these that provoke unfraternal strife among brothers?

We have neglected much and we have dallied too. But there is yet time, if only we take heart and muster our moral courage, to stop this fratricidal virus of ours from poisoning the embittered and beleaguered Diaspora as well. I dare not contemplate disunity in Israel at this hour! But if divide we must, let us not carry schism into broken Europe. Let us bestow on Europe only the blessing we all may share, the little, that is yet so much, accomplished here. This little, done in partnered loyalty and uprightness, will sustain our tortured brethren until, united, they join us. Then we, perhaps, may reunite for their sake.

* * *

It is thirteen years since I was taken out of active work in the Labor Movement and assigned to deal essentially with Zionist politics. The assignment deepened my conviction that if political activity is not founded on communal partnership and accountability, on a community awake and alive, then it is a hollow fraud. I have grown more and more aware that it must stem from unceasing and invincible concern with the public weal, with the education of the public to pioneer, to bear responsibility, to give sober counsel. With all their zeal the workers cannot by themselves take the brunt of Zionist politics: nation and Yishuv must also help, lest all succumb. Neither can nation and Yishuv put straining shoulder to the wheel of Zionist politics unless the workers are their core and backbone, and Zionist policy and planning must never relax concern for the welfare of the worker. These are the keystones of the Zionism of the Labor Movement.

In the party, as such, youth and industrial worker must be trained side by side with the farm laborer. For the princes of pioneers—settlers in kibbutz and moshav, makers of the Yishuv and authors of the transvaluation of Zionism which is our greatest joy—there is, I aver, no privilege finer than that which they have yet to exercise: to see to it that workers everywhere be in all things their own equals, acquiring and applying all the virtues of halutziuth. Reform comes from within. The factory hand and the stonemason, the stevedore and the engine-driver, must each demand his place in the party, and partake in its leadership and in the molding of its policy on Histadruth lines, just as do they who work on the land.

This will be harder for hired laborers than for independent farmers. It is not merely a superabundance of halutziuth that has placed the settlements at the helm of our Movement, for its organization and structure are wholly encouraging to public activity by the many. Can we not provide conditions which will allow the hired laborer, the day laborer, to figure as he should in the party and in the Histadruth? Few workers' movements in the world grasp tools as powerful as we in Palestine do; if we once recognize the importance, indeed the inevitability, of activating our entire labor force, we will be ready to give the worker for hire an impressive and responsible say in directing the affairs of the party and the Histadruth, from the local labor exchange and secretariat up to the Executive Council.

It is the same with the attraction of youth into this orbit. Youth is not a personal achievement—we were all young once, and youth deserves no special credit for its years. But the Movement needs the freshness and daring of the young, no less than the knowledge and experience of the old. Youth must be taught to accept responsibility, for it is only by responsibility that a man is tested, shoulder to shoulder with the more tried.

My friends, you are met together in ravaged and stressful times. The problems you face are involved; and of those whom we were wont to gaze upon and raptly hearken to, some the powers celestial have taken from us, others, the powers below. The responsibility is great, the time is short.

I pray that the pure spirit of our Movement may abide with you and devotion to our historic destiny light your path. I pray that you may still man, proudly and with high courage, the ramparts of our fighting ideal, that you may rally workers and Yishuv entire to the standard of halutziuth and virile Zionism, and with force and with faith, vindicating the trust and task of your electorate, uphold the banner of unity and independence of class and people.

ADDRESS TO THE ANGLO-AMERICAN COMMITTEE OF ENQUIRY
1946

Sir, our case seems to us simple and compelling. It rests on two elementary principles. One is that we Jews are just like other human beings, entitled to just the same rights; that the Jewish people is entitled to the same equality of treatment as any free and independent people in the world. The second is that this is and will remain our country. We are here as of right. We are not here on the strength of the Balfour Declaration or of the Palestine Mandate. We were here long, long before. I myself was. Many thousands preceded me, but we were here far earlier still. Speaking from the legal point of view, it is the Mandatory Power that is here on the strength of the Mandate. Our case, and I think you will meet many such now in Europe, is that of one who builds a house for his family to live in and is evicted forcibly and the house given to somebody else. It changes hands and the owner return and wants to get it back. In many cases the Jew is kept out, it is occupied by that other tenant. To be more exact I will put it this way. It is a large building, this building of ours, with, say, 150 rooms. We were expelled from it and our family was scattered. Somebody else took the building away and again it changed hands many times, and then we came back at last and found some five rooms occupied by other people, the other rooms destroyed and uninhabitable from neglect. We said to the occupants: 'We do not want to dispossess you, please stay where you are, we are going back to these uninhabitable rooms, we will repair them.' And we did repair some of them and settled there. Now some other members of our family are coming back and want to repair some other of the uninhabitable rooms. But the occupants say: 'No, we are here, we do not want you, we do not live in these rooms, they are no good for any human being, but we do not want to repair them or make them better.' And again we do not say to them: 'Depart, it is all ours.' We say: 'You stay, you are there, if only since yesterday, you may stay if you please and we will help you repair your rooms too if you wish; if not you can do so yourselves.' At hand there are many big buildings, half empty. We do not say to them: 'Please move over to that other big building.' No, we say: 'Please stay here, we will be good neighbors.'

That is the case. That is my submission. It is simple and compelling, but I realize its intellectual difficulty. There are practical difficulties as well, but now I am talking of the intellectual difficulty of understanding our case, because it is an unique one. There is no precedent, there is no example in the world's history, of this problem of the Jews and their country. There is no example or precedent of such a people. It is a people and it is not. There is nothing like the history of the Jewish people. There is nothing like the fate of this country, no parallel for its significance and position. There is nothing elsewhere resembling the relations between the inhabitants. It is unique, and usually, when people are faced with a new phenomenon, if they cannot understand it, they simply deny it. But here it is—the unique case of the Jewish people in this ancient land.

I read a great deal of the evidence given to you in America and in England. I saw the difficulty of getting at the heart of it. What is this Jewish people? Is it a people? Are the Jews not citizens of Poland, Russia, America and England? Did we not treat them as brothers and as fellows? People say so sincerely and I have the greatest admiration for those who do so because they really think the Jew is just like themselves. It is true that there is a Jewish people and a Jewish problem. The Jews, or the greater part of them, have been ravished from this country for many centuries, and still it is theirs. But it is not empty. There are people in it, some of them have been in it for many hundreds of years, many are newcomers, and from afar it is not easy to see the light. I believe when you see things here, it will become less hard to understand.

What I am going to do is simply to tell you what we Jews are in our own country, who we are, what we are doing, what we are aiming at. Why are we here, and for what? Perhaps that will explain things.

There are now some 600,000 of us, more than one-third born in the country, some families here for many centuries, and not living in the towns only. There are Jewish fellahin, peasants who have stayed put for hundreds of years; they live in Ramleh and in Galilee. But the majority of us were not born here; I was not. We have come from all parts of the world, and from all countries. Not only where Jews were persecuted physically, exterminated or repressed as they were in Nazi Germany and Poland, in the Yemen and in Morocco, in Czarist Russia, Persia and Fascist Italy. Many of us are from free countries where Jews were treated as citizens, where persecution was not—Britain, the United States of America, Canada and the Argentine, pre-war Imperial Germany, Soviet Russia, France, Egypt and elsewhere. Why did we come? What is the common denominator which brought us all here? Let me tell you.

First it was escape from dependence and discrimination. I do not mean from anti-semitism. There was a great deal of talk in your Commission about anti-semitism and many of our people were asked to explain why it is. But it is not for us to answer. It is your baby, it is a Christian baby. It is for you Gentiles to explain. Perhaps we ought to set up a Jewish Commission to make an enquiry of the Gentiles, or perhaps a joint Jewish-Gentile Commission, with one Chairman Jewish and one Gentile, to interrogate leaders of the Church, teachers, educators, journalists and political parties on what this disease is, and what the reason for it in the Gentile world. To me it seems part of a larger problem which does not concern only Jews. It is a general human one. Wherever you have two groups, one strong and powerful, and the other weak and helpless, there is bound to be mischief. The strong will always take advantage of the weak, rightly or wrongly. Human nature being what it is, with people having power over others, you cannot expect that they will not sometimes abuse it, not always, not necessarily always. But I am not concerned with anti-semitism; as I say, it is not our business. I am concerned with why Jews have come here. They came because they felt it unendurable for many of them to be at the mercy of others. Sometimes those others are excellent people but not invariably, and you have discrimination. It need not be legal or political or economic discrimination; at times it is merely a moral one and, as human beings with human dignity, they do not like it. No, they do not like it, yet they do not see how they can change the whole world.

You ask me what is moral discrimination. Gentlemen, I do not know in Europe a more tolerant, a more liberal, a more fair-minded people than the English in their own country; perhaps the Scandinavian peoples are like that too, but I do not know them as well as I know the British, although I do not claim to know the British fully. I do not think anyone can claim that except the British themselves, if indeed they can. Recently in the House of Lords, one of the noblest institutions in the world, whatever one may think of it from the democratic angle, there was a debate on the Jewish question. Only in England, I believe, could you have such a debate. In it the Archbishop of York in very strong language condemned anti-semitism as unchristian. Coming from His Grace that means a lot—unchristian. Practically it may not help us very much, but we appreciate it very deeply as a moral aid. He then began talking about the Jewish criticism of the policy of His Majesty's Government in Palestine, meaning the White Paper of 1939, and the attack launched against it by Jews on both sides of the Atlantic, and he said these significant words: '(Such criticism) is being resented and may easily lead to a most dangerous reaction.'

Well, Jews are not the only people who criticize or attack the White Paper. In 1939 it was described, not by a Jew, but by an Englishman, a pure Englishman, a Gentile, as a mortal blow to the Jewish people. His name, Gentlemen, is Winston Churchill.

We agree with his description. It was and is a mortal blow. Well, Gentlemen, when a people is dealt a mortal blow, who would ask it to lie down and take it dumbly? Who should resent this criticism, this attack on a mortal blow? And in 1939 when our people in Europe were still alive! Since then tens of thousands of human beings, of babies—after all, Jewish babies are also babies—have had to perish. Because of that blow they could not be saved. I do not suggest that all found death because of it, but tens of thousands could have been saved, yet were not—because of it. Is it surprising that we, as human beings, should criticise or attack it? I am sure His Grace understands that. He is a great personality, but he knows the mind of his people and he said it may lead to a most dangerous reaction. That is what I call moral discrimination. We receive a deadly thrust; we must be silent. Else there may be trouble for us. Where? Not in Poland, but in the most liberal and tolerant country, I say it with the greatest respect, in England. Why discrimination? There are many Jews who submitted to it; there are some who refused to submit, and that is what brought them over here. There they were at the mercy of nice people, but nice people may sometimes become very nasty, when they have the power and are dealing with a minority. Why is there this discrimination? As I see it, it is for two reasons: because we happen to be different from others, and we happen to be a minority. We are not the only people who are different from others: and in truth we are not different at all, for difference is a term of relativity. If there was only person in the world, he would not be 'different'. We are—what we are. Others are different, but, as they see us, it is we who are. But we are what we are and we like to be what we are. Is that a crime? Cannot a man be what he is? Cannot a people be what it is? On the continent I know they consider the British very different, and so they are; but no Englishman will think himself different. He is, but he is not different; he is just what he is and we are too: we are just what we are. We happen to be different because other people are different. For that, our people suffers. The English do not suffer because they are different. On the contrary, for them it is a great compliment, a great strength. They have their own individuality and people are brought to respect it. As for us, not only are we different, we are in a minority. We are at the mercy of others, in that people do not like us being different. It becomes very hazardous sometimes for us, because other people want us to be like them and from time to time to renounce either our nationhood or our religion or our country or our language. Many of us made the renunciation—not all, but some of us, and still do. You have perhaps met some such. The Jewish people as a whole defies any superior material power that asks us to surrender spiritual values which are dear to us and are ours. And we pay the price, sometimes a very high price, for sticking to our spiritual principles.

It is a long story. It goes back 2,300 years, to when the known world, Egypt, Syria and Persia, became Hellenized. Judea did not bow to that higher culture—for it was in many respects a higher one; the Jews preferred to be just what they were. So they suffered. There was another clash when Rome became the dominant power, and we were asked to accept the divinity of the Caesars, and again we refused. Here were the most mighty rulers of the world, above all other men, and recognized divine, but not by us. So again we suffered and fought and were foiled, but not in spirit. We defied the material power. Then it happened again with the rise of Christianity. I must be careful what

I say. The whole of Europe was converted to Christianity, many by force. We stood out, though we perhaps had more to do with it than other peoples; for St. Paul was a Jew. We refused, and we paid the price. We are still paying it, and it is a very high one. I read the evidence of some Moslems and I felt that what came with Christianity recurred with the rise of another great religion. I will say no more.

Then the French Revolution asked us to give up our nationhood. Some Jews did, but not the Jewish people. And now this last phase. I am not going to speak about it. What happened in the last few years is unspeakable. Why should I harrow you with Jewish sentiments? It happened to us, and to no one else. I will tell you only of one emotion I experienced when I knew of what had taken place: it was this—at least I and my children are happy that we belong to a people that is being slaughtered and not to those who are slaughtering us, nor to those who look on with indifference. I know many Christians in France, in Holland, in Belgium and other countries who risked their lives to save a Jew or a Jewish child. We will never forget that—never. But there were other things, not things that happened in Nazi Europe, which are outside the pale of humanity; I am not discussing them. There was a conspiracy of silence in the entire world. When we suffered and tried to tell you of our sufferings, the answer was: it is Jewish propaganda, just Press publicity of the Jews. I merely ask myself—would you suffer if a million Gentile babies were slaughtered in Europe?

Just imagine a British fighting division captured by the Japanese, put to the sword then and only one platoon surviving. Then the war is over, and the Americans occupy the concentration camp where the platoon languishes and for some reason prevent it from going back to England. Can you conceive the feelings of every Englishman in the world? Can you conceive ours when this remnant of us are kept confined after the war is over and the country liberated, when they want to get out and cannot get back to their home? They are Jews, and is not their home the National Home of the Jewish people? Here is a people bleeding to death, a few shreds remain. Why are they tortured? For it is torture. Not physical torture, no. I saw them being treated nicely, very nicely in the American and British camps. I have not seen the Russian camps. I have not seen the French. All the same, it is torture. There is such a thing as spiritual torture. We too are being tortured. Every one of us in this country is here for their sake. They are our flesh and our blood, they are our brothers. Many of them are our brothers literally, but all of them are our brothers because they suffered for the same crime that we are guilty of, for being Jews.

Why are we tortured? Why these subterfuges to lock up that hapless fragment of Polish Jewry? Some 30,000 Jews remain in Poland out of three millions, and every day they are massacred. Why imprison them? They are human beings. Why this discrimination in your Christendom? Why must we wait, why cannot we escape from this dependence, this being at the beck of others?

That is one reason why we want to get back here, and there is a second. It is love of Zion, a deep love, passionate and undying. It is unique, but a fact; you will see it here. There are 600,000 of us here because of it.

In evidence given to you in America, an American Arab, I believe it was John Hassan, said no Palestine was ever known as a political and geographical entity; and another American Arab, a great Arab historian, Dr. Hitti, went even further and said, and I am quoting him: 'There is no such thing as Palestine in history, absolutely not.' And I agree with him entirely; but when he speaks of history he means Arab history, he is a specialist in that and knows his business. In Arab history there is indeed no such thing as Palestine. Arab history was made in Arabia, Syria and Persia, in Spain and North Africa. You will not find Palestine in it. There is, however, something more than Arab history; there is world history and Jewish history and in that history there is a country named Judea, or as we call it Eretz Israel, the Land of Israel. We have called it Israel since the days of Joshua. There was such a country in history, there was indeed, and it is still there. It is a little country, a very little one, but it made a very deep impression on world history—and on ours, because it made us a people: and our people made it. No other people in the world made it; it made no other people. It entered world history by way of many wars, of Egyptians, Babylonians, Assyrians, Persians, Greeks, Romans, Byzantines. It gained a place in world history, because in it our people created perhaps a limited, but a very great, civilization, and here the Jews were shaped to be as they have been until this day: a very exclusive people on one hand and on the other a people universal; very national and very international. Exclusive in their internal life and attachment to their history, to their national and religious tradition; universal in their religious, social and ethical ideas. We were told that there is one God in the entire world, that there is unity of the human race because every human being was created in the image of God, that there ought to be and there will be brotherhood and social justice on earth, peace between peoples. Those were our ideas; this was our culture and this made history here. Here we created a Book, many books. Some were lost, some survived only in translations, but twenty-four remain in their original language—Hebrew, the language, Mr. Chairman, in which I am thinking now as I talk to you in English, and which the Jews in this country are speaking now. We went into exile, but we took that Book with us, and in that Book—which was more to us than a Book, it was our very selves—we took with us our country in our hearts and in our souls. These three, the Land, the Book and the People, are for us forever one. It is an indissoluble bond. There is no material power which can undo it, only our physical destruction can.

 The distinguished British Chairman quoted a book by Sir Ronald Storrs and from another writing. Sir, our rights and our attachment and our significance in this country you will find in the Book of which I speak, in that Book alone. That, and that alone, is binding upon us. Whether or not it is binding on anyone else is not for me to say. I know many Christians who believe it binding upon them too. You cannot contemplate our people without it, not in the far away past nor in the present, nor, in my conviction, in the future either.

Somebody may tell you: 'All this is merely a mystical attachment to a mystical Zion, not to this physical Zion.' But now you will see 600,000 living human beings whom the love of Zion has brought here and kept here. They are attached to the living Zion, although it has for them a profound spiritual significance as well.

Then we are asked what seems a very common-place question: 'When the Arabs conquered Spain, did they not create a magnificent civilization there?' Yes, they did. They created it and then were driven out. Can they claim Spain for the Arabs? Have they a right to Spain? I know of no retort which proves our case so forcibly as this, and I take it up. Is there a single Arab in the entire world who dreams about Spain? Is there an Arab in Iraq or in Egypt or anywhere who knows the rivers and mountains of Spain more than he knows his present country? Is there an Arab in the world who will give his money to Spain? What is Spain to him?

There are many who want to conquer countries and possess them. But I am speaking about love of country. Is there a single Arab in the world who loves Spain?

Here are Jews who have been parted for centuries, some of them for many centuries, some of them for thousands of years like the Jews in Yemen, yet they have always carried Zion in their hearts, and finally came back, and came back with love. Where in the world will you find people loving their country as the Jews love Zion?

I wonder whether all the American members of this Commission know this: in the first World War thousands of Jewish boys from the United States of America, myself fortuitously among them, came over to fight for the liberation of this country in a Jewish Legion in the British Army, in the Royal Fusiliers, under Allenby.

I know what happened then in Palestine, but not what happened in Egypt. There were Semitic soldiers in this country, many thousands. Some of them fought on the other side, and I do not blame them. It was their right and perhaps their duty.

What brought over these thousands of American Jewish boys with the consent and blessing of President Wilson? What else but the love of Zion? Perhaps it can hardly be explained, but there it is.

You have heard how Jews strove to settle on the land in many other countries. It was tried in Russia by Czar Alexander Nicolas I. The Soviet Government tried it. It was tried in Argentina; and in the United States. It failed everywhere. It succeeded here. Elsewhere there was no love of the land: there was that love here. As much as I love this country, I must confess that Argentina is much richer and more fertile. America certainly is, and Russia too, yet there the Jews failed, and here they succeeded. And the answer?—love of Zion.

Why? What is it? A man can change many things, even his religion, his wife, his name. But there is one thing he cannot change—his father and mother. There is no way of changing them. The father and mother of our people are this country. Once more a thing unique, but it is so.

More than three hundred years ago the ship 'Mayflower' left Plymouth for the New World. It was a great event in American and English history. I wonder how many Englishmen or how many Americans know exactly the date on which that ship left Plymouth, how many people were on board, and what was the kind of bread that they ate when they sailed.

Well, more than 3,300 years ago the Jews left Egypt. More

than 3,300 years ago, yet every Jew in the world still knows the date exactly. It was on the 15th day of Nisan. The bread they ate was matzot. And still today all Jews throughout the world on that same 15th day of Nisan eat the same matzot, in America, in Russia, and tell the story of Egyptian bondage and recount all that befell, all the sufferings of the Jews, since they went into exile. They end the recital with these two sentences: 'This year we are slaves; next year we will be free. This year we are here; next year we will be in Zion, the Land of Israel.' Jews are like that.

There was a third reason for our coming, and it is the crux of the problem. We came here with an urge for Jewish independence, for what you call a Jewish State. When people in the world outside talk about a State, it means power, domination. For us it means other.

We came here to be free Jews. I mean in the full sense of the word, 100 percent free and 100 percent Jews, and that we could not be anywhere else—not Jews, free. We believe we are entitled to be Jews, to live a full Jewish life as an Englishman lives his English life and an American lives his, and to be free from fear and dependence, no longer to be objects of pity and sympathy, of philanthropy and 'justice,' in the eyes of others. We believe that is our due, both as individuals and as a people.

We here are the freest Jews in the world. Not in a legal sense. On the contrary, we are deprived here even of equality before the law. We are living under a most arbitrary regime. I know of no regime in the entire world as arbitrary as this of the White Paper. But that is not what I wish to emphasize now.

Freedom begins at home, in man's mind and spirit, and here we have built our Jewish freedom more securely than any other Jews in the world. Why do we feel freer than other Jews? It is because we are self-made Jews, made by our country and making it. We are a Jewish community which is, in fact, a Jewish Commonwealth in the making.

DAVID BEN GURION

I will tell you in a few words how we are making it. When we say 'Jewish independence' and 'a Jewish State,' we mean a Jewish country, and by that we mean Jewish labor, Jewish colony and Jewish agriculture, Jewish industry and Jewish seed. We mean Jewish language, schools and culture. We mean Jewish safety, security and autonomy as complete as for any other free people.

I will begin from the beginning. You heard from Dr. Hitti that there is no such thing as Palestine, absolutely nothing. But we are not coming to Palestine; we are coming to a country which we are re-creating. When we came here as newcomers, or, as you say, immigrants, we found hundreds of Arab villages, inhabited by Moslems and Christians. We did not take those villages away. We established hundreds of new Jewish villages on virgin soil. We did not produce the soil, for that is made by God, but what nature has left to man is not enough; man must work. We did not merely buy the land, we re-fashioned it. It was rocky hills. You will find a description of it in the Royal Commission's report. In Hedera hundreds of Jews died of fever, yet because of love of Zion they clung to the marshes, because of the urge to make their own acres. Or it was the sand dunes of Rishon, and by our labor and love we are remaking them to plow at no one else's expense.

Now you are here and you may visit our villages. You will find the land reclaimed by our own efforts. It was uncultivable, or it was certainly uncultivated. We made it cultivable and we cultivated it. Land for us is not a commodity of trade. We consider it as belonging to the whole world, as the foundation of humanity; from it everything comes. It is a sacred trust to men and they should not spoil or neglect it. We should fortify, fertilize and preserve it. That is what we are trying to do to the best of our ability, and we have not altogether failed, although for so long we have been town-dwellers. We are told there is a law about this. It is not in any Statute-book, there was no question of our doing anything illegal, but it was a scientific law that people from the country go to the town, not people from the town to the country. We did not like that law because it works against our existence, because we believed we had to go back to the land. And so we did and we broke the law. I hope it was not a heinous offence, anyhow we committed it and will continue to.

You heard the evidence presented from an Arab State about this country, that more than 60 percent of its area is uncultivable. It is without doubt uncultivated. These tracts which are uninhabitable, we want to make cultivable, perhaps all of them, perhaps some, I do not know. We will make the effort. Is that a crime? We do not consider manual work a curse. It is a bitter necessity. It is a means of making a living. But in our eyes it is also a lofty human function, the basis of human life, the most dignified thing in man's existence. It ought to be free, creative. Men ought to be proud of it.

Our boys and girls, middle-class boys and girls, are encouraged to go out and work on the land before they finish high school, and if they cannot find land, to work somewhere else. The Jewish Commonwealth means Jewish work. You cannot buy a Commonwealth; you cannot get one by conquest. Your own work must build it.

We mean a Jewish economy, Jewish agriculture, industry, seafaring trades, fishing. We do not want to say that it is our country because we conquered it. We want to be able to say it is ours because we made it. Or rather, because we remade it. That is what we are trying to do, and you will see the testimony whereever you go.

If you had come here, not now, but 40 years ago and I had told you that we were going to revive Hebrew and make it a spoken language, a language of work and trade, of industry and schools, of universities and science and art, you would have said that we were mad; it could not be done, it is a dead language, it is archaic, it lacked all the modern terms. Well, it was done, and by Jews who came variously from America and England,

Canada and Russia and Poland, Persia and Yemen. With all their many former languages, they now speak their own Hebrew. We have educated their children in Hebrew, and it is today the everyday speech of our children and our grandchildren.

Man cannot live by bread alone, and in constructing a Jewish society we seek to base it on high intellectual, scientific, cultural and artistic values.

There are two Hebrew theatres in this country. There is a Palestine orchestra; there is an opera; there are scientific institutes. I question whether anywhere else so many books are published in original and translation, considering the size of our population. We are a people who practised universal education: for 2,500 years we had all the educational needs and we satisfied them in our own tongue.

A Jewish State means Jewish security. If there is one thing a Jew lacks everywhere in the world it is security, and after all he is entitled to feel secure. Why the lack? Because, even if he is safe, he is not safe of himself. Somebody else provides for his security. Well, we want to provide for our own security, and we have been doing it here from the start.

I came to Palestine 40 years ago and I went to work in Sejera, a little village in Galilee. I had never before been a worker or a farmer and I had to learn two things at once, how to hold a plow in my hands and how a rifle. I had to provide for my security, for the security of the village, and I went to work in the fields with a rifle on my shoulder. We had a special organization to keep watch. There were very few watchmen, and from time to time they were attacked. When I stood watch in the long nights and lifted up mine eyes, I understood the magnificence of the full meaning of the words in the Book of Solomon, that the heavens tell the glory of God.

We tried to make friends with our neighbors. It was not easy. I do not know what their reasons were for attacking us. They sometimes attacked others too, but us a little more. They have a great contempt for people who are afraid. They learned to know we were not like that, that we could take care of ourselves, and so they respected us, and we did our best to win their friendship and often succeeded. We are still doing our level best all the time in all our settlements, to maintain decent human relations with them. But we have had to look after ourselves. We held on to our weapons, but never used them save for self-defense.

It means Jewish independence to be our own masters, not to depend on others, to make our own laws, to live according to our own needs, desires and ideals. For we do have ideals of life, Jewish ideals and human: they are not opposed but complement each other.

We are striving to build up a new society, a free society based on justice, on human justice, and on the highest human intellectual and moral endeavor. If you find time to visit our agricultural settlement, you will see something of that spirit there. We seek also to help solve the tragic problem, the great historic dilemma, of the Jewish people throughout the world. Because, Sir, only a Jewish State can build a Jewish National Home. We need the State in order to continue building that National Home, for those Jews who for one reason or another, even if their fate be death, will be impelled to come just as we came; only the Jewish State can do it.

We began building the National Home under the Turkish regime. I am not going to describe it. We continued its building under the British Mandate, but I am not going to describe that either or make any complaints. At least we know now that no foreign administration, even of the best friends of the Jews and of the National Home, is capable of doing the job—of establishing that Home and bringing to it all Jews who want and have a right to come. No foreign administration can develop the country, or can raise it to the requisite level for the benefit of all the people already in it and those yet to enter. That is very difficult and requires complete identification with the purpose. You cannot expect from the best of the peoples—and I do not consider the British to be the worst—that special ardor and devotion. It can only be done by Jews.

Not that we are more able. Oh, no. I know what the British people have done in many countries, in Canada and New Zealand and Australia for example.

Even then, I am afraid that Englishmen in America some 150 years ago revolted against a British administration. They made war on it, although it was their own people. They thought that, coming from London, it could not satisfy their needs. Well, really it would be too much to hope that what the British could not do then for their own kin in America they should be able to do for the Jews. It is not an ordinary function of colonial administration, in which they are very competent; it is a dynamic one, constructive and creative, and beset with great harassment.

Perhaps we are not in greater trouble than anybody else. They are our difficulties, and we require not only knowledge but something besides. Not every woman can educate a child, but you can entrust every child to a mother. It is no easier bringing up a child than bringing up a Jewish National Home under these unmotherly conditions.

Therefore, we ask that the Jewish Agency, which means the Jewish people itself, be authorized to conduct this business of immigration. They know the needs and the possibilities and they will do it. They should be permitted according to the Mandate to develop the country to the full potentiality in agriculture and industry for the good of all the people here, and for those other Jews with the wish and warrant to come home, as only they can.

Our aim is not a majority, Sir. A majority will not solve our problem. It is not a question of the numerical relation between ourselves and the non-Jews in Palestine. That is an accidental thing. The number of Jews who need to come back is much,

much, more important. The majority is a stage, a very important but not a final one. You need it to establish the Commonwealth efficiently, but then we will have to continue, because we shall still have to build a National Home.

The State will have two purposes. One is to look after the welfare of the citizens of this country, all of them, with no least difference, to work for it and to raise them up higher and ever higher economically, socially and in intellect.

The second is to build a National Home. We will have to treat our Arab neighbors as if they were Jews, but so that they preserve their Arab characteristics, their language, culture and religion, their Arab way of life, yet become equal with Jews socially, economically, politically, intellectually.

We are not afraid of the unhappy conflict that exists now between the Arabs and ourselves. It is a passing thing. We are grown-up, and we see many, many changes in the world, little and large. We never accept a position if it is bad; it will alter. I know that the Arabs, or some of them, do not want us to return. I understand their attitude. I am conviced of its futility, but it is natural.

I heard two reasons given against the Jewish State by our Arab neighbors, one, I believe, in London by the Chairman of the Syrian Chamber of Deputies, Faris Bey el Khouri. I believe it was Dr. Aydelotte who asked him: 'Why are you afraid of this little Jewish State? Is it really a threat to the security of the big Arab States and the Arab people?' And this was the answer. 'Yes, a State like that is small in its place, but it would depend upon 15 or 16 millions of rich, qualified, able people outside who would always help it in everything. It will be sufficiently strong to threaten peace and security.'

Then in Cairo another representative of the Arab States said just the opposite. 'You cannot have a Jewish State. We will destroy it. It will have to depend on British bayonets.'

I think neither argument very serious. I attach little importance either to the threat or the fear; both lack foundation. As to the threat, we can take care of ourselves. We did it when we were but few, and I could tell you many a story of twenty or forty or sixty years ago. But I am not going to take up your time now with these tales. We will take care of ourselves. Still less is there any basis for fear that the Jewish State will threaten the mighty Arab nations, some 40 million souls or more, these big States of Saudi Arabia, Syria, Iraq. I have more respect for the Arabs, more faith in them, than I find in that Cairo answer. They, too, will take care of themselves. There is nothing to be feared and there is nothing to be threatened, and we, for sure, will not be moved by either.

There is tension at the moment, perhaps a little more than tension, between us and the Arabs. It is very unfortunate. But it is transient. It is not a danger. We may be of great help to them as they to us. I believe we need each other. We have something to offer each other as equals, but only as equals.

No people in the world can stand alone, whether it be a small nation or a great Power. There is an interdependence of peoples, and in that sense we too need to be dependent, as Belgium is, as are Sweden and Norway. Norway is the best example for us in many ways. They have something in common with us there, in human and social perceptions.

There will be not only peace between us and the Arabs, there will be alliance, there will be friendship. It is an historical necessity, just as much as is a Jewish State. It is a moral, a political and an economic necessity.

We are here as of right. We will not abandon Zion, as we never abandoned a Jewish imperative, whatever the price may be; and we will not abandon a Jewish Commonwealth.

It was Mr. Crossman in London who asked a Jewish witness a rather difficult question: 'If you had the choice of getting 100,000 refugees from Germany to Palestine or giving up the Jewish State, which would you do?'

For personal reasons, the witness could not answer the question. I want to answer it. It is my belief that every human being is a person in himself, with ideals which he cherishes. I will not sacrifice another man for my ideal; I will myself make the sacrifice. Put that question to the 100,000 refugees in Germany—well, they are there, and you know how anxiously they are waiting to go home. Ask whether they are willing to buy the certificates to Palestine, as you call them, by renouncing Jewish independence and a Jewish Commonwealth. They will give you your answer.

Suppose Hitler had in his hands a hundred thousand Englishmen—prisoners—and had said to Mr. Churchill: 'Either you give me the British Navy or we will slaughter every single one of them.' Would you ask Mr. Churchill which he would choose?

I know what the hundred thousand Englishmen would answer. Would not they gladly die, rather than yield their Navy?

I was in England, in the darkest hour of this war, when France collapsed, when invasion loomed, and there was only a small British army in England. I was there in the blitz when Nazi planes were raiding England. They bombed every night, and the British people took it. I saw the ordinary folk in the Underground. I saw the taxi-drivers; I saw the workers. They were not afraid. Many were bombed and more were killed. But I saw a people to which country and freedom are dearer than life.

Why do you think, what reason have you to suppose, that we are different? There are things that to us are dearer than our lives, and we love life. The Jewish religion was never an ascetic religion; we do not despise life—we cherish it. We are not going to give up, even if we have to pay a heavy toll, and there are hundreds of thousands of Jews, here and in other lands, who will give up their lives, if they must, for Jewish independence and for Zion.

PREPARING FOR THE STATE
*In the Elected Assembly, Jerusalem,
October 2, 1947*

Political developments have swept us on to a momentous parting of the ways—from Mandate to independence. Today, beyond our ceaseless work in immigration, settlement and campaign, we are set three blazing tasks, whereof fulfillment will condition our perpetuity: defense, a Jewish State and Arab-Jewish cooperation, in that order of importance and urgency.

Security is our chief problem. I do not minimize the virtue of statehood even within something less than all the territory of the Land of Israel on either bank of the Jordan; but security comes unarguably first. It dominated our concerns since the Yishuv began, from the start of colonization we knew we must, in the main, guarantee it ourselves. But recent upsets and upheavals in Palestine, in the Middle East and in the wide world, and in British and international politics as well, magnify it from a local problem of current safety into Zionism's hinge of destiny. In scope, in intensity, in purport, it is entirely different now. Just think of the new factors that invest the problem with a political significance of unprecedented gravity—and I could add a dozen others: the anti-Zionist policy pursued by the Mandatory Government during the past ten years, the obliteration of European Jewry with the willing aid of the acknowledged leader of the Palestine Arabs, the establishment of an Arab League active and united only in combatting Zionism, Bevin's ugly war against the Jews, the crisis in Britain and its political and economic aftermath, the creation of armed forces in the neighboring States, the intrusion of the Arab Legion. And not a single Jewish unit exists.

We can stand up to any aggression launched from Palestine or its border, but more in potential than yet in fact. The conversion from potential to actual is now our major, blinding headache. It will mean the swiftest, widest mobilization, here and abroad, of capacity to organize, of our resources in economics and manpower, our science and technology, our civic sense. It must be an all-out effort, sparing no man.

It is the duty of this Assembly to decide upon a defense scheme that will gear our economy, our public life and our education to instant needs.

There is the possibility, how near in time I cannot say, but very real, that we may be sucked into a political vacuum. Politics, pre-eminently, abhor a vacuum. If we do not fill it, others will. Let us, once for all, slough the fancy that others may run our errand, as Britain promised twenty-seven years ago. The polemics which agitated our Movement this last decade—the 'to be or not to be' of the Mandate—are meaningless now. You had to be purblind ten years ago not to see that the Mandate was disintegrating, the Mandate as we came specifically to interpret it in Palestine: a form of administration deputed by the nations to facilitate Jewish entry and settlement for so long as the Jews themselves could not stand alone in their Homeland and conduct the work of government by right of majority. Some, doubtless with the best of Zionist intentions, wanted to turn their backs on the truth, although it had been proclaimed long since and unequivocally by Britain and recognized by the Mandates Commission, than which no more skilled and conscientious organ of international vigilance could be imagined, when it laid down that the Mandate had become impracticable once the Mandatory itself was persuaded that it was. Good, true Zionists were obstinate and could not admit that, for practical purposes, the Mandate, in its purely Zionist meaning, was a dead letter. Palestine remains a British province, but acknowledgement of Jewish entry and settlement under international sanction—where is it now!

Many hoped by reprimands and reproaches to shame the interloper into fulfilling the task that is ours.

Others abused and scolded—even the workers' movement barked with the rest. There was withering criticism by the Mandates Commission and the Anglo-American Committee of Inquiry, but it fell on deaf ears. Now final judgement is passed by the United Nations and the Mandatory. The Mandate is to end. That is the common denominator uniting majority and minority at Lake Success and in Whitehall, and dispelling the friction between the Council of the United Nations and the British Government. No one can predict how things will go in the General Assembly. It may not decide at all, but one thing is certain: the Mandate is doomed, not just the British Mandate, but the principle. There is neither prospect nor proposal that Britain be replaced as Mandatory by another Power or an international body—in either event pledged to Zionism and the principles and aims which shaped the British Mandate a quarter of a century ago.

Whether we like it or not, there is one vivid conclusion we must draw—if governance has to be in Palestine, for the sake of the immigration and settlement which are unthinkable in a void, it will be a governance by the British or any one else: it will be our very own, or not at all. That, for good or ill, is the significance of recent political developments, external, world-wide, mightier than any will or influence of ours.

So much for the common denominator. Specifically, now, as to the recommendations of the Anglo-American investigators.

There were eleven findings, of which only the first four need concern us here, for their carrying out—and the British Government has said it accepts them—entails our taking new and difficult steps, which we would not take so long as we thought that others might manage Palestine for our benefit.

The findings are these:

termination of the Mandate at the earliest practicable date;

the soonest feasible grant of autonomy to Palestine, on the ground that the Arabs and the Jews, after a tutelage of over twenty-five years, wish to translate their national aspirations into fact, and assuredly no arrangement will be accepted by either with the slightest willingness which does not imply swift independence;

a brief inter-regnum to create the prerequisites of full sovereignty;

the transitional administration to be responsible to the United Nations, a link representing the indispensable element of compulsion where any scheme is bound to be unpopular with Jew and Arab alike.

Unpleasant or not, we may dismiss the idea of a successor Mandatory. After not more than three years, Palestine is to be independent. The British Secretary of State for the Colonies announced that his Government would prepare a speedy evacuation of the army and Administration. Should there be, in the end, an unagreed adjustment, it would suggest that someone else give effect to it. In other words, British control would cease immediately a new entrepreneur came forward.

There are two proposals before the United Nations—the majority proposal to set up two States, the minority to set up a federal, or, in Zionist jargon, a 'bi-national' State.

The minority proposal indulges in sonorous theory concerning the assurance of equality between the two nations and their historical link with a common Homeland, but warrants no solid inference. Behind it, instead, is denial of our age-long connexion with Palestine. For equality between Arabs and ourselves it substitutes Arab precedence in all things, even in immigration, and, in short, produces an Arab State in the false feathers of bi-nationalism.

The federal State embraces a Jewish district to which the name of 'Jewish State' is given. As to its area, to my regret I did not see the map that ought to have been annexed, but it looks to be about that of the Jewish province under the Morrison-Grady plan, though I would not vouch for it.

There will be two Chambers: one elected proportionately and therefore ruled by the Arab majority, the other based on equal representation. To pass into law a measure must get a majority of votes in each Chamber; if not, an arbitral committee of three Arabs and two Jews would decide and the decision become law. The President of the State would be elected by the Arab majority of both Chambers in joint session.

Over and above this, a Supreme Court with wide jurisdiction was invented, to interpret the Constitution, and we know what interpretation can lead to. It would adjudicate whether a federal or 'State' law was compatible with the Constitution, and pronounce in cases of conflict between local and federal laws. Its judgment would be unappealable. It would, under the Constitution, have an assured Arab majority of at least four to three. This majority could interpret and veto Jewish 'State' laws as it pleased. The federal Government, with an Arab majority, would wield full authority in national defense, foreign affairs, currency, federal taxes, waterways, communications, transport and immigration.

At any moment, therefore, Jewish immigration might come under ban. Only in the three transitional years would it be guaranteed, and then into the Jewish district alone, in numbers not exceeding its economic capacity and not necessarily to the full absorptive extent; the rights of the citizens of the Jewish district would have to be considered, and the rate of natural increase. And all as determined by a committee of nine, three Jews, three Arabs, and three of the United Nations representatives.

Liability for the immigrants during the triennium would fall on the Yishuv. The Jewish Agency disappears. Thereafter—immigration is in the hands of the federal Government, as I have explained, and that is as much as to say in the hands of an Arab majority. The Arabs have lost no time in declaring that not another Jew will be let in.

The status quo cannot go on: it has been condemned on all hands. It is hard to guess when the British will actually leave—three months, three years, or thirty, there is no telling. We know of 'provisional' occupations that lasted sixty. So let us be neither over-sanguine nor cast down. The main thing is not 'when?', but 'what next?.' We are vitally concerned that Britain should not, under any pretence whatever, keep on implementing the policy of the White Paper. What we want is mass immigration. The majority proposal provides for 6,200 persons to enter during the transition period beginning on September 1, 1947. There is an account to settle with Britain for shutting out thousands of Jews since the White Paper appeared, and we may let history make that settlement. But a new chapter is opening—the instant chapter of what is to befall in immigration now: this month, this year, next year. For us, now, there is no countenancing the White Paper's policy one moment after the Assembly of the United Nations ends, for is it not shorn of all international sanction, constitutionally and morally indefensible?

Moreover, we must at all costs prevent chaos and anarchy ensuing.

To sum up, it is all a question of effectuation, for both the United Nations and ourselves. Perhaps the whole design of Mr. Creech-Jones' statement was to stampede the United Nations, and make the decision harder. Very well, let us provide the catalyst. Britain assures us she will not carry out any United Nations' decision, but neither will she resist any, so be she is rid of the concomitant task. We, therefore, tell the world that we will ourselves discharge it, that we are willing, fit and ready to gather up the reins of government instantaneously.

We are twain—the elect of the Jewish people and the elect of the Yishuv. Alone, neither can perform the task. The Yishuv, indeed, is also a part of the people, but is so nearly concerned that it must here be a vanguard as well, as it was before in reconstructing Israel and vindicating Zionism. But this is no personal issue of us who live in Palestine. The majority upon the Committee sees it as a problem of world Jewry, and so, we think, does public opinion generally.

The majority framed its conclusions under the impact of two compelling revelations. First, it found here not just one more Kehillah, but the nucleus of a Jewish nation, a Jewish State in embryo. Second, words exchanged in curiosity with an unknown Jew in an unnamed camp in Europe, words that should be broadcast in every spoken tongue, a simple story of past sufferings, and of why he wants to come here and nowhere else. Thus the Committee learned that Aliyah is not shallow submission to Zionist propaganda, but a deep compulsion, elemental, mocking death. This the members saw again with their own eyes in ships that bore to Palestine the exiled and the slain, in camps that shelter those who ran the gauntlet.

There was, however, a tertium quid—and careful study of the report brings it out: the existence of an international commitment to the Jewish people, the flickering still of a spark of conscience in the world, the widespread recognition that the commitment must be honored, even if only in part, even if only a helpless, homeless, stateless folk was its object.

All of Jewry was that object, not the Yishuv alone, all of Jewry broke into the Land, all of Jewry seeks independence. So, too, let all of Jewry demand that an interim Jewish Government be set up to execute an interim policy under United Nations supervision and with aid thence, and primarily an interim policy of large-scale immigration and rescindment of the White Paper.

If a final policy we could accept were propounded meanwhile, we should start on that likewise.

No more protests and clamor, not another day of a vacuum in theory, jurisdiction and ethics. We shall bear the grave responsibility ourselves, untried though we have been in the arts and burdens of sovereignty for the last eighteen hundred years. The strain will be terrific. There is a local pretender to the throne, backed by millions of common creed and speech. But between acquiescing in the White Paper, with its locked gates and racial discrimination, and the assumption of sovereign power, there can, in truth, only be one choice. Perhaps we are unready, immature—but events will not wait on us. The international calendar will not synchronize itself to ours. We are set the problem and must solve it. I have told you how: supervised by the United Nations, helped by the United Nations, but in our own name, answerable to ourselves, with our own resources.

One more thing. If we have reached the parting of the ways, let us at least part with dignity, and not in the estrangement of recent years. Bevin's is not the only Britain; there is the Britain of Balfour, of Wedgwood, of Wingate. We expect no help from Bevin's Britain, we ask only that it keep its word and not interfere.

We have not absolved the Labor party of its pledges, nor will we, but we shall not entreat it to carry out a new policy against both inclination and ability. Well and good—the British wash their hands of us and depart! Go in peace, we say: we can manage—and at once—if you will just let us be.

* * *

To establish a Jewish Government will not be enough. Defense incalculably stronger and more up-to-date than anything improvised in the past seventy years—even that, be it never so vital, and succeed in it as I am sure we will, even that will not be enough.

The British episode was important, but transient: intrinsically, and from the outset, short-lived. The Mandate was a temporary thing, and so were its obligations. The cooperation it promised was fleeting, we may hope the quarrel it provoked will be as evanescent. But we cannot look upon dealings with the Arabs in that way.

This is our native land; it is not as birds of passage that we return to it. But it is situated in an area engulfed by Arabic-speaking peoples, mainly followers of Islam. Now, if ever, we must do more than make peace with them; we must achieve collaboration and alliance on equal terms. Remembering what Arab delegations from Palestine and its neighbors say in the General Assembly and in other places, talk of Arab-Jewish amity sounds fantastic, for the Arabs do not wish it, they will not sit at the same table with us, they want to treat us as they do the Jews of Baghdad, Cairo and Damascus.

That is the attitude officially proclaimed, and it is not to be scoffed at, considerable forces in the Arab realm, and beyond, are behind it. Neither should we overrate it, or be panicked by it. As Jews, and more so as Zionists, we must forego facile optimism and barren despondency. Basic facts are our allies and no concatenation of events can shake or alter them: the tragedy of the Jews, the desolation of the Land, our unbreakable bond with it, our creativity—they have brought us thus far, whether other things helped or hindered.

There are basic facts in the Arab realm also, not only transient ones, and understanding of them should blow away our pessimism. They are the historical needs of the Arabs and of their States. A people's needs are not always articulate, its spokesmen may not always be concerned for them, but they cannot be stifled for long, eventually they force their swelling way out into expression and satisfaction.

History has been harsh to us, perhaps, setting burdensome conditions which complicate our homecoming; but it has set conditions too which, in the final accounting, will not only allow but will compel Arab and Jew to work together, because they need and complement each other. Just two examples. Egypt is the biggest country in the Arab world and in the Arab League. More than three-quarters of its population are fellahin, with an average monthly income of a pound sterling, nine-tenths of the fellahin are disease-ridden, all but five percent illiterate. You cannot go on forever feeding this people on anti-Jewish incitement.

Iraq is thrice as large as Britain; of its 450,000 square kilometers only 67,000 are tilled; after twenty-five years of independence, 85 percent of the population are illiterate, half are infected and there is one doctor for every 8,500 persons. And this is among the richest countries in the world, watered by two rivers—and what rivers! An anti-Jewish diet will not do indefinitely in Iraq either.

I will not discuss ostensibly independent Trans-Jordan, its poverty and neglect—many of us have visited it and know.

A final fact. From our work in Palestine, from the society we are constructing, our economy and science, our culture and humanity, our social and fiscal order, and from no other source, must enlightenment come to our neighbors, for if they do not learn from us and labor with us, it is with strangers, potent and tyrannous, that they will find themselves partnered.

They in turn have much to give us, they are blessed with what we lack. Great territories, ample for themselves and their children's children, even if they are far more prolific than they are today. We do not covet their expanses nor will we penetrate them —for we shall fight to end Diaspora in Arab lands as fiercely as we fought to end it in Europe, we want to be assembled wholly in our own Land. But if this region is to expand to the full, there must be reciprocity, there can be mutual aid—economic, political and cultural—between Jew and Arab. That is the necessity which will prevail, and the daily fulminations of their leaders should not alarm us unduly—they do not echo the real interests of the Arab peoples.

Come what may, we will not surrender our right to free Aliyah, to rebuild our shattered Homeland, to claim statehood. If we are attacked, we will fight back. But we will do everything in our power to maintain peace, and establish a cooperation gainful to both. It is now, here and now, from Jerusalem itself, that a call must go out to the Arab nations to join forces with Jewry and the destined Jewish State and work shoulder to shoulder for our common good, for the peace and progress of sovereign equals.

THE WAR OF INDEPENDENCE

INTRODUCTORY

This group of essays and addresses makes no pretense to be a history of Israel's twentieth-century War of Independence. The time to write that history is not yet: we can only gather material, recount single episodes, or unfold certain phases of the great adventure. For many reasons, vital chapters telling how we turned the scale in procurement of arms and equipment for our soldiers, sailors and airmen must remain unpublished still. The disposition of our forces before and after the invasion, our strategy and its tactical developments, are best withheld, too, for unhappily we may not regard the war as ended. No peace treaty has been signed—we live in no more than a state of truce, prolonged, we hope, and tantamount to an armistice. But that is all.

Besides, the chronicles of the Haganah are unwritten; without them what would be the history of a war that was both the splendid epilogue to Haganah's story and the opening of a new era in the annals of Nation and Homeland? Once more, those annals, long divided, are blent almost together. This war of ours is a turning point in Jewish history as were the wars of Joshua and the Hasmonaeans. It was no impromptu diversion, on the spur of the moment. Nor did the State suddenly emerge on May 14, 1948, by being proclaimed—no, its beginnings were set by three generations of pioneers, from the builders of Petah Tiqvah to the pipelayers in the northern Negev. May 14 marked but the historical climax of their work of creation, to which we owe our new-found national dignity, our economy, culture and administration. Our resistance to the Arab States, likewise, was no magic combustion or conjuring of strength out of the thin air, no explosion from some uncanny, invisible source. Our youth and Yishuv were trained for it by the acts and education, the organized planning, of the Haganah for years past, by the first Jewish watchmen and the heroes of Tel Hai. Therein lies the secret.

The Israel Defense Army was fitted out as no underground Haganah in Mandated Palestine ever could be, and who does not know the crucial importance of artillery and machineguns, fighter planes and bombers, armored cars and tanks, anti-aircraft and anti-tank guns? Lacking these, we could not hope to resist—but there was something else. In equipment the enemy was our superior at all points. It was the man that decided, the fighting man, heir of the Haganah, of Jewish contingents in the Allied Forces in two World Wars, of the Palmach and of Wingate's raiders, of all who were schooled for combat through the Arab disorders up to 1939, and in our campaign against the policy of the White Paper. They gave us the Israel Defense Army and brought us to May 14.

The Arab invasion started 'officially' at the midnight which 'officially' terminated British trusteeship. That same night I broadcast to America from the Haganah transmitter in Tel Aviv, openly sending for the first time. I reviewed events since the United Nations resolution of November 29; the declaration of war by Arab States, members of the United Nations, in defiance of that authority; the dangers facing us and our determination to resist. As I spoke the first Egyptian bombs fell. The summer of 1940 in London had inured me to being blitzed and I finished what I had to say, not omitting to mention the air-raid, and hurried to the airport and the Reading Power Station which had been the first objectives. Returning home, I saw the faces of all Tel Aviv peering through its windows: it was just sunrise. There was no hint of fear or panic, and I knew in my heart: they will stand up to it! This was the inner strength that faith in the Haganah had given the Yishuv. Of course, the people was troubled, knowing we needed arms, but by that faith it was sustained, then and in the bitter trials of the emergent State, by a faith that sprang, not from a count of guns or accoutrement, but from remembrance of gallantry and devotion in every corner of this Land, from deep conviction that the Haganah is steadfast to the end and must win. And so it was.

Much ink has been spilled already into books about our war, but, touching the plain soldier, its history is told most truly and poignantly in memoirs of the rank and file.

Little of this grand but mournful testament has seen the light, but enough to raise a monument, not of brass or marble but of deathless spirit, the victorious spirit its pages enshrine, to the heroism of a new generation. Precious material is held by parents, and in Army records: not until it is published in full shall we know how much we have lost, what fount it was whence these youngsters drew their courage, subtlety and strength, how blessed the mothers and fathers who gave Israel its liberators. Whom shall we put first: the gallant sons who died that Israel might arise again, or the loved ones who bore and bred them?

We have our armistice agreements; we have had five years of independence, and the recognition of most nations; we are a full member of the United Nations. But the Arab States still ignore and execrate our free and sovereign Homeland, and certain world Powers are not less intransigent. So danger persists, and with it an urgent and acute concern for our security. Things have been done and done for good: the transition from an underground defense in a Yishuv under foreign domination to the Defense Army of an independent nation, a change attended by internal mishaps and vexations much more serious than the public knew or than the reader will learn from my pages. All that belongs to history. But armed readiness in the face of external threat is as necessary today and tomorrow as it was yesterday. Our past successes must not bemuse us or puff us up. The weapons and ways of 1948 would never suit a second war. To be sure, traditions of Haganah and the Defense Army will mean much if that day should come, but only if we discern the future with the vision of the future, and make ready for tomorrow with tomorrow's means.

Immigration and settlement, too, are no longer what they were: a difference not only of quantity or tempo, but of quality rather, and so the conditions of security alter every day.

The spectacular changes in the make-up of Yishuv territory, the vices and virtues of mass influx and mass colonization; shifts and turns in the political and economic fortunes of our neighbors, their military organization, their technical and industrial development, their health and educational services; growing international tension and the interests and ambitions of world Powers in the Middle East and Israel; the continuous advances in the development of means of warfare and in man's control of natural forces—all demand unremitting vigilance and up-to-dateness in security thinking and planning and recension of our state of preparedness each new morn to meet the next.

WITH STRENGTH AND UNDERSTANDING
*An Address to the Central Committee
of the Israel Worker's Party, January 8, 1948*

The disturbances have already lasted six weeks. We recall others that went on for three years. We recall the brief and bloody events of August 1929, when a whole community was wiped out. But it would be well if those of us with longer memories could forget the past and learn something new. For what faces us is altogether new and memory may trick us into outdated conclusions that spell ruin. This is no 'incident' or 'disturbance' but open honest-to-goodness war. In our days and earlier there have been undeclared wars—the one we are waiting for will be declared. Arab representatives have said so at Lake Success, in newspapers, and in their parliaments—that they will make war on us. This time we need not doubt their word.

Every war has a political object, and the object of this one is Arab dominion over Palestine—and it is threefold at that. It is a war to destroy the Yishuv: the Arabs know their object is unattainable so long as the Yishuv exists, even though it be a minority, and the interference must be obliterated. No use deceiving ourselves on that score.

Secondly, it is a war to prevent the establishment of a Jewish State—even in a part of Palestine. It means to upset the General Assembly's verdict of November 29, and we know of old that international verdicts can be upset. We remember the adjustments of the all-powerful Allies in the Near East after their victory in the first World War, parcelling out Turkish territory. Mustapha Kemal came along, and turned the tables.

Should neither principal object be gained, the war will be manoeuvred toward contracting our boundaries in the Negev and Galilee, and possibly elsewhere.

The war defies the United Nations, but we must bear the brunt of it. It is too soon to attempt conclusions—fighting may be prolonged, but a survey of these first six weeks can show us clearly what betides.

We have lost more than two hundred men. According to reliable sources at least twice as many Arabs have been killed. Fighting has been restricted to Jaffa, Haifa and Jerusalem, to the highways and the Negev.

In Jaffa and Haifa, we have had the upper hand so far, not just because of military strength, but because both towns are surrounded by our settlements, in effect they are Arab islands in a Jewish sea; we can cut off the Arabs there and invest them, and that, to a certain extent, is what happened.

It is credibly reported that between 15,000 and 20,000 Arabs have fled Haifa and more are shutting their shops and preparing to go: the masses are fleeing to Arab territory in the interior; those who can, abroad. It is worse in Jaffa—a vast exodus, alarming unemployment, panic; the Arabs themselves speak of chaos. Not that the Arab will to fight is feebler. The war goes on without sign of stop or pause.

Things are different in Jerusalem, and not just because of our military weakness, but because the city is not protected by Jewish villages. There are one or two enclaves which we use as bastions and defense bases, but they inevitably tie up considerable forces that are needed for Jerusalem.

We are on top so far in the New City. In the Old, the reduced and resourceless community, about 1,600 souls, is in bad case, in veritable fear and trembling. Some Jews have left the Jewish quarters on the fringe, and all have left the Arab quarters, but they are nothing so affrighted as the Arab population is.

At the beginning of January an Arab leader described the

situation in Arab Jerusalem as follows: 'It is very serious. The inhabitants are furious. They come to our homes and curse us right and left. Wounded everywhere. The hospitals full to overflowing. There are no bandages. The British Army is disarming us. There are no supplies in the Old City. On all sides frustration and despair. Control is impossible'.

Another of our handicaps is that Jerusalem must rely on the coast for its food and sustenance: its survival depends upon safety of communications, and they are, I am afraid, the reverse of safe. Maintaining communications is one of our most exacting problems, and Jewish Jerusalem is its victim day after day. There is no famine yet, but it is never far away, for the Arabs have four ways in, from Bab el Wad and Ramallah, and Hebron and Jericho, and we only the way from Tel Aviv.

Elsewhere the roads are still fairly clear, and only skirmishes have taken place.

* * *

The Administration is neutral only when the Arabs are the attackers and we the attacked. If it is the other way round—and there have been such cases—neutrality disappears. We behold a perverse complacence in the unhappy state of things, the immoderate satisfaction of a Mandatory persuaded that now, in the eyes of the world, events acquit it of thirty years of failure, a scoffing at decisions of the United Nations which it tried so hard to obstruct.

* * *

And now to the real adversary—the local Arab, and—much more than in 1936—his border friends.

As yet, the Arab townsmen of Jaffa, Haifa and Jerusalem have alone been involved, with support from Nablus and Lydda and the Negev tribes. The fellah has made no move, which is a significant but not necessarily a continuing fact: it is up to us to prolong it all we can.

But we have to deal with others. If it were just a matter of the Palestinian Arabs, we could end the fighting reasonably soon. Jaffa and Haifa are easily taken, and even in Jerusalem, but for the British, we would win out, if perhaps less easily, and occupy the Old City as well. The difficulty of keeping open the enfiladed link with Tel Aviv is great but not insurmountable, and remember that we can paralyze the Arab lines of communication, and Arabs are far more dependent upon motor transport than they were ten years ago. They may have more arms than then, and the supplement, I suspect, is larger than ours has been, but I am positive that without the British, and without their frontier confederates, their capitulation would not be long delayed.

In their covenant—it is in no sense a changeless line-up—the Arab States fall into three groups: the violently hostile and belligerent: Syria and Iraq, and to a lesser degree, surprising and unnatural as it may seem, the Lebanon; the more restrained, but unrestrained enough to declare war: Egypt and Arabia; and, in a class by itself, Trans-Jordan.

The principal training center is in Syria. Egypt and Saudi Arabia are not yet actively engaged. Iraq has a tolerably equipped army and is trying to send troops to our frontier. So far the ruler of Trans-Jordan has refused them passage. This may be a paradox, but then so is Trans-Jordan a paradox: it has the best army of them all, superior in quality, training and equipment, the greater part of it, the Arab Legion, actually encamped in Palestine. Abdullah has wanted peace and would willingly accept the decision of the United Nations. But how long can he stick to his guns? After all, he is an Arab and under tremendous Arab pressure.

* * *

Then the international factor—the United Nations, whose attitude is so valuable a moral support. We urge the speedy arrival of the promised Commission to set up our Provisional State

Council and our militia without delay. These issues are not in our hands, however. Everything is contingent, and we must be ready to stand on our own, on the Jewish resources at our disposal here and in the world at large.

The United Nations fixed a series of dates. One, indefinite, for the arrival of the Commission. The second, whose voiding I fear, is February 1, when the British are to hand over to us a Jewish port and enough hinterland to permit a substantial immigration: I wish we could be sure of it.

And the third: not later than April 1, each Provisional State Council must be established, with full territorial authority of its own, under the supervision of the Commission.

The fourth, set by Great Britain, is May 15: withdrawal of British forces and end of the Mandate. Will that date be kept, I wonder? At all events, the Mandate *must* be relinquished by August 1, for on that day, by resolution of the United Nations, all British jurisdiction here ends.

Finally, October 1, whereon the two States, or at least one of them, must come into being.

The Arabs are out to undo these assignments. It is risky to predict in our highly complex situation, but I believe that if in fact we see the British Mandate ended, we may expect war to begin or, I should say, the conflagration to spread on that same day. It means a test we have not undergone for thousands of years, a test, above all, of how soberly we have assessed the gravity of things. The start of preparedness is seeing things clear and true. The Yishuv and Jewry must be taught how serious things are, for only if we know how great the danger shall we find the strength within ourselves—and I am sure it is there—to withstand it.

When the war breaks out, we shall have the immense problems of the Negev and the North, of Jerusalem and of communications.

The Negev is a special problem—not of protecting a handful

of settlements, but of securing an integral part of our State. Bluntly, conquest of the Negev.

To contract our boundaries is easier in the Negev than at any other point. The United Nations has given us it to colonize but force of arms, not formal resolutions, will determine the issue, and unless we muster armed strength there, we may soon lose it. Every settlement there must be a garrison, and every Jew a soldier. We must be strong enough to occupy the whole far-reaching terrain, and not only for the width of our pipelines or our scattered farmsteads. Mobility and provisioning—food, water, fuel, equipment and vehicles—these are paramount. If our links with the Negev are safeguarded, no one can take it from us; but it will have to be by air and sea, for our land-lines pass through Arab areas.

Water-supply is crucial in Jerusalem also. While the British remain, water from Rosh Ha'ayin will probably reach the city, but all the same the pipeline may be sabotaged and the people die of thirst. Arab Jerusalem is less affected for it has cisterns, but the Jewish suburbs are modern and many houses, indeed whole quarters, have none. If the piped supply is cut off, we will have to seize the Arab quarters for their water. There is no sea-way to Jerusalem, and the airway over the encircling hills is risky. The only way to guarantee access—and we can do it—is to occupy the approaches.

Perhaps trouble will start in the North and the Arabs now training in Syria seek to overrun and isolate Galilee. We must see to it that, even so, Galilee is supplied by air and, as far as the Arabs let us, by the coast road through Naharia.

This is not the place for details of our plan of campaign. I can only affirm most solemnly that it calls for our supremest effort, physical and economic, in money and in morale. We must be prepared for setbacks. We will not be always or everywhere victors. We will take many a hard knock. And we must lift up our spirit to endure what is to come, for spirit will turn the scales of war, so be we are strong and many in the field.

This is life or death, and we shall prepare by every means and with all our energies, but welcome, nonetheless, any will to peace the Arabs show. We still pursue, as before disturbances broke out we pursued, a threefold political object. But it is unlike theirs. It is security, a Jewish State, an Arab-Jewish pact. Those, in that same order of time and significance, are our articles of faith.

A brief program and not easy, but neither is it impossible, if we do but attain the heights of strength and understanding.

THE FOUR-MONTH BATTLE
*At a meeting of the Zionist Executive,
April 6, 1948*

Since we were first assailed on November 30, more than 900 Arabs have been killed; the Jews in the Old City have been beleaguered for months; Jewish Jerusalem has been partly cut off all the time, for ten days marooned entirely, and the danger of famine still threatens it. Almost all roads are beset, and any Jew using them risks his life; settlements in Galilee and Samaria, in the Jordan Valley, Judea and the Negev have been raided, sometimes in great force; and in Haifa, Jaffa, Tel Aviv and Jerusalem there are incidents day and night. Thousands of armed Arabs, many of them regulars, both officers and men, have invaded Palestine, and their number is growing. They come chiefly from Syria, Iraq and Trans-Jordan, and, less so, from Egypt, and at least some carry arms the British Government sent to their countries. Many, if not most, local Arabs have private arms, and those who have not try to buy them at any price. The Arab Legion is encamped here still, ostensibly a Trans-Jordan unit, but in reality under British aegis.

Public services already are chaotic. Effective administration has ceased, functions are collapsing and disintegrating. Confusion reigns and it will be worse confounded on May 15. Then we will be exposed to the full force of the enemy's attack, his well-nigh limitless reserves, his odds of forty to one, his sovereign status in the United Nations and his British ally and arms. We have neither sovereignty nor government, nor international recognition; lacking statehood, we may not openly buy arms. Against us are arrayed seven States, with drilled armies, more or less, an air force in some cases and the Egyptian navy. That is the essence of it: not for over one thousand eight hundred years have we been so grimly circumstanced.

* * *

When I say: 'We have no choice', I am thinking of those Jews in Israel and beyond who can live only one way of life: independent, Jewish and in the Homeland. Such, be they here or still to join us, have no choice. They will never bend the knee to the Mufti, to the masters of the Arab League, or to Bevin's policy and its supporters. They are bound to defend themselves and their nation's right to Homeland and independence. Try to rob them of this right by force, and by force they will guard it. To them it is a right of ages won by their forefathers, by the creativity of pioneer generations, a right recognized by international authority, barter of Jewish suffering and tragedy down the years. For them there is no choice. Gentlemen, that is the simple question: how to fight for a victory that will make certain the freedom of our people, the unbroken development of its creativeness in Israel, its sovereign future and international status.

At our last meeting in Zurich in August 1947, I endeavored without success to convince the Movement that the Yishuv's security is overwhelmingly our most vital and pressing problem, that in domestic and external relations it is the needs of security that must guide our every step.

Today no one, in the Movement or, surely, in the Yishuv, has to be persuaded of the gloom and peril. Yet I doubt if all have drawn the bitter conclusion and are prepared to align their lives, their works and ways to the call of the hour.

You know the odds against us. You know that we must give all we have, absolutely and without reserve, if we are not to succumb, that the Yishuv must mortgage every scrap of its economy, its manpower and transport, its science and techniques, its financial resources and moral strength, its Press and public life, the agencies and political influence and material of the Zionist Organization.

Nowadays wars are not fought just by armies; the whole nation is mobilized and we are no exception. It is not our Army that is being warred against, but the Yishuv: vanguard and rear are indistinguishable, every child is in the front-line perforce. Every settlement is a frontier outpost, each of us a border scout. However much we expand our Army, only all-out marshalling and concentration of our material assets and, no less, of our stamina and spirit, will do. Even professional soldiers admit that morale is two-thirds of victory. Yishuv and Movement must be transformed in outlook and action to answer this burning challenge.

But the anxious query in your hearts is—Will we come through? With all mine, I say we will, though not I, nor anyone else, can prove it as you would a theorem in mathematics. Economists or tacticians, who do not know the soul of the Yishuv or the inwardness of Zionism, would see only 650,000 men and women of certain ages, a certain agriculture and industry, such and such possessions, military skill and equipment, so much money. They would see the Zionist organizations overseas, all very eager and ready to help the Yishuv but under official restraints and thousands of miles away. They would see one million one hundred thousand Arabs here and thirty million others next door, with States and Governments, budgets and armies, with British military and financial backing. And they would at once pronounce the hopelessness of our case. So indeed they would have done five months ago. But the months are behind us now, and we abide. Gentlemen, mark well the lesson.

To begin with, we had only defense units under a loose territorial plan, but essentially localized each to its post. Personnel were not trained soldiers—not even as the professional watchmen of forty years since, but busy farmers and workers who every week gave a few leisure hours to drills, and were prepared, if need be, to defend the settlement. There was one central unit of some thousands permanently mobilized, though still only part-time, but essentially mobile and on call. There were also the beginnings of another unit, in theory mobile and trained but again part-time, for more than local defense, made up of volunteers from office and factory.

Our budget for defense was not even a third of what Great Britain spends on the Arab Legion, and you can imagine the poverty of our equipment.

In spite of all, the enemy has failed to enter a single one of our settlements, central or distant, populous or unpeopled. None has been destroyed, none abandoned. True, in the main towns Jews have had to leave homes on the boundary to escape the incessant fire and shelling; yet never a Jewish quarter has been captured, while we have taken many enemy strong-points and penetrated the Arab defenses far from any Jewish settlement. We have hit the Arab guerrillas hard, villages have been emptied in panic, even from Haifa one-third of its Arabs have fled. A fierce battle is raging in and for Jerusalem. So far, we have not done too badly, but it is not over yet—the peace of Jerusalem is still in peril and the way thither unsafe. Since the destruction of the Second Temple, there has not been in Jerusalem so Jewish a precinct, for a great stretch of the city is basically as is Tel Aviv: one hundred percent Jewish, dwelt in only by Jews. But there are also islands of Jews among Arabs as of Arabs among us. All the Arab islands have been deserted; after two months of unabated assault, and not by Arabs only, every Jewish island is still manfully held.

There are isolated cases of individual Jews fleeing the country, but the Yishuv everywhere is firm and unyielding. At this moment, the Arabs are evacuating villages between Tel Aviv and the Carmel: it may be strategy, for guerrilla troops are moving in as women and children depart; it may be fright but anyhow we do not, and will not necessarily, leave them unoccupied.

Yes, we may be proud of our successes when you consider how few we are and outarmed, no allies, no British Government on our side, and the initiative with the Arabs, who can, to enormous advantage, choose where and what to attack. And we may be reasonably hopeful, without assuming that to be spared disaster hitherto is to be completely secure: we must know that only a part of the Arab fighting potential is yet committed—some six or seven thousand guerrillas. Thousands more may enter. And there are the Arab regulars in readiness.

All this is, as it were, negative. But there has been positive improvement as well: our fighting power has grown and not merely in numbers—you will not expect details, and under all reservations of political and military chanciness the prospect is that it will keep on growing.

The littleness of the Yishuv and the Diaspora's difficulty in furnishing extra manpower limit the numerical expansion of our fighting strength. But manpower is not everything, the determinants of victory are logistics, money, morale and intellect. Flouting the experts, I dare believe in victory, but only on one surmise, that the British Army, or something like it, will not be fighting against us—at least, no more than it has so far fought; that it may hamper, aggravate or interfere, but not actually make war on us.

Let us then exploit our quality to the utmost.

Let us muster our whole manpower for battle and for production as rationally as possible, with nothing but the needs of security in view.

Let us prepare, produce and procure the necessary equipment, vehicles, aircraft and ships according to plan.

Let us organize industry, agriculture and business, external trade and the distribution of food and raw materials, as the emergency requires, to maintain and enlarge the Army and preserve our war-time economy.

Let us set up one central, supreme authority with control over manpower, the Army, labor, finances, and all public services, and enjoying the loyal and unstinted support of the Zionist Movement and world Jewry.

And let us resolve not to be content with merely defensive tactics, but at the right moment to attack all along the line and not just within the confines of the Jewish State and the borders of Palestine, but to seek out and crush the enemy wherever he may be.

REVIEW OF THE MILITARY AND POLITICAL SITUATION
At the second session of the Provisional State Council, May 19, 1948

Just now, the enemy rules the air. What that means to him, to Tel Aviv, you all know. We have reason to trust that it will not be for long; but I can fix no dates. The Yishuv has not been stampeded: it needs no compliments, but I cannot refrain from praising its splendid fortitude. I watched with awe Londoners' wonderful display of courage in that pitiless and unending bombardment. Our people are as valiant. For all my profound faith in the Yishuv I must confess to being astounded by its self-control, calamity has not made us cowards.

There are several fronts of battle and on no two is the situation alike. Western Galilee, save Acco, is wholly in our hands. In eastern Galilee there was ground to expect an enemy attack and concentration of forces, but we took the initiative instead, attacked and pursued the enemy across the border. The Jordan Valley is tense: strong columns of the Arab Legion, supported by armor, are operating with Iraqi and Syrian reinforcements and using planes, artillery and tanks. We reinforced our troops there yesterday and more will have to be sent. In the center, all appears quiet, but an enemy attack seems to be developing. We learn that Kaukji has been ordered to withdraw to Trans-Jordan and hand over his positions to the Arab Legion, which is approaching Jerusalem and, according to latest news, has reached Sheikh Jarrah. We hold the New City almost entirely, and have forced our way to the Old. In the Ramleh sector we have captured

Sarafand.* As you know, it had been sold to the Jewish Agency, but the Colonial Office annulled the sale and the British Army handed the camp over to the Arabs. Now it is ours, as spoils of war. Our attack on Ramleh is making no progress. In the south there is nothing new. The situation in the Negev is strained, and large formations oppose us. We are mobilizing additional forces against them, and within the next fortnight our effectives ought to be much more numerous and better equipped.

At the third session,
June 3, 1948

The invasion began even before the Mandate came to an end, and it began with the covert aid and open protection of the Mandatory. It is no secret that the invading forces received most, if not all, of their equipment from the British Government, and there is some foundation for the belief that tactics and command do not altogether lack the benefit of close association with the same leadership. While the Mandate lasted, this interplay was discreetly camouflaged: neighboring Arab States themselves were careful not to admit responsibility for the guerrillas, and the Mandatory was at pains to appear neutral. Now it is all in the open—we have been invaded by the Lebanon, Syria, Trans-Jordan, Iraq and Egypt, liberally fitted out with modern munitions of war, thanks to the good offices of Whitehall. The Arabs planned a lightning overthrow of the young State. According to captured documents, Haifa was to have fallen on May 20, Tel Aviv and Jerusalem about five days later, when Abdullah was to enter the city and be crowned king of his wider realm.

Looking back on what we have gone through in three short but hectic weeks, we cannot allow ourselves to be complacent.

* Site of the largest British military installation in Palestine, extensively used in the second World War.

We may be worse off very soon, for the British Government has blatantly joined in the Arab blockade. The representatives now in Israel of that Government affect ignorance of the State and acknowledge only our Jewish mayors, and so it was that the British Consul in Haifa 'arranged' to let us know that if we dared again bomb Amman the Royal Air Force would shoot down every Jewish aircraft it saw, for Amman is the main British air base in this area.

We may nevertheless pay ourselves some little meed of praise. The enemy has met with a decided reverse so far as his political designs are concerned and militarily he has suffered a considerable defeat. A quick subjection of Israel was foiled, the State endures and its conquest is farther distant than it was three weeks ago. Its entire territory as set by the United Nations is in our hands and substantial areas outside it have been occupied besides—more particularly western Galilee and almost the whole Tel Aviv-Jerusalem highway, except for two short but very difficult interruptions, and certain stretches through the Shephelah.

The New City, saving a few places, is ours, though our losses were heavy. After an heroic stand, the Etzion group of settlements in the Hebron range laid down its arms, and, having held out with perhaps even greater gallantry for many months, the Jewish pocket in the Old City had to surrender.

The details of the fighting and of our casualties are known to every Jew here and to every newspaper reader in the world. But I must cite the valor of our few practically unarmed settlers in the Jordan Valley, who for weeks beat off heavy attacks mounted by armored columns with air support and artillery; they are not yet out of the wood—nor are we anywhere, but for the moment we hold the whip-hand.

One fight, above all, I shall single out—the fight for Jewish Jerusalem. There have been few encounters in our annals where the ordeal was so frightful, the courage so high. In fortitude unexampled, the city stands—cut off from every Jewish succor, under the shadow of hunger and thirst, bombarded day and night with ruthless inhumanity in insolent and cynical mockery of the meaning of the Jerusalem that is called holy by Christians and Moslems alike. And the guns and planes are British, manned by the Arab hirelings of Bevin's policy, while the Anglican Church, which must answer in part for this barbarous outrage, is strangely mute. The Jews of Jerusalem resist because they know the State is with them. The flower of Israel's youth will give their lives to free Jerusalem. The oath we swore by the Waters of Babylon is no frigid speech, it flames still in their hearts and ours. Today, the chances of relieving Jerusalem are good: a strong link with it has been established, not only along the narrow highway, nay, a broader living link of Jewish soldiers.

Right at the beginning, I declared this to be, for us, a defensive war. We did not want it; it was thrust upon us, and we are only defending ourselves. But we shall defend ourselves not by being on the defensive, but so far as possible by keeping up offensive pressures—not only within the State, not only within Palestine. We have been as good as our word.

The Army has done its job well. We are attacking the Arab Triangle, we stand in the approaches of Jenin, and at the gates of Tulkarm, and in Nablus the people tremble. We have fallen upon concentrations of Syrian and Lebanese troops in their own territories, and in our bombs upon Amman the invaders had warning not to be gulled into thinking that only the soil of Israel and the Palestine heavens will be theatres of war.

I read in the Press today that Nokrashy Pasha complains that we displayed less regard for the spokesman of the United Nations than did Egypt, that the Egyptian air force was ordered not to raid Tel Aviv while Count Bernadotte was here. The Pasha errs. We were careful to hit Amman before Count Bernadotte got there, indeed we tried hard to stop his trip, for we did not specially want him to see what a Jewish air force can do to the country where the Arabs think themselves secure.

With all this, with our Jewish air force created and a Jewish navy founded, deliverance is still far. The war has only begun. Perhaps our greatest trials lie ahead. I cannot too often warn you against the enemy. We have dealt him many shrewd blows during the past six months, I know, but he has yet to deploy his full strength, and it would be wrong to think that he will always be nerveless and inglorious.

Luckily we, too, are not full out, either in the Yishuv, or, even more so, in world Jewry. If we are to go on to the end—and it must be final victory—those tremendous sources of might must be drained to the last drop.

* * *

In the political sphere I have, perhaps, less news to tell. You know that the two great Powers which bestride the world have recognized us. This is doubly important, for they seldom find a common language, and with equal significance they were united on the vital issues on November 29.

Here again, peace and comfort are still seek. Enemies, declared or secret, are astir; openly or by stealth strings are being pulled in many capitals to hinder acceptance of the fact we now are. It may be, indeed, that out of all the difficulties, political and military, in which we are toiling, not only strength but sweetness also will come forth. We know that not by the grace of nations was our freedom won, not upon their bounty will its continuance depend. We built the Yishuv with our own sweat and blood. So too we built, so too we shall guard, the State. Never have we lost faith in the conscience of mankind, always we shall demand of the world what is justly ours. But morning and evening, day in and day out, we must remind ourselves that our existence, our freedom and our future are in our own hands—our own exertions, our own capacity, our own will, they are the key.

And now a word or two about the home front. The State was not created for war. It is an unveiling of Zionist hopes and Jewish vision. It was created so that the dream might come true, and its high purpose is to bring home the weary of Israel and refresh the desolation of the land. Alien influences, far beyond our control, enveloped it in war at its first breath, its first struggles are now spent on war, and who can tell how long our sons must fight and fall? Yet, in the midst of war, we are charged with mighty tasks of construction and of reconstruction. Much that was wicked the Mandatory bequeathed us. Not the least of its malevolence was the disruption or disorganization of all services. So now, while the battle rages, we must strain to renew them. We must re-establish touch with the world: for the Mandatory was so evilly-disposed that it made known to the Postal Union that after May 15 Palestine would be sponged off the map. We cannot claim to have restored completely the few services we rescued: perhaps the emergency, perhaps our own inadequacy, is to blame. But at least Bevin's ugly plot went astray, and today we have more order, more regular and dependable services, than the expiring Mandate vouchsafed. There is a great deal still to be done, and done under difficulties, in air-raids, in the front-line: we are all in the front-line, and you of Tel Aviv know it in your very bones. But the work does not stop, valiantly we are forging a new panoply of State day after day, and, in like measure, we fulfill the twofold duty for which the State was born: Aliyah and settlement. Over these distracted weeks, more immigrants have come in than ever in our generation during the same length of time. We believe the tide will rise, and, cease-fire or not, we shall add everywhere to the score of our settlements.

THE CEASE-FIRE
A radio broadcast, June 10, 1948

From the Provisional Government, I bring a brief message to the nation. The Government has decided to accept the will of the Security Council that hostilities should cease for four weeks on all fronts. The Arab States, the State of Israel, and the Arabs of Palestine were all required to comply, and the cease-fire begins tomorrow, June 11, at 10 a.m. local time.

Our decision was only taken after deep thought and long debate, for we saw clearly the disadvantages and detriments involved. But we were moved by two main considerations:

First, from the very beginning of aggression by neighbors egged on and aided by foreign elements wishful to stir up strife and contention between Jew and Arab, we have affirmed over and over again our readiness to cease fire the moment the enemy did.

Second, this State is building its future on the creative and fighting quality of its people and its foreign policy rests squarely on the paramount principle of mutual understanding and adjustment with the United Nations.

We, therefore, will hold our fire if and as the enemy holds his —in good faith, and all Army Commanders have had unequivocal orders accordingly. The Jews in Jerusalem, all inhabitants of the State, all dwelling within our occupied areas, are bidden strictly to desist from breach of the agreement. Always and peremptorily, independence demands perfect discipline, national unity, a closing of all ranks around constituted authority.

The Government will permit no attempt to violate our pact

or break our promise to the United Nations. It will treat any offender as an enemy of the State, and punish him with martial rigor.

Israel is undiminished by this wanton and sinister war: our bounds are set wider, our forces multiply, we are administering public services, and daily the new multitudes arrive. Entrenchment and construction are in crescendo. All that we have taken we shall hold. During the cease-fire, we shall organize administration with fiercer energy, strengthen our footing in town and hamlet, speed up colonization and Aliyah, and look to the Army. We have shown what we can do not in defense alone, but in sweeping offensive; that, ready as we have always been for peace, we can meet crisis with new fortitude and force.

In full consciousness of our right and strength, we shall keep the truce, and on that awareness rely until the peace of Israel is certain and redemption a dream no more.

PEACE AND WAR
*At the fourth session of the Provisional
State Council, June 17, 1948*

It is the first week of the cease-fire. You know why we agreed. It is but four weeks since we established our State. You know what marvels, peerless in history, we have worked in that spell— an infant State under the unreasoning onslaught of five powerful and populous neighbors. A small and young State, 700,000 against twenty-seven millions, one brave man victorious over forty, and they with weapons and officers, money and influence, supplied by a great Power. Much of what befell must now be unspoken, but I cannot be silent on the grim glory of Jerusalem. For centuries Christendom and Islam claimed holy to themselves this city hallowed by our Prophets. Therefore was it decided, upon the establishment of the Jewish State, to place the treble sanctuary under international control. It is this sacred citadel that has endured long bombardment by Moslem legionaries, its shrines demolished and its churches wrecked in unspeakable vandalism and cynical excess. Wordless, the Christian world looks on. The Church of that same England that loaded and laid the murdering Arab guns, has lost its tongue. All saw and heard, yet no denomination speaks. The holiness of Jerusalem is forgotten, and oblivion buries memories sacrosanct to the greatest faiths on earth. It has no shield but Israel, no savior but a small and lonely people, wittingly stripped by Britain of all defense, which in suffering and valor beyond the ken of man has shown all the world who truly holds the city dear, and who renders its worship lying and empty lip-service.

Of one exploit of our Army few may have heard, and few can have appraised it fully: for it was not spectacular. At the end of May, the Seventh Brigade was sent to a crossroads on the Latrun front. Jerusalem was not only cruelly shelled, the enemy was out to stifle and starve it into submission. Thanks to British design and its Arab disciples, the plan almost came off. The Seventh Brigade was thrown back at Latrun although its armor penetrated the village and fired the police post; but two obscure villages, Bet Jiz and Bet Susin, were captured while the fighting at Latrun was still in progress, and it was possible then to send soldiers, material, engineers and equipment for the building of a second, parallel road to Jerusalem.

Our troops now hold a continuous front from northernmost Ras el Nakura to Tel Aviv, from Tel Aviv through the southern settlements to Bab el Wad and the western entrance to Jerusalem, thence southward to Talpioth and northward to Sanhedria; and from the Lebanese border straight to the north and south of Jerusalem.

Throughout this pause, we must prepare ourselves for peace and war. There is little more we need do for peace: are we not immemorially the people of peace and forever? Have we not held out our hands in peace to all who dwell with us and on our borders, since our third homecoming? We will give all possible help to the peace envoy of the United Nations, but not for peace at any price. It is as well the world should know—the United Nations, the Arab peoples with whom we have no quarrel, and the Arab rulers too—that if those rulers seriously mean the preposterous conditions they stipulate in advance—annulment of the State or any trespass upon our people's absolute right to return to its Land—then the envoy will only be wasting his time and breath.

We are ready for peace as an independent State, a sovereign

nation, whose very life and soul is Aliyah, free and full. The peace we want must be one between equals, based on the vital principle of our foreign policy—reciprocity, and no other. But are the Arab rulers and their foreign advisers as anxious as we are to have peace? Will the cease-fire last even its twenty-eight days? Rumor has it that the British garrison will evacuate Haifa even before the month ends, and it is very likely. Who knows if that will not be again the signal for a surprise attack on the State, and on Haifa especially? If fighting is renewed, be sure it will be violent. We must be much, much better, more confident, more responsible, and bolder and bolder still.

This war will settle our fate, and all Jewry's. We cannot look to external aid. We must depend upon ourselves. There is no truer picture of our present case than in the words uttered by the Prophet Isaiah thousands of years ago: 'wherefore art thou red in thine apparel, and thy garments like his that treadeth in the winevat? I have trodden the winepress alone; and of the peoples there was none with me . . . For the day of vengeance was in mine heart, and my year of redemption was come: and I looked, and there was none to help; and I wondered and there was none to uphold: therefore mine own arm brought salvation unto me; and my fury, it upheld me.'

THE 'ALTALENA'
*A statement made at the fifth session
of the Provisional State Council,
June 23, 1948*

My friends! We are assembled this day to reflect upon a lamentable story, an attempt, pregnant with calamity, by the Irgun Zvai Leumi to wound the unity and sovereignty of the State, its military power and its international status.

You are only too familiar with the unhappy record of violence which this body of so-called dissidents has successfully engineered. When the State was established, we thought it wise and well to forget all that had gone before, and allow every member of the Yishuv alike to open a new chapter, the chapter of equal part in the rights and duties which State building and defense must mean.

On May 6, we proclaimed the establishment of the Israel Defense Army. This was no routine measure setting up a public service: it would decide whether the State itself, whether the hopes of Israel, would flourish or die. We had to suffer the wanton turbulence of our enemies before the State. Then, with the State, came concerted invasion by Arab legions. On repelling this aggression our ultimate survival depends.

The Army Order forbade the formation or maintenance of any armed forces other than the Israel Defense Army. And that was not only for the sake of administrative tidiness, important though that is; it was naked, imperative self-defense! Only a united army, loyal to one Government, obeying a unified High Command, can resist a foreign invader.

The law, and our serious circumstance, gave us reason and right beyond a peradventure to break the dissident organization. But we chose not to, for we wished to encourage voluntary disbandment, and engender an atmosphere in which the members would feel heartened to join the regular forces. And indeed Lechi (Fighters for Freedom) seems to have resolved itself to disband, for its members joined the Defense Army without any special fuss. Agreement to similar effect had been concluded with the Irgun before the State was established, in accordance with a decision of the Zionist General Council. The Irgun, however, did not follow Lechi's suit; it made its own conditions for obeying the country's laws, its undertaking to the General Council was not honored.

The Government was not anxious to stress formality overmuch, and when it appeared that the main purpose had been gained—dissolution of Irgun and enlistment of any members liable for military service—we made a number of concessions. On June 1 of this year, the Irgun leader signed a new undertaking in which the following points were specified:

1. Irgun members would join the Defense Army on the terms prescribed in the Government's draft law and would take its oath of allegiance.

2. Arms and military equipment in Irgun possession would be surrendered, and placed at the disposal of the High Command.

3. By its own freely affirmed decision, the Irgun would cease to exist as a military unit.

4. It would end all independent activity to obtain arms or military equipment, and would make its sources of procurement available to us for the defense of the State.

These promises were only kept in part. Some thousand Irgun members joined up, in special units, and a small stock of arms and equipment was handed in. But the most important pledges were broken—the Irgun and its Command continued to operate; arms and equipment were still obtained independently, and the sources thereof denied to the Army. Such is the dark background, at this most critical hour, of the grievous doings of the past three days at Kfar Vitkin and in Tel Aviv.

Defying our statutes and its own unforced professions, the Irgun brought to these shores a ship laden with arms. United Nations truce or no, this would be grave enough, for no State can countenance private citizens or organizations thus importing on, as it were, personal account even the tiniest armory, much less the wholesale consignment of rifles and machine-guns that the Irgun tried to land this time.

A venture of such a degree of indiscipline and faithlessness, and running counter, besides, to an international requirement laid down by the United Nations and accepted by Israel, is a frightful threat to the State and might set the fuse for a disastrous civil war.

When the intention became known to the Ministry of Defense, instructions were given to require that the Irgun yield the ship to Government. The Irgun declined, save on conditions. Again the Government was indulgent, perhaps too much so and, if it was, the responsibility is entirely mine. Details, not by any means unimportant, were shelved, and we asked only that the ship be made over absolutely to Government, and not unloaded by the Irgun. When that too was rejected, my duty was clear. The safety of the State must be preserved, the law carried out—and I knew that only by force could it be done. I placed the issue before the full Cabinet, and after heart-searching debate we decided ourselves to carry out the Government's stipulations.

I regret to say that certain former Irgunists deserted their units and went to Kfar Vitkin to join the rebellious hazard, but it collapsed quickly there; overcome by our regulars, they capitulated, were disarmed, and signed undertakings to report to Government when called upon.

I should like to commend the skill and effect with which the Commander of the Central Area discharged his mission—doing all that was required with the least bloodshed.

It looked as though the episode were closed. But the ship slipped away from Kfar Vitkin, once the immigrants aboard had been disembarked, and reached Tel Aviv. There it would not heed our orders to stand away from the shore and give itself up to the State.

An extraordinary meeting of the Cabinet was summoned. Its decision was that the mutinous craft must surrender with its arms, on pain of military measures. Again defiance, with what result you know. Our artillery scored a direct hit and the ship caught fire. As I speak it is a smoking hulk on the beach of Tel Aviv.

Was it not enough to undergo the murderous ordeal of Arab hatred, that this bitter aftertaste of blood should be proffered us by fellow-Jews?

The momentary danger may be past. Our Army can put down any rising. But the evil will not be rooted out by punitive action alone. The dissidents in their stratagems are encouraged greatly by the support they get from various quarters. Once we might understand, if we could not justify, this partisanry; now it is hard even to understand. We are fighting for our lives. There is a truce, but no end of war: Arab columns are inside our territory and Jerusalem is under the guns of the Arab Legion; the road to the Negev is in the hands of a powerful Egyptian force, and Mishmar Hayarden occupied by Syrian troops. Beyond our frontiers wait larger concentrations.

In such straits, armed revolt in Israel spells ruin of the Yishuv's strength to defend itself and its future. If that fails, the State is lost, and failure looms so long as there remains in the Yishuv or Galuth a single Jew who cannot see that the existence of rebel gangs in Israel, that to give them moral or material comfort, prolongs the awful risk and invites disaster. This is not just a job for the Army: the whole nation has a duty to perform.

Firm and swift Government intervention has repaired much

of the damage inflicted by the Irgun hitherto. But if yesterday's folly had not been averted, I doubt if we could have undone the consequences. 5,000 rifles and 250 machine-guns would have fallen into the hands of terrorists, and they might have wrecked the State and the freedom of its Yishuv.

* * *

Why did the Irgun refuse to surrender the ship and its cargo of arms?

One member of this Council asked: 'What does it signify? Why this fear of an armed minority?' There is good cause to fear, to fear greatly. I am hardly among the cowards of Israel, yet I am very much afraid of an armed minority. For what purpose or function is it armed, on whose behalf? It is not for show. Arms are for killing, literally killing, and nothing else. Alas for mankind, that it must produce weapons of destruction! And so civilized peoples limit strictly the carrying of arms, and those handling the instruments of death are placed under rigorous discipline and under the overriding command of superior officers. They are distinctively uniformed and segregated in special camps or barracks, with all manner of restrictions and subordination. All this is so that the bearers of arms, the army, shall not use them as they please. That is my answer to the question.

A second member with deep emotion protested against the shedding of blood. That is the very crux: we do not want bloodshed, but with an armed minority we may be sure there will be. More than once has the Irgun spilled Jewish blood, and the blood of others: these things must not happen again. Why were 5,000 rifles brought? Not for Army or State. For what, then? Was it to fight the Arabs? But for that we gave the Irgun official arms. Government and the Army have not been altogether idle during the past six months in evidencing that they can stand up to the Arabs. Of course, there were reverses: there always are, even with an Army generations old and a State ancient, rich, and powerful. But our young Army has defended us not unsuccessfully. Give it its due! There have been blunders; certain things must be changed, certain practices put a stop to. But let us have no more vilifying of the Army, no loose talk of 'wild men with sten-guns.' Those of us who never in our lives carried a gun to defend the Yishuv ought to respect the men with the guns who saved it and are ready to risk their lives for us.

A Government embattled for survival, sorely needing arms, and here are Jews, not just any Jews, but incomparable patriots and warriors as they would have us believe, bringing in arms but withholding them from us, with whom they pledged their word, from the menaced State, from the Army to which they swore allegiance, in which their own comrades are serving. Why? There were three Army battalions of Irgun soldiers and men deserted from all three, to prevent transfer of the arms and ensure their remaining in Irgun hands. Why? One member here ingenuously suggested that the ship should sail away from Israel. But as luck had it, he was not the Irgun commander, and could not chart the course! The ship got its sailing orders at Kfar Vitkin, but disobeyed and made deliberately for Tel Aviv, and there deliberately ran aground. But let us imagine that the member spoke not in his own name, but for the Irgun, and was proposing that the ship should escape entirely. Did he think the dangers out to the end? Fortunately for us, all this has happened during the truce. But suppose the ship is at large at sea when the truce soon ends, and our troops are committed at Ashdod, at Latrun and Jenin. While we are busy with the Arabs these gentry will bring in 5,000 rifles, for themselves. That even now, having lost so rich a prize, they seek to dictate terms is because many still side with them, wittingly or not, like the previous speaker, who, I am sure, detests them consciously no less than I. Where, then, would we be if they had their rifles and bren-guns? What, then, would be their accents to Yishuv and State? You can envisage it for yourselves. Unhappily this is a nettle we cannot grasp with velvet gloves. It is tragic that we should have to use force against fellow-Jews. But it is a far greater tragedy that they should have forced us to, that they should have broken their promises and belied their declarations. I had misgivings, but the agreement was written down and signed. I have it here before me, subscribed by the 'Commander-in-Chief' himself. He and his friends betrayed it, nevertheless, and yet you ask me: 'Why this fear of an armed minority?' Now that we have seized the arms there is little fear, though even one rifle may do murder. We do not want to resort to bodyguards in Israel: it is humiliating. Besides, a bodyguard will not avail. If the assassin has willed to murder, murder he will. With one rifle you may take more than one life; with 5,000 a whole Yishuv is at your mercy, and unless such mass murder is in your mind, you cannot want 5,000 rifles.

To burn this ship was the most loyal service we could render the Yishuv. A truce infringed, our sovereignty risked. Perhaps these things are secondary, although it is surely enough for Bevin and Nokrashy Pasha and their like to deny that sovereignty, without the Irgun baying in chorus. No, worse is the crippling of our defensive resources. Suppose yesterday had never been, and the Irgun had landed the entire lethal cargo and cached it. And here am I, as a plain man, not a Minister, and I ask myself sensibly, 'What does it all mean? There is a war. Its men are in the Army, and at the same time Irgun has arms of its own. What for? I know it cannot be for fighting. So it must be for persisting in domestic terrorism, for attacking and even killing, as they killed before, Jews who do not want to give them money. I am one of those who hate truckling to terrorism from any quarter, but my Government seemingly cannot protect me and is frightened to confiscate the arms.' So I decide to take matters into my own hands, and there are many like me in Israel, of the stuff that no terror weakens. Are we all to arrange to get private arms? Why should the Irgun enjoy a monopoly? What of myself, my son, my friends? We too know how to get arms, we knew it forty years ago; and how to bring in ships—as Bevin will admit. One after another will do it, except the member of this Council who is not afraid of the Irgun, and can dispense with private arms and a private army. But I and all the fainthearted who fear every man with an unlicensed gun will have our private armies, and as many agencies for buying arms, as many ships bringing in arms, as there are parties and organizations. This realm of chaos will not be civil war, not at all! It will be the 'brotherhood' and 'unity of Israel' which the champions of the Irgun long for so ardently.

There used, of course, to be people who had private arms. There was a time when any Jewish armament in this country was unofficial, when there was as yet no National Council, no Agency, no communal organization for the Yishuv's protection. Our 'private entrepreneurs'—young men, laborers and pioneers—made themselves responsible for guard and defense, and not of workers' settlements, for there were none such in Israel then, but of 'bourgeois' farms, as we called them. Rogochevsky of Sejera was a 'bourgeois,' and I watched his lands. Nissanov, a Zionist laborer like myself, was willing to give his life for his employer's yoke of mules, and did. His fellow-watchmen were no different; and it was all on private initiative. But when the Yishuv organized itself collectively for defense, the watchmen made over their arms to the common store and rallied to the ranks of the organization. And now that there is a State, which has the duty to protect its citizens, and the Irgun sets itself up as a private army with private arms, is it likely that the Irgun will hold an exclusive concession in that dangerous commodity? The regime you recommend is civil war, and ruination of our war effort. Men will fight side by side only if they know a true comradeship and equality, that each is prepared to guard his friend's life with his own. But not if, of two soldiers, each equipped from Army stocks on identical terms, one also has a secret gunroom to which the other has not access. So long as the Irgun or any gang of terrorists clings to its private arms, our Army must be split in twain, perhaps even worse divided, every faction fearing the next, and vying with it under independent arms.

It does not lie with us to prolong the truce or cut it short. It may end tomorrow, and the war go on. But can we still fight on if authority, Army and equipment are disunited and any gangster flagrantly apes the Irgun? Even before the ship reached Tel Aviv, the Irgun was not ashamed to invite the Press to witness and publicize its exploits, and so slander a Government that dared take away its arms for the State.

No, not that way can we fight on! In war rekindled, we will be, all of us, dependent again on youngsters of the Palmach of whom two members here spoke so contemptuously today, and we will be praying, all of us, for the united Army that alone can deliver us.

The Irgun brought catastrophe about, the Government, at whatever cost, brought about deliverance and did not, dared not, give way to false sentimentality.

None among us seeks revenge: we have enemies and to spare, outside Israel. I and many are willing to forgive and forget—if the Irgun stops, and stops first, and not just by signing a second worthless scrap of paper. It must surrender arms and military equipment and the members must report for Army service like anybody else; no special agreements, simply enforcement of the law made by the State for every citizen without discrimination.

Much depends on you as well, you men of good intention. If you will refrain from siding with the Irgun, if you will insist, as every Jew should, that all its ranks join the Army, there to defend the Yishuv, exactly as their fellows do, it may be that a real halt will be called. Then, and only then, will the past be forgotten.

That is the position as of now. That is where the Government stands. I know as well as the next man what a ship is worth, and

5,000 rifles. But better far that the ship was blown up and burnt out and its cargo destroyed. The arms could be a boon only in Government hands. So give praise to the gun that sank the unsurrendered ship. Greater still had been our joy if no shot or shell was fired and the ship was ours unscathed. But the defiant Irgun wished it otherwise, and the Altalena and all it held are at the bottom of the sea.

It has been argued here that a Provisional Government has not the right to do such things. This is certainly a Provisional Government, and I hope you will be soon rid of it, as soon as we win the war and can hold elections. But its very short life determines the future of the Jewish people perhaps for centuries to come, for decades undoubtedly. If we can now hold fast as one man, at least while we are still at war, under a single authority and with an Army united, we shall prove the saviors of posterity in Israel.

PREPARED TO MEET THE FUTURE
*At the eleventh session of the Provisional
State Council, July 22, 1948*

Another cease-fire, Gentlemen, and this time without terminal date. We cannot be sure, for all that, of the war being over, but there is not much doubt that we are on the brink of a terrific political struggle. So we must stick to our guns, prepared for the worst, and doubling our preparations. There is no other way to success in war or politics.

It is, then, too early yet to expatiate upon the campaign, or on how and how far, outnumbered and alone, we made headway through eight months of fighting against local guerrillas, against armed infiltration by irregulars and lastly against a full-scale invasion.

Our greater concern must still be with a continuance of fighting and how to end it to our satisfaction than with retailing events past, and we are, I doubt not, too near them, too much a part of them, to judge them aright.

The first phase lasted from November 30, 1947, to May 14 of this year. The second for four weeks until June 11, and faced us with the armies of Syria, the Lebanon, Iraq, Trans-Jordan and Egypt. The third, the ten days from July 9 to July 19, when Saudi Arabia joined the incursion.

All three phases strangely resemble the Bible story. Chapters from Joshua and Judges might have been written today.

'And it came to pass, when all the kings which were on this side of Jordan, in the hills, and in the valleys, and in all the coasts of the great sea over against Lebanon, the Hittite and the

Amorite, the Canaanite, the Perizzite, the Hivite, and the Jebusite, heard thereof: That they gathered themselves together, to fight with Joshua and with Israel, with one accord.'

'And these are the kings of the country which Joshua and the children of Israel smote ... in the mountains, and in the valleys, and in the plains, and in the springs, and in the wilderness, and in the south country ... all the kings thirty and one.' Only the names of the 'kings' have changed.

But there is one great difference. In Bible times, the children of Israel fought only the inhabitants of the land and the sheikhs of towns and villages who were grandiosely styled 'kings'—the king of Jarmuth, the king of Lachish, the king of Jericho, the king of Eglon, the king of Gezer, the king of Debir. Were we to do the same today, we should be calling our adversaries the king of Bet Susin, the king of Bet Nabala, the king of Bet Machsir, and so forth. That, however, is of little import. What differs is that never before had we to join battle with all our neighbors at once. None of our recent foemen are strangers to our history. More than once have we met Egypt and Assyria, Babylon and Aram, Canaan and Amalek, but always singly, never in concerted aggression, never the whole Middle East together against us, never in our 3,500 years.

One likeness there is between us now and our forefathers in the war of Saul and Jonathan against the crafty Philistines. 'Now there was no smith famed throughout the land of Israel: for the Philistines said, lest the Hebrews make them swords or spears. So it came to pass in the day of battle, that there was neither sword nor spear found in the hand of any of the people that were with Saul and Jonathan.' Not less vindictively, the British took care that there should be no smith in Israel, neither sword nor spear. They blockaded us by land and water, so that no arms might reach us, their constables pried and probed for our arsenals. Who will forget the searches by massive detachments of troops and police in our villages, our schools, and synagogues, to uncover and distrain on every sword and spear of Israel? Drastic laws were passed against military training, and it was at the Yishuv they were aimed. Who would have ventured, nine or ten months ago, that we should hold on? Yet today history records we did, that we withstood and broke the full shock of the grand Arab alliance.

Disappointed of the lightning victory they had schemed, the conspirators could not see or would not admit facts, and when the United Nations envoy called for an extension of the cease-fire, and we agreed, the Arab States would not. Some thought our agreement a sign of weakness, the Arab refusal a sign of self-confidence. The ten days that followed July 9, ten glorious days in our history, have given the Arab peoples and leaders, and the whole world, the plainest and most final of answers. Victim though it had been of an intensified embargo so that neither sword nor spear should come into its hands, our Army opened a general offensive upon all Arab concentrations as soon as the truce ended, and laid low the 'kings' of Lydda and Ramleh, the 'kings' of Bet Nabala and Deir Tarif, the 'kings' of Kolah and Migdal Zedek, the 'kings' of Tzorah and Eshtaol, the 'kings' of Artuf and Ain Karim in the lowlands, the 'kings' of Chatah and Kretiya in the south, the 'kings' of Shfaram and Zipori, the 'kings' of Ain Mahil and Kafr Kana, Nazareth and Nimrin in Galilee, the 'kings' of Lubiyah and of the Horns of Hittin where Saladin vanquished the Crusader hosts. And, within the selfsame ten days, it smote the hosts of Egypt and Trans-Jordan, Babylon which is Iraq, Syria and the Lebanon and the famed Kaukji, and slew more than five thousand men. A thousand square kilometers have been added to the State.

Soon we shall tell the whole wonderful tale of the Army, from its furtive birth to its triumphant arms and organization today. But one thing I can and do now reveal—the secret weapon that helped us most to stand fast and win. It was the spirit of the Jew, pioneer and fighter, the spirit of vision, faith and devotion shining in our youth, our settlers, our Army, that for seventy years created here the soul of man and earth, and gave us strength to build this Land and all that illumines and sustains it. With the spirit victory came to us in the past. And if we are again to be tried in war, it will make us victors again. In that, Gentlemen, I do solemnly believe.

MEETING THE FUTURE
July 23, 1948

Have we won the war? You may find my question very odd. You will point to the undeniable fact of our successes through every stage of the fighting—against local gunmen, then infiltrators and, in the end, standing armies—until the second cease-fire five days ago. Still, I ask the question, for it is only the final victory that counts, that decides the issue. You may win every battle from the start almost to the finish of war but if you lose the last you lose all, and your earlier victories are in vain. To know whether we have really won or not, we must have fought the last battle, we must know whether this cease-fire marks the end of the war or just a brief respite. If it is only a breathing space, then the issue is undecided, unless we make sure now of winning the last battle when it comes.

Actually, there is good reason to suppose that we are nearing the end. The great Powers do not want the war to be prolonged. The whole world—so far as the world has a collective will—does not want it. That is the meaning of the cease-fire order of the Security Council, against which only Syria voted.

Moreover the military weakness of the Arab States has been exposed, and those who trusted in them have begun to doubt the wisdom of continuing. There is also the disclosure of disunity among the Arabs, and their incompetence to stand up to the ordeal. But let us not minimize our own troubles: we were all jubilant at the Army's triumphs, yet we breathed more freely when enemy aircraft stopped bombing Tel Aviv and Jerusalem was spared cannonade at last.

So beware of hasty self-congratulations and concentrate on the concluding round. Even if all goes well, and peace is formally arranged, we must be strong to be secure, for in the present world there can be no enduring peace.

Meanwhile, take heed that only destruction of the enemy is the final verdict. That verdict we won against the Arabs of Palestine and they quailed before us. But it is, as we knew it would be, a duel between us and the Arab States; and though they have taken a hard beating, they are not knocked out. Politically as much as in the field, they still have plenty of fight left, and for us, therefore, military preparedness is still the central theme. We need, above all, combatant reserves. All our effectives are in the front-line and committed to battle. Had we only had one or two reserve brigades beforehand, the truce would have 'broken out' in totally different circumstances. We cannot do without them hereafter.

We need a large supplement of tanks, artillery and aircraft, and we need shock troops, commandos and paratroops to land behind the enemy lines in surprise forays.

* * *

We now approach a momentous, an unprecedented, turning-point in our history. We are the actors in a revolutionary drama, protagonists in an epic struggle: to gather in the exiles, to rebuild the wastes of the Homeland, to create a society of workers. These aims are not distinct and separate, but in all truth diverse manifestations of one vision of perfect redemption, and by military and political victory the attainment of our threefold ideal will be ensured.

You may ask: why all this talk and theorizing now? What will be our job after victory? Is it not our duty to strain all our resources and strength without stint or qualm to achieve our sole objective—victory? Let us win first—then we shall settle what to do.

Napoleon, who knew his business, has given the simple answer. He used to say that two forces govern man's history: the sword and the spirit, and that in the final reckoning the spirit prevails. Regiments and armor mean a lot, but the Arabs have more of those than we, and it is in the spiritual asset that we must ascend, complementing but outweighing the physical. The events of the last eight months have confounded the wastrels, the spineless, who are blind to ethical superiority. The essence of it is that the soldier knows what he is fighting for, that it is worth fighting and dying for. The Jewish soldier is irresistible and unconquerable because he knows he is fighting for the full deliverance of his people, its perfect redemption. No part of our threefold ideal will be realized without military victory. But neither military nor political victory of itself can make a realization endure; it only makes it possible, and even so there are tremendous difficulties in the way.

Our Arab encirclement is one: even after decisive victory we shall remain neighbors of the Arab nations, we shall live in a backward environment of poverty and disease, illiteracy and exploitation, where persist cheap labor and low standards, a feudal society and the habits of serfdom. Therein we must develop in all its diversity an advanced economy based upon Jewish labor with its multifarious needs and at a high social and cultural level, upon freedom and mutual help, upon a lofty concept of civilization. We must set up a Government consecrated to the principles of democracy, to the rights of man, civil and political equality. We know from our own experience of settlement here how hard it is going to be. There will, of course, be changes in the Arab countries, but ancient traditions of society, economics and statecraft are not swept away overnight. Thirty years ago, Russia was the scene of the most violent revolution in human affairs, a revolution more audacious and venturesome than any in history. Today, the masses and workers of Russia languish in conditions far inferior to their counterparts in America, and their paradise may still be very far away.

Next, the colossal productivity of highly developed States. On one hand, the sloth of our Arab periphery will be a drag upon our forward-looking system, on the other, we will be outdone contrariwise by such wealthy and progressive countries as the United States where production and the capacity to produce have risen to fabulous heights in the course of the second World War, where techniques are being fantastically improved day after day. How are we to compete with that prodigious output, and others hardly less startling? That is the problem for us, who for immigration's sake must build up a wide industrial range, not only for the home market, but for export as well.

And again, how shall we reconcile the demands of security, which are bound to swallow up a good deal of the post-war energies and finances of the nation, with the needs of Aliyah and colonization, that weigh us so heavily down? And what of our deserts, bleak and waterless?

One difficulty I shrink from speaking of: shall we find Jews enough for the Jewish State? Ten years ago such a question would never have leaped to our lips. Now, after Hitler's savagery, it rends our heart. Only a remnant of European Jewry survives, most of it behind bars. Will they soon be free? Our doors are open wide!

I hope I have said enough to make you understand that victory alone, be it the most conclusive in war and in politics, will not solve all our problems. Even if we emerge into the light, our path will be beset by stumbling-blocks and vexed by misadventures. How to win through? By two means: by science and halutziuth, by intellectual and moral primacy.

Science is man's dominion over the forces of nature and its elements. It is his quality, of intellect and thought, to unveil nature's secrets and master them. We live in an age of scientific upheaval, the discovery of the atom, its amazing structure and the tremendous power unleashed in its splitting and radiation.

Well-nigh infinite reserves of vast energy have been given into the hands of man. We go forward nowadays with giant strides, speaking across the ether and annihilating space. Chemical and bacteriological inventions are revolutionizing the principles of agriculture, and the immense outputs made possible by new techniques open up undreamt-of vistas for industry. We exist and work in three dimensions: on land, in the air, under the sea. To escape the atomic bomb, men are beginning to dwell in the bowels of the earth, and the human spirit spurns all bounds of time or place.

We fall short of other nations, being few, and less imperial, but in intellectual gifts we admit none our better. We do not lag behind others in science and research. Till now, it is true, we wasted spiritual treasures in foreign climes and it was for others and not ourselves we helped to bring about the great scientific feats of the nineteenth and twentieth centuries in physics and chemistry, in mathematics, biology and technology. Why doubt that the scientific genius of the Jew may find as nourishing soil in its Homeland? Wrapped in a new cloak of freedom and statehood, heir to spiritual perfection in a society of his own countrymen, surely the strength he draws from his native earth, the robust encouragement he receives from his prideful brothers, will launch Israel's science winging to the skies! The State must fail in the performance of developmental works and in the absorption of mass immigration unless science is king of all, unless the furthest advances, technological and scientific, are pressed into the service of our agriculture, industry and crafts, our seamanship, aviation and housing, unless the maximum incentives are held out to scientific workers, pure and applied, to extend their enquiry. Only so can we raise our productivity, enhance the quality of our products, and exploit to the full the riches that nature has stored in our earth, and in our seas and rivers, in our sunbathed air. We shall harness the urgent winds and tumbling waves; our research will pry, for our boon, into all nature's secrets. Only with the powerful aid of science can we dispel the destitution and neglect of this Land and withstand the impact of its near and distant environs. We must apply our finest minds to scientific discovery and innovation, uphold the hegemony of science and set its mark on all we do.

But that is not all—there must be the pioneer spirit. By science, man governs nature; by halutziuth, himself. Science serves the needs of humanity, good or evil; halutziuth awakens the dormant strength of will and mind, the sleeping soul of man, and guides them in a new flowering to ends that ethics and history discern. Science is a mighty instrument and does wonders, but it is blind and subject, docile as clay in the potter's hands. Halutziuth charts the actions of man, judicially it measures their spiritual content and inspires him to his highest flights. It unites his intellectual and moral greatness and makes him even greater. It will not compromise or yield, it will not despair; it does not bow down to circumstances. It challenges and rebels, it dares and it transforms, it sees coming events, and perfection is its aim. It alters the present for the sake not of today's wants, but of generations to come, not to gratify the individual but for the common good, not for personal gain but to profit all society and each member of it. It makes every scientist a saint, every man a giant.

Halutziuth will not recognize the conventional grouping of men into a talented elite, the thinkers and leaders, on one hand, and the colorless clay of lesser mortals on the other. As in nature, so in man are concealed forces and skills whereof little has yet come to light, unplumbed depths of impulse and ambition, dynamic aptitudes waiting for release and the stimulus of creating.

For halutziuth there are no good and bad impulses. The pioneer, dedicating the virtues of his spirit to the ultimate purpose he serves and which ennobles him, can offer up his vices, if we may so call them, no less. Soldiering affords a vivid illustration.

We all fear death. But the innocent fool does not understand that his only salvation is to stand firm beside his comrade in a joint effort to defeat the enemy: he runs away and brings disaster upon all. Unreasoning fear makes him a poltroon and most often, victim of his own panic, he falls into the very trap he sought to flee. The wise soldier, no less fearful of death, charges the enemy with his comrades, and most often survives; savior reason has turned his fear to courage. The difference at bottom is between the man of faith in his comrade and in himself, and the man of no faith. One conquers fear, the other is its slave; one follows the hard way that is easier in the end, the other sees the easy path and finds it painful. Halutziuth elects the line of greatest resistance, to make its triumph the greater. Heroism is not the monopoly of a few, but the gift of every man who would use it. Two World Wars have given proof of it in millions. Without the need and opportunity for courage in the mass, none of these countless heroes of accident would have suspected the valor in themselves. There are no peaks to which man cannot climb, no handicap he cannot surmount—that is the simple, proven faith of halutziuth: its first commandment is to defy circumstances and facts, to refashion our lives as our historic vision bids.

It is a product of human liberty. Its outpourings are willed by self-control, that checks impulses or heightens them, that draws creativeness and courage from the wellsprings of the soul. Without freedom we cannot discipline ourselves. A robot cannot be a pioneer, for he patterns his life to others' designs, a decadent personification of submission, impotent over his own desires and thoughts. A robot can do great things, like any lifeless machine, but only in the hands of a skilled engineer. He is no creator, but raw stuff. The pioneer makes his own life and his friends'.

And man must be equal, to be pioneer. Where discrimination is rife and creation only for a favored few, the fountain of halutziuth is choked and runs dry. Only where men are peers does the rich fountain flow of man's secret worth. And last, the cooperation of man is necessary: his trust in society, an attachment to his fellows, a will to unity.

Halutziuth is service to commonalty, that is its beginning and its end. Those that prey upon their brethren, that rouse discord and faction among peoples or aggrandize themselves over their fellow-men and ill-use them—all such flaunt the banner of service and, pretending solicitude, oppress and rob. Has service the public interest at heart, or is it only a mask for social ambition, the lust for power, domination, and glory? The test is simple but sure: can the service, should the service, be an act of the whole community and of each separate member? Only what is proper and worthy to be so performed is true halutziuth.

Not even goodness of intent is enough. What you do must be a public example, and become public property, not just service to the public, but service by the public. To serve the public faithfully and truly, halutziuth must be undivided in its faith in the people, by the people it must be invigorated and to the people dedicate itself. All else is contradiction and glorified betrayal of its very essence and origin.

What halutziuth has done for us in the past, what it will yet do, I need not say. But it is my duty to enjoin upon us all a redoubling of our united effort to establish for ever the conditions of the intensive halutziuth we shall need to meet approaching tribulations—and those conditions are liberty, social equality and public spirit. Already calamity has overtaken the pioneer movement in Israel. First it was split by Hashomer Hatzair, then by Hapoel Hamizrahi, and lastly by the left wing of Hakibbutz Hameuhad. But let not your spirits droop: it was not halutziuth that failed, but its lack and counterfeit. For there are degrees of it and only those who are half, or third, or quarter pioneers would dream of schism and disintegration. Therefore will our trust be unimpaired in the pioneer capacity of man and worker in Israel, and we shall not strike our colors so long as the spark of halutziuth is alive in us. Unity is not out of reach; the more we fan the spark and with it ignite our ranks far and wide, the higher the hopes of solidarity.

In the last half-year we have seen events and exploits that rocked the people. We believed these things would be, we heralded them, though many scoffed, and sought to prove they could not be. But faith, resolution and foresight did not betray us. We are yet in the anteroom of our new palace of history, and the portals of its great chamber are heavily barred. One key to them is pioneer strength and will. Let us take on new vigor, let us gather the scattered embers, let us unfurl our banner in all its radiant hues—the banner of halutziuth that is one with equality and freedom, with unity of labor and nation. Let us have in our hearts confidence in individual man and in society. Let us cherish the vision of utter redemption, and for its sake assemble the searchers for truth and accomplishment. Let us proclaim a partnership of men of action in creativeness, of scientists and executants together. Then will all our troubles be as the snows of yesteryear.

FREEDOM AND INDEPENDENCE
August 13, 1948

We live in time unique, for vision has become real. Real, but fragmentary yet and infirm, nor are we, or is the world about us, accustomed yet to the wonder of it. The transformation is still imperfectly viewed in our thoughts and planning, and in current affairs.

We live through days that may shine brighter than any in Jewish history and we have witnessed in them two events of superlative moment.

First a vicious attack launched upon us to destroy our life and hopes: we threw it back, and till now our arms have been victorious.

And then, we set up a Jewish State. Three months have passed. and there is no sign of tremor or weakening. In concept and reality, the State is strengthened day after day. Here, then, is cause for joy, and here, too, dangers lurk.

We have yet to end the war, to win its final victory. As the war went on, the surer did our successes become; but they have not brought decision, yet. The enemy besets our borders, even stands somewhere on our soil.

The truce is no milestone on the way to peace, nor even a true armistice. And what strange truce is this that the Arabs break again and again in hostile acts, crowning their sullen moods by destruction of the pumping station at Latrun, a wanton sabotage aimed at Jewish Jerusalem?

Even were it kept to the letter, and all the Arab States scrupulous in observance, we still could not accept it indefinitely. For it means foreign oversight of our State and foreign oversight especially of immigration. Neither the one control nor the other can we countenance for long. If the United Nations lack the power or the will to bring about an early peace, we must try to do it ourselves. If the United Nations cannot evict the invaders from the territory of Israel, we must try to do that ourselves as well. This little Land will have to do what the United Nations will not or cannot—and we must be so prepared.

That is why we dare not regard as firmly set or settled what we have so far achieved. For all our resounding victories, it is what still may happen that will decide. We cannot be certain, even, that the State will yet live. It is not to disparage the part of the United Nations, of the General Assembly in November 14, it is not self-glorification or an overweening conceit of our powers, if with simple honesty we claim the right to say that this Jewish State was established, not by the United Nations, but by our own hands. The fact some may aver with chagrin, some with satisfaction: none will gainsay it.

The United Nations felt no urge, it seems, to carry out their own Resolution; perhaps the grace was wanting, perhaps the means. At all events, had we been left to the sole mercy of the Resolution, the State would have been still-born, and Israel given over to bloodshed and chaos.

The Jews, the Jews in this very Land, established the State; they have persevered in its establishment these three months past, pitting their strength against the massed Arab assault.

It is only very slowly that the State's being impinges upon the consciousness of the world: many Governments have yet to recognize it, even if their citizens already see it as a pulsing and dynamic force. It is delusion to think the work done.

The edifice of State is unfinished, perchance the fatal battle has still to be fought, our frontiers are undetermined still and undecided, if ever indeed frontiers can be irrevocably fixed. Domestic controversy about them neither helps nor hinders. We must strive to fix them by Jewish-Arab agreement, but be ready, if need be, to hack them out with the sword's edge should accord be unattained. It is already patent that the Resolution of November 1947, in its bearing upon frontiers, was set at naught when, striking at us, the Arabs struck at the authority of the United Nations, and the United Nations, unwilling or unable, shrank from the challenge. The plan we steeled ourselves to accept in the last resort, for the sake of its international endorsement, is relevant no longer: after all that has happened in Israel and in the Middle East, and within the United Nations, it has lost all point whether touching Jerusalem and its approaches, or Galilee, and much besides.

But even when, out of history's crucible, there shall come the solid metal of our boundaries and of our place as State among the nations, a metal clear-cast and finally assayed, we shall still be distant from our statehood's purpose the ingathering of the exiles.

I hold the basic determining premise at the heart of all our thoughts, our whole Movement, our policy, to be this, that the State is not in itself an aim: it is a means to an end, the end of Zionism. A State of seven hundred, eight hundred, thousand Jews cannot be the climax of a vigil kept unbroken through the generations and down the patient centuries; nor could it last for long.

That we defeated six Arab nations was miraculous, a miracle of superior intellect and moral strength, and, if a second encounter must be, I believe we shall defeat them again by the same advantage. But we cannot construct our present or our future on the weaknesses of others, on Arab frailty. The Arabs too will arm themselves in the course of time; they will not always lack learning and technical skills.

No, even if unperturbed by external dangers, so empty a State would be little justified, for it would not change the destiny of Jewry, or fulfill our historic covenant.

Immigration in the myriads that only sovereignty allows, settlement upon a scale never before possible—these alone will justify it. It is without wit or profit to argue whether immigrants are to be counted in thousands or in hundreds of thousands: the duty of the State is to end Galuth at last. Perhaps our generation will not live to see a homecoming from the New World or from Russia in the Old, but when the war is over and the State made strong, what let or hindrance will deny us early sight of the ending of the Diaspora in Moslem lands of North Africa and the Middle East, in Western Europe no less? What the Zionist Organization could not accomplish under foreign rule, hostile, indifferent, or even friendly, a Jewish State can and must, so be it commands the loyal aid of world Jewry and the nations do not wholly forsake us.

We must rid ourselves of the attitudes of mind and ways of thinking that once were rational and warranted, but are antiquated in the new age of Israel. Not that I believe the State all-powerful. No State, however rich and mighty, can be that, least of all Israel. We must not blind ourselves to difficulties imminent within and without, to our own shortcomings and the troubles which the Gentiles, kindly or cruel, will make for us, or to the economic and financial tribulations that will vex the State and bow it down. Plainly, the State in isolation is not equal to the task, but with all the drawbacks and defects of a young republic beset by enmity and peril, no other instrument, no other agent to vindicate the dream of Zionism, can compare. In the State new horizons open and prospects dawn we dreamt not of before; and we need a new approach and re-orienting of all our relationships and systems.

We are still only at the lintel of the State, for our chief concern at this moment is not its building but its safety. The ordinary budget is, I think, some IL700,000 or IL800,000 a month: the budget for defense is several times as much. Our best men and women are held fast in the Defense Army, and pitilessly must there be held, I cannot say how long, whether weeks or months; and I know full well the tragedy my words may forebode. The time is not yet, or so I, at least, in my secret heart avow, to think seriously of anything except security. I am very willing to learn from those of our friends, less backward than I, who have already contrived to delve into other problems that concern the State and its coming enterprises. One thing, however, is clear to me too, the necessity of the Zionist Movement and Organization as the core of the whole Jewish people, helping to shape and safeguard the State. I find it hard to credit that there will not be far-reaching changes in the relationship between State and Organization, but I do not echo the lamentations and plaints lately voiced that the magic of the State has somehow dimmed or diminished the light of the Organization.

The candle of the State still casts only a fitful gleam. Key though it is to the heart of the nation, the State cannot open the portal of fulfillment if Jewry stands aloof.

Inherently, the strength and capacity of the State will depend a great deal on the place within it that the Labor movement occupies. Alas! in the very days of our most acid test, when in Europe millions of Jews were horribly slaughtered, the movement split, and split yet more widely in the momentous phase of the War of Independence and the State's establishment. This was a stinging self-defeat, and a tragic one, and no present hope appears of mending the rift. But let there be no furling of the flag that proclaims the unity of the workers: for it is the pennant of truth and of deliverance. Let there be neither fear nor shame that we are 'Utopians.' Let us not estrange ourselves from a vision radiant with truth and the high call of history. It might seem that in the conditions that irk us today the vision could never come to pass. But those conditions are not immutable. We bore aloft the symbol of the State when practical men, men who talk realism, derided. Unity of the workers is vital; without it, what chance is there for divided mankind? And that unity we will miss until we understand that it cannot come out of talking with one voice or thinking with a single thought, such as unites only robots or slaves. We have ourselves seen that you may turn men into robots, but, even so, the transformation cannot last forever. In any movement of free men there is bound to be discord, and unity must stem then from a common way of life, an historical vision shared. It is not accident that certain political groups of workers, Israel not excluded, deny freedom of thought and discussion, deny the right of the majority to decide, and bow to the dictatorship of the few or one. In Israel the crucial party argument was whether to declare a State or not. In the end, it was history, not a majority, that cast the die. That issue, I think, our opponents accept, but at the same time it has given rise to new sources of conflict, and sharpened older differences. However we debate, there are three essentials upon which we must uncompromisingly insist. First is independence, and not just national sovereignty, or political and economic self-government. Independence must begin in our hearts. Without moral and intellectual independence there is no anchor for national independence. No enslavement is as deadly as the spirit's. No nation can be free whose thoughts and actions a foreign tyranny dictates. Not that we must quarrel with every way of government that we cannot admire, or with every ruler who dissents from us. Historical forces impel each nation along its own path, and each, in turn, directs them according to its own desires.

Nor does independence mean standing alone. There are necessary links between nations and States, economic, political, and in ways of thought. Just as economic autarchy is inconceivable, so is intellectual. We may learn from other nations, and gain by the stored-up experience of mankind. But there is a fundamental difference between learning from others and truckling to their opinion, an essential gap between employing the experience of others and being slaves to their mind.

The second is freedom of the individual. Neither the workers' movement nor the State is a theocracy that can lay down what is truth. To no form of government are a man's thoughts subject, not even to government by majority. A man may, of full right, defy the world entire if in his eyes it is led astray, pursuing vain things and in its ideas deluded. Freedom of the mind is not limited or fenced about. A man may choose to differ from every agreed opinion, to challenge every accepted axiom, and still no government, no party, no world-wide organization has authority to prescribe to him what is truth and what untruth. Indeed, each new truth is first revealed to some single man. Government holds no sway over that which is in a man's heart, or over aught concerning science, aesthetics and art.

The third is free choice of the people's representatives, in political idiom—democracy. Man is not instrument but end, each man is as free as his fellow, his rights and freedom of action restrained only by his fellow's. What goes beyond the personal concerns of the individual and is done on behalf of the people must be determined by the free choice of the many, unbound by wish of ruler or rival. A nation that is not free to challenge its rulers, and replace them as may be its will, is no free nation, but a miserable multitude that exists only by a despot's favor.

For these three things we shall fight, as workers, as men, as Jews and as Zionists. We will not surrender them, for they are of our very souls. Zionism and socialism, both, are reft of their meaning and become ghosts if our independence, our liberty, our free choice of leaders, are spoiled or are destroyed.

THE SOUTHERN FRONT
*At the twenty-fourth session of the
Provisional State Council,
October 28, 1948*

Councillors! I am come to survey briefly before you the Battle of the South. It lasted exactly one week, from the fifteenth to the twenty-second of October. It was important in many respects: the authority of the United Nations, the competing strength of forces in the Middle East, the future of Israel. It tested the practical value of the truce, how efficient were the United Nations observers in execution and how capable, how united and effective was the Arab League, what substance there was in the Gaza Government, the prowess of the Egyptian Army, and the skill of ours. I venture to claim that only our Army stood the test.

At no time did we approve the truce, nor do we now. But we accepted it, being instructed by the United Nations so to do. We demur because it rather implies 'legality' of the invasion and gives an internationally recognized status of a kind to those who perpetrated it, by equating aggression and defense. In our opinion it needlessly lengthens the way and harms both Arabs and Jews. It is in no wise a means for peace, as three previous truces showed. We agreed because our policy stands true with the United Nations. We are sensible of the weakness of the United Nations, but think it shortsighted to seek to exploit it. We believe that our interest as Jews and as men is to enhance the jurisdiction and efficacy of the United Nations. Were the United Nations to perish, it would be the blackest day in man's history, and the most tragic in ours. No less than other nations, maybe more, we are concerned with world peace, with international cooperation, with the universal rule of law, with peaceful settlement of international squabbles, with amity between East and West. That is why, in loyalty, we agreed to the truce: the veriest child knows it was not out of military impotence, and we did not, nor ever shall, agree to a one-sided truce. And right from the start it was obvious to us that the truce laid upon the Arabs and ourselves was one-sided on all fronts and at all times. Hardly a day passed without its violation by the enemy. You had only to spend a night in Jerusalem to hear and see and feel that it was non-existent. There was almost no halt in the enemy's shelling or in his attacks. It is not only violation by gunfire. The fundamental principle is that neither side should profit, augment its forces or gain any military advantage. But the Egyptians, all along, brought up reserves and arms, and pressed the local inhabitants into a labor gang to build a defense-line. They went even further—flagrantly, again and again, they flouted a vital decision of the United Nations observers, on which turned the genuineness of the truce.

When the second truce began, on July 18 I think, the situation in the South was curious. The Egyptians held the east-west line from Majdal to Bet Jubrin. We held the north-south line, and the lines intersected near Kartuja. Each side could have cut the other's communications, and so the United Nations observers decided that convoys of either might proceed: Egypt using the east-west line in the afternoons, and we the north-south in the mornings.

The Egyptians disregarded the decision on two counts.

First, they thought the observers were unwilling or unable to enforce it, and indeed they had ground to think so after what happened at Latrun, when the Arabs defied them and would not pump water to Jerusalem, and even blew up the pumping station, all with impunity.

Secondly, they assumed that Israel and its Army would not and could not themselves enforce the decision. And not entirely without cause, for of all the Arab hosts only the Egyptian could boast a little that it had not been defeated. Our successes were won in the main against the Arab Legion, the Iraqis, the Syrians and the Lebanese. Not that the Egyptians did much more than capture two of our villages: their victories, such as they were, in Ashdod, Beersheba, and Gaza were over Arabs.

At all events, they felt safe from military reversal and expected no challenge on our part, so for three months they barred the way to our settlement and Army convoys.

Their first assumption came true. The United Nations—and who am I to sit in judgment and pronounce the verdict?—either would not or could not carry out the decision and uphold the cardinal purpose of the truce. The Egyptians had not asked for a truce; the United Nations decided on it. But it is no truce if it disallows free access to our settlers and soldiers in the south, and the United Nations failed of their duty.

Week after week we appealed to them to enable us to pass convoys through, each time the answer was: 'You are right, but the Arabs say no. We shall try.'

We waited weeks, months. Not by any means stockstill, for we discovered another way of bringing supplies to the southern outposts. But it was our right to do so by the simpler way, and eventually our patience gave out.

On Friday, the twelfth of Tishri, a convoy left for the Negev. The United Nations had still to get Egyptian consent, but this was now three months after the decision on convoys had been taken, and longer since the beginning of the truce. The Egyptians attacked the convoy and our men were obliged to fall back. Several lorries were burned out. Thereupon our Army was ordered to clear the road, and did.

DAVID BEN GURION

A statement to the Security Committee,
January 7, 1949

The Battle for the Negev which ends today, like the Battle of the South before it, was due to Egyptian refusal to obey the directions of the United Nations observers. On November 16, the Security Council called upon the Egyptians and ourselves to start peace talks. We were entirely ready and willing. The Egyptians held back at first, but on the eve of his departure for America Dr. Bunche informed us that they had agreed and he asked us to permit the phased withdrawal of the Egyptian army from Falluja. We were agreeable, provided evacuation and peace talks went on simultaneously—we would permit the first stage of evacuation and talks would open at once, and as they progressed, the evacuation would enter on its second stage.

Dr. Bunche regarded our attitude as prudent and correct. After he had left, however, the United Nations supervisor conveyed to us what was tantamount to an Egyptian change of heart, to wit, a claim that, before talks could begin, the Security Council's decisions of November 4 should be fulfilled and our Army withdraw to the lines it held prior to the Battle of the South and give up Beersheba. We replied that we saw in the claim a repudiation of peace talks and of the Council's decisions of November 16, and that we must now allow ourselves freedom to act for a speedy peace and the defense of our Negev territory.

The military operations we undertook from December 23 to January 7 were successful in both ways: the Egyptians, beaten in the field, soon avowed willingness to discuss terms, and the entire Negev was rid of their troops.

There were enormous difficulties of transport and communication. The only road in is from Beersheba to Auja, and the Egyptians straddled it, so we had to make new paths through deserts untracked before by modern chariots of iron. Phenomenal labor was expended to move materials and net the sand for tanks to cross. It was, in fact, the engineers and transport services that largely turned the scales.

There were supply troubles too. We were fighting very far from our bases, and had to stock a great deal of food and fuel against the possibility of our communications being interrupted, for which purpose we were obliged to commandeer many civilian vehicles, though our plans were kept secret until the very last moment. Traffic was badly tied up, for from the North there is a proper road only as far as Bureir; thence to Saad, along the Beersheba-Gaza road, the surface is shocking, and to add to our trials heavy rain fell on zero day and the area was flooded. Lorries had to be hauled by tractor, and the tractors were often bogged down themselves.

The Egyptians were extraordinarily well dug in and we knew we could only beat them by surprise. We feinted at Gaza to draw off their forces from the Negev. As it was, they had large concentrations with tanks and heavy artillery in the Gaza sector as well, so after we had taken several strongpoints there a considerable Egyptian force engaged us, and our 13th battalion— one of the best—was compelled to retreat with serious losses.

These encounters near Gaza lasted four days, and the Egyptians were convinced that it was our objective. Our main attack at Auja had to be put off for twenty-four hours when the heavens intervened, but then Auja was captured by a surprise sortie, next Bir Asluj, and the road was cleared. Many of the enemy were captured, the rest fled. A few high ranking officers among those taken told us it had never entered their heads that an attack would be launched from the east, which is trackless and all sand and rocks.

Three days afterwards we had crossed the Sinai frontier and on the fourth day reached Abu Ageila, where is the junction of the roads to Ismailia southward, El Arish westward, Rafa to the northwest, and northeasterly Beersheba.

With Abu Ageila gone, the Egyptians had only one line of

communication left—the railway, which our aircraft bombed with effect, and we advanced toward El Arish, as far as the airfield, where we found dummy planes. At the same time we brought artillery and aircraft into action against the Falluja 'pocket' in the northern Negev. One battalion broke into Irak-Manshieh, but was thrust back by counterattack in strength from the 'pocket' and suffered heavy casualties. We still encircle Falluja and it is under constant bombardment, but the Egyptians are making a gallant stand and though their supplies are running out and their situation is desperate, they will not surrender.

All three armies took part in the Battle for the Negev. The navy shelled the Egyptian coast and the long-range shore batteries did not score a hit against it; patrols steamed right to Port Said without meeting a single enemy craft.

Our pilots did terrific mischief and virtually paralyzed the Egyptian fliers. Just once, six enemy planes appeared near Falluja: one was brought down, two were damaged, and the rest turned tail. In a second dog-fight we shot down several more, and that was the end of Egyptian air power in the campaign.

In Sinai, we risked collision with the British garrison, and our troops were consequently ordered to withdraw from Abu Ageila and take Rafa, so as to bottle up the Egyptian detachment in Gaza. Near Rafa there is a circular network of roads, and one links Rafa with Auja, crossing the border in a semi-circular alignment. Thereafter the Army had instructions not to enter by that road unless Rafa operations necessitated. The Egyptians were much too heavily entrenched on the Gaza-Rafa front, however, and though we seized some commanding positions, we failed to isolate Gaza or take Rafa. The Egyptians were stubborn fighters, with great quantities of heavy armament, and their fire-orders were amazingly effective.

* * *

Today at 1400 hours, hostilities are to cease. A Committee of the Security Council meets today in New York to determine the fact. The Egyptians have declared that 'if the cease-fire goes into genuine effect on January 5 their Government is prepared to instruct its representatives to open negotiations at once with representatives of Israel concerning the carrying out of the decisions of the Security Council of November 4 and 16.'

This announcement was only passed on to us by the United Nations after the time set, because it had been forwarded from Cairo to New York, and relayed thence to the United Nations people in Haifa. We were asked if we would be ready to cease fire on January 6, and said yes, provided we had timely intimation of similar assent from the Egyptian Government. Finally, owing to circuitous communications, the cease-fire agreement was fixed for today, January 7.

This was the first declaration by an Arab State of parleys with the Israel Government, and it has a political significance beyond the bounds of the local dispute. The Arab States—and Egypt is the largest of them—have protested hitherto their unwillingness to recognize Israel or negotiate with us. It is true that Egypt cites the decisions of November 4, which entail withdrawal to the earlier lines and the evacuation of Beersheba, but the decision of November 16 is also cited which makes no such demands but specifically requires the parties to start peace talks. Obviously the November 4 conditions are out of the question: only November 16 counts, and that means an armistice—and peace.

Until negotiations begin, we cannot, of course, be sure, but at least there is a change in Arab policy, and it may be a radical one; and we can point to the attainment of our double objective in the fighting—the Negev wholly ours and peace sped.

IN LIEU OF A SUMMARY
Introduction to 'From Riots to War'
by Yosef Ulitzki, Spring, 1949

This is no story of the Haganah from its birth in the far-off days of Tel Hai, but a chronicle of events in the short space, less than six months, between the decision of the General Assembly that there should be a Jewish State and that State's establishment. But within these narrow bounds, in this brief interval, the fates of Haganah and Jewry entire were entwined. Tel Aviv was the nerve center. Tel Aviv manpower had to defend not only the city and its suburbs, but every part of the country. Tel Aviv youth were sent to the villages of Galilee, the wilderness of the Negev, the hills of Jerusalem: wherever crisis and danger called. Without the men of Tel Aviv, roads could not be kept open, nor lonely farmsteads in Upper Galilee or the southern steppes be protected. The defense of Tel Aviv itself was defense of Yishuv and land.

The book deals with a dramatic transition from foreign rule to Jewish independence, from underground maquis to the Israel Defense Army, from self-defense against guerrillas to tactical defense against regular troops. The events, political and military, which followed May 14, 1948, were more richly spectacular and prolific than all the Haganah did in the five and a half months that preceded it. But they would never have come about had not the Haganah, outlawed though it was by an unfriendly Administration, taken heart to step into the breach, multiplied its numbers, and drafted and equipped and drilled and made them ready to pit themselves against the Arab hosts in mortal encounter.

Understandably enough the magnificent derring-do of the Israel Defense Army after the invasion threw the previous exploits of the Haganah into the shade. There were sixty-one days of battle and in them our little Army, victorious against an overwhelming multitude, changed the destiny of the Land of Israel and the whole Middle East to boot, pushed forward the frontiers of the State, gave us an outlet to the Red Sea, fortified our approach to Jerusalem and secured it.

The Haganah did not fall short of the Defense Army in gallantry, dedication or spontaneity. There have been brilliant, unforgettable chapters in the annals of our defense in Israel between the World Wars, but the passage of intense and critical time from British Mandate to Jewish Republic saw the Haganah charged with its sternest task, saw it display its most splendid courage and most consummate preparedness.

Without in the least detracting from the historic, political or military value of the Army's sixty-one wonderful days, I think our security forces reached the zenith of moral courage precisely during that passage of time. It is right to speak of the 'miracle' of a State that rose from the fire and fury of battle, from the political and administrative chaos left behind by the Mandatory, from famine and from the sword and shot that menaced the Yishuv, but you will misread events if you fail to glimpse the fountain-head whence the Yishuv drew ardor and armor on the glorious eve of the State—that 'illegal' Haganah which schooled us for the acid test, and fore-ran Israel's Defense Army, testator of our honor and sovereignty.

The magic of this stand by an infant soldiery amazed the world, this uprising, over-night almost, to meet a six-fold invasion, the resplendent victories.

A few weeks before the Mandate ended, the Haganah had

not a single cannon: the coast was effectively blockaded by destroyer patrols of the British navy. When trouble started here—I had it from the High Commissioner himself—the British garrison numbered 75,000, not to say thousands of British and Arab constables, and a Frontier Force— practically all Arab, and the Arab Legion.

The Administration closed its eyes to the infiltration of armed bands from Syria and Iraq, the High Commissioner confessed it was not within his power to seal the frontiers—but police force and British army were wide awake to our 'illegal' arming. To smuggle in arms was practically impossible, to move them from point to point difficult and hazardous, and our ordnance men, storekeepers, lorry drivers and Haganah men, and especially women, took frightful risks in shifting weapons from cache to combat.

The Haganah was under orders to avoid involvement with the British, for the real tug-of-war with the Arabs would come only when they had gone, and to localize the disturbances as far as possible. We had to gain time for the showdown, and for all that we were outnumbered even by the local Arabs we never for a moment doubted that, if we were left alone, only with them, our survival was in no danger.

Faithful to its trust, servant of a Yishuv ever peace-loving and ever desirous of cooperation with its neighbors, the Haganah neither attacked nor provoked. But it did not just defend itself when forced to fight. It stormed and destroyed guerrilla hideouts, scrupulous always to distinguish between peaceful and passive Arab villages and those which showed aggression or collaborated with the enemy.

We expected the attack on the Yishuv in that last half-year of the Mandate, and the Haganah had its operational plan long ready.

It was, of course, completely different, in strategy, tactics and arms, from the one the Army later used. Equally it diverged radically from the scheme blueprinted before the second World War. It had to fit a new set of conditions, and the main differential was that we no longer counted on the Administration to help. From 1920 to 1938 our defense plan assumed that the Government was responsible for security and for protecting the Yishuv against Arab violence, and that all our settlements need do was be able to look after themselves until official aid arrived. Now, however, we reckoned that the Government would be neutral at best, if it was not obstructive, and we also foresaw attack not by the local Arabs only, but by infiltrators as well, armed and fitted out by our neighbors. In practice, this meant more than a number of local defense problems. It meant regional defense guaranteeing inter-settlement communication, electricity and pipelines and the sources of staple supply.

Under the plan, the country was divided into defensive districts, sub-districts and regions, and manpower classified by age and training into a Home Guard of the age-group 26 to 40 and above, for static, local fighting; Field Troops of younger men for wider operations of defense; and Shock Troops (Palmach), the only fully mobilized unit on constant full-time all-purpose service, and—within existing limitations—superlatively trained.

The primary task of the Haganah, as I say, was to safeguard our settlements and lines of communications, but here the best defense is attack. Field Troops and Palmach in particular were thus deployed, and quickly showed the mettle that was soon to animate our Army and bring it victory. In Operation 'Nachshon' the road to Jerusalem was cleared at the beginning of April, almost all of New Jerusalem occupied, and the guerrillas were expelled from Haifa, Jaffa, Tiberias and Safad while still the Mandatory was present. It needed sagacity and self-control not to fall foul of the British Army.

The Haganah did its job: until a day or two before the Arab invasion not a settlement was lost, no road cut, although movement was seriously dislocated, despite express assurances of the

British to keep the roads safe so long as they remained. Arabs started fleeing from the cities almost as soon as disturbances began in the early days of December. As fighting spread, the exodus was joined by Beduin and fellahin, but not the remotest Jewish homestead was abandoned and nothing a tottering Administration could unkindly do stopped us from reaching our goal on May 14, 1948, in a State made larger and Jewish by the Haganah.

How, and by what means, did it ride out the storm?

At the outset it had only rifles, machine and sub-machine guns, automatic rifles, two-inch and three-inch mortars, pistols, hand grenades, and Molotov cocktails—very widely distributed, and none easy to get hold of, since everything was cached, and to open a cache or carry arms from place to place was a risky business, as I say.

The Administration's searches for arms, regardless of promises given to the Jewish Agency, put us in hideous jeopardy. Often the British police sided openly with the guerrillas against the Haganah.

The answer to the question is here—in the spontaneous dedication and boundless gallantry of thousands of Haganah men and women, seeking neither material reward nor honors and rank. Save for a small permanent staff, all gave their services voluntarily, and all in modesty, in that saintly namelessness which seeks not praise, nor citation, nor publicity, nor honorific title nor public thanks—but only fulfillment of a duty felt deep within conscience and spirit, a sacred duty for which a man would give his life simply and without vainglory, as a thing universally accepted, as a natural law of existence, unrequited and unpaid in cash or in spiritual kind. That was the Haganah's distinction and its strength—the loyalty of volunteers to the last, no stint or reservation, no payment, no prize.

The Haganah was a free-will band of brothers sworn to guard us with their lives, night and day and everywhere: boys and girls of sixteen were runners and connecting links, men of fifty and more, and all the ages between, manned the trenches tirelessly and unrelieved.

Our Defense Army had not to fight underground, behind it was a recognized and more or less patterned Government. So in training, equipment and organization, in physical and material capacity, it transcended the Haganah. But not even it nor any other army in the world could surpass the Haganah in devotion and dedication. And it is that heritage we must preserve, not just as a valuable memento of the past but as an indestructible asset of our upbringing rare and poignant, finer than the finest gold. The youth, the people, the Army itself, all must be brought up in this shining tradition.

We have today new tools to hammer out the vision of redemption but they lack edge if we cannot perpetuate and exalt the pioneer self-abnegation which was the soul of the Haganah.

THE ROAD OF VALOR
Spoken on December 12, 1948

In the road we open today there is set the crown of our fight for the Homeland and freedom. Into its making went the most tragic heroism and the greatest grandeur of that fight since the day we were called to face our many enemies and save Jerusalem.

This was the heart and soul of the War of Independence that has ranged over the country now for more than a year. It was, it still is, a struggle in the eternal city and round about it, and even more a struggle for the road to it. On mastery of the road hangs the city's fate.

Our Third Return to Israel took a course opposite to the First and the Second. We have come now not westering from the east, but from the Occident moving eastward, not from desert to sea, but from sea to desert. Of the three regions of the Land—mountains, lowland and valley—we possessed the valley first. We took only little of the lowland, and late. Of the mountains, we held almost nothing except for Jerusalem, which in every generation from every quarter drew Jews to it. Within the last century this magnetism has turned Jerusalem into a Jewish metropolis, with a great and growing Jewish majority. But it also meant that Jewish Jerusalem stood severed from the main centers of rural and urban settlement, for it was the coastal belt we held for the most part and the Valleys of Jezreel and Jordan, north of Lake Tiberias and south of it. In normal times the threat to Jerusalem did not strike the eye. An hour's journey to Tel Aviv seemed of little concern, so long as it was safe. How deadly was the danger soon appeared when the Arab States sought to encompass us. Many and bitter were the hurts our settlements endured in this War of Independence: the suffering of Jerusalem alone was seven-fold. Our enemy knew the mortal stroke he might with ease deliver was to seize and destroy this city of ours, distant from all concentrations of Jewish force and surrounded on all sides by a numerous, compact and daring Arab population in towns and villages whence every road led to Jerusalem. The Jews had only one and almost its entire length traversed Arab areas up hill and down dale from Abu Kebir near Tel Aviv to Lifta at the gates of Jerusalem. With strategic astuteness the enemy deployed his strength from the start in the effort to sunder Jerusalem from Tel Aviv and the lowland, to halt all Jewish traffic to the city; and this while the Mandate was still in being, as long ago as December 1947.

The Mandatory undertook to maintain freedom of movement on the road: its promises were not kept, and while yet British troops garrisoned Palestine, hunger and the sword were menacing the Jewish capital. The State was still far off when we realized that, unless unaided we could blast a way through to Jerusalem and occupy a sufficient space on either side of this corridor, the city was doomed and our whole campaign might be lost.

With the incursion of Arab regulars right upon the Proclamation of the State, the concentrated wrath of the enemy was vented upon Jerusalem. As it was in the days of the Prophet Ezekiel: 'For the king of Babylon standeth at the parting of the way, at the head of the two ways, to use divination; he shaketh the arrows to and fro, he inquireth of the teraphim, he looketh in the liver. In his right hand is the lot Jerusalem, to set battering rams, to open the mouth for the slaughter, to lift up the voice with shouting, to set battering-rams against the gates, to cast up mounds, and to build forts.'

In our days the king of Babylon was joined by the king of the sons of Ammon, but the Army and champions of Israel, its builders and engineers, its warriors and workers, set the schemes of Babylon and Ammon at naught; they broke through to right and left, they thrust back the invaders and scattered them. Jerusalem was liberated and a broad, untroubled approach secured.

Thus, as April began, our War of Independence swung decisively from defense to attack. Operation 'Nachshon', to free the road, was launched with the capture of Arab Hulda near where we stand today and of Dir Muhsin, and culminated in the storming of Kastel, the great hill-fortress near Jerusalem, where Abdul Qader el Husseini, perhaps the only real commander among the Arabs of Palestine, fell in action. Jerusalem drew breath freely again, but not for long: reinforcements arrived from other Arab States, and it was beleaguered a second time. Upon it the enemy rained his fiercest blows indiscriminately, viciously, night and day without surcease. British guns, primed by British gunners, bombarded it. Our relief column was led by a gallant and honored American Jew, Colonel David Michael Marcus. He was not fated, alas!, to enter the Jerusalem he came to free, and on the very eve of the first truce he died in the Judean hills.

Here, in the Valley of Ayalon, the Defense Army of Israel, only just taking form, made its first assault on the Arab lines at Latrun. In the van was the Seventh Brigade, newly mobilized, in the main of men landed a few days earlier from the detention camps of Cyprus. Its units in a brave engagement penetrated the village and burned it down, but were forced back by massed artillery. A Palmach Brigade, with typical courage, renewed the assault but it too had to withdraw, not unscathed.

So the Arab Legion held the key still to Sha'ar Hagai, the portal of the valley-way, and Jerusalem was in the toils.

It seemed as though we had been worsted at Latrun, yet the fighting there in actuality saved Jerusalem, even before the first truce gave it a brief respite, for we had compelled the enemy to shift a large part of his strength from the city to the valley; the shelling was more fitful and the citizens were heartened to hold out until the end. And more: the fighting gave us a new and open access from the coast through the foot-hills to Jerusalem. At the end of May the Eleventh Brigade took Beit Jiz and Beit Susin and the Palmach entered Zar'a, birth-place of Samson. These actions hewed out the line of shock and valor we call 'Burma Road,' on to deliverance and the salvation of Jerusalem. Afterwards, it was retraced along an easier and apter line, no longer to be makeshift in emergency but an established and enduring link, flanked by multiplying settlements that will unite to form a living brigade of men and husbandry from the principal zones of Jewish occupancy and power in the State to imperishable Jerusalem.

As we dedicate today this Road of Valor, this path of deliverance, let us remember in deepest thankfulness the soldiers and workers in their thousands who helped in its making, the battalions of infantry and the armored cars, the artillery and the engineers who contrived it, the men who laid the pipe line, the men of Solel-Boneh, from Jerusalem and Tel Aviv, the stout-hearted drivers. They had a proud share in this feat of combat and development, one that will be immortalized in the ageless annals of Zion set free, that will be a monument to Jewish prowess in arms and in labor, the passport, now and always, to victory.

THE NAVY, ISRAEL AND THE SEA
*To the Graduating Class at the Naval College, Haifa,
February 5, 1950*

The Israel Defense Army of today is very young, but Jewish military history is ancient. Our first warrior was the Patriarch Abraham, who did battle with Chedorlaomer and the attendant kings, to rescue Lot and his people. Our first war was fought some centuries later, soon after the Exodus from Egypt, against Amalek at Rephidim. Our first general was Joshua, and Moses, with Aaron and Hur by his side, watched the campaign from the hill-top.

For 2,500 years the hosts of Israel warred in their Land against Canaanite and Philistine, against Egypt, Aram and Edom. So too, they encountered Assyria and Babylon, Greeks and Romans, Byzantines and Crusaders.

At the end of the eleventh century the Jews fought a last battle on their own soil at Haifa, against the Crusaders. In that century the Caliph of Baghdad had given the city to the Jews in return for a yearly tribute. It was a ship-building center and its Jews played an important part in the life of Palestinian Jewry, and in 1084 we find the Gaon Rabbi Eliyahu ben Shlomo Hacohen of Tyre visiting them to renew the gaonate and rabbinical authority in the congregation. But the victorious Crusaders were now upon them; Jerusalem fell in 1099, and in the following year Tancred, made governor of Galilee, launched a powerful attack on Haifa. The Jews defended themselves bravely but the odds against them were too great—the Venetian fleet, to aid Tancred, blockaded Haifa from the sea, and after a siege of fifteen days the city was taken and its population destroyed.

So the Israel Defense Army, if only two years old, has yet a tradition that goes back into antiquity, and its enemies are still those that faced us then: Egypt and Babylon, Aram and Ammon. But Israel had no navy then and it has, at last, one today, the youngest navy in the world.

Our air force is young as well, but so, comparatively, are all such, for the conquest of the air is only a matter of two generations, whereas the conquest of the sea is as old as history and throughout history has been vital in war and in politics, and in the economic development of great nations.

Athens, in the fifth century before the common era, was a smallish town, about half the size of Tel Aviv, but seapower enabled it to found no inconsiderable Mediterranean empire and become the directive power of the Greek world and the apotheosis of poetry, philosophy and art. When the Athenian fleet was worsted in the Sicilian war, and that seapower lost, the genius of Athens perished and her political and cultural brilliance faded.

The might of Britain these last three hundred years and her far-reaching hegemony until the first World War were the reward of conquest and rule of the sea. While they held watery dominion, Venice and Spain, Portugal and Holland, in turn were great; when they relinquished it, greatness quitted them.

For the nations strengthened by it, that same dominion ensured freedom of export and import, and an unending flow of merchandise, raw material and foodstuffs; it enhanced their productivity by overseas trade, allowed them safe transport of armadas, munitions and supplies wherever they were wanted, and denied all these advantages to the enemy. Most of the great wars of history were decided by command of the sea—the Persian wars, the struggle of Rome and Carthage, the two World Wars in our time.

But not Greece nor Rome nor their modern heirs were the

first to steer a course over the waves and sail the sea. The fathers of seafaring, prime instrument of economic progress and the spread of culture for three millennia now, were Semitic tribes, speaking Canaanitish Hebrew and dwelling of old on the shores of Palestine—in Tyre and in Sidon and their off-shoots Acre, Achzib, Kanah, Zarephath, Gebal and Arvad. The Sidonians, as all the inhabitants of the northern coast were called, were masters only of a narrow strip of land running the length of it, and could not subsist on farming. So they turned to trade, Canaanite became a synonym for merchant and the word kina a synonym for wares.

International trade was the mainstay of Tyre and Sidon, but they were not content to traffic overland with their near and distant neighbors; they became the first great maritime powers. To the very ends of the earth their vessels ventured: to all the islands of the Mediterranean and its ports in Asia, Africa and Europe. On many shores they founded colonies; 2,000 years before Vasco da Gama they circumnavigated Africa, they burst into the Atlantic Ocean and the Indian and brought their wares as far north as the British Isles, to Arabia southwards, and to India in the Orient. They came into contact with peoples primitive and civilized, helping to educate the contemporary world and endowing it with the alphabet, the most potent agency of human enlightenment.

The Prophet Ezekiel has left us a glowing description of the wealth and power of Tyre, and its sea-borne trade: 'that wast peopled from the seas, the renowned city that wast strong in the sea, thou and thy inhabitants, that caused your terror to be on all that inhabit the earth.'

What Jerusalem was in the annals of religion, Athens in the annals of art and philosophy, Rome in the annals of law and administration, Tyre and Sidon were in the annals of seafaring and the commerce of nations.

Listen to Ezekiel's prophecy on Tyre—'that dwelleth at the

entry of the sea, that is the merchant of the peoples unto many isles . . .

. . . Thou, O Tyre, hast said: I am of perfect beauty. Thy borders are in the heart of the seas, Thy builders have perfected thy beauty. Of cypress-trees from Senir have they fashioned all thy planks; they have taken cedars from Lebanon to make masts for thee. Of the oaks of Bashan have they made thine oars; thy deck have they made of ivory inlaid in larch, from the isles of the Kittites. Of fine linen with richly woven work from Egypt was thy sail, that it might be to thee for an ensign; blue and purple from the isles of Elishah was thine awning. The inhabitants of Sidon and Arvad were thy rowers; thy wise men, O Tyre, were in thee, they were thy pilots. The elders of Gebal and the wise men thereof were in thee thy calkers; all the ships of the sea with their mariners were in thee to exchange thy merchandise. Persia and Lud and Put were in thine army, thy men of war; they hanged the shield and helmet in thee, they set forth thy comeliness. The men of Arvad and Helech were upon thy walls round about, and the Gammadim were in thy towers; they hanged their shields upon thy walls round about; they have perfected thy beauty. Tarshish was thy merchant by reason of the multitude of all kinds of riches; with silver, iron, tin, and lead, they traded for thy wares. Javan, Tubal, and Meshech, they were thy traffickers; they traded the persons of men and vessels of brass for thy merchandise. They of the house of Togarmah traded for thy wares with horses and horsemen and mules. The men of Dedan were thy traffickers, many isles were the mart of thy hand; they brought thee as tribute horns of ivory and ebony. Aram was thy merchant by reason of the multitude of thy wealth; they traded for thy wares with carbuncles, purple, and richly woven work, and fine linen, and coral, and rubies. Judah and the land of Israel, they were thy traffickers; they traded for thy merchandise wheat of Minnith, and balsam, and honey, and oil, and balm. Damascus was thy merchant for the multitude of thy wealth, by the reason of the multitude of all riches, with the wine of Helbon, and white wool. Dedan and Javan traded with yarn for thy wares; massive iron, cassia and calamus were among thy merchandise. Dedan was thy trafficker in precious cloths for riding. Arabia and all the princes of Kedar, they were the merchants of thy hand; in lambs, and rams, and goats, in these were they thy merchants.

The traffickers of Sheba and Raamah, they were thy traffickers; they traded for thy wares with chief of all spices, and with all precious stones, and gold. Haran and Canneh and Eden, the traffickers of Sheba, Asshur was as thine apprentice in traffic. These were thy traffickers in gorgeous fabrics, in wrappings of blue and richly woven work, and in chests of rich apparel, bound with cords and cedar-lined, among thy merchandise. The ships of Tarshish brought thee tribute for thy merchandise; so wast thou replenished and made very heavy in the heart of the seas. . . .'

The tribes of Israel, Zebulun and Asher were close by the seashore and were on good terms with the people of Tyre. 'Zebulun shall dwell at the shore of the sea, and he shall be a shore for ships, and his flank shall be upon Sidon.' 'Asher dwelt at the shore of the sea, and abideth by its bays.' And Hiram, king of Tyre, sent David cedar-trees, and carpenters and masons, to build his house, 'for Hiram was ever a lover of David.'

'And there was peace between Hiram and Solomon; and they two made a league together . . . So Hiram gave Solomon timber of cedar and timber of cypress according to all his desire. And Solomon gave Hiram twenty thousand measures of wheat for food to his household, and twenty measures of beaten oil.'

Yet the children of Israel and Judah learnt not seamanship from the Tyrians, for the way was barred to them by those that dwelt upon the shores, in the north the Canaanites and the Philistines to the south. The tribe of Asher 'drove not out the inhabitants of Acco, nor the inhabitants of Sidon, nor of Ahlab, nor of Achzib, nor of Helbah, nor of Aphik, nor of Rehob,' and all through the lifetime of the First Temple we find not one Jewish harbor on the Mediterranean.

Not that, even then, our leaders and teachers lost sight of the sea's importance to us. 'And I will set thy border from the Red Sea even unto the sea of Philistines' says the Torah. And the bard foretells in the Psalms: 'May he have dominion also from sea to sea', dominion from the Red Sea to the Mediterranean. And surely the words have at long last come true.

Our ancestors came here from the East, from Aram and across the Jordan, and could not subdue the inhabitants of the valley 'for they have chariots of iron'. Jaffa certainly was the port of Jerusalem and already, in the time of Solomon and Hiram, wood was cut out of Lebanon and brought to Solomon 'in floats by sea to Joppa,' and Solomon carried it up to Jerusalem, but there is no sign that there were Jews in Jaffa in those days. Therefore the kings of Judah sought to gain to the southern sea and make on its shores a Jewish haven for trade with oriental lands. The work was begun by Solomon. The Gulf of Elath was within the bounds of Edom, and only when Edom was overthrown could the Jews find foothold there, but when Edom waxed strong again, they were ejected.

David enlarged the borders of his kingdom and conquered Edom. 'And he put garrisons in Edom; . . . and all the Edomites became servants to David'. Rest came to Israel in Solomon's days: 'and he had peace on all sides round about him. And Judah and Israel dwelt safely . . . all the days of Solomon.' So the son of David might give himself to building, development and the conquest of the sea. And king Solomon made a navy of ships in Ezion-geber, which is besides Elath, on the shore of the Red Sea, in the land of Edom.

But then there were no mariners in Judah and Israel, and again Solomon besought help from Hiram, his friend, who sent him 'in the navy his servants, shipmen that had knowledge of the sea, with the servants of Solomon.'

Solomon's heir was a weakling. In his reign the monarchy was cleft, and of the claim staked out in the Red Sea nothing remained.

Only when no king reigned in Edom did Jehoshaphat, fifth in Solomon's line, build ships in Ezion-geber to voyage to Ophir. The Jews, however, were still untried in seamanship and the ships were wrecked in the Gulf.

In the days of Jehoram, son of Jehoshaphat, 'Edom revolted from under the hand of Judah and made a king over themselves.' Once more Elath was lost to Israel, and again five generations were to pass before it was re-won in the days of Uzziah. Of him the Book of Chronicles tells thus:

'And he built cities in the country of Ashdod, and among the Philistines. And God helped him against the Philistines, and against the Arabians that dwelt in Gur-baal, and the Meunim. And the Ammonites gave gifts to Uzziah; and his name spread abroad even to the entrance of Egypt; for he waxed exceeding strong. Moreover Uzziah built towers in Jerusalem at the corner gate, and at the valley gate, and at the Turning and fortified them. And he built towers in the wilderness, and hewed out many cisterns, for he had much cattle; in the lowland also, and in the table-land; and he had husbandmen and vinedressers in the mountains and in the fruitful fields; for he loved husbandry. Moreover Uzziah had an army of fighting men . . . And Uzziah prepared for them, even for all the host, shields and spears, and helmets, and coats of mail, and bows, and stones for slinging. And he made in Jerusalem engines, invented by skillful men, to be on the towers and upon the corners, wherewith to shoot arrows and great stones. And his name spread far abroad; for he was marvellously helped, till he was strong.'

This great king turned his thoughts to the sea as well: 'He built Elath, and restored it to Judah.' The port thenceforth stayed in Judah's hands for three generations, until the reign of Ahaz, when 'Bezin king of Aram recovered Elath to Aram, and drove the Jews from Elath; and the Edomites came to Elath, and dwelt there, unto this day.'

The Jews had to wait until Hasmonaean times to reach the shores of the Mediterranean and occupy Jaffa, and it was the first and only Jewish port on that littoral in the period of the Second Temple. We remember that, when the land was divided in the days of Joshua, Jaffa fell to the portion of the tribe of Dan, but the Jews did not capture it then. When Jeroboam II was king, it came under Assyrian rule, after the victorious wars of King Rimnon-nirari. In those days Jonah fled to Tarshish by way of Jaffa. The great storm that smote the sea, so that his ship was like to founder, is no rarity, and even steamships today will sometimes cast about for days seeking without avail to drop anchor in the angry waters, especially during the rains, when high winds whip the breakers against the treacherous reef that blocks the shoreward approach.

Hezekiah, king of Judah, threw off the yoke of Sennacherib, and Jaffa too rebelled: in his triumphal inscription Sennacherib tells how he punished Hezekiah and enslaved him, and subjugated Jaffa, Bnei Brak, Chatzor, and Bet Dagon, the cities of Zedek, king of Ashkelon.

In the era of the Second Temple, Jaffa was long a bone of contention between the successors of Alexander the Great, and Syrians and Egyptians ruled there in turns after its capture by Alexander in 333 BCE. The quarrel between the Ptolemies and the Seleucids over the coastal cities of Palestine—Jaffa among them—lasted until the rise of the Hasmonaeans. The population was a mixed one, Greeks and Hellenized Syrians and Jews.

The Greeks of Jaffa committed an ungodly crime. They beguiled their Jewish fellow-citizens, with their wives and children, to sail on a harmless outing and then drowned them all in the depths. Judah the Maccabee was roused to avenge himself upon the murderers of his brethren, and he came with his men in the dead of night and set fire to the haven and burned all the ships.

Any that fled the conflagration were put to the sword. But the city itself was shut up and he could not overcome it and he went up from it.

But what the greatest of the Hasmonaeans failed to do, his younger brother achieved after his death. In 148 BCE, with his brother Simon, Jonathan stormed the walls at the head of a Jewish army of 10,000 men and Jaffa was his.

When it became known to Simon that the Greeks in the city conspired to deliver it over to the officers of Demetrius, he went up again and set a Jewish garrison in it to keep guard. And still the Gentiles would rebel against Jewish governance, until Simon sent troops in force to master the city, and he drove them out and held it firmly, 'and it was a haven for ships to go thence to the isles of the sea.'

This, then, was the garland of victory of one of our mighty liberators, Simon the High Priest, and his prowess a grateful nation resolved to engrave 'on tablets of brass and fasten them to pillars on Mount Zion.' So signal an honor was paid to no Jewish dynast and redeemer since the Jews became a nation.

And, indeed, Simon wrought much—he consummated the enterprise begun by his father and his elder brother, to free the land of Judah from a foreign yoke and culture. The chronicler of the First Book of Maccabees describes in panegyric the happiness of the Jews in Simon's sway:

'Then did they till their ground in peace, and the earth gave its yield, and trees their fruit. The old men sat in the streets communing together of the good that was in the land, and the young men put on glorious and war-like apparel. Simon provided victuals for the cities, and set in them all manner of munition . . . He made peace in the Land and the House of Israel rejoiced with a great joy.'

The prosperity of the Jews stirred the envy of Antiochus IV, who had formerly made a pact with Simon, and he set up a pretence concerning Jaffa and Gezer which Simon had conquered, for, said Antiochus, 'they are cities of my kingdom.' Wherefore he sent one of his henchmen to demand that Simon return the cities to him. The answer Simon gave was worthy of the giver and it is as apt today for all that hate Zion and bedevil her:

> 'The Land where to we have returned to inherit it, it is the inheritance of our fathers and within it no stranger has part or parcel. For our enemies did steal our inheritance and possessed it by iniquity and evil. And now the Lord hath made prosperous our way, and we have taken unto us our fathers' inheritance and have dwelt in it.'

Twice the Syrians seized Jaffa and twice John Hyrcanus, son of Simon, came back and retook it, and the Roman Senate, with whom John had renewed his father's treaty, solemnly confirmed that Jaffa, city and shore, would belong to the Jews.

In 63 BCE, Pompey tore Jaffa and the other coastal cities from Jewish hold and added them to Syria, but after sixteen years Julius Caesar decreed the restoration to the Jews of all that had been theirs, and, in Josephus' words, 'that the city Joppa which the Jews had originally, when they made a league of friendship with the Romans, shall belong to them, as it formerly did; and that Hyrcanus, the son of Alexander, and his sons have as tribute of that city from those that occupy the land for the country, and for what they export every year to Sidon.' So we see that even then the Jews exported their produce through Jaffa's harbor.

Jaffa was then the chief maritime city of Judah and the only port in Palestine where Jewish culture and the Jewish spirit reigned absolute. Gaza and Ashkelon, Migdal and Startonos' Tower—afterwards called Caesarea, Dor and Acre, were populated in the main by Syrians, Greeks and Romans, none of them overfond of the Jews, and the alien spirit of Greek enlightenment lay upon them. All of them, and some cities of hybrid population in the interior, had Gentile names as well; Jaffa held to its name and kept its national character inviolate. Even Herod the Idumaean, lover of Greek culture though he was, who built palaces and circuses, baths and theaters, in the Grecian and Roman styles all along the coast, did not dare in Jaffa to set up these affronts to Jewish worship and national sentiment. Perhaps that is why the Hellenizing monarch moved the center of his seaborne trade from Jaffa to spacious, elegant Caesarea.

Jaffa was near the nation's capital in spirit as in space. And when in 66 BCE there came the great uprising against the tyranny of Rome, all the other cities of the coast were divided in allegiance—Gentiles and Jews clashed furiously and in Caesarea itself twenty thousand Jews were slain. But Jaffa stood fast, as one man, by the side of the insurgent zealots in defense of liberty. So, when Cestius Gallus marched on Jerusalem, he first dispatched a legion to fall suddenly upon Jaffa, where the inhabitants had made no provision beforehand for a fight, and slew more than eight thousand of them and burned the city down.

The Jews returned, however, for all that, and rebuilt it. Refugees from the Roman havoc, from every part of Palestine and from the coast towns above all, gathered there, and a new community arose on its ruins. They were embittered and thirsted for revenge. The country round about was devastated. The legionaries had utterly destroyed all means of livelihood, and the soil no longer sustained the townspeople, who consequently set their minds to the building of ships so that they might foray and plunder the Phoenician coast, and Syria and Egypt also, a meet retribution for the murder of their brethren and the desolation of their land.

When the news came to the Emperor Vespasian, he sent foot-soldiers and cavalry by night and they attacked Jaffa unawares. The Jews took to their ships, but the rocky, turbulent sea of the place was their undoing: a great wind blew toward morning and

and in the seething vortex the ships were hurled one against the other or dashed upon the rocks. For all their straining oars, the giant breakers swept others shoreward, where the enemy waited. Many Jews went down with their ships; not a few fell despairingly upon their swords before the end came, and any that clambered ashore were taken by the Romans. The sea was crimsoned with blood, and the beach piled high with corpses—four thousand two hundred dead the sea gave up. The Romans then entered Jaffa and razed it to the ground. That was not all. So that the Jews would nevermore seek to rebuild the city, Vespasian placed a body of horse in it and built a fort where the city once stood. The soldiers were bade spoil and strip the countryside and cut to pieces the neighboring hamlets and boroughs. And they did it with a will.

The Jews were not seafarers in the First or in the Second Temple. Truly a most ancient hymn of Israel is Moses' song of the sea, but when, in departing out of Egypt, the Jews crossed the waters, that was an exploit overland: 'And the children of Israel went into the midst of the sea upon the dry ground; and the waters were a wall unto them on their right hand, and on their left.' In the whole Bible there is only one hymn that evidences a bard who knew the sea and they that go down to the sea in ships. It may have been written in the Hasmonaean days after the Jews had struck the sea at Jaffa and sailors and shipmasters arose among them. It is preserved in the Book of Psalms:

> 'They that go down to the sea in ships,
> That do business in great waters—
> These saw the works of the Lord,
> And his wonders in the deep;
> For he commanded, and raised the stormy wind,
> Which lifted up the waves thereof;
> They mounted up to the heaven,
> They went down to the deeps;

Their soul melted away because of trouble;
They reeled to and fro, and staggered like a drunken man,
And all their wisdom was swallowed up—
They cried unto the Lord in their trouble,
And he brought them out of their distresses.
He made the storm a calm,
So that the waves thereof were still.
Then were they glad because they were quiet,
And he led them unto their desired haven.'

Today, for the first time in its history, the sovereign Jewish nation borders two seas. Ours is the only State in the Mediterranean with egress to both Atlantic and Indian Oceans without dependence upon the Suez Canal, from our western seaboard and from Elath's gulf in the south. This hold upon the shores of two seas sets apart our third Return to Zion.

From Egypt and from Babylonia the Jews entered the Land of Promise by land, coming out of the east. This time, it was out of the west, by sea. This is cardinal in our contemporary repatriation, a fact of economic, political and strategic moment, and it stamps the value of our young navy.

Landward, we are surrounded by Arab States which made war upon us and are intransigent still. It is not an historical imperative that they should hate us interminably. Of this I have written elsewhere. But hopes of an early peace are insubstantial. Armistices only exist, and at times our neighbors speak of a second round; whether they mean it or not, it is a fact that there is still a state of war, we are beleaguered on land, and the sea is our main route of free access to the Diaspora and of contact with the world. Realization has come to the splendid verse of Isaiah: 'That made the depths of the sea a way for the redeemed to pass over: And the ransomed of the Lord shall return and come with singing unto Zion.' Never before was the sea, to us, a way for the redeemed. And now Aliyah is as an ocean current, and what the sea does not bring, the eagle wings of aircraft bear aloft.

Not only immigration, but our security also, depends upon the sea, for it carries all our needs and all our trade. Lacking seapower and command, we shall not profit from our ground and air forces, be they never so strong. Let us not, however, disparage them. We shall not emulate Themistocles, who counselled the Athenians to abandon the land and fight the Persians at sea, and verily then he brought them victory. Without ground troops that can carry the war into enemy territory and aircraft to rule our skies from the very start and be first to batter the enemy's military bases, there is no holding our own, but unless we command the sea Israel will be as a city under siege. One neighbor, and the most powerful, is maritime Egypt, mistress of one of the greatest harbors in the Mediterranean, the key to the Suez Canal in her hands, her navy growing. In the War of Independence we sank two Egyptian warships at no cost to ourselves, but rich Egypt can recover easily from this brief reverse and we cannot allow her to deny us outlet in the Mediterranean, for on that our lives depend.

But the sea is not of political and military importance only: our economic hopes largely rest in it, in its boundless possibilities for colonization, paradoxical though that seem. The sea is no waste of waters, as many think, but a sealed store of infinite treasures. It is the most facile and the cheapest method of communication to all the ends of the earth, it has inexhaustible supplies of food, a multitude of raw materials, and reservoirs of force and power. The sea covers the greater part of the earth's surface, it has no frontiers, it is free. It is not divided among the States and the peoples that are on land, there are no partitions between the oceans, no barriers or confining bounds. A people with a territorial base and port may sail the world over and sound every sea, it may put a girdle about the globe and seek out every folk and speech. Land severs the nations, the sea unites them and brings them close, it advances the unity of mankind, opening new horizons and spaces invisible to us that stand on shore.

Our forefathers, who had never sailed its length as their kinfolk of Sidon did, called the Mediterranean the Great Sea, but it is just a land-girt lake with a narrow exit to the Atlantic. That ocean the ancient Jews never saw. And the Atlantic itself is but a small segment of the great fluid mass which surrounds the large islands we call continents. On the broad bosom of ocean man sees the elemental immensity of nature, for the mightiest man-made vessel imaginable is no more than a minute speck of sand in an illimitable expanse of water. He also learns his own greatness and the tremendous strength that is in him to control natural forces and rule the vasty deep. The man who bridges gigantic oceans in a frail craft of his own making is proof that quality transcends quantity, that the human spirit is superior to nature's measureless wealth of matter in the raw.

There is nothing, nothing, like the sea to widen our worlds, to increase our sense of security, to develop our latent powers, and bring out our courage, to draw us near to nature and give us dominion over it.

The conquest of the sea is among man's most glorious and creative adventures: without it the story of civilization, of the spread and associations of the human race, could not have been written. It is an adventure still to be fittingly ended in Israel and our navy is only a humble beginning.

Fishing and navigation promise to furnish livelihood to thousands of our sons, if we come to understand what the sea means to us, and are bold and skilled enough to govern its denizens and its wares. As we must make the Negev fruitful, so must we turn to profit the multitudinous sea. Our small country will flourish and expand once we perceive that the coast-line is no boundary, but corridor into a colossal empire that stretches almost to infinity on waves abounding in life and riches, in power and might. Riding the sea, Israel will voyage throughout the world, and in every ocean its trawlers and freighters, its passenger-ships as well—under our national flag—will vouch for the sustenance of myriads of immigrants and moor fast the economic and political independence of the State.

MISSION AND DEDICATION
An Address to the General Staff and Commanding Officers of the Israel-Defense Forces, 1950

> The Lord did not set his love upon you, nor choose you, because ye were more in number than any people; for ye were the fewest of all people: But because the Lord loved you...
> (DEUTERONOMY, VII - 7, 8).

> I will bring thy seed from the east, and gather thee from the west; I will say to the north, Give up, and to the south, Keep not back: bring my sons from far, and my daughters from the ends of the earth... (ISAIAH, XLIII - 5, 6).

In the history of mankind to this very hour, there has always been political conflict between nations, and over and over again it turned into physical, into military strife. Like others, the Jewish people has fought its duels of politics with neighboring peoples, and more than once its real wars. Thus it was in the days of the Judges, in the era of the kings when the First Temple stood, and during the Second Temple.

Generations passed, centuries receded and again we were an independent nation. Even before the State came into being, war was declared upon us, and the State was founded and its building began in the heat of battle. For the moment, the fighting is stilled, but the political struggle goes on and on and no one can say how long it will last, or whether it will not once more be war.

To prevail in the contest, whether political or military, we must know ourselves, the circumstances and terms of our existence, the factors that are basic and enduring and those of time and place which, in their constant change, condition our being and our historic work.

We shall not truly understand things, we shall not fulfill many a vision of our history, past, present or to come, we shall not be ready and equipped for the political or military combat—and remember that the armament that counts is the armament of the spirit—unless we plainly comprehend the ideological and moral warfare that is waged among men and our place in it.

*   *   *

It would be profitless to indulge in metaphysical argument whether this opposition of ideas stems from economic, social or political antagonisms, or is itself their cause. Nor is it necessary to decide whether the ideological and economic differences are bound together inseparably or not. There is no practical value in these abstract speculations, any more than in deciding whether the chicken came first or the egg. Obviously one cannot exist without the other; there is no way of raising chickens without hatching eggs and no way of getting eggs without raising chickens.

We have seen it happen that ideas change regimes—political and economic, that regimes renew ideas and infuse strength into them. Men fight for their ideas no less than for power or property. Since man grew up, there is no end of the conflict of ideas. It has perhaps played a greater part in our history than in any other. Hardly a quarrel in that history, of politics or soldiery, but was linked with it.

We are now at odds not only with our Arab neighbors, but to a certain extent with the greater part of the world organized in the United Nations. The issue is Jerusalem. Only the blind will not see that the heart of it is not just politics, economics or tactics, but ideology as well.

When the Syrians, Iraqis and Egyptians support the internationalization of Jerusalem with outward enthusiasm, their motive is clear—better to have the Mosque of Omar under Christian guardianship than a large part of Jerusalem under Jewish. The stand taken by several Latin American States, which usually backed us in the United Nations but have rounded on us on this issue, is difficult to explain on the score of political motive alone. Nor can such motive explain the attitude of France, which had a substantial political and military interest in helping us and did help us no little, both in the General Assembly and in many more concrete and effective ways. The same may be said of Czechoslovakia. Yet here these countries voted against us, underlining the presence of warring ideas in the world.

It was, indeed, a strange tripartite alliance that we saw. On one side not the whole Christian world, but the most universal group within it—the Catholic bloc; on another, the Moslem; and on the third, the Communist. No doubt each had its own reasons. But there is no doubt either that all had a similar, although not a common, cause. What united them is not a political interest, but an idea. Islam, Catholicism, Communism—each has its ideology. Again, for the understanding of our problem it is not important to know whether the idea governs policy or the other way about: idea and policy derive from a single source. To ignore the idea is to ignore one of history's major factors and forces.

* * *

The Jewish people is not merely a political and national unit, and from the time it first stepped upon the stage of history it has personified moral will and historic vision. That will and vision do not wholly accord with any of the three great ideologies which made common cause in the General Assembly on the issue of Jerusalem, nor with other ideologies which have fought for world domination since the dawn of time.

REBIRTH AND DESTINY OF ISRAEL

You will never understand the annals of the Jews, their struggle to exist, their stand in all periods and places, as a nation dwelling in its own land and more or less autonomous, and as a wandering race dispersed in exile, unless you can see down to their ideological unity in this lone, stubborn fight. Fight not only economic, political and military, but spiritual, moral and intellectual; a fight they have waged without respite from the beginning and will go on waging to the end of days, until the vision is fulfilled.

* * *

One physical fact in our history is constant, and from it much has flowed, and flows still: numerically we were always a small nation and such we have remained. Seemingly it is our fate so to be forever, small in comparison with our near neighbors and with the nations we meet in the wider world. The material, mathematical fact has affected our destiny profoundly to both our disadvantage and our gain.

In ancient times our great neighbors were Egypt and Babylon, outvying us in their size and wealth, their military power and spheres of rule, and in certain intellectual qualities and scientific achievements no less.

Our conception of Egypt, as we drew it from the Books of Genesis and Exodus, is somewhat one-sided. According to what we learned at school, Egypt was a land of serfdom where our forefathers were enslaved and down-trodden. The Exodus from Egypt to this day is regarded by Israel as an escape from slavery to freedom. But Egypt was one of the few nations in the ancient world to create an original and comparatively advanced culture. Five thousand years ago, in the reign of Pharaoh Senseru, it had already attained a high level of civilization and laid the foundations of many branches of science, mathematics and engineering, chemistry and medicine. It had written a rich and diversified literature, on religion, history and ethics, on science, poetry and fiction, of which indeed very little has been preserved or re-discovered. But the little that is extant testifies to wide intellectual interests and a distinctive culture: in one story we find the Joseph-and-Potiphar's-wife motif, and the love songs recall the Song of Songs. There are hymns not unlike our psalms. The Egyptians were great architects too, as witness their pyramids; and they excelled in sculpture and painting.

Much the same may be said of Babylon, which in her copious literature outdid even Egypt. The epic of Gilgamesh was preserved and stories of the Creation, the song of Ishtar, lamentations, prayers, stories of wisdom and morals, hymns and historical writings and records. Babylon developed the sciences of astronomy, medicine, and engineering, and was the first to perfect the art of jurisprudence. For a long time its language was the international medium of diplomacy for all the countries mentioned in the Bible, in modern parlance for the Middle East.

The struggle of the Jews with these powerful neighbors was not only political and military; it was as much spiritual and cultural. The vehemence of the Prophets was pointed in the main against the influence of neighboring nations upon the religious and ethical conceptions of the people of Israel and their social order. The controversy of orientation, which seems to have been revived, is ancient in our history. The military captains, with Johanan son of Kareah and Jezaniah son of Hosaiah at their head, had their own alignment on the question of Egypt versus Babylon. But Jeremiah had his toward Israel, and Israel's God, and—it bears repeating—he said to the captains in prophetic wrath:

'. . . If ye wholly set your faces to enter into Egypt. . . . Then it shall come to pass, that the sword which ye feared, shall overtake you there in the land of Egypt, and the famine, whereof ye were afraid, shall follow close after you there in Egypt; and there ye shall die. . . . If ye will still abide in this land, then I will build you, and not pull you down, and I will plant you, and not pluck you up. . . . Be not afraid of the king of Babylon of whom ye are afraid; be not afraid of him, saith the Lord: for I am with you to save you, and to deliver you from his hand'.

Of a surety, this argument did not come suddenly to life in the days of Jeremiah; it had been vented a long time. Jewish history in the First Temple was charged with the clash between the alien influences exerted by neighbors and the national spirit expressed by the Prophets. It is not chance that political thoughts on the relations of bordering peoples are found in the words of the Prophets, with social and ethical aspirations and predictions. The small nation surrounded by neighbors who ruled the world —the only world our people then knew—was always under a twofold pressure: political and military, spiritual and cultural. The neighbors not only inspired dread; through their formidable culture they exercised a powerful fascination. This enchantment was the source of the inner conflict in the life of our nation from its rise until the Babylonian exile, and from that exile to the present day. Faint echoes reach us of combat between the false prophets and the true. The words of the 'false prophets' have not been preserved and we do not know what they said or meant, but all that is left of the words of the 'true prophets' bespeaks a tremendous spiritual effort to withstand not only foreign domination but the intellectual spell cast by mighty nations over a puny neighbor weak in the political and military sense yet endowed exceptionally with spiritual courage and ethical individuality.

The people of Israel, whose heirs we are, were not the only ones in the land and roundabout to be subjected to this dual strain. There were other Semitic folk living there and speaking a form of Hebrew, as is seen from the records of the Canaanites (Phoenicians) and the inscriptions of Mesha, king of Moab; but no vestige of them remains. They could not hold out against the cultural pressure of their great neighbors and were utterly swallowed up.

The Jews did hold out and prevailed, to reappear now in the same corner of the world where first they made their bow in history four thousand years ago. But the original environment, political and cultural, of this region of the Bible has altered out of recognition. The chain of development of ancient nations broke forever. Their language and religion, their culture, tradition and name disappeared completely from the face of the earth. Only the people of Israel, parted though it was from Homeland for almost two thousand years, preserved its traditions in its own language and culture as though the thread of its history was never twisted or torn.

'As though', I say. But it is obvious that the Jewish people today is not as it was in the period of the First Temple or even the Second. The whole world has changed meanwhile, and it is natural that the Jewish people should have changed with it. We do not intend, nor wish, to revert to the condition of Judea overwhelmed by Babylon or the reign of Bar Kochba ended by the Romans. In Babylon itself, and in all it underwent since that exile, our people absorbed new learning, new *mores* and customs under the impact of the nations which it encountered and reflecting changes in the life of society. The early Jewish outlook was intuitive and theocratic. In the Middle Ages, beginning with Saadia Hagaon and his successors, Jewish thinkers sought to synthesize Jewish theocratic thought with the Greek philosophical outlook in vogue among the intellectuals of the age. From the time of Spinoza and onward, the experimental scientific outlook grew and deepened among us, as among all contemporary civilized peoples. Jews have occupied a prominent and honorable place in the progress of science in the last hundred and fifty years, perhaps a higher place than their numbers among the Gentiles might warrant. They were full partners in the profound intellectual revolution which came to pass in the perception of the world of matter and in the revelation of nature's secrets. Yet not all the changes and mutations in matter and spirit, in political and social conditions, during the thousands of years of our existence could destroy or even shake the remarkable vital force which upheld our people in times of stress, nor shatter its national unity. The contrast with many of our historical contemporaries in different lands is astounding. There is some wonder-working vitamin stored in the Jewish nation which safeguards its existence and independence, and gives it an unconquerable strength to withstand all external pressure inimical to its national and moral being.

* * *

Of course, not every individual Jew possessed the unusual attribute. Many fell away—individuals, congregations, classes and entire communities. In every generation and in every country, even in their own Land, there were Jews who could not stand up to the onset, physical or intellectual, and were eliminated or converted, but the stout core bore the ordeal, wrestled, fought and won.

We know little of our history during the Persian governance, from the return out of Babylon in the days of Zerubbabel, Ezra and Nehemiah to the emergence of Alexander of Macedon. That was perhaps the only interlude in the life of the Jewish people in its country when it was not vulnerable to foreign influences and had not to fight for political and cultural survival. Persian rule was, in general, based on tolerance and autonomy; each subject nation might live according to its own customs and beliefs and enjoy a large measure of self-government.

There were, of course, instances of persecution and oppression, as we may infer from the story of Esther and from the historical allusions of the Greek writer Hecataeus. It may, however, be assumed that, broadly, the Persian period, which lasted more than two hundred years, was a time of inner consolidation for the Jews. Their spiritual character, was molded and made steadfast then, perhaps more than in any other period, even though they could not altogether escape Persian suasion, unconsciously breathed in.

With Alexander's conquest of the East in 331 BCE, and of the Persian empire within it, the Greek period begins. Here we behold a desperate rivalry between Judaism and the rich and superlative culture of Hellenism, a culture unparalleled in previous history, and one which, more deeply than any other, has influenced human society. In poetry, literature and philosophy, in science, sculpture, painting and the other arts, it has given the world treasures of the spirit which are the culminating glory of man's creativeness for all time.

The struggle between the Hasmonaeans and the Greek overlords was not only the political and military revolt of a subjugated people against foreign rule and oppression. It was essentially a contest of cultures and one of the most dramatic such in history between two nations original in character, entirely opposite in material welfare, in political strength, in world philosophy, but alike in the individual stamp of spiritual greatness.

The Jewish nation was small and poor, confined within the narrow borders of part of its ancient land, claiming no more than a local autonomy. The Greek nation governed the whole world—those regions of Europe, Asia and Africa then known to man; its language and civilization were widespread, from the western shores of the Mediterranean to India and to the banks of the Nile. The Greeks conquered not by the sword alone but by their copious and brilliant civilization. When the heirs of Alexander entrenched themselves in Egypt and Assyria, and Alexandria and Antioch became centers of Greek culture, tiny impoverished Judea could not but be affected by it too, though in the tarnished form of the Hellenistic period.

Hellenized Jews in Israel were not just sycophants. The part of Greece in history was not as that of Rome in later times, a manifestation only of military and absolutist strength. It was a cultural phenomenon which opened a new era in the works of the spirit. No other nation has given so much richness to the treasure-house of civilization.

In our literature, as I say, there live the writings only of those who challenged the Hellenizing faction and fought it, and the scene their words evoke is not altogether objective or complete. But there is no doubt that the joust enriched and sublimated the Jewish spirit and left an abiding mark on the Hebrew writings of Israel. With the advent of Alexander, a profuse and diversified Hebrew-Hellenic literature was born, historical and poetic, interpretative and philosophical. Yet easily as it had absorbed other nations in the East, the civilization of Greece could not absorb the Jews, who preserved their unity and individuality, and, what is more, it even strengthened and deepened them.

The victory was not without its casualties. We cannot tell how many were lost, by death or by assimilation. But the nation as a whole was victor, and the Hasmonaean period will ever be one of the most remarkable political, military, and spiritual chapters in our chronicles. The few defeated the many, the poor overcame the rich—solely by virtue of the great spiritual forces which animated both the elect and the masses of the nation, even if they did not stir the ruling caste of privileged and clerics.

The longest and hardest trial came with the flourishing of Christianity. The culture of Egypt and Babylon, of Greece and Rome, was foreign to Judaism. Not so Christianity. It was born in the very bosom of Judaism, from within it, and out of it. The man to whom the new faith was accounted was a plain Jew living in the midst of his people. His religious and moral conceptions did not overstep the bounds of those accepted by the Jews of his time. Even the idea to which Jesus gave special emphasis was not, in essence, different from the thinking usual among the sects which abounded in Israel before the destruction of the Second Temple. As a Jew of his generation, Jesus refused 'to take the children's bread and to cast it unto the dogs', and when the Canaanite woman cried out to him for help he answered her, saying: 'I am not sent but unto the lost sheep of the house of Israel'.

The anti-Jewish bias was imparted to the new religion by Saul of Tarsus, the apostle, and perhaps also the author, of the 'New' Testament in contradistinction to our Old. Saul, son of a Roman citizen who lived abroad, was brought up as a Jew and was the pupil of Rabbi Gamaliel. Like the other pupils, he was a fanatical Pharisee, but he had travelled and taken in something of Greek culture. At first, he was one of the spirited adversaries of the Christian sect in Jerusalem, but after he had 'seen the light' on his way to Damascus and become one of the believers in Jesus as the son of God, a new direction was given it. Unlike the disciples of Jesus in Palestine, who regarded themselves as Jews in every way, Saul of Tarsus, now named Paul, held that his mission was mainly to the Gentiles, and turned the sect into a religion and a church, defying the fundamental principles of Judaism as a nation, a religion and an ideal.

At the moment when Jesus is quoted as saying: 'Think not that I am come to destroy the Law of the Prophets. I am not come to destroy but to fulfill. For verily I say unto you—Till heaven and earth pass, one jot or one tittle shall in no wise pass from the Law till all be fulfilled', at the self-same moment Saul was striving with might and main to uproot the Torah and its commands, and to bring an end to Jewry as a national entity pursuing a better world. Saul was perhaps the most potent assimilationist the Jewish people has ever had. He denied the practical precepts which constitute the essence and foundation of Judaism and based all religion on faith alone. He recognized only the individual and not the nation. He tried to destroy the faith and hope of the Jewish people in national and territorial redemption. Rejecting the ultimate vision of the Prophets, which looks far into the future and there makes one the redemption of the nation and of the whole world, the dignity of Israel and the kingdom of peace and justice on earth, Saul founded Christianity on faith in heavenly redemption through a Messiah already come.

Christianity throve and spread when the last vestige of independence was lost to Israel. The fierce, despairing wars fought against its Roman tyrants, from the days of Yehuda the Galilean and Zadok to Shimon Bar Kochba and Rabbi Akiva, ended in total defeat and loss of liberty. It was a deep-seated spiritual and social shock, a political reverse the like whereof Israel had never before endured. The forsworn and gallant warriors had fallen in battle or were taken captive. The people's freedom was shattered. The Temple was burned down. Much of the land was laid waste. Jerusalem was blotted out and its name was changed. It seemed as if Judah had fallen never to rise again, that the Jewish people was dead to memory. There was left only the Jewish faith. That too had to undergo a gruesome ordeal.

The Emperor Hadrian, conqueror of Bar Kochba, banned the practice of circumcision, the observance of the Sabbath, and the teaching of the Torah in the schools. These prescriptions were enforced with vicious severity, and great men of Israel, who imperilled their lives for the learning of the Torah, were put to death. Among them was Rabbi Akiva, vital spark in Bar Kochba's uprising.

But the deadlier attack came from within, from the adherents of that Christianity which sprang from the heart of Judaism. They had claimed at first that they put their faith in the Prophets and in the beliefs, hope and ideas which had taken root in Judaism during the period of the Second Temple, especially the beliefs in a Messiah and in the resurrection. For a long time the first followers of Jesus behaved completely as Jews, fulfilling all commandments and canons. But they discarded the national hope of Israel, hope of a redemption destined yet to be. The attraction of a number of expatriate Jews, who had little knowledge of Judaism or connection with the Jewish people, the adoption of the new religion by the Greeks and other nations which had been idolaters, and the proselytizing work of Saul accentuated the differences.

The Christian Jews did not take part in the national struggle against Rome. They were wont to inform the Roman authorities explicitly that they had no link or association with contumacious Jews. Saul bade his followers submit to the Roman authorities and accept their judgement. Jesus too is quoted as saying: 'Render therefore unto Caesar the things that are Caesar's; and unto God the things that are God's,' but Saul went further. Every man, he preached in one of his epistles, must yield to his superior, for there is no authority that is not there by the will of God, every authority that exists was by God appointed, and whosoever rebels against the appointed rulers rebels against the word of God.

The terrible losses and setbacks inflicted upon the Jews in the wars of Vespasian, Titus and Hadrian, the sore frustrations in their wake, prepared the ground for the teachings of Christianity. Many Jews in Palestine embraced the new religion and, even more, those living abroad in the lands of the Roman empire. In less than two hundred years after the fall of Bar Kochba, Christianity had become the dominant religion of that empire and was imposed by force on all the peoples of the Graeco-Roman world in Europe, Asia and North Africa. Only the Jewish people continued to resist it, suffering great hurt on that account over endless years, but faithful to its trust.

The people which was the first harbinger of the vision of universal redemption, of peace and freedom and justice for all nations, which based its Torah on the golden rule: 'Love thy neighbor as thyself'—this people was not drowned in the new creed, one attired in raiments of universality and preaching a meek submission, yet, when it came into power, suppressing and persecuting all who would not yield to it.

Christianity enthroned, which could subdue a world under the rule of Rome and its heirs, did not forgive the Jewish people for its obduracy, and in the name of a religion of love used them ill. Whole communities perished for the sake of hallowing the Name. But the people did not give in. It stood alone for centuries in this fearful welter and in the end it was not vanquished.

* * *

About five hundred years had passed since Bar Kochba, when Palestine was over-run by the Arabs. This invader, unlike most who preceded him, was not only a military power, but came armed with a new idea and a new doctrine, the teachings of Mohammed. The doctrine did not start in Palestine or develop within Judaism, although it did not lack a marked and recognizable Judaic influence, coming from the commercial and intellectual contact of the Prophet of Islam with Jews. The conquests of Mohammed and his disciples were more rapid and remarkable than Christianity's. The spread of his gospel among the Arab tribes in the seventh century, and soon after throughout Asia and Africa, was unique in its vast scope, its amazing swiftness and its strong cultural and linguistic impact. In a comparatively short space, the greater part of the Mediterranean had become an Arab-Moslem empire and Arabic the speech of the peoples of Mesopotamia, Assyria, all of North Africa and the Iberian peninsula. All the peoples of the Middle East and North Africa adopted the new religion, some willingly, some under compulsion. The only ones to weather this terrific storm were the Jews.

Jews had been living in the Arabian peninsula from the earliest times. There is a tradition among the Jews of the Yemen that they settled in that country during the reign of King Solomon. There is, however, no doubt that Jews had penetrated to the remotest parts of north and south Arabia as far back as the period of the Second Temple. King Herod sent a Jewish battalion of five thousand men to south Arabia to aid Caesar

Augustus in the conquest of the territory. Jews had come to Arabia from Babylon and Persia. In excavations at Beit Shearim near Haifa, the graves were discovered of a Jewish family from Himyar dating back to the second or third century of the Christian era. At the end of the fourth century Abu Karib Assad, a king of Yemen, was converted to Judaism and proselytized his people. The tragic fate is known of the Jewish king Du-Noas, who ruled in Himyar at the end of the first quarter of the sixth century and was vanquished by the Christian armies of Ethiopia. Many who were persecuted by the Ethiopians fled to north Arabia and settled in Yatrib (Medina) and its vicinity.

In the time of Mohammed (570-632) there were many Jews in the peninsula and a number of them were farmers and cattle-breeders. The Prophet used to meet them in his trading journeys and listen to their stories of the Torah and the Patriarchs, and hear them speak of the one-ness of God and the sacredness of Jerusalem. In the first phase of his prophetic evangel, Mohammed bade his followers face toward Jerusalem in their prayers. Thus he sought to win over the Jews. It was only after the Jews had put aside his teaching that Mecca, his native city, was made the orientation of Moslem devotions, and that he gave an Arab national character to the new religion. His hatred of the Jews was then intensified and he went forth against them sword in hand, and demanded that they accept his word. They would not submit, although refusal cost them dear. Save those who lived in the Yemen, all the Jews of Arabia were exiled or put to death. The remnants of the Jewish community in Palestine, especially the rural population, likewise failed to hold out. Some were assimilated by the conquerors, some left the country. But the nation as a whole was unshaken, despite recrudescent persecutions. As late as the twelfth century, five hundred and fifty years after Mohammed, Maimonides was moved to write to the Jews of the Yemen and encourage them to stand fast in face of the harsh decrees, the vexation and violence of Islam.

A new ideological onslaught was launched upon the Jewish nation, its unity and moral independence, in the aftermath of the great revolutions of recent times, the French at the end of the eighteenth century, the Russian at the beginning of the twentieth.

The French, with its slogan of liberty, equality and fraternity, was not confined to France. It powerfully affected all the countries of Europe, shook the foundations of monarchical dictatorships and feudal regimes, and provided the first impulse toward the liberation of the Jews, their emancipation, and equal rights for them, in the West.

By design, however, it demanded of Jews that they jettison their heritage, and many willingly did. A movement of assimilation began and threatened to engulf the nation.

'It seems that this ancient race, which fought for its life for thousands of years and had stood firm in the face of the storms of history the whole world over, could not endure against the blizzard of the nineteenth century, but succumbed, disavowing its essence and lowering itself to the level of a religious sect whose parts are incorporated in the bodies of other nations' (Dubnow). Assimilation claimed its many victims in the East no less than in the West. Still the eternal will of the Jewish people checked the fresh invasion; and emancipation led not to assimilation but to a new expression of national unity and of messianic longing. Judaism shed its theocratic form and put on lay garb, but its bonds with origin and Homeland were strengthened and its age-old speech was infused with new life. A secular Hebrew literature was created and the Zionist Movement was born. The trend toward emancipation, which had come from outside, became one toward auto-emancipation, towards escape from the shackles of foreign dependence and exile in strange lands. The first foundations were laid for the renewal of national autonomy in the Land of our birth.

Just as the French, the Russian revolution did not keep within its own frontiers. Its repercussions, like a tide, were felt then and are still being felt throughout the world. It faced the Jewish nation with one more ideological dilemma and evolutionary ordeal as grave and difficult as any before.

In 1917, the Balfour Declaration. In 1917 too, Russian revolution. But the new regime, if it promised mankind redemption, spelled ruin for us. The Jewry of Russia, largest and most virile community, was forcefully sundered from our nation and native land.

The revolution had proclaimed that it would give national equality to all peoples and races of Russia, and it kept its promise in its own way. Territorial autonomy was granted. The Soviet Union was formed as a federation of nations with equal rights, each in its nationally autonomous territory. As is the rule in all organization in the Soviet Union, the autonomy is subject to the absolute dictatorship of the Bolshevist party, with its center in Moscow. This central authority over all nations and inhabitants determines every economic and civil, every cultural and political regulation in every part of the gigantic republic. Nevertheless, within the framework of the Bolshevist dictatorship, all the peoples, small and large, were given equal rights. The culture, language and economy of each, to the extent that it was autonomous, developed in accordance with its needs.

Only one ethnic group, the Jewish, was in effect condemned to national and spiritual extinction. This was not because of any particular antipathy of the regime toward Jews, but because it took no account of the objective reality of a dispersed people without a country. The other groups, concentrated in specific areas, in large measure control and develop their own schools, Press and literature in their own language. Not only are national traditions undisturbed, they are positively encouraged and fostered as never under the Czars. But the language of the Jewish people, its education, literature and links with the national past were paralyzed, severed and strangled. Contact with nation and Zion was forbidden. The oldest culture among all the peoples of the Soviet Union was robbed of its heritage. The Hebrew book was thrust aside. All Hebrew schools were closed. Silence and national bereavement were laid upon a community of millions, which for generations had been the mainspring of Jewish creativeness.

Not since the war of Bar Kochba and Hadrian had the Jewish people been dealt so numbing a blow. It affected not only the millions of Jews living in Russia, but struck hard at Jews everywhere. To envisage the appalling deprivation which Jewry endured from the events and consequences of 1917, let us reckon the loss had it all happened not in 1917 but in 1880. If the Jews of Russia had been atrophied then and cut off, we would have lost the Bilu immigration, modern Hebrew literature—Mendele, Achad Ha'am, Bialik and their literary contemporaries, the Zionist Movement and the Jewish workers' movement, the Second Aliyah, the creators of collective settlement and of Hashomer, the builders of the labor villages and the founders of Tel Aviv, all the outstanding personalities of the Zionist Movement and the Yishuv for the last forty years, all the help rendered by Russian Jews towards the upbuilding of this country. We would have lost, as well, the Jewish workers' movement in America, the creative work everywhere of Jews from Russia.

The failures and triumphs of the Bolshevists in the first years after their seizure of power—setbacks in the international sphere and conquest and victory at home—led to far-reaching changes n the direction and objectives of the new regime. From assumption of rule by force they went on to its retention by force, and dictatorship became a permanent system instead of a temporary expedient.

The doctrine in effect became a narrow national ambition, which substituted for international socialism the interests of the one country. Reliance on the working classes throughout the world as the liberating force of every land and nation was replaced by trust exclusively in the Soviet Union and its military strength. The behest to workers' movements outside Russia is not that they bring about each the realization of socialism in their own country in harmony with its historical needs and circumstances as taught by Marx, but give unquestioning loyalty to the internal and international requirements of the Soviet Union as interpreted from time to time by the leaders of its ruling party.

The same absolute discipline is, of course, demanded of all its citizens, its working masses, farmers and intelligentsia; the same implicit obedience is exacted not only in social and political issues but also of scientific and cultural elements in literature and art, in history and language, in family life and personal conduct.

Since the founding of the Catholic Church and the universal sway of its Pope, no other power in the world has claimed such unreserved and world-wide authority. Backed by tremendous military might, it runs up the standard of a revolutionary socialist ideal and professes a wish to better the world and redeem humanity. Assuredly its rulers believe that what is good for Russia is necessarily good for other countries, and that Russia is in truth the world's redeemer. But precisely in this belief there is nothing new, either in Russian or in other history.

The Jewish nation had never yielded to superior physical force; it had kept itself free morally and intellectually even when it lacked the strength to preserve political and economic freedom. It was now meeting the cruelest of trials. There was no nation in whose life and records, in whose spiritual development, the vision of universal redemption played a larger and more constant part. No other people longed for peace among the nations and the unity of mankind more intensely. The great figures of its latter generations were men who had probed deeply into the ideas of social revolution. The best of Jewish youth in all countries, above all in Czarist Russia, were in the front-line of every fight for liberation. Almost all of Russian Jewry stood for the men who were breaking the tyranny of the Czars, and Jewish champions were in the vanguard of revolt.

The terror of pogroms, which had darkened Jewish life in Russia for decades, ended only with Bolshevist victory. The Jewish millions knew at last that pogroms could not be. Lenin, prophet, law-maker and commander-in-chief of the revolution, had Jewish friends and followers, and even when almost all of them were successively 'liquidated,' the persecution and humiliation borne under the Czars were not so soon to fade from Jewish memory. Within Russia and outside it, many who could not square the socialist watchword of the Bolshevist party with the acts of its leaders still felt they must acknowledge the change wrought in the legal status of the Jews.

Yes, the new regime destroyed all trace of Czarist discrimination. The *individual Jew* has the same rights as the non-Jew. For all that, the Jewish community was smitten fatally by the Bolshevists and their totalitarian demands striking at the soul of Judaism, and the Jewish people the world over sensed the thrust. Yet thirty years of its pounding and more have proved that the steamroller of dictatorship could not crush the Jewish spirit, and though many excellent men in the community agreed with the dictatorship without reserve and accepted its total requisitions willingly or perforce, among the masses the spark of spiritual independence was not quenched nor their spiritual bond with the Jewish people and Homeland broken.

Instances of spiritual self-abasement, of self-contempt and slavishness were not wanting among Jewish revolutionaries long before Bolshevism. Even in Czarist days they did not frown on pogroms against the Jews; for them pogrom was a rising of the Russian peasant against the propertied class, and Jewish blood a lubricant of the wheels of revolution.

Those who now proscribed Hebrew and the Zionist Movement were members of the Jewish section of the Bolshevist party

(Yevsektzia), whose hate of Zion and of the sacred tongue exceeded their communist zeal, and the personal intervention of Lenin had to be invoked to allow the Hebrew theatre 'Habimah' to play in Moscow. When, in 1923, the Histadruth asked to take part in the World Agricultural Exposition in Moscow it was the Yevsektzia which opposed its coming, but the authorities disregarded the odious advice.

Yet this same Russian Jewry, even since the Bolshevists came into undisputed power, has given Israel the best of its pioneer youth, whose achievements here speak for the capacity dormant in it, the urges which live on in it unseen and not all the physical and moral coercion in the world can kill.

When the State of Israel came into being, it seemed as though the prolonged struggle of the Jewish people had at length been crowned with final success. This is a false and dangerous illusion, not only because the work of building is not finished and the ingathering of the exiles only at its beginning, not only because political and economic independence is not yet won, but because the ideological battleground of our moral independence is become bloodier still. The seriousness does not lie in an intellectual and moral encounter between any world Power or Powers and ourselves. Here force or numerical superiority is never the decisive factor and the Jewish people, though it be the 'least of peoples,' has no reason to dread the outcome even if world aggressors and the mightiest of Powers are banded against it. True to itself, it will not kowtow to moral-ideological domination by any foreign Power. On social and scientific, or spiritual and cultural questions, and concerning values of liberty and equality, of justice and peace, it will not bend the knee to those who appoint themselves, by the force of their authority and military or economic resources, to be the supreme judges of mankind. No, the seriousness lies in inner strife. In a nation as small as ours, there are always groups attracted by the dazzling appeal of great Powers, whose political, economic and military strength is tremendous and their influence in the world inordinate. They are not attracted only for their private good, although one should not dismiss that prosaic factor, but by the potentialities, the breadth, the power, the riches of rulers of the world. This weakness of obsequious toadying before the 'poritz,' the squire, has been styled 'mayofes' in our modern history, and 'mayofes' Jews are to be found in circles without self-respect or enough faith in their nation. In Rightist circles, they are called the Council for Judaism, headed by American millionaires; in Leftist or revolutionary, it is the Yevsektzia, headed by writers out of whose mouths their master's voice is always heard.

* * *

Since the establishment of the State, these open and obvious assimilationists and separatists have ceased to be specially dangerous; at the moment we have a faithful and a sure support for Jews wherever they may be—the dignity of Israel in its own Land. But even in the State there are many in whom the cleavage persists between the man and the Jew, which cleft the Jewish soul in the Diaspora. The misguided and miserable doctrine of the wise men of the Diaspora: 'be a Jew in your own tent and a man outside it,' has followers even here, where all is Jewish of a new brand. It is easy nowadays to be freed from physical Galuth: one has only to settle in Israel. But it is not so easy to turn one's back on spiritual and moral Galuth. That cannot be done by external change, by moving from one place to another. It comes from within, through great spiritual, intellectual and moral effort, and of such not everyone is capable.

'Be a Jew in your own tent and a man outside it'. In the State this would mean that we should only determine our Jewish affairs—immigration, and settlement; but as for human affairs, problems of society and international policy, who are we and what is our strength that we should meddle in them independently? On these issues we are to accept the judgment of the great and aggressive, who know all, who are empowered to do all, who decide everything. There is an omnipotent power 'somewhere', apostle of the redemption of mankind—and our part is just to chant Amen to all that its autocrat tells us to think and do and say. And if what he tells us today is the exact opposite of yesterday, we may not ponder on his ways; he knows what he is doing, only he knows.

The loyalists of Jewish independence will not adopt foreign judgments. They realize the limited province and restricted capacity of the Jewish people. They respect and esteem the great Powers responsible for the fate of hundreds of millions, whose vast authority goes beyond the boundaries of their countries and extends over most of the world. But there is one empire in which the Jewish nation regards itself as the equal of any in all respects, even in the capacity to influence mankind today and the coming generations. It is the empire of the spirit and of vision.

The great Powers, the nations which rule far and wide, have no monopoly in deciding for all men on a new course to freedom and peace, justice and equality, to redemption and the betterment of the world and the realizing of man's finest hopes. When strong nations use power even for a good cause, in the nature of things it is converted from a means into an end. All the great conquerors, Persian, Greek and Roman, Arab and Mongol, French, British and Russian, have always claimed that they were bestowing the blessings of their superior civilization upon the conquered. It was not always an empty pretext. Many did in fact give their subject nations better government and a higher culture. But history records not a single instance of a 'charitable' conquest which did not eventually oppress and enslave. Rule by violence, not resting upon the free will of the ruled, has its own ruthless, inescapable logic. You cannot maintain it without force and suppression, and the need and desire to hold on to it overbear all other considerations.

But to bring about cultural and moral advancement one need not possess material strength and military power; small nations no less than great may be capable of pointing mankind the way to scientific, spiritual and cultural progress. In their long experience, there is nothing to make Jews feel inferior to the strong or the aggressor.

After millennial wandering and woes, they have at last reached the land of their origin, where they first were sovereign. They will not give up their historic vision and spiritual heritage: the hope that their national redemption should be part of the redemption of all peoples. Their independence now will keep its universal purpose, they will not be vassals or in alien bondage when they shape their future and chart the way to attainment of their ultimate ideal. In Israel, there is no rift between the Jew and the man. Intellectual and moral dependence is irreconcilable with its dignity. *Independence is indivisible.* There cannot be independence in Jewish and subservience in world affairs. Jewish life embraces the world and all that is in it. Independent Israel means affirming the essence, the root, the origin. It means that we plot the course we are to follow now and hereafter, in internal and foreign relations and on present and future issues, in complete and utter freedom and in harmony with our will, and our needs, our circumstances, our desires and our vision, subservient to no external or foreign dominion, large or lesser.

Spiritual independence does not rule out a bond with all humanity, any more than political independence is incompatible with international ties or economic independence implies economic autarchy. Mutual bonds between States and nations are eternal facts and historical imperatives. Each nation takes sustenance from others, from the legacy of all the ages, from every conquest by the human spirit. Inter-relation is cosmic law. There is no thing in the world, of whatever magnitude, from the invisible and impalpable electron to the powerful elements in infinity, that is not related to its own kind and to other things. All existence is one endless chain of inter-relation, in the world of spirit as in the world of matter. The thought and poetry, the art and literature, of generations and peoples influence and feed each other, and less than ever before is it possible today for a people to live alone.

With the coming of political independence we have become more citizens of the world than once we were, although, scattered as we were in all corners of the earth, wandering from country to country and from nation to nation, our citizenship had in it more of the universal even then than other nations showed. Our independence puts that citizenship on a sound and normal basis. Only through sovereign and territorial status are we immersed in all human problems and aware of human needs and troubles, equal partners at last in them all.

Modern means of communication on land, by sea and in the air, and radio links, have wiped out distances and demolished barriers.

Jewish dispersal is also a potent factor in our universality. The Jews who fought in the Israel Defense Forces came from fifty-five countries and from five continents. Knowingly or not, we are nourished through these channels by all the people in whose midst Jews have settled. Just as we shall eat Argentinian beef and Russian grain, plough with American tractors and smelt Belgian steel, burn Mexican petrol and wear British cloth and furnish our homes from Canadian timber, so we shall read the literature of all nations and seek wisdom wherever it may be found. Into our language we shall pour the treasures of the spirit and the intellect, science and poetry of all nations, so that the spiritual inheritance of men everywhere becomes ours too. No one can read our Book of Books without listening to echoes of the mighty civilizations which once encompassed us. We may proudly admire the singular capacity of our people in Maccabee days to resist the pull of such rich and great cultures as the Greek. Still we must regret that our finest minds in the past could not distinguish the dross and trivia of Hellenic culture in its declining phase from the magnificent spiritual values of Greek genius in ascendancy, in the days of the Return from Babylon and the Great Assembly. Perhaps much in our history would have been different and in the history of the civilized world, if, when our sacred literature was turned into Greek, our scholars, who knew that tongue, had turned the works of Sophocles, Thucydides, Plato and other Greek thinkers into Hebrew, and striven to learn military art and statesmanship from the Greeks and Romans.

* * *

Having so viewed world history and many lands for four thousand years, we have come back to our starting place and for the third time established the sovereignty of Israel. We shall not now shed our precious and diversified international experience. We shall not shut ourselves up in our shell. We shall be open to take in all the cultures of the world, all the conquests of the spirit. We shall not segregate or isolate ourselves. We shall maintain our bond with the great world: a bond but not bondage in any form. The criterion of spiritual and moral freedom is free judgment and free conscience. Only if we use our own judgment to determine for ourselves what is good or bad in itself, and what is good or bad for us, are we free men acting of our own accord. To bend to the judgment of a foreign Power is to surrender inner freedom and personal independence. Independence springs from the heart, the soul, the will of the people, and only through that inner strength is outward self-sufficiency attained and upheld.

That is the essence and content of the spiritual struggle of the Jews ever since they became a nation: against their conscience, they will not submit even when foreign judgment is backed by superior physical force.

The Jewish people have always spurned physical supremacy.

DAVID BEN GURION

To deny that physical power is supreme is not to deny its worth, for that would mean rejecting Jewish history from the days of Joshua to the Israel Defense Forces. Nay more, to deny physical force is a denial of the world, of life itself, and was always alien to the spirit of the Jewish people. Herein lies one of the fundamental differences between Jewish and Christian doctrine.

From the Prophets down to the days of Einstein, Jewish genius opposed the theory of the duality of matter and spirit, Jewish intuition, religious and scientific, has always believed in the oneness of creation and experience, despite their numerous forms and phenomena. And although the greatest of our Prophets, thinkers, and teachers affirmed throughout the ages that the highest destiny of Israel was in the kingdom of the spirit, they did not decry the body or its needs. For no soul is without body, nor any universal human mission without sovereign nationhood.

The victory of Jewish over Arab arms played a decisive part in the establishment of our State. The root and source of it were in the moral and spiritual superiority of the Jewish nation; it was the Jewish spirit that sent our arms victorious. Faith in the spirit's sublimity accompanied the Jewish people throughout its long journey down the years from the revelation on Sinai to our own War of Independence. It was cherished by all the great ones of Israel, who shaped the nation from its beginnings, who created and fostered its Torah and its song, its prophetic yearnings, and its literature, its justice and its laws, its ultimate vision and the messianic hope of its unity and of its racial and universal mission. It was cherished by the men who led Israel's wars of spiritual and political independence and who, sanctifying the Name, perished in the massacres of the Crusades, at the stake of the Inquisition, in the pogroms of Chmelnitzki and in the Nazi holocausts. It was cherished by the men who founded, built and developed the work of settlement which led to the State.

It was bound up with the belief by the Jews in the *dignity of man*. Man was created in the image of God. There can be no more profound, lofty or penetrating expression than this of the greatness, worth and dignity of man. Our conception of God embodies the ultimate of goodness and beauty, justice and truth. To us human life is sacred and dear. Men created in God's image are equal. They are an end in themselves, not a means. No wonder then that our sages based the Torah on the golden rule—'Love thy neighbor as thyself.' Not only the fellow-Jew: 'But the stranger that dwelleth with you shall be unto you as one born among you, and thou shalt love him as thyself: for ye were strangers in the land of Egypt.'

From the earliest times Judaism held a universal outlook and embraced all of humanity: the echoes reach us in the prayers of King Solomon as he finished building the Temple. He prayed first for his people, then for all men saying: 'Moreover concerning a stranger that is not of thy people Israel, but cometh out of a far country for thy name's sake; . . . when he shall come and pray toward this house; Hear thou in heaven thy dwelling place and do according to all that the stranger calleth to thee for. . . .'

The whole Book of Jonah is given up to the idea that the mercy of God enwraps all in equal measure, those who worship idols as well as the Jews themselves. When Jonah cried out in anger against the Lord because He had spared Nineveh, the Lord said to him: 'Thou hast had pity on the gourd, for the which thou hast not labored, neither madest it grow; which came up in a night, and perished in a night: And should not I spare Nineveh, that great city, wherein are more than six score thousand persons that cannot discern between their right hand and their left hand; and also much cattle?'

And last, jewelling this faith of Jews that the spirit must prevail is the distant vision, the source of messianic hope and the longing for national and universal redemption.

The Jewish people conceived primordially an original epoch-making thought, unfamiliar to the people of Egypt or Babylon, of India or China, of Greece or Rome or their modern descendants in Europe. Unlike the rest, our people did not pine for the past, for the legendary Golden Age gone without return; it turned its gaze to the future, to that final day when 'the earth shall be full of the knowledge of the Lord, as the waters cover the sea' and the nations shall beat their swords into plowshares and 'nation shall not lift up a sword against nation, neither shall they learn war any more.'

Not a feeble craving for a fictional splendor of the past, but a vision of the future, of a reign of justice and peace between all nations—that was the historical philosophy which the Prophets of Israel instilled into their people, and which was handed down by the people to the best among the nations in all lands. The vision sustained us in distress and affliction and brought us to this wonderful stage, to the beginning of national redemption and, with it, to a faint glimmering of redemption for the whole of mankind.

For long, the Jews regarded themselves as a chosen people, and had reason enough to think so, while their only yardstick was a credo, a moral consciousness. A modern Jew, however, will remember the cultural distinction of other nations in all eras, their discoveries and social progress. We have much to learn from foreign peoples in economics, State administration, research and technology. Let us honor all such without genuflection or surrender, nor seek ourselves to reign. Let us go our own special way with our conscience to guide.

To differentiate between good and evil we need draw only on our own moral genius, which has ever made luminous our lives. We will make ours the true way to freedom, justice and fraternity, in absolute intellectual and moral independence, neither servile nor plagiarist.

This, then, is our intellectual struggle, never to be decided by force of arms, but by the spirit only. Fear not, for the spirit of Israel will not betray us. Of that surety, four thousand years of history are witness.

* * *

We have seen two transforming wonders: the rebirth of the State, and the victories of the Israel Defense Forces. But they do not fill the revolutionary content of the new era. They are only a beginning and a preparation for the most vital event, the homecoming of the people.

This is not the first time that Jews have come back to their country and to sovereign status in it. It happened before, some two thousand five hundred years ago in the days of Zerubbabel, Nehemiah and Ezra, when exiles returned from Babylon and founded the Second Temple.

The present ingathering is other and more arduous. Then the people was exiled in one country, and had not been there long. Only about seventy years had passed since the expulsion. The Homeland was not far away. Many had family ties with those who stayed behind. In those days Cyrus, high-minded lord of Persia, 'made a proclamation throughout all his kingdom, and put it also in writing, saying, Who is there among you of all his people? his God be with him, and let him go up to Jerusalem, which is in Judah and build the house of the Lord God of Israel.' The number of those that responded was not large, indeed only about a tithe of arrivals in Israel in the past two years. In the Book of Ezra, detailed and seemingly accurate statistics are preserved of the immigrants from Babylon, their property, horses, mules and camels. It says:

> 'The whole congregation together was forty and two thousand three hundred and three score, beside their servants and their maids, of whom there were seven thousand three hundred thirty and seven; and there were among them two hundred singing men and singing women. Their horses were

seven hundred thirty and six; their mules two hundred forty and five; their camels, four hundred thirty and five; their asses, six thousand seven hundred and twenty.'

It is otherwise with the exiles of the twentieth century, and still today many languish in Babylon who heeded not Cyrus. Jewish dispersion is ancient. It preceded the destruction of the Second and even the First Temple. As long ago as the seventh century BCE we find Jews in Egypt. It is possible that they were exiled after King Hosea fell in battle against Pharaoh Necho. At any rate it is clear that the Jews who went down to Egypt in the days of Jeremiah found Jewish settlements in Tahpanhes, Noph, Migdol and Pathros. At the gate of the Egyptian Negev there was a Jewish garrison village in the sixth century BCE and it was joined by Johanan son of Kareah, with the 'captains of the forces and the remnants of the people' who had refused to listen to Jeremiah.

There were Jews in Syria and Asia Minor even before the Hasmonaean period. Inscriptions in Delphi tell of the liberation of Jewish slaves during the Maccabee Wars. Earlier, the Prophet Joel upbraided Tyre and Sidon, because: 'The children also of Judah and the children of Jerusalem have ye sold unto the Grecians, that ye might remove them far from their border.' In the Book of Isaiah, too, there is a passage on the scattering of Israel across the seas: 'And it shall come to pass in that day, that the Lord shall set his hand again the second time to recover the remnant of his people, which shall be left, from Assyria and from Egypt, and from Pathros, and from Cush, and from Elam, and from Shinar, and from Hamat, and from the islands of the sea.'

The Greek geographer Strabo, who lived in the time of Herod the First, writes that the Jewish people had reached every city and country, and that 'there was not to be found a place in the populated world which had not absorbed members of this nation or was not seized by them.' Philo the Alexandrian, who was born ninety years before the destruction of the Second Temple, wrote: 'No one country can contain the Jews because of their great numbers, and therefore they make their livelihood in most of the rich cities of Europe and Asia, in the islands, of the sea and on the land. They consider the Holy City as the city of their origin, where on a hill there stands the Temple of the Lord. The countries in which their fathers and forefathers have lived for generations they love as their native land, because there they were born and brought up.'

And so the wandering went on—to all parts of the Old World and still on, to the continents of the New.

The wrathful chastisement—mark it well again—had come to pass:

'And the Lord shall scatter thee among all people, from the one end of the earth even unto the other . . . And among these nations shalt thou find no ease, neither shall the sole of thy foot have rest: but the Lord shall give thee there a trembling heart, and failing of eyes, and sorrow of mind: And thy life shall hang in doubt before thee; and thou shalt fear day and night, and have none assurance of thy life . . . for the fear of thine heart wherewith thou shalt fear, and for the sight of thine eyes which thou shalt see.'

* * *

While usurpers ruled the Land, all efforts to return were frustrate, try as we would. Now, with Bar Kochba and Rabbi Akiva in their graves these nigh on two thousand years, the State of Israel has re-arisen and the gates of the Homeland are open wide to the scattered folk.

It is hard, nearly impossible, to decide just where the thing began. Who will identify the first wave of the immigration that led on to the State? With the establishment of Mikveh Israel and Petah Tiqvah, the foundations were laid for our modern agricultural settlement. But immigration had preceded these experiments and there are people here who belong to the fifth generation, or earlier, of native-born. Before the first World War the community was less than 100,000; its number fell off during the fighting and at its end there were less than 60,000. By the second World War it had multiplied ten-fold, and when the State was established it had about 650,000 Jews. In the two years that followed, more than 400,000 Jews have come to Israel. Not only the tempo and numbers are different; there is a fundamental change in the essential character of immigration. Entire territorial groups are being transplanted from their foster-countries and brought to their ransomed Homeland, from Bulgaria and the Yemen, Yugoslavia and Morocco, Germany and Algiers, Austria and Tunis, Turkey and Egypt.

The greatest ingathering of all is taking place in the Israel Defense Forces. During the War of Independence, there were volunteers from twenty-one European countries, from fourteen North and South American countries, from ten North, South and Central African countries, from five countries in Asia—Burma, India, China, the Yemen and Turkey, and from the remote Antipodes. I doubt whether there has ever been such a cosmopolitan Army. And that was only a foretaste of what was to come. When the fighting was over, a tidal immigration began, veritably a new Exodus, not from one but from many Egypts. Now, in one month, more Jews arrive than in a year of the Mandate. On the American scale, this represents an immigration of forty millions a year, on the Russian, of fifty-three millions.

This unparalleled return, this staggering, challenging, unheard-of movement of men, is the cardinal fact and the primary task of our generation. Without it, our independence will not be established nor our State attain full stature. This year we have the first million in our Land, in a way the greatest event in our history since the triumph of the Maccabees. But it is only a beginning, that can promise no security, no completion, if it does not broaden out into swift continuance.

No one can foretell if all of Israel will be reunited in this Land. The Diaspora has those who do not hold themselves exiles nor mean to settle here, and those who cannot and do not want to stay where they are because their life is unhappy, poor and unsafe. The dividing line is not fixed or unalterable. The fortunes may change of a community appearing content and rooted, and it may all at once be humbled and banished as were the Jews of Germany. But what matters is not whether complacency in the Diaspora is justified or not in the long run. It is not the prognosis by ideologists that determines the wish to come to Israel, but the feeling of the majority in each community, and the feeling does not depend on being a Zionist or an anti-Zionist. The Jews of America of all trends are firmly convinced that they have no need to emigrate to Israel. Of course, even such countries may sponsor an immigration prompted by a pioneer and Zionist impulse, but this is a *personal* immigration of individuals, though for all that their number may yet reach hundreds, even thousands.

Our first and urgent duty now is to gather in those communities *which have no choice*. If only they are allowed to depart, they come, and will keep on coming, in masses. Those in East Europe and the countries of Islam want to come, and they must, though for some the gates are shut against departure. But all who may go we must bring, even if Israel is not yet ready to absorb them. The great majority have nothing left. Property or capital, all was taken away. They have been cheated of education and deprived of culture. They come to us without means or trade, without learning or training, without our language, without knowledge of this country or national values.

The tremendous business of absorption, far more exacting than to win the War of Independence, depends upon two undertakings that call for the nation's utmost effort: land settlement and education.

The people cannot be restored to the Land if the Land is not itself restored. To make the wasteland bloom, to subdue the elements, to do an enormous job of housing, irrigation and power projects, to build a variegated economy up to self-support in agriculture and industry—these are the material conditions. But material and economic absorption is not the whole answer. Nor are housing and settlement and work. Nations, like men, need more than loaves.

The communities which are being dissolved in the Galuth and assembled in Israel do not yet constitute a nation. They are a mixed multitude, shapeless clay, without a common speech, untutored and rootless, not nurtured on the traditions and ideals of the race.

The Jews are of those rare breeds that for two thousand five hundred years, have maintained a system of general education, and even after forfeit of independence and Homeland, in all of their wanderings guarded jealously the teaching of their sons. Yet a large proportion of the immigrants come to us illiterate, with no Jewish or general lore. Time and place have brought this about. They are the children of an age of ruin and destruction, of world wars and of that material and spiritual decline which sets in when the very foundations of the universe quake. They come from backward, isolated and victimized countries.

The spiritual absorption of this immigration, its synthesis and reshaping, the transformation of the rawest of matter into a cultured, creative and independent nation, aspiring to a vision, is no easier than its economic absorption. It needs a gigantic moral and educational endeavor, a profound and pure love, to unify these long neglected creatures, to share with them our national treasures and standards, to integrate them into our society and culture, our language and creativity. And this we must do not as dispensers of charity, but as partners in destiny.

The progress that we, veterans of the Yishuv, achieved, our spiritual and material attainments, were not won altogether by our own hands. We had the rich bequest of our forefathers and we climbed upon the shoulders of preceding generations. What we here possess is the estate of the whole Jewish people, and only as such can it continue to exist. In the un-lettered immigrants are latent all those attributes and potentialities which made the builders of this country what they are. Nothing has been done by us in the economic or political sphere, the military or spiritual, that will not also be done, in time, by those immigrants, if they get from us the help and care we once got from our parents and our kibbutzim.

This education, on which depends the future of State no less than of immigrants, will not be confined to the schools. No doubt the new generation, born or brought up here, will assimilate and adapt itself as did the children of the earlier settlers. But we dare not, we cannot, wait until that new generation grows up. The work of educating and helping in assimilation must be extended to all immigrants of all ages. The deep and rapid change which can be effected in a child cannot be effected in an adult immigrant at the same rate or with the same ease. But we have a powerful instrument for education besides the school, and it is the Army.

The most vital task of the Army is to safeguard the security of the State. It deserves all the talents, time and energy of the best of our young people. But it is not the only task. It is incumbent on the Army to pioneer and educate, builder of the nation and redeemer of the desert. If we are not a unified people, if we do not plow our wastes, we shall have no security. Our security is a problem different from any other nation's, and not only because we are few, but because we are not yet fully a nation and have no real country. A population in which one man does not grasp his fellow's language, which does not know the Land, which is not held together by bonds of a common culture and a national ideal, is no nation to stand fast in the hour of trial against enemy or inquisitor.

It was no liking for 'luxuries' that passed the Military Service

Act, which makes it obligatory for every young man and woman of eighteen to undergo training in agriculture. When the Bill was put to the Knesseth on August 15, 1949, we explained that our Army would necessarily be small and our limited manpower needed for works of development and the absorption of immigrants, and for basic economic and cultural duties. The foremost aim of the Army should be superior quality. The technical and professional knowledge which every modern army has, the physical and spiritual qualities every soldier needs, the improvements in organization which increase total military effectiveness, all these we must have. But alone they are not enough. For the urgency of our unusual circumstances, geographical and historical, demands that the Army add an important element— pioneering. In the Knesseth we asked that this be not regarded as a monopoly of 'privileged' groups. It is not the special province of specially gifted individuals. It abides in the soul of every man. In every man are hidden powers and gifts and spiritual riches, whereof only a tiny part finds expression. Historical needs and directed education will find a way to them. They will open and quicken the springs which flow unseen, and lift every man to heights of courage and adventure. Every capable commander knows this secret, and can transmute his army of ordinary men into a host of heroes. So intuition blazed our trail to vanguard virtues buried deep in young Jews of villages of Lithuania and Poland, Galicia and Rumania, and of American cities. The immigration of the next few years will be largely from the Orient, the countries of Islam, of Asia and Africa, whose recent generations of Jews lacked means or opportunity to enjoy the blessings of Jewish and Gentile culture. But there is no ground for assuming that they are essentially and fundamentally different from the others. They also have untapped sources of pioneering courage and creativeness. If we devote to them but a fraction of the effort we invested in those others, the same success will attend us.

The Army has been entrusted with the training of our pioneers; it is an instrument for the synthesis of the ingathered communities, their unification and cultural advancement. Suffer not the nonsense of detractors saying that an army by its nature engenders stupidity, careerism, idleness and vanity. To the youth which it is to instruct, beginning with the cadet corps, our Army must hand on fundamental traits of physical and moral purity, knowledge of the language and the Land, agile body and mind, love of Homeland and true comradeship, strength of spirit and creative initiative, and discipline and order. All these, and, as well, the military skill and qualities required for the strict purposes of security.

The Jewish army was almost always a people's army. In Joshua's time the warriors were men who had settled and built up the land. It was a fighting nation that conquered then, not mercenaries who made war for hire. The greatest sin was to take 'of the accursed thing.' For a soldier to put enemy booty among his belongings was shamefully to violate the Covenant. For such a deed Achan, son of Carmi of the tribe of Judah, was put to death by Joshua, his property confiscated, and the place of shame called the valley of Achor 'unto this day.'

When Othniel, son of Kenaz, brother of Caleb, took Debir in the Negev, and was moved by Achsah his wife, daughter of Caleb, to ask her father for springs of water: 'for thou hast given me a south land . . . And he gave her the upper springs and the nether springs,' that was perhaps the first 'Nahal'* in the Israel army to irrigate the Negev.

Not for nothing were the Jews allowed to go home to watch over their plantations in times of war, even during a siege. 'When thou shalt besiege a city a long time, in making war against it to take it, thou shalt not destroy the trees thereof by forcing an axe against them: for thou mayest eat of them, and thou shalt

---

* Pioneer combatant youth movement.

not cut them down (for the tree of the field is man's life) to employ them in the siege.'

The rules of mobilization which Moses laid down are also eloquent. 'And it shall be, when ye are come nigh unto the battle . . . And the officers shall speak unto the people, saying: What man is there that hath built a new house, and hath not dedicated it? let him go and return to his house, lest he die in the battle, and another man dedicate it. And what man is he that hath planted a vineyard, and hath not yet eaten of it? let him also go and return unto his house, lest he die in the battle, and another man eat of it. And what man is there that hath betrothed a wife, and hath not taken her? let him go and return unto his house, lest he die in the battle, and another man take her.'

And because it was a people's army and the whole nation fought, they did not want cowards in their ranks, and this too was one of Moses' rules: 'And the officers shall speak further unto the people, and they shall say, What man is there that is fearful and fainthearted? let him go and return unto his house, lest his brethren's heart faint as well as his heart.'

One of our great scholars, Rabbi Johanan ben Zakkai, who lived at the close of the Second Temple, commented thus: 'See how God has regard for the honor of men: what man is there that is fearful and fainthearted, let him go and return, and the man who built a house, who planted a vineyard, who betrothed a wife, all had to bring their witnesses, except the fearful and the fainthearted for his witnesses were with him. He heard the sound of closing shutters, and started, the sound of horses neighing, and trembled, the blowing of horns, and was terrified, saw the drawing of a sword—and water came down from between his knees.'

This was the custom only in wars undertaken without God's bidding. In a holy war, when the nation was attacked, everyone went, the bridegroom and the bride, for to defend the nation against the aggressor was the bounden duty of every man and woman, none exempted.

Remission they gave not in disregard of the army's grave responsibility, but on the contrary, to strengthen morale and to free it of men who could not devote themselves to warfare whether because they had made new family ties or because their affairs at home were not arranged, or because of an organic or moral frailty which could not be cured. Once the fighting forces were rid of such elements strict discipline was imposed, and severe measures were taken against those who ran away, for flight is the beginning of defeat. They would place armed men in front and behind to strike down those who tried to turn back.

Israel had no regular army until the period of the kings. Saul was the first to organize a standing force of three thousand men: 'whereof two thousand were with Saul in Michmash and in mount Beth-el, and a thousand were with Jonathan in Gibeah of Benjamin: and the rest of the people he sent every man to his tent.' Solomon maintained a cavalry of twelve thousand.

Military perfection was reached in the reign of Uzziah, son of Amaziah, king of Judah, in the middle of the eighth century BCE. He was a contemporary of Jeroboam the Second, son of Joash. These two kings extended the boundaries of Israel, a thing not done since the united kingdom was split on Solomon's death. Jeroboam pushed back the northern line and restored Damascus and Hamath to Israel, and Uzziah extended the border of Judah in the south. He fought the Philistines at Gath, Jabneh and Ashdod in western Palestine, and the Arabians living in Gur-Baal in the eastern part. He not only enlarged the territory but developed it, built new cities in the over-run regions, increased their agricultural area, installed irrigation systems in the arid lands of the south, and encouraged cattle-raising and orchards. I say the lovely words again. 'Also he built towers in the desert, and digged many wells: for he had much cattle, both in the low country, and in the plains: husbandmen also, and vine dressers in the mountains, and in Carmel: for he loved husbandry.'

One of his principal enterprises was the building of Elath. Solomon before him had realized the value of the Bay of Aqaba for the economy and status of his kingdom, had opened and exploited copper mines in Wadi 'Arabah and built a foundry at Ezion-geber. He gave thought as well to seafaring and shipping, 'and made a navy of ships in Ezion-geber, which is beside Elath, on the shore of the Red Sea, in the land of Edom.' Soon, however, Edom once more possessed Elath, and not until Amaziah, son of Joash, 'slew of Edom in the valley of Edom ten thousand, and took Selah by war' did his son Uzziah succeed in reaching Wadi 'Arabah, once more to build Elath and restore it to Judah.

But Uzziah's greatest work was to uplift the army in organization and equipment. No earlier king in Israel did so much to strengthen the security forces and improve their fighting caliber. It was not as in the days of Saul when 'there was no smith found throughout the land of Israel.' Uzziah made sure his army had all types of weapons known to Egypt and Assyria and the neighboring countries. He invented new weapons too, and formed the first artillery of Israel. Who can weary of the tale? 'And he made in Jerusalem engines, invented by cunning men, to be on the towers and upon the bulwarks, to shoot arrows and great stones withal. And his name spread far abroad; for he was marvellously helped, till he was strong.'

The historian records the size of Uzziah's army as 'three hundred thousand and seven thousand and five hundred, that made war with mighty power to help the king against the enemy.' Another figure given in the same chapter seems more likely: 'the whole number of the chief of the fathers of the mighty men of valour were two thousand and six hundred.' Still it is evident from his boldness and courage, and his excursions into the lands of the Philistines in the west, the Arabs in the east, and Edom in the south, that Uzziah had a large army whose might was not only in numbers but in up-to-date armament. 'And Uzziah prepared for them throughout all the host shields, and spears, and helmets, and habergeons, and bows, and slings to cast stones.' These were all the weapons of defense or offense known then and for long after.

The classic instance of labor and defense combined was in the first Return to Zion. Those who came back from Babylon found that 'the walls of Jerusalem also are broken down, and the gates thereof are burned with fire.' At the bidding of Nehemiah, they began to build the city wall and gates. But when the enemies of Israel, 'Sanballat the Horonite, and Tobiah, and the Arabians and the Ammonites, and the Ashdodites, heard that the walls of Jerusalem were made up, and that the breaches began to be stopped, then they were very wroth, And conspired all of them together to come and to fight against Jerusalem, and to hinder it.' Nehemiah bade again that the work of construction go on: 'For the builders, everyone had his sword girded by his side, and so builded.' Nehemiah relates: 'And it came to pass from that time forth, that the half of my servants wrought in the work, and the other half of them held both the spears, the shields, and the bows, and the habergeons . . . They which builded on the wall, and they that bare burdens, with those that laded, every one with one of his hands wrought in the work, and with the other held a weapon . . . in the night they may be a guard to us, and labor on the day. So neither I nor my brethren, nor my servants, nor the men of the guard which followed me, none of us put off our clothes . . . '

* * *

This double burden has to be sustained by our generation too, but it is much heavier now. We must rebuild the walls of Jerusalem, we must make fertile the barren lands. We must teach the hundreds of thousands returning how to work and how to fight, raising up a nation that will make the ruins of its country gracious again, and defend it against foes.

Our Army cannot be just a military weapon. It must be a medium of learning and absorption, of settlement and reconstruction. Within its framework young immigrants will acquire a knowledge of language and country, and our youth be taught to reclaim desolation, to establish border villages, to colonize the desert, the approaches to Jerusalem, the plains and the hills; and in navy and air force how to control the forces of nature at sea and in the skies.

Not all the immigrants will or can get their training in the Army. The civilian community is not spared the duty of material and spiritual absorption. All settled places, urban and rural, kibbutzim, colonies, cooperative villages, cooperative societies, business firms, workers' organizations, craftsmen, farmers and manufacturers' associations, associations of the free professions, municipalities, local councils, every working man and woman, clerk, physician, teacher, writer, contractor, landlord, manufacturer, merchant, householder—all are enjoined to outstretch a loyal and brotherly hand, to guide the immigrants and educate them, help them settle and take root, not for one or two, but for many, many years, and respite there will be none. There is no higher call.

This conglomeration of humanity, flooding in from foreign lands of exile, will be purified, tempered and cleansed in the crucible of fraternity and military discipline. Sectarian differences will be wiped out and patriotic unity forged in a nation renewing its youth and drawing its strength from an ancient past of great events and myriad struggles. It will be a nation made anew and exalted by the deeds of free men and pioneers. It will be a nation fired by a valorous, daring and powerful spirit, embracing its vision of the last days, for the time of fulfillment is come.

PERFORMANCE

TWO YEARS ON
A Broadcast on Independence Day, 1950

With feelings of deepest joy we celebrate the second anniversary of our independence. Already we have seen great things but the most difficult and fateful test of all awaits us. The ingathering has begun: can we of this new State receive it wholly?

In the first year we made the Defense Army: we met and mastered the invaders; we opened wide the gates of the Homeland to all the people of Israel. We enlarged our bounds, even unto Elath and the Red Sea, held tight the approaches to Jerusalem and peopled her hills, restored its services to the young State and set them in motion. We won for Jewry international and sovereign status and Israel became a State-Member of the United Nations Organization, with full participant rights and obligations.

The endeavors of three pioneer generations and of our defenders for seventy years prepared the way for twin achievements that posterity will see as a glorious symbol and fulfillment of justice: Israel reborn and its soldiers triumphant. More than once in our long annals, storied both in rise and fall, a lost independence was regained, and even two thousand years ago warriors of Israel were victorious in the field. But never before, in our strange and separate history, has the world seen the miracle of the ingathering.

The years had brought us bitterness and confusion: 'And the Lord shall scatter thee among all people, from one end of the earth even unto the other; and there thou shalt serve other gods, which neither thou nor thy fathers have known, even wood and stone.'

Now, at long last, is the beginning of comfort and redemption —'I will surely assemble, O Jacob, all of thee; I will surely gather the remnant of Israel.' In our sight and in our days the scattered people is homing from every corner of the globe and every point of the compass, out of all the nations among which it was cast away, and it is coursing over its Land, over Israel redeemed.

Four hundred thousand exiles have come back since the founding of the State, almost as many as entered in the thirty years of Mandate. Some two hundred settlements have been established, almost as many as in the entire period of Zionism's first colonization.

There was an earlier homecoming, an earlier rekindling of our nation's pride. We turned back from Babylon to found the Second Temple and make a mould of national intellect and society that shaped the likeness of our people forever. Truly it has been said: 'Ezra merited that the Law be given to Israel by his hand, had not Moses come before him.' Then, as in no other day, Jewry was fashioned and its spirit steeled. Else had it not survived through the consuming ages. Nehemiah tells how the folk returning to Zion kept again the feast of Tabernacles: 'for since the days of Joshua the son of Nun unto that day had not the children of Israel done so. And there was very great gladness.'

The ingathering of today is vaster far and different. Now the wanderers return after two thousand years of divorcement and manifold dispersal, not as single spies from clan or city, but in territorial groups, whole communities and tribes of Israel, taken from unloving step-countries in every continent and set anew in their own Land.

Our freedom and statehood alone made possible this great-hearted thing, and without it, no less, they cannot be. It must go on apace and in swelling volume: there can be no end or limit to the resources we must marshal in Galuth, of energy, enthusiasm and exchequer, for reception and integration of the newcomers.

Most of them that come today and most that will come hereafter will be poor in possessions, as in education and culture: unskilled, knowing not Hebrew, strangers to the Land. We must all help: Government, the Zionist Organization, the Yishuv in its every sector—landlords and laborers, writers and teachers, doctors and nurses, contractors and clerks, artisans and farmers, soldiers and officials; and the newcomers must do their part manfully, prepared to speak Hebrew, to learn a trade, to better the sown and conquer the desert, to defend their country. On the outcome of their striving and ours hangs the destiny of nation and State; not for many morrows will we know the issue, after long, long, and selfless perseverance.

Step by step with the ingathering, we must construct the Land and make the wilderness to flower. We have doubled the area under the plow, but that is still not a tenth part of the State, and on the heights of Galilee, in the Jordan lowlands, and by the western sea, in the Shephelah, and in the great untilled expanses of the Negev, the wilderness challenges us in its many-patterned acres. It challenges the young and venturesome to press on as pioneers for the shaping of our economy and our philosophy of life, mastering the forces of sea and air, and of that element whence flow independence and civilization themselves—the earth.

Tradition has it that, when the Almighty redeems Israel, the Prophet Elijah will stand forth upon the hill-tops on the third day before the coming of the Messiah, and he will weep and bewail our hills, saying, 'Mountains of Israel, how long shall ye remain desolate, arid and unfruitful?' And all will hearken unto the ends of the world. So let our sabra youth and young immigrants hearken now and spare us the shame of our wastelands.

At the close of our first year of independence the Army made its way securely to the farthest marge of the Negev, to Elath and Ein Gedi. Now we have driven tracks through the desert, with the help of Nahal battalions and military engineers, and a road from Beersheba to Elath. The navy has transported craft to the Red Sea anchorage, and Israel planes land at Elath's airport almost daily. This year our search for water in the Negev was crowned with success and a good sweet supply, discovered north of the town, will be piped in. Thus do we carry forward the aim of three kings of Judah: Solomon, Jehoshaphat and Uzziah, who ever strove toward Elath and Ezion-geber. So do we set up in the South our new centers of farming and manufacture, of fishery, shipping and aviation.

The United Nations, which shrank from fulfillment of its own decision of November 29, 1947, and was powerless to prevent a murderous Arab onslaught against Israel and upon the Holy City, saw fit nonetheless this year to decide that our eternal capital should become a corpus separatum under international control; a decision backed by the Catholic, Moslem and Eastern blocs. Our rebuttal of this wicked counsel was unequivocal and resolute: the Government and Knesseth at once moved their seat to Jerusalem, and made it Israel's crown and capital, irrevocably and for all men to see.

The Trusteeship Council went on to plan a dismembered Jerusalem according to the will of the General Assembly, though many of the planners knew their task to be fanciful. It is comforting to find today that Russia, the only great Power which voted for internationalization, has changed its opinion: a few days before we celebrated Independence Day the United Nations Secretariat was told that the Soviet Government now desired that the wishes of those that dwelt in Jerusalem be met.

Long is the way and uphill. Years yet of heroism and sacrifice, of matter and spirit, struggling to build and make ourselves the main arbiters and agents of our success or failure.

Therefore let us say unto Jerusalem: 'Fear not, Zion, and waver not!'

LAWS OR A CONSTITUTION?
*At the 117th session of the First Knesseth,
February 20, 1950*

The Assembly of the United Nations prescribed six stages in the establishment of the Jewish and of the Arab State: the setting up of a Provisional Council of Government, democratic elections to a Constituent Assembly, enactment of a democratic Constitution and election of a Provisional Government, recognition of the State's independence, election of a permanent Government, and, finally, acceptance of the State into the membership of the United Nations.

In other words we are already three stages beyond the Constitution, and you cannot put back the clock. We have already chosen not a provisional but a permanent Government, in accordance with a Constitution drawn up by the Provisional State Council and by the first Knesseth, or Constituent Assembly as it was then known. Our independence has been recognized, Israel is a member of the United Nations in full function. So that the juridical argument of my learned friend, Mr. Nir, falls to the ground.

First, we should define what we mean when we say 'Constitution,' how a 'Constitution' differs from a law, and why, if at all, there should be this difference.

But at the outset I want to explain in what respects I disagree with the opponents of a Constitution.

Mr. Levinstein defined the attitude of the Agudah in delightful Hebrew, in plain, transparent phrases. The way he spoke was vastly different from the version of earlier Agudists, and that is gratifying. The following sentences, which I quote from his speech, sum up his case:

'Only Holy Writ and its tradition possess sovereign force in the life of Israel.'

'A Constitution made by human hands can have no place in Israel.'

'We shall regard a secular Constitution as an attempt to set for ever aside our sacred Torah.'

Like many of us, I have a wholesome respect for his simple, untroubled faith, whether we agree with him or not. I would rather we did not speak, in this place, of the faith that is in men's hearts, for controversy on such a topic may wound the feelings of the faithful. He, however, deemed fit to say what he did—and with perfect right. I hope he will not be angry if I too say what I must.

I do not know whether, in the first quotation, he was referring to the State. If he was, he has surely in mind a theocratic State. I must remind you that the representatives of the Mizrahi and the Agudah publicly declared, before the State came into being, that they did not plan such a State, nor will Israel be one. The Agudah is entitled to change its mind, but so are we entitled to assume that when it so declared it did believe that a non-theocratic Jewish State does not signify the ruin of Judaism or contradict the Torah. And if what it then declared was right, there is no substance now in his contentions.

And again, if he truly holds that, save Holy Writ and its tradition, there is no overriding authority in the State, he can only mean that members of the Agudah, and perhaps only its rabbis, are exclusively the repository of power in Israel to make laws and enforce them, and no one who does not belong to the Agudah may meddle in the State's affairs. I question whether such a thing accords with the Torah, or whether a State could be established under such conditions.

Next, he claims that a Constitution made by human hands

can have no place in Israel. Since when has man's handiwork been profane in Israel? He claims that a 'secular' Constitution is profane. Yet 99 percent of all the actions of himself and his friends are 'secular,' and bound up with the handiwork of men. The sewing of the tailor who made his clothes is secular work, and the clothes are secular—but he wears them nevertheless. The electricity which lights his house, the accounts rendered by his book-keeper, the by-laws of the township where he lives, the train or car in which he travels, are secular and 'made by human hands.' All the State does is naturally secular: it levies taxes, mends roads, carries out public works, engages in agriculture, housing, settlement, health and communications—all of them secular undertakings. Are they therefore profane? Of course he believes that all is done according to the will of the Creator; but the laws that men make for their own needs are also made that way. He partakes with all of us here in the promulgation of 'secular' laws, and I fail to see the difference in this regard between a Constitution and a law. By passing laws for itself, in the light of its own will and wants, the people affirms its sovereignty. Does he play the heretic to the people's sovereignty?

It seems to me that his 'constitutional' ideas do not square with the Torah. We find in the Bible two constitutional cases, and both were decided on 'secular' lines, not anti-religious, but stemming from the needs of man or nation, as man and nation see them. And neither decision affronted the law of Moses, for one Moses himself made, and the second was as God commanded.

The first case is thus narrated in Exodus:

'And it came to pass on the morrow, that Moses sat to judge the people; and the people stood by Moses from the morning unto the evening. And when Moses' father in law saw all that he did to the people, he said ' What is this thing that thou doest to the people? why sittest thou thyself alone, and all the people stand by thee from morning unto even? . . . The thing that thou doest is not good. Thou wilt surely wear away, both thou and this people that is with thee: for the thing is too heavy for thee; thou art not able to perform it thyself alone. Hearken now unto my voice . . . thou shalt provide out of all the people able men, such as fear God, men of truth, hating covetousness, and place such over them, to be rulers of thousands, and rulers of hundreds, ruler of fifties, and rulers of tens, and let them judge the people at all seasons; and it shall be, that every great matter they shall bring up to thee, but every small matter they shall judge: so shall it be easier for thyself, and they shall bear the burden with thee . . . ' So Moses hearkened to the voice of his father in law, and did all that he had said.'

Jethro was not a Jew, but Moses took his constitutional advice, and organized the judiciary as this experienced 'Gentile' statesman from Midian had counselled him, and no conflict with the law of Moses was seen.

The second case is even more remarkable, for it involved a specific clash between secular and theocratic authority, and the judgment, for the secular, was given by the Almighty. The story is told in the first Book of Samuel:

'Then all the elders of Israel gathered themselves together, and came to Samuel unto Ramah, And said to him, Behold, thou art old, and thy sons walk not in thy ways: now make us a king to judge us like all the nations. But the thing displeased Samuel when they said, Give us a king to judge us . . . And the Lord said unto Samuel, Hearken unto the voice of the people in all that they say unto thee: for they have not rejected thee, but they have rejected me, that I should not reign over them. Now therefore hearken unto their voice, howbeit yet protest solemnly unto them, and shew them the manner of the king that shall reign over them. And Samuel told all the words of the Lord unto the people that asked of him a king . . . Nevertheless, the people refused to obey the voice of Samuel; and they said, Nay; but we will have a king over us; That we also may be like all the nations, and that our king may judge us, and go out before us, and fight our battles. And Samuel heard all the words of the people, and he rehearsed them in the ears of the Lord. And the Lord said to Samuel, Hearken unto their voice and make them a king.'

'The manner of the king' which is spoken of here—and the English word 'constitution' is more apt in this connection than the Hebrew chukka—means the law a king gave out as the custom was among all peoples at that time, and as the Jews pleaded of Samuel, and he was divinely bidden to grant the people its wish, completely 'secular' though it was, borrowed indeed from the other nations. And if we now call 'the manner of a king' a Constitution, there is nothing in our idea which offends the Torah, so that again, in my humble opinion, rebuttal of the Constitution in the name of Writ or tradition is overthrown.

It all goes to show the futility of much of a debate whereof the subject matter is not precisely defined beforehand. When people demand a Constitution, as something intrinsically different from the other laws, and of different validity, what have they in mind? A supreme legal charter, privileged and rigid, which lays down the principles of sovereign administration and to a certain extent of all legislation, but cannot be amended like the rest of the statutes.

In this sense a Constitution is, generally speaking, a modern invention, not yet two centuries old, devised in the aftermath of certain political events. We must consider very closely whether our State is in need of the novelty.

It is true we are an infant State, not yet two years old, but we are also an old race, its memory reaching back into a past of several thousand years, and we are not bound to snatch with our eyes shut at every new idea, before making up our minds whether, in our present historical circumstances, it is a need or a blessing. I know of three ancient peoples, that bequeathed to civilized mankind the foundations of morality and justice, of law and imperial order. They were Judea, Greece and Rome: so far as I am aware, they did not distinguish between 'constitution' and 'law.'

Even the Romans, protagonists of law and jurisprudence, were ignorant of the modern concept of constitution, although the word is derived from the Latin; there was no written Constitution under the kings, the republic or the Caesars. The early meaning of the word was a collection of the emperor's ordinances and decrees.

The Greeks were equally unaware, although at the dawn of history the City-State of Athens did develop a democratic form of life. The oldest term for the current idea of constitution is 'politeia,' which meant primarily a form of government; subsequently, however, Aristotle uses it also to mean a written Constitution.

The present sort was introduced in America mainly, if we overlook Cromwell's 'Instrument of Government' of 1653. America became independent in 1776, and it was not until eleven years afterward, in 1787, that the text of the Constitution of the Union was ready, a Constitution in our acceptance—an overriding and eclectic State Paper, unalterable except in extraordinary circumstances. It came into effect only in 1789, but it has stayed valid ever since, with one or two amendments. The second State to pass a Constitution was France, after the Revolution. There was first, in 1789, the Declaration of the Rights of Man. I am not sure if it had formal legal force, but it was a political and human document of immense historical significance which greatly influenced contemporary and succeeding political thought in Europe. The first 'Constitution' was promulgated in 1791, limiting the kingly right, but it did not last long nor did its successors, replaced one by the next too often in the days of the second Revolution and of Napoleon. Similarly, other countries in Europe and Latin America gave themselves Constitutions as they threw off the tyrant—for example, Belgium in 1831, Sardinia and Switzerland in 1848.

The 'ideal' Constitution is North America's from every point of view: it was the first; it has lasted for 173 years, which may not be a very long time in the life of us Jews, but in the lifetime of Constitutions is a record; it has been the model for several other countries, especially in Latin America; it is hard to change, harder than any other. Indeed any amendment requires, first of all, a two-thirds majority in the Senate and the House of Representatives, and then ratification by three-quarters of the States; and it conditions all legislation, so that a Court may set aside any law it finds inconsistent with the Constitution. How did this come about?

In the founding of the United States, two political facts were merged: the ending of British dominion and the federation of thirteen States. Federation, perhaps, came less easily than insurrection, for the States clung to their sovereign rights, and it was essential to safeguard those rights in a document warranted to be of supreme authority. The Constitution therefore prescribed meticulously the jurisdiction of the Federal Union, and all else was left in the hands of the States. Amendment was, of necessity, rendered very difficult, to prevent trespass on their powers. The Supreme Court assumed the right, not expressly written in the Constitution, to determine whether any law passed by the people's representatives in Congress accorded with the Constitution or did not, and has the power, as I said, to set it aside, however 'popular' its backing, if found to be incompatible with the Constitution. Thus the Supreme Court became a hindrance, upsetting and reactionary, favoring the rights of property over the rights of man. When it was decided to levy income tax, the rich argued before the Court that the law broke the Constitution, and in fact the Court vetoed the tax and in the end the Constitution had to be amended. But if thirteen of the 48 States had voted against the amendment, the other 35 States plus two-thirds of the Congress could not have carried it through, and the people's will would have been balked. Another time a federal law was passed to protect child labor: and along comes the Court and vetoes it on constitutional grounds. Curious that with us it is just the parties which bandy about words like 'progress' and 'the forces of tomorrow' that wax enthusiastic about the American Constitution.

In France the origin of the Constitution was otherwise. There was no founding of a new State, the State already existed, and it was and remained unitary. But the despotism of an omnipotent monarch was replaced by a government of the people, and the rights of the people had to be enshrined in a revolutionary document. The Constitution made the people sovereign in the king's stead, democracy took monarchy's place. It was not an inflexible and privileged Constitution like the American—it had not to be, and it has actually been altered often.

Do we need a Constitution like the American? By all means let us profit from the experience of others and borrow laws and procedures from them, provided they match our needs. But an unbending and haughty Constitution, that fetters the Legislature and the people's autarchy, and makes the judge competent to decide whether a law the people wants is valid or not—is that what we need?

In this sphere, Israel must be assured of two things above all—the rule of law and the rule of democracy, for thereon our future hangs.

The liberty of the subject and the liberty of the people depend not on any pronouncements of freedoms, nor on the finest of Constitutions but uniquely on the rule of law. There can be no certainty of personal or public liberty save where the citizen—soldier, official, Minister of State, legislator, judge or policeman—is subordinate to the law and acts according to it, and where nothing is arbitrarily done by Ministers of State or governors, by the people's representatives or Civil Servants, or by political leaders. Where there is no rule of the law, no freedom is—even if the most vehement and liberal Bill of Rights in the world is inscribed in the Constitution.

We need laws of all kinds, to fix our form of government and our human relationships: for election to the Knesseth, the authority and responsibility of the President, the appointment and resignation of the Government, the Army, the Press and meetings, equal rights and obligations for all citizens both women and men, criminal, civil and commercial codes, taxes and customs, and the appointment of Civil Servants. A Constitution cannot possibly do all this. Only within the framework of laws that must be altered and improved from time to time as hurrying life demands, but while they last are binding on all citizens without exception, from the President himself and members of the Cabinet and Knesseth to the humblest—only therein is civic freedom truly alive and are the rights of every man upheld.

During the debate two stood out as champions of the 'liberties' of the subject: Mr. Begin and Mr. Yaari. Regrettably they did not define 'liberty.' Does it mean that every man does whatever is right in his own eyes? That, I think, is not liberty but license. For true liberty you must respect the rights of the community, the people and the State—its security, its administration, its honor and its needs. Only law can set the line that divides liberty —the plain man's liberty and not the monopoly of a particular group—from the rights of your fellow-man. No law, no liberty.

The Prime Minister and each of his colleagues may, as such, do only that which the law allows them, but the citizen may do anything but what the law forbids him. You may think the law bad, but you must obey it. Of course, you can suggest amendments, but meanwhile you obey.

Where the law rules, it is the people's prerogative to legislate, the judge's to watch over and safeguard the law. The people, as legislator, must not be circumscribed: it can make mistakes, but a free people, unfettered, will correct its mistakes. But safeguarding the law, interpreting it, enquiring into its incidence in particular cases—that is the business of the judge, who is independent of citizen and Government, and obeys only his conscience and his understanding. The judge neither makes the law nor unmakes it. Real life is complex and heterogeneous, the legislator cannot foresee all the possible cases, so the judge determines the meaning and intent of the law in any given set of circumstances. Where the law rules, the legislative power entrusted to the elected representatives of the people is totally sundered from the judicial, entrusted to a body of appointed judges, independent of the Executive, expert in the law and faithful to it.

The rule of law is inconceivable without the rule of democracy. The people respects the laws and patiently bears the burden, if they are enacted in its discretion, derived from its needs and linked to its will. Where the people is not free to make its laws, through representatives of its own free choice, not the law rules—but arbitrary dictatorship. If the law-making authority is not dependent on the people, the law is not a child of free men. No liberty, no law.

The hallmark of democracy is government, not for the people, but by the people. Even tyrants claim or honestly think they govern for the people's good. There never was a dictatorship that did not profess so to govern. More than once dictatorship has come about for reasons of public welfare, of national or social idealism; but government has an inexorable quality—if it be not of the people, not chosen by the people in free ballot, it becomes an end, however praiseworthy in itself, even if to start with it was only a means. History has shown the simple truth of this, time and time again.

There it is: law and democracy are the inseparable sureties of Israel's well-being. That is the cardinal juridic problem of the State, not the antithesis between 'law' and 'Constitution.'

Nowadays democracy is under question. The challengers dub it 'formal,' and I observe that those of our number who reject 'formal' democracy have strangely become the most fervent disciples of a Constitution. Is not the Constitution 'formal?' And the law? Indeed, in the countries of dictatorship, where is no 'formal' democracy, the law and the Constitution are nothing but dead letters, and 'law' is only the arbitrary will of a single tyrant, or several, but all above the law. I have said it often, I say it again—totalitarian government spells ruin to Jews and Jewry, and to Judaism, physical and spiritual ruin; it spells the end of our State, snapping the links between us and the Dispersion.

We Jews can breathe only in democratic air, where minorities are free, where votes and thoughts are free, where one can move freely, and freely appeal within the limits of the law. In totalitarian air—even if it be not of special malignancy toward us as Jews—we are doomed. Democracy's destiny is ours.

There the majority decides, and its will is the law of the land, by which the minority is bound. But the minority may without constraint express opinions, think as it chooses, vote as it sees fit; and the majority is not the determinant in matters of faith and thought, of art and science. Thinking man is not under tutelage of law and Government. The entire nation will accept a given view, yet an individual may fight a lone fight for his own. You are at liberty to criticize and discuss. You are not compelled to endorse a single list of candidates named by your rulers; you choose your representatives yourself, and hence they are the servitors of the people, not its masters.

But democracy itself will not endure if we emasculate it, make it inert, ineffectual and defenseless. I am not as sanguine as Mr. Yaari, who assures us that the rule of democracy is out of danger, the democratic certainty of the people forever safe from attack. He doubts the need for legal means to defend the State, democratic and sovereign. This, surely, is not just being naive. He must know there are men, in this very Knesseth and in this State, who aim to destroy our democracy and long for a totalitarianism. Not all of them dare make open avowal of it, but there are brave men like Messrs. Wilner and Mikunis, who forthrightly declare that their sole ambition is to inflict on Israel the domination of their party and only theirs, to suppress every other, to deny the people the right freely to elect or criticize, or be Zionist. This is no fanciful ambition, outside the realm of fact. Since the first World War, we have watched democracy go under in one country after another, with armed gangs within or armed force from without helping on the sad process. The totalitarian end-products, for all the variance and at times the contradictions of the purposes, have this in common: that none tolerates individual liberty or the rule of law, or free criticism, or the existence of any other except the party monopolizing government. The governors flout the law, and if there is a Constitution it has no real force—it is merely ornamental, for show and propaganda abroad.

A totalitarian country has one so-called 'advantage': 90 per cent votes for the dominant party. We must avoid this like the plague. In a democratic State there is nothing to stop you voting an anti-democratic opinion; but it would be suicidal of democracy to allow only the arraigners of democracy the chance to act, and to condemn itself to impotence by divesting itself of all means of defense. In Israel, you may even be a non-Zionist, we have an anti-Zionist party in this House, but we must not permit these gentlemen, as the liberal and openhearted Mr. Yaari would, to win control over us by non-democratic ways, and forcibly put down Zionism and democracy, as happened in the other countries where 'formal' democracy has been abolished.

We cannot stomach the preposterous creed of the Jesuits, who insist upon a liberal regime treating them according to liberal principles, while permitting them to treat liberals with Jesuitry.

Perhaps it is not surprising that the very people who yearn—by stealth or blatantly—for a totalitarian State and the absolute rule of a single party, whether the coming be slow or swift, are prating so much of liberty, and brand anybody that differs from them on the constitutional issue as out to rob the people of its charter of liberty and power. I, in my simplicity, had thought that the charter was given on the 14th day of May, 1948, the birthday of the State, and that the legal and democratic system we wish to fortify is designed to give effect and permanence to it.

Security, Aliyah and settlement are the mainstays of the State and in them we must make good, if the State is to be preserved. But they cannot exist at all without fundamental and ordinary laws. What we have to settle is whether the rule of law and democracy indispensable to Israel will be better assured by a Constitution or by a series of fundamental laws no different, in validity or privilege, from any other ordinance.

The circumstances which demanded and defended a Constitution in America or France do not obtain here. On the contrary, if we wish to bring up the people to respect the law, it must be by teaching it to respect every law, and not only that favored one we call a Constitution. For it is not the Constitution, but the ordinary law, which orders the thousand and one items that make up the everyday life of the citizen. The only cure for that scorn for the law which exile and dependence in foreign lands ingrain in us is to reject the strange doctrine of Mr. Begin and others of the 'constitutional' bodyguard that a law purporting to affirm the Rights of Man, which is not 'privileged' and is not a Constitution above all other laws, is just a worthless scrap of paper. If a law passed by the representatives of the people is nothing but that, what is a Constitution worth which they have passed? If Messrs. Begin and Yaari veto in advance—to put it in their own words—'the rule of the mechanical majority,' or 'the fortuitous fleeting parliamentary majority,' what are the effect and value of a Constitution which either majority promulgates? The mere existence of a Constitution will not add to respect and affection for the law, but the reverse. Disregard of the law will be encouraged by the argument that the law is out of step with the Constitution. If talmudic dialectics could find a hundred and fifty reasons for any ritual ruling, it is surely possible to discover five hundred for vitiating any law.

The Americans rarely made a fuss when the Supreme Court annulled a law on constitutional grounds. Will our public be so complaisant? Will our law and judges not be brought into dangerous contempt?

Democracy is strong in Britain simply because the British revere the law made by legislators they have elected and trust their judges as loyal servants, not satraps of the law. The King of England pays no less homage to the law than does the chimney-sweep, the Prime Minister no less than the shoe-black. Rule neither of law nor of democracy has suffered a whit for the want of a Constitution.

And if, to protect both rules, it is under certain conditions necessary to withdraw his freedom from a man who endangers them, British law does not blench from dealing thus even with a Member of Parliament. It is acknowledged universally that in Britain liberty of the subject is as complete as in countries which enjoy a Constitution, be they 'formal' democracies or 'people's.' Yet the law of England allowed Captain Ramsay, Member of Parliament, to be gaoled for several years by order of the Home Secretary, without reason assigned, under an Emergency Regulation for the defense of the realm—which a freely elected Parliament of the people had enacted and a Government answerable to Parliament enforced. Without those conditions of what avail is a charter of freedoms?

In a free country like Israel, we may dispense with it, for all are free to do aught the law does not expressly forbid. In an eighteenth century in the grip of despotism, it was needed, no doubt. It is still needed—where totalitarianism holds court today, but elsewhere it is a charter of duties that is needed, and for us that means what we owe to Homeland and nation, to Aliyah and ingathering, to upbuilding, to the safety of our fellows, the protection of the weak. More than any other free democracy that already treasures the Rights of Man, we need it for long, it must be self-imposed. Our mission of halutziuth calls for it.

In one respect the revolution in our lives and the revolutions of America and France, or Switzerland and Russia, were poles apart. There the people rose against the government and a change in government signified attainment of the people's aim. But not we. We rose against a destiny of the years, against exile and dispersion, against deprivation of language and culture.

The establishment of the State set free only six hundred and fifty thousand Jews then in the Land. The Jews of the Yemen were in bondage until they could make their way to Israel; the Jews of Morocco have yet to find freedom by Aliyah, thousands there are waiting for salvation day after anxious day.

In our plight we could not carry out instantaneous revolution. The redemption of Jewry, even to nationhood and no more, is only in its beginnings. The million of us here at this moment are still not wholly free, because we are not wholly secure. No one rates more highly than I the portent of that 14th of May; there have been few days so fateful in our long saga. But its significance is betrayed if we do not prolong with constancy and determination the revolution we began years before it. No short-lived happening will redeem us. It will be a tedious process of immigration and settlement, of struggle for security, a toilsome sequence of events and laws. It is in opening up new vistas on all three horizons that the significance of that great day lies.

That makes ours the most dynamic country in the world. It is a little country and its dynamism cannot vibrate far afield, but it can and does form the country's character and fortunes. Each day our State is born anew. Each day newcomers enter and are freed and the desert and desolation move further back. The laws of the State must be ceaselessly adapted to this rapid growth—no too-tight framework or mock tools will do.

Mr. Bar Yehuda demanded a Constitution that would proclaim colonization and the ingathering. Did he not forget that a Constitution is made up not of proclamations but of obligations? And the proclamation has been made, in the most striking document of our days, transcending even a Constitution. For the Declaration of Independence says: 'The State of Israel shall be open to Jewish immigration and the ingathering of the exiles; it shall promote the development of the country for the benefit of all its inhabitants; it shall be based on foundations of justice and peace in the light of the vision of the Prophets of Israel; it shall maintain complete social and political equality for all its inhabitants without distinction of religion, race or sex; it shall ensure freedom of religion, conscience, language, education and culture; it shall preserve the Holy Places of all religions; and it shall be faithful to the principles of the Charter of the United Nations.'

Is this statement legally valid in the formal sense? I do not know. But I do know that, morally, it has greater force than any other document we are now empowered to indite. Of course, we could put one together more high-sounding, but could we easily reproduce the resplendent, the incomparably historic occasion whereon it was approved and signed by every party in this House, from the Communists to Agudath Israel? So sure and cementing a unity is seldom experienced—let us prize it, for, whether valid in legal form or not, the utterance of that wonderful day, when the State came to life again, must always own superior moral force than what was said at other 'looser' times. There has been nothing like it in our lives for two thousand years.

Professor Dinaburg sought evidence in Exodus to justify a Constitution. He conceded that the Torah was given up scroll by scroll, and hence that one may enact fundamental laws from time to time, but his case was that the Constitution preceded the laws inasmuch as the verses which begin 'Now these are the judgments' follow those describing the revelation on Mount Sinai, and those in turn follow the announcement of 'a kingdom of priests and a holy nation,' that is to say, earlier chapters are the principles of the Constitution, and from them flow the laws set forth in Chapter 21 and what follows.

Since Professor Dinaburg is a distinguished historian, we must measure his words to the hairsbreadth and see if his assumptions fit the Bible narrative precisely. I wonder why he began with Chapter 19, telling of the third month after the flight from Egypt. The law-making had begun long since. Already in Chapter 13 Moses says, 'Thou shalt therefore keep this ordinance in its season from year to year.' The Hebrew is 'chukka,' and I have explained that in the Bible it is identical with 'chok,' which is 'law.' The chapters following tell of Moses' concern for Israel's economic affairs: Chapter 16 of the manna, and Chapter 17 of the supply of water, and moreover, of Israel's war against Amalek, the first of all the wars of Israel, fought 3,300 years ago and in the very same region where we fought our latest war only thirteen months back.

After the war against Amalek came the arrangement of administration and justice as Jethro counselled. And only after this constitutional reform came Mount Sinai. But it is by no means clear that the Decalogue represents principles from which the laws were derived. The Bible mentions the ten commandments in that express usage not in Chapter 20, from which Professor Dinaburg quoted, but in Chapter 34, long after 'Now these are the judgments.' The ten commandments of Chapter 34 are of altogether different tenor from the injunctions of Chapter 20, which Professor Dinaburg wrongly calls by the decalogal name, and Goethe in his time pointed the error out. How can we substantiate the need for a Constitution by so doubtful a plea?

In this crucial debate, I have heard thunder peal and seen lightning flash, or rather I read these splendors. But profoundly though I respect those that spoke, I am fain to say that I heard not the Voice of God speaking from out of the midst of the fire.

Mount Sinai is not vouchsafed us every day. Twenty-two months ago we made history once more, and we shall make it again—how illustriously I cannot tell. But we may a second time hear the Voice speaking from out of the midst of the fire—'with signs and wonders and battles, and with a strong hand and an outstretched arm, and great terrors,' and a new chapter of greatness be etched in our annals.

Till then let us do our work day after day, soberly, unassumingly, with perserverance, unafraid.

CIVIL DEFENSE
Speech delivered in the Knesseth, January 2, 1951, on the Civil Defense Bill

It would be a breach of duty on my part not to offer, at this opportunity, some general observations on the security situation and its major problems.

I said at the beginning of my speech that the Bill marks the nation-wide and total character of modern war and defense. That, however, does not exhaust the intense and fundamental import of Israel's security problem. If I seem needlessly to lay stress here on its gravity, which our stand against the enemy in the War of Independence, victorious though it was, has done nothing to diminish, it is because I fear that many of us are still unheeding of the hazards, the unprecedented demands and hardships it means.

Every country has its security problem, and with things in the world as they are, international feud and friction are possible, by reason whether of boundary disputes, treaties and alliances, or trade and markets—or even forms of government. Let any such divergence become sharp, and you may have a state of war.

With Israel, it is not just another detail of internal or foreign policy that is placed in jeopardy, but our whole existence. As men and as sovereign State, our enemies seek to compass our undoing—that is the brutal fact, that is *our* grim problem.

It is a problem which enfolds the basic issues of the Yishuv, of Zionism and of the State. As war in Israel strikes at every man and woman here and at every Jew in the world, so Israel's security rests on how each Jew here and throughout the world comports himself, reacts and perseveres, and there is no act or circumstance in Israel but somehow bears upon it.

Situated as we are, engaged in epic reforms and revivals, we must ask ourselves how are we to manage our lives, what sort of government to choose, on what to found our culture, what shall be the character of our society and the make-up of our economy.

There will always be differences of opinion on this controversial subject, and they are entirely in order, though the methods used to express them are not always so.

But a graver and more urgent question is how to make our lives secure. And it comes first, 'for the dead do not praise the Lord.' Indeed, it is so vexing and burdensome that the people tend to avoid it and shelve responsibility, in the spiritual and intellectual sense at first and soon also in the material and physical.

In the War of Independence we mobilized over one-sixth of the population. Our spiritual tautness was fulldrawn, but you cannot keep that up indefinitely, and it is natural that it should slacken off. The loosening of grip is, however, sadly before its time, and what is doubly serious is the fact that certain organizations assist the process and preach its virtues. There are also impersonal reasons: security work is essentially negative—and when we are secure we do not feel it, any more than we are specifically aware of a sound limb, or as for long we may not suspect the presence of cancer until it has grown malignant beyond healing.

The financial, administrative and human exertions which security consumes are in a way so much prodigality. No assets are created, no comforts, and success gives nothing tangible, since the main purpose is to safeguard peace and stave off ruin; and always where an ill is averted, people are happily oblivious. But not only human frailty is to blame: unworthy instances are reinforced by commendable. In this stupendous dynamo we call the State of Israel, creative impulses and capacities absorb all our energy, all our resources, and set them to gigantic and endless tasks of immigration, settlement, education, research and art. The demands of security are always colliding with needs of the will to create, and without our knowing it, security comes off second best.

One of the most alarming signs is the way our public are increasingly prone to look upon the State as there to be importuned and upon themselves as there only to make demands. As single spies or in whole battalions they entreat the State for everything essential and dispensable, important and not so, pressing and far from immediate, for good and bad purposes. They both fail to understand that, quite simply, the State can give only what it receives, and incline more and more to forget that every one of us must be prepared today to meet demands, not make them, for the daily survival of the State, which is to his personal interest, and for its continuing security and its upbuilding, on behalf of all Jewry.

Thus we may behave under parochial influences, as it were, until international developments refresh our sense of perturbation and remind us that we are living on the edge of a volcano.

Some simpletons—and some who affect simplicity—believe that in the cockpit which the world has become, one side will be armed from spur to crest while the other relies on the peaceful protestations of its adversary. We may take the declarations as sincere, but sincerity hardly convinces when pointed with bayonets, and the net result is that the other side arms all it can and with equal sincerity protests its peaceful aims.

It is not inevitable that a new World War should break out; it has not been divinely decreed. It can be averted—but who dares count on that? And so each nation must prepare as fast and as furiously as it can against disaster, while with ever greater intensity it labors for peace. Every year of peace is a clear profit for mankind at large and for each separate nation, but there is no shutting our eyes to the global armament race, and only time can tell how it will end. Manifestly, the central political fact of today is the rivalry of two titanic Powers for world hegemony, but that is not to say that the universe is divided into satellites and subordinates of one or the other.

There are puppet States, no doubt, and puppet governments, that chant the standard anthem, and are bound body and soul to a tyrant will. Perhaps it is natural for them to believe or make believe that all others are like them, that no free and independent countries are left. Totalitarianism knows no fine shades: it recognizes only the completely black and the completely white, only the wholly innocent and the utterly guilty. So crude a distinction of men and nations is quite untenable. There is attachment and there is mutual dependence; no people or State, the greatest as the least, is absolutely self-sufficient and unattached. This planet of ours is more nearly a single unit today, in that sense, than it ever was in history.

But apart from great Powers and their vassals, there is a large company of free peoples—as far as freedom goes in a world ruled by the law of interdependence—without prefabricated allegiances, determining their courses in every case on its merits vis-a-vis what is good or bad for mankind and for themselves, and with all their hearts wishful for the strengthening of peace. They and their hopes are by no means negligible in international policies.

The State of Israel is of their number. Not that the key to world peace is in our hands, for we are in numbers exiguous and overburdened with cares, and in our limitations to be boastful or presumptuous would bring us to scorn. But we are neither empty-handed nor helpless as men and soldiers, and our moral and political stock is high. We can, and ought, help other peace-loving nations to banish war forever, though it is not we that have the power to pronounce banishment; and we must meanwhile, with all the world, be filled with foreboding.

To this measure of our anxiety, already brimming over, is added the vendetta of our neighbors.

Only a child would suppose that the Arab States are arming to fight the United States or the Soviet Union. If those arms are used at all, it will be against us. They make no secret of their designs, but proclaim a 'second round' from the house-tops. Mounting international tension does little to lessen the risk. I am not counseling panic. I counsel prevention of war by preparing for every eventuality, by omitting no effort to ensure peace and maintain it, as far as possible through treaties of friendship with any neighbors who will meet us halfway.

Where security is involved, time is of the essence, and neglect may be, literally, catastrophic: our lives here are at stake—shall Israel stand or fall?

That is the question, and double-edged it is: Can we survive a World War, and can we a second round? Boldly I answer yes, and yes again—if we do what we must to defend ourselves. And the first condition is will and moral armament.

I have spoken of the sin of vainglory. Respecting our Army, that sin is most grievous, for the prospect there is not of ridicule, but of a crashing knockout. Israel cannot and will not pit itself against any Power worthy of the name, and that is not confined to the United States or the Soviet Union. Luckily we are in no such danger; outside the Middle East a duel between us and any State is just not conceivable. What we may have to engage in is not single combat, but global conflict, with world forces in counter-array in every thinkable arena, oceanic and terrestrial. Will we be able then to preserve our existence and our sovereignty? Again I answer yes, for sure—and again there are conditions, as I shall show.

A foreign aggressor must think twice before venturing to attack us and experiencing the full defense impact of this State, potent beyond its size in this vital corner of the earth.

That Israel will proffer aid to aggression on no pretext, I am convinced. We are entitled, in the mass and as individuals, to think well or ill of alien forms of government, although that gives us neither the right, necessity nor power to help aggression because we disapprove of this form or that. But we have the power, should there be global conflict—or a second round, to protect our lives and our national and international liberties and autonomy.

We are much stronger than we were three years ago, not least military, but wars are no longer exclusively military contests between professional armies, when the people themselves hardly felt the shock of war, but were just transferred from vanquished monarch to victor.

War now is all-enveloping in the hurt it does to men and in the might that decides it. It is decided not by armies, however excellent their training and equipment, but by the total mobilization of the people: in skill and production, in management and science, in money and, above all, in moral armament. In the second World War and in our own, the inner spirit conquered.

The clouds gathering in the skies of the world, the black fog that invades our sunlight here, compel us to examine how far we are ready for the next blow, not the Army only but all of us that dwell in Zion, all our groups and trends, the veterans and the newcomers. Deliberately I say it: that dwell in Zion. In all other issues, and most in the all-important one of ingathering, we need and expect the help of world Jewry—it has not, it will not, let us down. But to maintain our security, make no mistake, we can rely only on ourselves who are here, not because that security leaves world Jewry cold—nothing affects it more—but because you must be bodily of the State to defend it, and we might be isolated at the critical hour. Thousands of volunteers from the Diaspora abetted us three years ago—we cannot be sure that will happen again.

So let us see things as they are, not fool ourselves by using sweet-sounding misnomers. First, that the Jewish nation in Israel, our only certain rod and staff, is still a promise and not a fulfillment. Nine-tenths of Jewry are without, and, of those within, very many are only in interwoven process of becoming a people, and creating its Homeland. The transformation is a long business, and the threat imminent allows no breathing-space. Except we hasten toward our twin goals with giant strides, we shall be found wanting when the call comes. All along, the policy of the State has felt this quickening spur, all along we are driven to things in seeming contradiction to accepted logic and proved experience, and often to the personal interests and the proper needs of each one of us.

That is why the Government follows, in regard to immigration, a policy without historical parallel—one that many observers at home and abroad, not wholly unreasonably, deem fraught with danger and disaster to the State. In about two and a half years, our population has been almost doubled, by the entry of more than 520,000 Jews. Our good friends were startled by this enormous and hurried accretion of resourceless creatures, many of them uncultured too, and warned us that the upshot would be not only economic but also political and social reverses. Even leading Zionists of unexceptionable loyalty were against the policy, and they had a strong case. We all know the difficulties. The pity is that not a few in the veteran Yishuv are reluctant to lift the heavy burden, and do not lend a hand, in many ways, willingly or unawares, they show their disapproval.

There are other cogent reasons, but, primarily, this daring, even dangerous, policy, is imposed by the needs of national security. If our Army is twice as strong today—not merely in roll-call—as two years ago, we may thank the policy for it.

Immigration is not just shipping Jews from Rumania or North Africa, or flying them out of Iraq or Aden. You must work to absorb them, and absorption raises security as well as economic, cultural and social problems. The Army, as our principal agent of security, necessarily plays a special part here. Absorbing immigrants is not usually a soldier's duty, but then our security is unusual too. Unusual because it will be a figment and no more unless we teach the immigrants Hebrew and school them to cherish our national values and the Jewish vision of past and future, unless we help them to strike roots in a working livelihood, train them for self-defense, and bring the divergent, insubstantial tribes to coalesce into a solid national unit. Hence Nahal, which trains young people in the Army; hence the Army's assignment to ma'baroth,* where it has done much valuable work efficiently and with devotion.

By the tempo of immigration and the speed with which it is absorbed, both materially and in spirit, more than by any other factor, will Israel's security be determined. It cannot be left to the machinery of Government, to the Army or to the Jewish Agency. Without volunteer effort by every soul and section of the Yishuv, it cannot be done, and we are lost.

The colonization of the frontiers and the filling of the blank spaces is scarcely less important for security than immigration. It is alarmingly unsafe that half our population should be crowded into the Yarkon region and around Tel Aviv. The War of Independence proved the great tactical and strategic value of the settlements near Jerusalem, and in the South, in Galilee and the Jordan Valley. But in colonization as well, circumstances impose an extraordinary policy upon us.

We are an orthodox and conservative people, not excluding the free-thinkers and revolutionaries among us. When we seize an idea, a dogma, or an article of faith, we never budge, even if changing times and conditions empty such tenets of their meaning. We will not adapt our ways even after they have ceased, by alteration of circumstances, to answer a good purpose. We lack perception of facts as singular yet mutable within the cauldron of a reality that bubbles and seethes always, that is ever changing. Our every approach is influenced by prejudices formed in us by long-vanished causes.

Practical businessmen cannot see the point of sinking effort and expense in the cultivation of tomatoes in the wilds of Elath,

* Immigrant transit camps.

when it is so simple to grow them in the Sharon or buy them in the markets of Tel Aviv. From a purely commercial standpoint they are of course right—how can you, at any rate nowadays, justify tomato vines in Elath and watermelons in the 'Arabah? The development of the Negev and the defense of Elath are not, however, to be tackled at this juncture commercially.

Others plausibly criticize our colonizing methods. But massive, accelerated colonization cannot wait for the refined systems of 'the good old days' when there was only a thin trickle of immigration. Like unto the angel with the flaming sword that turneth every way, security bids us swiftly people the borders and the barren voids in new ways.

I believe that the developed Negev will come to be a boon and a profit: comfort and cash are immensely important, I know, but I am prepared hand on heart, morning, noon and night, to proclaim that security means more. To that view, I pledge my political faith.

In the third place, security depends on industrial capacity. Quite apart from its value as an absorbent of immigration, diversified industry with a high level of technical skills is essential to our existence. All branches matter but certain basic industries especially so, and these we are busy establishing or expanding. There are many openings for private enterprise by cooperatives, kibbutzim, companies and individuals, but in the interest of security the State itself must take first heed for basic industries, and not only those of a 'military' kind, with the aid of private capital or without it.

And last, but fundamental, the moral element. A large army fully-trained and equipped, disciplined and fighting fit, rapid communications by land, sea and air, not a spot in the country out of effective touch, technical, professional and scientific talent of the highest order, local farming and manufacturing that can supply our main wants, modern weapons of all types in sufficiency—all this we must achieve. But it will not avail, even so, if we be not a nation instinct with courage and with belief in its historic mission.

The spirit always and at the last the spirit! That is the tocsin I sound, that is why the spiritual and moral heedlessness that undermines the Yishuv is, in my eyes, the worst enemy of the State of Israel. We are living in a fool's paradise; sensuality and pleasure-seeking are rampant among the old guard and our newcomers chance the contagion. We ask more and more of the State, less and less, almost nothing, of ourselves. We forget that the State is not a milch cow but the palfrey of a messianic redemption.

A great Jewish thinker of the seventeenth century affirmed that all things must be viewed *sub specie aeternitatis*. This metaphysical criterion hardly suits the needs of any State, even ours, but let us at least apply the yardstick of a single generation, if not of several. It is a mortal risk we run if we look at all things ephemerally and in greed, saying: 'Eat, drink and be merry, for tomorrow we die.' We have to live tomorrow and again the day after that, it is today that decides what tomorrow shall be.

ISRAEL'S FOREIGN POLICY
In the Knesseth, February 4, 1952

Our problem is how to map our policy, external and domestic, now and henceforth. The starting point must be not our attitude to any particular national ideology, but solely Israel's fundamental values, and its historical as well as its current urges, and they are these: security, immigration and development, unhindered contact with the Diaspora; a Jewish-Arab peace, the strengthening of world peace, freedom and democracy; and, therefore, friendly relations with all States and nations, and I mean every single one.

I stress in particular the importance of being allowed touch with free public opinion, through the Press, through popular representation and party influences. That, however, can only be where rule rests on persuasion, where differences are permissible and natural, and government may be criticized, because it depends on public opinion, and public opinion determines its policy. Whatever is right, reasonable and worthwhile, even if the Cabinet does not yet favor it, gets a hearing; public opinion can be mobilized behind it and the Government brought round in time. Where the situation is otherwise, I fear it is not in our power to change things.

I alluded to security and immigration. Who here is indifferent to either? I recall the debate in the First Knesseth on the Law of Return. No member could rival the Zionist fervor of Tewfik Toubi of the Communist party. The Cabinet proposals I laid before the House were not far-reaching enough for him. We withheld the right of Aliyah from criminals and diseased persons who might endanger the security or health of the State. Tewfik Toubi demanded an ingathering of exiles without limit or restriction upon wrongdoing or hurtfulness. I confess, too, that where the State's security and independence are involved, the public patriotism of our Communists is peerless. But profession of principles is not the real loyalty of action. Security and immigration entail a certain foreign policy for their fulfillment. To reject that policy is to abandon security and immigration.

Security hinges primarily on our manpower, on the readiness of youth and, by its own will and choice, of people to guard the independence and liberty of their State. We want independence for the sake of the ingathering, to develop our country, and suit its social, cultural and moral order to our particular needs and ideals. We want to keep all these aspirations safe by the strength of the men of Israel themselves. That they can do, however, only with the training, the equipment, arms and supplies which outside aid provides. We have not yet the best kind of advanced military schools and must send our outstanding officers to institutions abroad. We do not compare in military experience, knowledge or skill with the Soviet Union and the United States. Others must make much of the equipment we need, the four-engined airplanes, warships and tanks, the rations for the Army, and much else besides. We are in a coil of local inadequacy in technique and production, of foreign currency, of official benevolence and popular goodwill. We try everywhere, by every channel that is open, and we do not always take no for an answer.

It is with deep satisfaction that I can say that the young men studying in Staff Colleges overseas merit the distinction of their secondment and will bring profit to the Army and the State. They are not ambassadors, they have no diplomatic function, but their simple presence, their talent, bearing and character inspire faith and respect toward Israel in the hearts of the peoples among which they sojourn. And public opinion means a great deal there, so that, while certain sources of armament are still sealed tight against us, others grow more and more responsive in the atmosphere we are creating, of friendliness, of mutual understanding and trustful solicitude.

For immigration we need such sentiments, and their practical outcome even more, I would opine. If we could confiscate all the gold and silver in the country, we would still be unable to get the necessary houses, tools, machines, raw materials and foodstuffs at home. The oratory, the figures of speech and the rhodomontade about the ingathering are senseless if the speakers evade the crushing issue of supplies. If you do not help to prepare the ground where supplies are, in fact, forthcoming, then, fine phrases or not, you renounce immigration. That is the way of it. Unless we are sightless and fond, unless we overlook the governing factor in our lives, our foreign policy is bound to be of such orientation as will search out the governmental systems and political climates, the accessibility and sympathetic helpfulness, failing which not all the hard cash in the world will buy the means of redeeming the Galuth and rendering Israel secure. I make no moan against those countries which so far have turned their back on us. Luckily there are others that do not, else we were indeed forlorn.

A word of warning. The champions of the Cominform divide the world into two: one part—the West, of course—is black, and the other, which, needless to say, is East, a dazzling light. We may reject this totalitarian approach, but let us be careful not to fall into the opposite blunder and blinker ourselves to shadows and shortcomings of the West as to illumination from the East. You can learn the frailties of politics and society without a visit in the United States. American newspapers and books are outspoken in the extreme; their chief concern, indeed, is to pillory those weaknesses. It is, regrettably, less easy to learn the virtues of the East, even our Cominform disciples cannot visit as they choose. But virtues there certainly are, and many, not least in the art of propaganda. The constructive and cultural advances in the Soviet Union command respect, which is not necessarily to accept the fairy-tale that it is governed by workers and peasants. Anyone with the slightest knowledge of Russia and the basic writings of its ruling politicians knows perfectly well that the Soviet Union, like the 'people's democracies', is run by a Communist dictatorship, which brooks interference from no quarter. Naturally there is no written law, nor any clause in Stalin's famous Constitution, which says so, but it is common knowledge that the Bolshevist party enjoys absolute power, and if you call that kind of concentrated oligarchy a 'Workers' and Peasants' Government', it is a parody of speech. To point the moral, is there a party in Israel so violently arraigned by our workers and peasants as is the Communist? Whatever else we may or may not know about the Soviet Union, of this we can be sure, that it is far removed from socialism, that the worker and peasant are much worse off than in many countries of the West. Otherwise thousands of Russian workers would be sent to the United States on propaganda errands, to gaze upon the oppression and penury of the American worker in chains, thousands of American workers would be invited to the Soviet Union to marvel at the blessings of the Russian worker: his food and dress, his culture, and terms of labor, his influence on government, his trade union organization and social privileges.

This hermetic aloofness does not imply that nothing great has been done. Provinces lost by the Romanoffs have been reconquered, countries the Czars never subdued are under the Kremlin's heel. It is understandable that every Russian should be proud of these national victories, and respond to his ruler's appeal to the patriotic instinct.

Not few are the failings of America and England. They are on view, as in an open book, which each one of us may read to his heart's content, and many of us have gone and have read it. So discussion is not difficult.

For centuries America has been the stage of a gigantic unfolding, a mighty phenomenon, whereof we here in Israel are making a little likeness today. America has given asylum and opportunity to millions of the Old World's oppressed and persecuted. In America, as never before and nowhere else, pioneers vanquished the desert and the unknown. America was rent by the most terrible of civil wars, fought for the emancipation of the African slaves its early settlers introduced. Swiftly, but not yet finally, the human mosaic of differing races and origins is dissolving into the pattern of a new nation, and a spectacular creativeness and enterprise are being born.

For over a hundred years the vast continental State, safe within its oceanic boundaries, obeyed the counsel of George Washington and steered clear of foreign alliances. But in the course of two World Wars it emerged from its isolation, and has begun to act a decisive part in world affairs. I was there in both Wars, when, after much searching of heart, America broke away from her past.

With some justice, members have spoken of the great role played by the Soviet Army in the second World War. But it was not friendless: America furnished it with immense stocks of arms, equipment and food. More than that, a colossal armada was marshalled in the United States, which fought conclusively against Hitler in Europe and Africa, and in the Far East against Japan.

The part of England was hardly less magnificent. No longer the illustrious power she was at the dawn of this twentieth century, entering the war in the name of freedom, almost unprepared, she held out, alone, for freedom's sake, even when Hitler had Stalin by his side.

A little while ago I spent four weeks in the United States. With typical Jewish curiosity and interest, I observed what was going on. I talked with the President and his principal advisers, labor leaders and captains of industry, with distinguished journalists, Senators and Congressmen, with State Governors, and city

Mayors. And I believe that in the consciousness of the nation something very hopeful for humanity is taking place. After all, America has escaped many of the pitfalls and trials that convulsed the life of Europe. It has had few wars and fewer border quarrels, and could expand peacefully from ocean to ocean. Providence gave it abundant natural resources, an enormous internal market, and a productivity without par. It can, unaided, satisfy almost all its wants, and its standard of living is the highest in the world. But more and more it is beginning to realize now that this comfort and security will not last, if the rest of mankind lives in poverty, in squalor and fear. Not every American perceives this, perhaps, but in all men of influence the conviction is deep—that the United States must dedicate part of their wealth and production to raising standards in impoverished lands and banishing the fears of lesser nations. Thus, in recent years, America has granted enormous sums—not in the way of charity—to strengthen other national economy and security. All in need might ask: not all were willing to be so assisted—and I will not discuss their reasons, but those that were have benefited exceedingly. But above and beyond all this, America shelters the greatest and freest Jewish community of the Diaspora. On that community our State has bestowed an enhancement of dignity and stature which no gold can measure; in turn it makes to us a contribution with which no other Jewry can vie.

American Jews rightly look upon themselves as a loyal element within the great republic, but bound still to their own people. And so without their prodigious help the upbuilding of the State, the ingathering of exiles, cannot be: only from a free, democratic, open America can such help come. They are not better Jews than the Jews of Russia, but they are given the chance to do their part. Take away the freedom of the American people, and American Jewry, too, is paralyzed. Jews can be free only where freedom reigns.

The righting of the immemorial wrong the nations did us will depend for many years on international goodwill and aid, and it is only through the hearts of a people that we find a way to the bounty of its Government. We must keep the friendship and trust of the American people, that as long ago as 1922, in Congress, proclaimed unanimously its favor of the Jewish National Home, and earlier still, indicted Czarist discrimination.

We do not seek identity with other States. Not so. Yet we have the right to praise freedom and democracy as inestimable boons to man, not least the Jew, and declare our resolve to defend our freedom with our lives.

I listened without surprise or alarm to yesterday's explanations by Communist members of their outpourings in honor of Nahas Pasha and King Farouk. Remembering similar eulogy of the Mufti, our arch-enemy, I have long ceased to find it strange that self-styled patriots, who never tire of professing devotion to independent Israel, should extend comfort to its enemies.

That the United States and Great Britain should invite Egypt to join the Middle East Command as a founder member does, however, both astound and perturb us. Do they really think that Egypt will fight to defend for the world the freedom and democracy its own borders do not know? Have they not yet marked the lesson of two World Wars? It was not the Egyptian Army that kept Rommel out of Egypt, but the British, the Australians, the New Zealanders and Indians, and the Jewish units that fought with them. If Egypt ever uses the arms the western Powers are about to supply, it will be against Israel, and we have told them so.

They and all other Powers concerned for the peace and prosperity of the Middle East will err grievously if they do not recognize that, geography apart, Israel is uniquely different from its neighbors in conduct and culture, and must be handled differently. We are no State of family cliques and powerful cabals trafficking in appointments. We live and die for a messianic ideal, the advance-guard of universal redemption. We are not for sale or hire, not for all the riches in the world. Tiny, poor and underpopulated Israel may be, but no earthly power can make it a protectorate or its Government a puppet. With all our modesty in material things, we shall hearken to none save who speak to us as equals. Neither sword nor gold nor false redeemer will beguile or browbeat us into denial of faith.

About peace with the Arabs. I have no illusions; it will not be achieved by ideological blandishment. But equally, why regard today's Middle East as immutable, why not plan ahead for a less imperfect reality? I am convinced that, given two conditions, not only peace but constant and honorable cooperation between us and our neighbors may be firmly hoped for.

The first condition is so to strengthen the State in its economy and political values that no enemy can harbor fond notions of its collapse.

The second is liberal and democratic governments in the Arab States, and in time, have no fear, they will come. This may to many of you sound far-off and unreal. Yet I hold it a goal we shall assuredly reach beyond today's narrowed horizons. Toward that goal let us set our faces steadfastly, and in that aim instruct our children and ourselves.

THE CALL OF SPIRIT IN ISRAEL
*From the Government Yearbook,
October, 1951*

> So my spirit remaineth among you; fear ye not.
> (HAGGAI, 2:5)

> If it be marvellous in the eyes of the remnant of this people in these days.
> (ZECHARIAH, 8:6)

The State of Israel will be judged not by its riches or military power, nor by its technical skills, but by its moral worth and human values. We must make one more tremendous and concerted effort to become like all other peoples. To be that and no more, a normal, vigorous, free and sovereign nation, is not easy, but by setting up the State we guaranteed the principal condition of fulfillment. Each one of us, however, is entitled to cling to the conviction that merely to be like all other peoples is not enough. We may pridefully aspire to bring true the words of the Prophet: 'I the Lord . . . give thee for a covenant of the people to the Gentiles.'

History has no other record of a people that suffered and struggled so much, that paid so high a price for its dedication over the centuries. The causes of this distinction lie deep indeed, and its source is undying. Through generations untold we, and no other people, believed in the vision of the last days. It cannot be that a vision which for so long inspired a people's faith, its hope and patient expectancy will disappoint it now of all times, when the miracle which is the State of Israel has come to pass.

It was destined that the State should rise amid the storms of war, and our liberated people first reveal its fighting quality and military prowess, not its creative and spiritual virtues. In the first months of independence we had to apply all our strength to the main purpose of routing our enemies. In retrospect, that was all to the good. It was well for us, and for history and the world, to know that independence was no gift, that we paid for it the supreme cost of the lives of our dearest sons, and with our own hands set up our State.

We shall have to render up the best of our means and energies for many years to come, to maintain the security of the State. Yet security is only one condition of our existence and independence. Every country must safeguard the peace, prosperity and progress of its inhabitants; Israel is under like obligation, but that is not the main thing. The redemption of the people of Israel comes first.

Even in the hour of crisis, the first months of the State's life, when we were forced to defend ourselves against the armies of six Arab States and, out of Mandatory chaos, establish law and order, services, administration and a Government, even in that tempestuous period the tide of immigration did not ebb, but flooded fuller and higher yet.

When the fighting ended, the duty was laid upon us to bring in countless multitudes of our people, to roof them and place them in agriculture, in industry and handicraft; to build new towns and villages to absorb hundreds of thousands, maybe millions. That this might be, we are adjured to carry out a project of colonization far greater than all of the last seventy years. We shall have to devote ourselves on a tremendous scale and at lightning speed to afforesting the hills and flowering the sands. We must install irrigation, improve the soil, and erect farm buildings, dwelling-houses and schools, factories, hospitals and laboratories. We shall have to construct a network of local, national and international communications. We must organize an extensive export and import trade, lay railways and make roads, and much more besides.

But all that is only one side of the coin. We are not just bringing in droves of creatures whom it is enough to employ, feed and house. These are Jewish men and women. This is a people unique, hurled to all the ends of the earth, speaking with many tongues, apprenticed to alien cultures, asunder in different communities and tribes within the House of Israel. We must melt down this fantastically diversified assemblage and cast it afresh in the die of a renewed nationhood. We must break down the barriers of geography and culture, of society and speech, which keep the different sections apart, and endow them with a single language, a single culture, a single citizenship, a single loyalty, with new legislation and new laws. We must give them a new spirit, a culture and literature, science and art. We must draw them into new social and political orbits and attach them to our past and to our vision of sovereignty, in self-government, in liberty, in Jewish unity, in brotherhood, in mutual aid and collective responsibility. And, at the same time, we must take thought for their security, for the security of the State, its freedom and its place among the nations. All this we must do in a tempest-tossed and riven world, when peace hangs by a slender thread and we are encompassed by malevolence and enmity.

How can we get through this immense and difficult task? How lift this heavy load, at once administrative, economic and political, at once cultural and organizational—and we so few? We were hard put to it to garner what little assets we have in the Land; and they are not enough for our multitudinous immigration. We are an oppressed people, the sport of history, we have no material heritage. Yet within a short space of time, with the resources of a little State, there is work to be done which never before we did, which perhaps no other people has ever done.

It can only be done by enlisting fully the one superiority we have, our moral and intellectual greatness.

History has robbed us of many things. We did not inherit a spacious land; we were not a numerous people. Political power was not given us. Only now, after seventy years of pioneer striving, have we reached the beginning of independence in a part of our small country. But one thing history granted us from the very start—incomparable moral strength. By this virtue, even in ancient days, we withstood mighty empires which overtopped us not only in numbers and material and military resources, but also, in many respects, in culture. There is no parallel in human memory for a people driven from its native land and dispersed among the nations, yet holding triumphantly to its sworn purpose and independence for thousands of years. Moral strength has made us what we are today. There are nations not inferior in intellectual fibre. There were nations excelling in diverse branches of culture and in the creations of their art and thought. The culture of the Jewish people when it dwelt in its Land was one-sided. In religion, ethics and poetry we ranked high, but had almost no say in metaphysics, in science, in most of the arts, in architecture and road-making. Perhaps, from that standpoint, the Almighty did right by the people of Israel when he scattered it among the nations. Our life among the peoples of Europe and America enriched us with values we lacked. In our wanderings we imbibed modern culture and took part, too, in its making. Now, in spiritual resource, we are not less than any other nation. The Jewish contribution to the achievements of spirit and science in recent times is as fine as that of the finest nations.

*   *   *

In fulfilling its missions, our State cannot depend entirely on the apparatus of Government, on members of the Cabinet and the Knesseth. We shall need them, but with them alone we cannot harness completely the pioneer energy within us and marshal all the superior qualities of Jewish heart and brain. I do not mean only the gifted individuals with special talents and unusual attributes. Within each man and woman are hidden tremendous powers: it is only a question of knowing how to reach their source, and reveal and exploit them. The halutzic youth which carried out, in this country, one of the most productive revolutions in the history of man and set up undertakings without precedent, these were no supermen or wonder-children, but just ordinary boys and girls. That revolution brought our independence but will not fulfill its purpose if it remains political and military and nothing besides. The decisive phase is still ahead. We have yet to revolutionize the land, the people, all our ways of life.

This demands from each of us a new accounting of self. Our former habits of thought, our internal relations, the old manners and methods and measures, no longer apply. None are exempt, be it civil servants, teachers, lawyers, physicians, Army officers, engineers, men of science, literature and the arts; least of all those animated by the pioneer spirit, whether they be pioneers of labor or of settlement, or in the realm of spirit itself.

Let me begin with the Army.

For no other people is the contrast so startling between steadfast aspiration toward peace and lack of security. Even before it emerged into the light of day, the State was put to the test of blood and fire, and came forth with honor and victory. This must not lead us into vainglory; we must not be drunk with success. We have signed armistice agreements with all our neighbors and are working for a peace that will endure. But there is reason to fear that, even if the best befalls, it will only be an armed peace. So long as war between nations is countenanced, the danger of a new onslaught and a new invasion menaces Israel, and the object will not only be to crush our independence, but to wipe us out. We must be prepared.

From the moment that threat of war loomed upon the horizon,

it was evident that we could not hold our ground with the strength of the Haganah solely, its resources and methods. Nor if, Heaven forbid, a second war awaits us, shall we hold it with the forces, the means and organization which we disposed in the first.

First of all let us rid ourselves of the foolish error that with the Army alone can we maintain the security of the State.

A paramount and deciding factor in our security is mass immigration in swift tempo. Nothing is as forceful for security as intensifying immigration. Immigration is not only our commandment and purpose, to render the State secure; as that agent it is unsurpassed in effect, finality and speed. No economic or such-like considerations can be allowed to slow down the rate of immigration any more than they braked our resistance to the Arab armies.

Of hardly less significance is the factor of settlement and of balanced distribution of population. Two perturbing facts imperil our security: only a tithe of the Jewish people dwell in the State, and only a tithe of its area is cultivated by our hands; there is excessive concentration of population in one city, or in two or three large cities. We need a policy of settlement, so far as possible, to populate all parts of the country in equal measure. To transfer immigrants to agriculture and establish a complex of villages in the east and south, and in the approaches of Jerusalem, that is not only a biological and economic need, it is an indispensable protection.

But the State cannot just lean upon pioneers. It must extend maximum aid to settlement through law and order, financing and planning. It must direct colonization, and so create a belt of defensive outposts along the frontiers and in danger-zones, to serve as its first line of defense.

We dare not be blind to our geographical placing. In a quarrel with our neighbors we have no overland communication with the outside world. Our agriculture and fishery, therefore, must supply the inhabitants with foodstuffs: fruit and vegetables, milk and bread, fish and meat. Defensive weapons must be made locally, so that we be not wholly dependent on outside sources. We must foster Israel shipping and the expansion of national marine services to all quarters of the globe, and pay special heed to building up a large fleet of fast merchantmen, and a young generation of seamen. We must improve domestic and international air routes, procure freight and passenger aircraft, train ground and air crews, perfect and extend radar.

In the general mobilization of our war it became painfully clear how high was the percentage of unfitness among our youth. And present immigration now coming to the Land is less fit still. The physical healing of the nation, improved nutrition of children and healthier youth are vital requirements of security.

And lastly, security rests on a foreign policy of peace: a sincere intention to be at peace with our neighbors, and with all nations; a determined effort to establish relations of friendship with countries great and small, in east and west; avoidance of all and any belligerent provocation from whatever quarter it come, in whatever form it be revealed; unswerving support of every step aimed at punishing aggression and achieving peace in the Middle East and all over the world. Our neighbors, too, depend in no small measure on world opinion: to the extent that the world recognizes the true aspirations of our State, by so much will our security be strengthened. But so long as wars are possible, without an Army our security would be short-lived.

When war was declared on us, while yet our hands were still tied by an alien and a hostile Government, and we mustered to defend ourselves, we had no choice. You do not examine recruits too closely at the hour of danger. We had one objective only, to drive out the enemy, and the selflessness and heroism of our youth, and experience won in Haganah and Allied units during the second World War, helped us to gain it. Now, in a prolonged truce, is our chance to build up an army on preconceived lines, free from the cramping pressure of an enemy at our gates. We must plan and organize carefully upon two principles: the best military experience and science; the particular needs and conditions of State and people.

We must scout the fallacy, borrowed from backward and untended lands, that an army by its very nature stupefies, coarsens and demoralizes. True, there are armies of that decadent kind, each in turn produced by an unsuccessful and decadent regime. In a normal nation the army can become an instrument of education, uplift and health. Our Army must. It will not do its duty by the State, if service is not designed to raise the physical, cultural and moral status of our youth, nor will it satisfy the needs of our security, of national reconstruction, *unless it is transformed into a cradle of combatant pioneer youth,* sound of limb and healthy in mind, daring and ready to act, fleetfooted and energetic, undismayed by difficulty or danger, and faithful to our missions. We are not a normal people yet. The veterans among us, firmly settled here in the culture and life of Jewish independence before the founding of the State, overlook the lamentable fact that they are only a fraction of the Jewish people and that, Jewishly, the bulk of it is still no more than formless clay, without language or tradition, without roots in sovereignty, with none of the ways of a free-born society. We are now only at the outset of mass immigration, and we suffer the birth-pangs of absorption, economic and social and cultural too. We must stitch the torn seam in the fabric of the Diaspora and join hearts estranged by distance of time and place. We must knit exiles together and communities far withdrawn each from the other in cultures, and remould them into homogeneity.

Even in the State, separatist and schismatic forces are still at work. Partisan and ideological cleavages split us as widely as the most backward nations, which scarcely makes for rapid mending of rifts in the Galuth. Apart from the school, itself not yet immune, only the army can, and it must, be a means of solidarity and uplift in reshaping the nation, and integrating it truly into the civilization and society which are today being formed in this State. An army of mercenaries, scornful of national independence and vision, will not stand the test when the battle has to be joined, battle of the few against the many.

Not only men of brilliant spirit, but military geniuses like Hannibal and Napoleon, have recognized the decisive military value of a spiritual lead. Being few, we need that advantage more than any other army.

Our soldier must first of all be a citizen of the State in the noblest meaning of that word, a citizen set solid in the Homeland, in his nation's past, in its culture and language, in its creative efforts and vision. The Army must be established upon a brotherhood in arms. Only in such do barriers of community, party, class and the rest disappear. Every soldier is equal to the next in standing, in rights and rations, in quarters and uniform. We must give this fraternity a full and positive content, make it one of mission and duty, of comradeship and cultural progress.

In the general mobilization there met for the first time young men and women of all classes and communities, from farm and factory, slum-dwellers and the underprivileged, and there was revealed in its immensity the widening gap, not of ideology and politics but in ways of life: between the directive class of the Yishuv and the less fortunate ones deprived from childhood of opportunities of education and refinement, and growing up in ignorance, squalor and mannerlessness, with no fundamental Jewish or human graces.

They were good soldiers and displayed in battle an unsuspected moral courage. But our whole existence hung in the balance. We could not disengage ourselves to be educators in the Army, and so, educationally, we failed them. From now on there can be no excuse for failing.

DAVID BEN GURION

* * *

The Defense Service Law is designed to give the Army the two basic characteristics our security requires: military capacity and the capacity to pioneer. The first year is devoted principally to education in pioneering: after a preliminary military training of from six weeks to three months, the 18 year-olds and over are sent for agricultural instruction. This is accompanied by intensive cultural activity, to inculcate a knowledge of Hebrew in a youth that never went to school or was taken from it because of family distress and poverty, and to foster a bent for partnership in labor and mutual aid, a sense of responsibility, order and discipline, familiarity with the Land, with a life of nature. This is combatant and creative service in one.

The agricultural instruction has two objects: military and colonizing. Experts hold that an effective army cannot be built up in this country of immigration unless the youth, and particularly the immigrant youth, receive above all else an education in agriculture which will enmesh them in its life, accustom them to physical labor, and acquaint them with the language, and with culture and discipline before they enter the regular forces. This will stimulate the establishment of frontier settlements, the first rampart of defense, a rampart of flesh and blood. The State cannot bid citizens go forth and settle on the land, on the frontier of all places. No one becomes a frontiersman by order. The whole of our education in school and outside it, in literature and in the Press must be directed to one end, the upbringing of a pioneer generation that will regard it as its sacred duty to revive the desert, master the elements and create, in economy, society and culture, a lodestar to the exiled children of Israel, and an example to all the world.

Over the past three generations there has become manifest in the Land that exceptional virtue we call halutziuth, pioneering, instrument of our every success, not least the military, from the founding of Petah Tiqvah to the establishment of the State. Pioneering is not the exclusive property of the elite and eminent; it is in the soul of every man, one among those rarer spiritual powers, traits and treasures, of which only few find expression. The pressure of historical needs, and guided educational activity, finding the way to man's secret heart, can stir the silent springs to flowing life, so that each of us may show himself hero and pioneer with the best. All skilled commanders know this, and can transform an army of ordinary mortals into a phalanx of heroes. Springs like these came alive in young Jews in the little towns of Lithuania and Poland, Galicia and Rumania, and in America.

The immigration of today is mainly from the east, the countries of Islam in Asia and Africa, where Jews of late could draw little enlightenment from Jewish or any other culture. But that does not make them different in character and basic quality from other Jews. They, too, have a rich potential of pioneer talent, courage and creativity. If we invest in them only a trifle of our zeal for the Jewish youth of Europe, we will get results as splendid. The wonders of yesteryear in Israel stunned the universe, but here was no sudden miracle of the day the State was born, or one conceived with the Second Aliyah or Petah Tiqvah. It was one link in a valorous chain stretching back thousands of years. It was manifest in the martyred congregation of Worms, the sainted disciples of Rabbi Akiva, the warriors of Massada. Without it, our people would not have survived. It has not grown less nor will it now, when the magnificence has come to pass for which the people waited with mystic yearning for generation on generation. Tremendous forces are dammed in us, to gush forth at the touch of a loving hand. The fount of courage will not be choked, nor our youth fail us.

There is nothing like this in any other army; but for us it is a categorical imperative of security and existence. The frontier villages will not be military cantonments but farms like any other, where a man may live his own life and bring up his children. We need men and women pioneers in equal measure. These settlers, likely to be the first attacked in any incursion by troops or irregulars, must know how to carry firearms and use them.

We must train a soldier capable of acting as well in formations as in small groups. He must not be an inert cog, unable to move independently within the vast military machine. In our first war, guerrilla tactics were important and our young men, Haganah-trained most of them, showed a special aptitude. Personal initiative, adaptability to plainland or valley, field or street, by day or night, heat or cold, foul weather or fair; knowledge of Land and its environs, swift reaction to unforeseen difficulty or obstacle, and physical and spiritual self-sufficiency—these are an essential condition of military success. Every man must be so drilled that he can take command of himself in any instant of need.

But education and personal training are not enough. The effectiveness of a modern army rests primarily on the power of collective, coordinated action by large units, battalions, brigades and divisions; and on combined operations of land, air and sea forces.

So there must be group discipline and action as well. Undisciplined, the Army would degenerate into an armed rabble, dangerous to the external security of the State and even its inner welfare. Our individualism does not easily accept the yoke of discipline, inside the Army or outside it, and it is for us ourselves to mend the fault, mindful that discipline is not denial of personal freedom, but has its origin in reciprocal responsibility, in a common destiny and loyalty to the common cause.

Haganah, Palmach and the Jewish units in the British Army gave the Defense Army of Israel a cadre of trustworthy, daring and experienced commanders. Whatever an ideal commander in the most advanced of countries must be, so must also a commander in our Army. And something more: *he must be a man of model character and educative example.* Technical and professional skill, administrative and fighting ability, loyalty and devotion, physical and moral courage are not all. The human material of which our Army is made, the historical conditions in which we are placed, make it vital that a commander *be endowed with a great spirit,* and serve, in life, bearing and behavior, as a *living example* to his men. He is charged with a high, a twofold, responsibility: for their lives and honor, and for the security of the State. The born leader commands not so much by orders and instruction as by the witness of his conduct and personality, embodying moral values and an ideal for which one cheerfully lives and dies. He must hold the affection of his troops and their trust. Without orders or discipline an army cannot be, but the courage it needs, the readiness to hazard all, infinite devotion—these plumb the depths of man's spirit. Only that commander will succeed who is fitted by intrinsic quality, by a moral character that wins respect, esteem and confidence, to start in his every soldier the current of courage. Our War of Independence, the earlier stand of our pioneers, have proved there is in us this precious stuff of which perfect soldiers and officers are fashioned.

The education and training of commanders are never really at an end; they study and qualify all their lives. This will be made possible in part in military academies to be set up in the State, in part by special courses abroad.

Two years' conscription will not answer all the needs of Army and security. We must have volunteers as well, from among the better commissioned and other ranks, to serve from three to five years more and longer. The finest and truest of our young men, those of surpassing moral and intellectual mettle, must come forward for regular enlistment, pioneers to nation and Government alike—in that highest form of service, keeping Israel secure.

So shall we create, in constant readiness, a striking force to ward off sudden onslaught and hold its ground until the whole fighting power of the nation, which we are now equipping against the hour of need, can move to its side. So, on the anvil of the Army, do we forge the pattern of a people compact, uniform and peace-loving, reliant on its strength and taking the place proper to it in the society of nations.

* * *

Defense and settlement have been interlocked ever since the new Yishuv began seventy years ago.

For forty years the kvutza was the focal point of Jewish resurrection, in Land and Diaspora. Upon it centered age-long yearnings for redemption. To myriads of our generation it pointed the way of Return, and taught them labor, farming and the lore of Hebrew, to develop creative personality and exalt woman's place; it taught them to live free, equal and independent. It spread its benison afar upon the scattered communities, lit up the face of youth, enriched it with new values, and gave birth to a brave new generation of halutzim. It transformed Zionism and tracked new and surer paths to the building of the Land and the shaping of the nation. It changed the physical and spiritual scene of our country. With pride and faith forthright we can proclaim that it has served and will serve again to augur a new life, not for us alone, but all mankind.

Did its founders foresee all that their simple, modest undertaking on the banks of Jordan was destined to bring about in Jewish and universal values? They probably did not give it a thought. They did not enquire much into the tremendous significance beneath what was, to them, the plain and natural course. They just did what was their life's aim, they attached themselves lovingly to their native soil, spent lives of honest labor, honest with themselves, honest with their comrades. Only now, forty years after, we perceive how rich the blessing borne in that seed; perhaps, even now, we see only a tiny part of the final harvest.

In the Galuth it was the power of vision and faith that sustained us, but we were not redeemed, not could we be, by that alone. Only when it was fortified by pioneer will, *the will to achieve*, galvanizing the faculties of man to make his ambitions and dreams come true, was the road to redemption opened at last. All through our history the vital spark shot up, flamed and sank again; only in the last seventy years did it glow into steady, splendid incandescence. The morn of vision dawned.

By the grace of twin forces of the spirit, faith in a vision and the will of pioneers, we established the kvutza and we built the State. At the outset those who created our labor settlement can have theorized little concerning the solution of social problems, concerning the unimaginable hardships of settling an exiled nation upon a desert land. But in their hearts was timeless, envisioned resolve for a life of decent toil, of brotherhood and freedom. They believed in the truth, patent yet profound, that man is not man's enemy, but his partner and friend, that society must be founded, not upon exploitation and rivalry, but upon mutual help and cooperation.

The commandment to act is of the essence of Judaism. The Law of Israel was not based upon abstract principles with no binding force, or faith that is only in the heart—but upon a code of ordinances, of what to do and from what to refrain, by which man should live.

The sublimated love to which Christianity was bidden did not pledge it to deeds, and so became illusory. Judaism stands on *precepts*: on a duty to do things. This law of action, of positivity, is the law of halutziuth.

Now the State is in our hands, an instrument mighty and manifold in performance, some hold that we no longer need the pioneering of kvutza and moshav. From now on, they argue, everything will be done by the State, its staff, its statutes and budget. Great though they are, and although they have given us almost everything achieved in Israel these past fifty years, apart from the significant contribution of private enterprise and private capital, neither the Zionist Organization nor the Labor Federation can compare with the kvutza, and in capacity and possibilities the State outstrips all our public bodies to this day. What *it* has done in a brief space the Chovevei Zion, the Jewish National Fund, Baron Rothschild, the Palestine Jewish Colonization Association and private capital all together could not accomplish in seventy years. In immigration, it did more in a year than we had done previously in ten to fifteen. Our Defense Army restored in a swift campaign more than tenfold the area won back in three preceding generations.

But no mistake is more harmful or hazardous than to imagine that the hour of pioneering has passed. It is just the reverse. Only in a State are there substantial prospect and reward for pioneer enterprise. There are things to be done by the State and by its power alone—opening wide the gates of the Land to every Jew who wishes to return, offering basic education to every child, providing health services and the like. But immigration, education and absorption are lost without pioneer inspiration and ways of life.

Where there is no vision the people perish—and it is just because of the greatness of the everyday purpose, and the heaviness of the load, that it is our duty to kindle the ultimate flame and illumine our every act with the visionary spirit. Only if we hold the vision close will we chart a safe course through the mounting billows of this vexed sea of our times. The vision will be realized in a partnership, full, faithful and enduring, between the State and its pioneers: making the kvutza dream a pervasive and all-embracing fact, accomplishing Israel's historic purpose, vindicating its Prophets, through the transcendent exertions of dedicated youth. We are untrue to ourselves if we take not heed of the moral testament of our Prophets and sages. In our great labor venture and, first and foremost, in that venture's settlements are implanted the brotherhood of man, social justice and creative liberty. It is for the State to further these ends, but not at the expense of reconstruction and absorption; there is no such dilemma. Nay, rather, they help to build our economy and absorb immigrants, and will be encouraged for their own sakes, for truly are they the way and the vision, they are the teaching of seers, and will mold a nation worthy of its glorious tradition and its yearning for deliverance.

Great things have been done already, in quantity and quality: that at which many of our best had scoffed is no myth. A Jew can be a first-class cultivator and still a man of culture, knowing how to blend farming with industry, manual with spiritual labor, and, worker that he is, how to fight as well.

We stand only on the edge of our colonization. More than half the southern expanse of the State is barren yet, and in it perhaps lie hid our richest natural resources. One such treasure has been uncovered, in the waters of the Dead Sea. Many others are blanketed by the sands; we must unearth and work them.

And the sea calls to us, with its bounteous sources of food and raw material.

Against the vistas thus unfolding to us, we need a colonization that will embrace husbandry and industry, fishing and shipping, communications by land and communications by air, civilians and soldiers, and will flourish on toil and sweat as on scientific attainments and cultural values. We shall have it, if youth be but bold and better the instruction of its forerunners, if it will renew the pioneering we have dared so far, and march on, with heart courageous, to make the vision real.

Our first step was the land. Landless for centuries, plucked from the bosom of nature, we have now, returning to the Homeland, bound ourselves again to every acre, and our townsfolk become farmers and makers of homesteads.

The second step is seaward. Thirteen years ago the Arab 'Fuehrer' tried to destroy us by fire and sword and famine.

Jaffa port, where no Jewish seaman or stevedore had been allowed to set foot, although it prospered entirely on Jewish passengers and cargoes, was paralyzed by the Mufti with intent to starve the Yishuv and throttle immigration. But the plot failed. Instead, seafaring sense and gallantry were aroused in a Yishuv that knows not fright nor capitulation. The foundation of a Jewish port was set overnight; and our mariners, fishers and trawlermen, our sailors and steersmen sprang into being, to spread an empery of Jewish creativeness and labor over the oceans.

This saga of Israel is in its maritime prelude, and much is yet to be wrought by our masters of the sea.

Man's dominion over land and sea is as old as civilization itself. Expelled from our birthplace, for two thousand years we had been cut off from these springs of national life. Our lusty endeavors to strike roots in the earth anew and make our way across the waters prepared us for sovereignty. Without the Jewish villages of seventy years building, there would have been no State; without Jewish seamen, the ports would not have stayed in our hands. Our future and fulfillment depend upon how far and how fast we settle the barren wastes, with what array of manpower and science we go down to our seas.

The air was conquered by man only in our generation. The first experiments of our fearless and unassuming vanguard, Dov Hos, Ben Ya' aqov and their companions, were frustrated by an alien and obstructive Government. An illegal Haganah built ordnance factories and arsenals in secret places, but you cannot fly aircraft underground, and without independence we could not conquer the air.

We were hemmed in a vicious circle: our enemies marshalled all their might to kill the unborn State. 'Primus' monoplanes, acquired in the days of the Mandate, did marvels during the disorders before real war broke out. They supplied food to besieged villages—the Etzion bloc, Yehiam and the Negev; they flew the wounded out of isolated places and bombed guerrillas.

But they could not stand up to the enemy's fighter-planes, and the grave, uneasy people asked: Where are our planes? For weeks enemy aircraft raided us, dealt wantonly with our settlements and struck at women and children. We had not long to wait. Soon our air force soared into the cerulean lists. At once it proved its superiority, technical and professional, even when it was numerically weaker. The ascendancy grew, and in the final battle in the south it played a decisive part: at the very outset of the operations it shattered the enemy's air base and ruled the Negev skies.

The second World War and ours have shown that you cannot break the enemy's will or fighting power by bombing, even if it be carried out by great squadrons over long periods, as when England was bombed and afterwards Germany. It was not less clear that without superior air power you cannot win. We could not have driven back invading Egypt nor freed the Negev had not our air force got the upper hand. That the State exists today, and its bounds reach from Dan to Elath, is due markedly to the air force. We would not, before proclamation of the State, have kept in our hands many points north, east or south, were it not for the 'primuses,' nor fared as far as we did without an air force organized, and in the main equipped, in the actual stress of war.

Mark this: the pioneers of the air force, and in the first stage its personnel, were sabras; the part of native-born pilots in operations and victories, and no less in casualties, was considerable.

But we could not have built up the force, or maintained it, without overseas volunteers, men who had gained skill and experience with the Allied Forces in the second World War. Volunteers from 50 countries served in the Defense Army; never before had Israel's unity been typified so brilliantly and so vividly, and never, it seems to me, was there a Jewish organism embodying so complete an ingathering of the exiles. The volunteers did their duty loyally and with success, in all formations, though many did not know the language and were not even

Zionists. But nowhere did they fill such an important, responsible and successful role as in the air force; and from young Jewry of South Africa, Great Britain, America, Canada and other countries specialists and experts offered their services, and their lives, for Israel.

But conquest of the air is not just a matter of security. A sound economy, a high standard of living, a rich culture, and spiritual, political and economic independence are not to be got without it, and without mastery of the earth and the sea.

Aspiring to peace, freedom and justice as we do, we condemn all domination, save over the elements. To rule the elements, we must develop all the more intensively our spiritual valor, bodily health and quality of action; we must follow the search for truth, the spiritual and moral virtues of pioneers and heroes. Only by these can a nation climb to grandeur.

* * *

In the realm of legislation and justice, we know two codes: our ancient Jewish canon, and the laws of the Gentiles among whom we dwelt. Our jurisprudence flourished on its own hearth, inspired by the reality and spirit of an evolving nation; but its free growth ended when independence was lost to Rome. It did not wholly wither, it developed still, but as in a vacuum, and it was foreign statutes which governed our lives though they could not satisfy our needs, even when not aimed with malice against us.

Here, if ever, we stand before a tabula rasa. We cannot for any length of time retain the laws of the Mandatory, designed not for the facts nor the developments of the State. We are no neophytes appearing suddenly upon the world's stage. We are a nation of great age, rejuvenated, and shall not be as we ought to be if we do not drink deep and always at the springs of our former life, and cling to the tendrils of our past.

Yet we should not now go forth to war with the arms of the hosts of Joshua or the Hasmonaeans. Likewise the ordering of our sovereignty goes beyond the laws of Saul or the prescripts of Nehemiah, though, truth to say, not all such are yet too old for our times. Ours must be a code of laws and justice blending the claims of an eternal ethic, the imperial requirements of the time and the purpose of the vision of the last days. We are like no other State and dare not be content with passing needs. Israel was established not by the grace of its present inhabitants or for their sake alone. It is not only an end in itself, it is a means also toward fulfillment of the age-long mission of Jewry, and its code must serve that mission no less than the State.

It is a mission we may spell in two brief ways: one, the ingathering of the exiles; the other 'and thou shalt love thy neighbor as thyself.'

Our code must be framed to speed the absorption of immigrants into our economy, culture and society; to fuse the returning tribes into a homogeneous national and cultural unit; to forward our physical and moral healing and the cleansing of our lives from the trivia and dross which gathered upon us in dependence and exile. To maintain the status quo will not do. We have set up a dynamic State, bent upon creation and reform, building and expansion. Laws which lag behind development, merely a digest of experience and the lessons of the past, are useless to us. We need to anticipate the character of the times, discern embryonic forms emergent or renewed, and clear the path for circumstantial change. The revolution which is the State is only an overture to the two-fold revolution, in man and nature, which will come when our people is at last gathered together and resettled in Zion, at peace. The code prepares the way and buoys the course.

We have rebelled against all controls and religions, all laws and judgments which the mighty sought to foist upon us. We kept to our dedication and our missions. By these will the State be judged, by the moral character it imparts to its citizens, by the human values determining its inner and outward relations, and by its fidelity, in thought and act, to the supreme behest: 'and thou shalt love thy neighbor as thyself.' Here is crystallized the eternal law of Judaism, and all the written ethics in the world can say no more. The State will be worthy of its name only if its systems, social and economic, political and legal, are based upon these imperishable words. They are more than a formal precept which can be construed as passive or negative: not to deprive, not to rob, not to oppress, not to hurt. Jewish law was not content with that; it is not enough not to trespass on another's rights. Human relations must be constructed on partnership in destiny, mutual aid, reciprocal attraction; on a comradeship of equals and on love of mankind. Only on the rock of the commandment 'love thy neighbor as thyself' will a State arise, faithful to the great call. This is the one and only key to the legislation and laws of Israel.

To erect a State on this rock-like foundation is not only the business of lawyers and legislators. The builders of the State and its defenders, the men of the spirit among the people, its seers and teachers, its craftsmen, all these will mold its shape; and the visage will be as that of the nation. But in the newly-established State the legal profession has now a special responsibility and an inestimable privilege.

Exiled the Jewish lawyer, at best, would appear in a foreign country, to defend prisoners against alien laws and judges, to prove the law unjust to the Jew or its circumvention inevitable: not to fortify but appeal against it, as inimical, subversive, discriminatory and cruel. He might not make laws or pass judgments; he was in Jewish duty bound to oppose the State and its ordinances. In Israel, things have changed. In a people robbed of independence for thousands of years, the lawyer, more than any citizen, is charged to implant instincts of reverence and esteem for State and the law, for those who do the State's work and make its laws, for its judges and its constables.

Galuth sapped our respect for the law, and we must take pains to protect not only the State but the law also and its honor. Every citizen must obey the law; our legal system is unsafe unless the generality of citizens respects it, but defense of the law is the lawyer's part above all.

In Israel he must not seem as one wrestling with oppressive legislation in a strange land, but championing the rule of law and teaching the community to understand it. The attitude of the public will then be judged much by its attitude towards the policeman. Will it be unhelpful, evasive, hostile or fearful, or show appreciation, obedience, trust and goodwill? Naturally, it depends on the policeman as well. We feel that the State is organizing and training a police force as loyal and efficient as anywhere. The public must be brought up to see the policeman as friend and aid, its servant and instrument of the law. He in turn must accustom it to see the law not as persecution, but an expression of its own will for the general good. The law does not fetter individual liberties, it imposes no obligation on the subject save out of concern for the common weal, for the welfare of each and everyone. Effectiveness lies not in punishment of transgression, but in veneration of the law and the public's determination to uphold and observe it. We will do more, we will love the law, if it flows from that sure fount 'love thy neighbor,' if our legal and social structure rises upon reciprocal attachment and succor of all citizens, Jews and non-Jews, and if all know that, in Israel, man is no ravening wolf to fellow-man but helpmeet and friend.

The moral and mental standard of our lawyers will determine largely our legal system and law-mindedness. A lawyer is not like an engineer, physician or teacher. He is not, as it were, tied to one trade, but has a hand in everything, and every one a hand in his affairs. He comes in contact with all businesses and classes, the economy, the State and its institutions; and his behavior, his speech and deportment, his attitude and standing, his professional and personal qualities will, in no small measure, stamp on the whole Yishuv its legal and moral character.

* * *

It is, however, the Civil Service which will cast the character of our Government; here not the form of the law, but its execution, signifies.

The modern State has left far behind the primitive stage of two basic functions, justice and security. These our people defined in its constitutional dispute with the Prophet Samuel: 'and that our king may judge us, and go out before us, and fight oui battles.' Year after year the bounds of State activity are extended; to justice and security are added the public services: education, health, development, trade and industry, the heightening of the standard of living.

Israel must do all this, and bears besides the crucial burden, the charge no other State can know—the in-gathering of the exiles. So, for us, the law and the Civil Service will not suffice. In any free and democratic country, the law must rely on the public will, and the Civil Service do that will. The more cultured and free a people, the stronger the rule of the law, the greater the honor in which all men hold it. The more advanced a State, the deeper the loyalty of its officials, the surer the trust and respect of the people towards them. An administration truly sovereign is never tyrant, it serves the people and ministers faithfully to its needs.

But the ingathering and all it entails, land development, attraction of capital, further productivity, promotion of cultural enterprises and security, are beyond our reach without self-denial by the whole people, without *pioneer initiative* in the whole gamut of our endeavors, in the Land and in Galuth still. This is not to decry the essential value of the Civil Service.

The will and the way of the people is expressed in the promulgation and enforcement of laws, and there, in the forefront, stand Civil Servants to do duty for the State. Thus is our mission committed into their hands.

We had a public service in bygone days. There were parnassim (presidents), both elected and others who were not; the Zionist Organization for fifty years and more has had a capable staff of whom no one need be ashamed; there was an officialdom in the Yishuv, in the Labor Federation and in various communal institutions, and on the whole it did its duty well. Now we have an officialdom of the State.

The qualities sought of public officers everywhere and always —capacity to act, industry and loyalty—ours too must have, and more besides, if they are to match the superhuman effort of sustaining the triple burden of security, absorption and settlement. The burden may be more than we think we can bear, but it makes or mars our existence, freedom and growth, and we must sustain it, to live and be redeemed. What cannot be done by routine, halutzim may achieve. We must show the initiative and unconquerable spirit of pioneers, if we are to have merit in our greatest hour.

Never was so vital and so precious a charge entrusted to Jewry's public servants, as the Israel Civil Service now assumes. The State holds in fee all who serve it. Into their care are given security and absorption, development and reconstruction, education and health. On them the honor of the State and its repute depend.

Let us be frank. This is a calling we knew not formerly or, at least, have not followed for centuries past. We have to ply a new craft, create something out of nothing, almost. The spiritual possessions, the practical experience and the intellectual assets derived from our work in Yishuv, in an alien Government, in our own institutions, will not satisfy. We must outdo ourselves, electrify our hidden talents and deploy our ethics and intellect superbly. We are few and poor, our needs are many and burdensome. We must fulfill enormous tasks with scanty means. We must keep on unpausing to ascend our mountain and reach the peak, knowing full well, when we reach it, that no pinnacle is permanent and unmoving, that yesterday's is but a stage today toward a new one, loftier still. Every one of us, in military or in civilian service, must labor unflaggingly to enhance his skill and diligence, his output and knowledge, his calibre and quality.

Not Government, as an employer, makes this exacting bid: our history makes it of us, the last generation of serfdom and the first in manumission.

It will not answer for the Civil Servant to be only trustworthy and efficient, industrious and loyal. That utter devotion he must give the State as a pioneer would, but we must never lose sight of the precious element whereof the State itself is compounded, the citizen, the common man. Day after day in the course of his work, the Civil Servant must meet with the human being whose wants the State supplies. He encounters him abroad, when a Jew applies for an immigration permit and asks how to live and earn in Israel. He encounters him at the port on his arrival; in the customs shed and in the camp; in reception-center and training depot, when the young immigrant enlists in the Army; in the labor bureau and the health office, when the newcomer seeks work or medical aid, or a chance to settle on the land, or other help from the State. The ordinary person who appeals to a Civil Servant does not see the State; he sees only its emissary and sizes up the State by him. Truly to do his duty, the Civil Servant must greet the common man with sympathy and liking, with a sense of full cooperation, with a sure instinct of his pangs and straits, his resentments and frailty.

Israel must needs be rebuilt by a people racked and impoverished, decimated and rent; we have no other. And a Jew tends to multiply his demands upon his fellow-Jew; the State particularly, being all-powerful, ought, he protests, to satisfy his every importuning, and at once; he neither knows nor cares if it can. Sometimes his solicitation is preposterous or impossible, and how wearisome and exhausting, how vexatious it can be for the kindliest of us to handle inflated complaints or impossible claims!

But the Civil Servant will belie his special trust if he regards the seeker of aid or counsel as just another number in a neat card-index, not a human being with troubles and wants; or does not welcome him radiantly, as though there were no other case to settle, with warm understanding of his plight and state of mind. He must be filled with *love of man and love of Israel*.

It is our lot to gather a mortal dust that has been flung on foreign lands and unfriendly soil, to knead it into national, cultural and social unity, and enshrine it forever in the Homeland, framed within our law and State, within a brotherhood of Jewry and all mankind. That those appointed to this imperial mission may not fail, their skill, loyalty and love must know no bounds.

I speak not only of Civil Servants who draw pay from the Treasury and work in Government offices. All who work in Israel, in field and factory, at seaport and airport, as soldiers and civilians, in office and school, in trade and craft, in public or private employ, in manual labor or mental, directly or indirectly —all are helping to lay the plinth of the State, to make a free nation and carry out its unforgettable purpose.

* * *

Even greater the charge laid upon writer and teacher.

Three generations of venturers, prolific of toil and heroically girt, brought us to our present state. But not alone. Behind them was the steadfast resolution of their forebears. The gallant modern vanguard was refreshed at the wondrous spring of suffering and vision, which temper the spirit of our people to press on toward redemption, be calamity never so frequent, or obstacle and difficulty never so mountainous. Over this ancient source and secret of Israel's imperishability, the Hebrew Book stood watch. What other nation's destiny, so closely and so long, was the destiny of its writ? For thousands of years we safeguarded the Book, and it has kept us safe. When we lost our independence, it too, was ripped from its birthplace, its horizons were contracted, its contents diluted, and it was immured into a narrow corner which yet was the sole refuge of our spirit.

Then, miraculously, Israel was restored.

Although its roots strike deep down to the immemorial past, the young State is foredoomed to grave trials, for to maintain peace, to gather in the wanderers and reclaim the wilderness are tasks that call for incredible exertions.

Yet, just because the difficulties are many, the burden grievous and the uphill road flinty and unsafe, let us be mindful always of the fountainhead of spirit and dream whence we have drawn and again will draw strength to defend our gates against attack, to bring exiles home, to subdue the soil and make the desert green.

The work of seventy years of pioneering and the first years of resurgence has braced and reinforced Jewish power and built up the vigor of Israel. Plows and tractors, mattocks and bulldozers, machines and forges, rifles and machine-guns, aircraft and ships, farms and factories, transport and laboratories, stables and granaries, installations and shelters, barbed-wire and trenches, roads and plantations—for our survival, we must assure their multiplication and perfection without remission or surcease. Therefore must the spirit abide within us, in our heart and soul, wonderful, invisible. Only if so, only so long, are we worthy of a life of creativeness, venturing and valor, appointed unto us in our generation to hand on to generations yet to come.

If spirit be not patrimony of all, of people and youth, the

Hebrew writer labors in vain. His to give faithful expression to it, to magnify and ennoble it by the power of his inspiring and fertile imagery; no 'scribe of State' fawning on authority, submissive to invitation and instruction, but recorder of Israel resurgent, obeying only conscience and the vision in his heart, speaking his glorious message to the people at freedom's call. Only then will he design the fabric of our national re-birth and universal dedication. Only then will the Hebrew Book make past and future one, link the values of Judaism and mankind, fit the Jew in a brilliant setting in the great world entire, and on the brow of Israel place again man's loveliest guerdon, the diadem of the spirit.

* * *

No one profession can pride itself on giving whole form and finality to the nation's ends. But if there be in the Yishuv a group which might advance the boast, it is the teachers, for into their care we have delivered the nation of tomorrow. Teacher and school are not the only educators of the rising generation. The family and the Press, literature, the various movements, the institutions and undertakings of the State, events in Israel and throughout the world—these play no small part, at times they are decisive. But an up-to-date school system, and teachers who see their duty clear and its performance, are the main architects of the new design. Security, immigration and settlement bespeak a tremendous educative impetus. Our security is not solely or even principally dependent upon material resources, it rests upon the fitness of the whole nation to man the breach in the moment of peril. This all-embracing national preparedness requires organization of education.

The Army is to be a school for growing youth, a nursery of the nation's singleness, its culture and courage: here then our teachers must be mobilized in full strength.

Immigration, too, is not just an exercise in housing and employment, not just a complex of material struggles and difficulties. To absorb immigrants calls for a herculean effort of education, no less among the Yishuv than the immigrants. It has been said: 'We all love immigration, but only few among us love the immigrants.' That is the sad truth: except for the appointed institutions, the Jewish Agency and Government, and moshavim, the Yishuv has not yet responded warmly. Few have visited the immigrant centers, fewer than visited the camps of displaced persons in Germany after the second World War. Vouchsafed this supreme grace to welcome home hundreds of thousands of its lost brethren, the Yishuv must learn once and for all that the ingathering is the climactic duty of our generation, perhaps the greatest event of Jewish history, that the fate of the exiles turns upon our individual efforts. The immigrants must be taught our language and a knowledge of the Land and of the pains of immigration. They must conceive what the first settlers did with their bare hands, how they fought with the desert, with an inept Government in Turkish days and obstruction under the Mandate; and what nevertheless they did. Being privileged to enter Israel, they must be told that they too must toil, if perhaps less than their forerunners; that they too can create as did the men of Petah Tiqvah and Rehoboth, Sejera and Ain Harod, Nahalal and Kfar Vitkin; and that, like every one of us, they not only seek but are besought.

Nor can there be settlement without pioneer education. We must teach our youth and childhood not to brook naked hills and barren dunes. Boy must vie with girl, and school with school, which shall plant the greater area, which take most productive part in the upbuilding of the Land, in the regeneration of the desert.

The State in being makes us answerable for our own destiny, and so our inherited concept of education, its nature and functions, must now be changed. Among few peoples, we have kept general education alive over the past 2,500 years, except for some 500 of them, in an alien milieu of dependence. In the kingly days, our forefathers saw the ideal of manhood, marked out for greatness, predestined leader, in one that possessed the qualities of David: minstrel and hero, warrior, sage and stalwart. Education in the Diaspora could not fashion a character of such content and color. There, circumstances emptied the vessel of Jewish education and cut away its living base; a psychological gulf yawned between Jew and man, between matter and spirit, between creature and nature, between the Jewish community and the State and Government. Education shrivelled up in a corner. True, the little left did great things; it was our mainstay in tribulations no other peoples endured. And, with our return to the Land, gaps are being closed and sovereignty allows us to render our education complete and comprehensive. Not, however, only in book-learning. We must magnify the value of the written word, but also teach the young what are nature, spirit and society, in the State and in the world.

Till now, we were changelings everywhere. Today, equal citizens of the world, we are on the threshold of statehood upbuilt. Let us be sure, then, that the book we place in our children's hands is the book of life, and all its outpouring of revelation, problem, task and hope; the book of living universe, of moral power, of man's freedom and creativity, of an autonomous people hammering out its destiny, acting of its own right in every sector of life, nature and history: a book that will inspire the young ever to enrich and enlarge the spiritual and material treasures of their nation.

But not even then can we be complacent. Education must be attuned to the needs not only of the hour but of the future. We betray the nation's purpose if we hide from our youth the great vision of the Prophets. Our hearts yearn for the historic morrow. Yesterday has gone, never to return, and man cannot live in the past. That is so. But we, being an especial people, robustly refuse to accept as immutable what exists today in our country, in ourselves or in the world. We do not suffer our wastelands to abide. We are at odds with the fortune which has been ours hitherto; we struggle against it; we will not yield to it. We are resolved to master it and frame it anew and in the spirit of the vision that lights us. It can no longer be the lot of our people to be dispersed, for is not Israel sovereign and erect in its own Land? The danger that threatens the Diaspora is not only persecution or discrimination. It is the 'kiss of death,' the loosening of ties which for centuries kept fast the unity of Israel in exile.

We shall not join in the scramble for power and the fear of war now universally rife. We will not find ease so long as nation lifts up sword against nation, and man lords it over his neighbor. Never have truth and justice been utterly silent, nor was their power halted in the affairs of nations. Yet the principle of evil has triumphed till now, and might prevails. The nations will not know peace so long as, in their dealings, rivalry and armed strength, not amity and cooperation, rule. The terrible instruments of destruction which modern science has created may blast our whole civilization to pieces, perhaps the very globe itself, unless, while there is yet time, a sure way to peace and unity among nations is revealed, and to liberty and equality for every man.

We are not vain enough to suppose that, by will-power alone, we can frame a future that will change the face of the Land and its people, and of the world besides. We are as a bagatelle in an array of mighty forces. In international decisions, as in decreeing our own fate, in our own hearth and home, we are bound by circumstances and conditions which we do not control. But we have neither wish nor right to surrender the responsibility. In number and in material measure we are few and weak, but quantity is not always decisive in the annals of men or States. To carve new ways of life in the cycles of history is not a prerogative of the populous. Not always have great masses been the guides of mankind. The most crowded nations are not in the van today; not China or India, but the United States of America and Russia lead in the world. Judea and Greece played a far greater part than any of the great nations of their times or that came after, and their influence persists still. The qualities of the spirit, moral and intellectual, are no less determinant in history than material wealth and great numbers. Even if our part was in quantity less, we were not accounted worse than other nations. A small people, fighting for its life in the infancy of independence, must contend with circumstance, and each moment balance the possible and the barred; but it need not submit to circumstance and tamely accept it. If its spiritual valor, its creative and martial mettle, prove not traitor, it will not be overawed by contemplation of greatness and glories to be won, be they never so distant, difficult and perilous. We are not swept along by a blind fate in the tideway of time, unknowing whither. We are making for a historic haven and to it the compass needle of our vision steadily points.

'Whither' is compounded of 'Whence'; nature's 'Yea' is never changed to 'Nay'; history loses naught. Our past is not only behind us, it is in us; not as blank parchment or dead clay, shapeless and without form, do we march onwards to our future, nor with empty hands; we bring to posterity the gift of a great and ancient heritage. At each of the many stations in our wandering, we acquired something of which the mark is graved in us for the rest of time; by each contact with the culture of the peoples among which we dwelt long or briefly we added a jewel to our spiritual crown. But it was here, only here, in the land of its origins, that the Jewish nation was born, and grew and was made one. Here it fashioned the eternal talisman which made its spirit forever safe—the Book of Books. Its ventures and growth will rest hereafter on the Land and the Book.

We partook in the making of modern civilization and we will partake in the splendors of the spirit, the wisdom and the arts of all ages and lands. We will spare no effort, spiritual, intellectual or bodily, to grasp the achievements of technology and the sciences of nature, biology and sociology. We will heighten our talents and capacity in agricultural, industrial and maritime pursuits, in all branches of art and handicrafts. In the lathe of this Land we shall turn a household and economy for all communities in Diaspora. Tending its very earth and soil, its sources of water, the fish in its lakes and seas, the mines in its hills and rocks, its natural riches, we shall construct a husbandry and industry, sea and air communications, to support all that return. By the moral and social light veiled yet in the everlasting cipher of the Book, by the sermons of peace, justice and charity preached by our Prophets, by the message of the image of God which is in man, and by the commandment 'love thy neighbor,' we shall school unborn generations, and shape our society and our government.

* * *

For the doing of the great thing we have yet to do, our acquaintance with the Land and the Book is sadly meager. Few lands or books had treatment so extensive, prolonged and diversified, from explorers, commentators and travellers. The writings on our Land and Book in ancient days, in medieval and modern times, are almost beyond count. Authors in Greek, Latin and Arabic of old, in English, German and French, in Russian, Dutch and other languages more lately, have bequeathed to us innumerable works on the nature of the Land, its scenery and climate, its inhabitants, boundaries and wars. Historians, theologians and natural scientists, travellers, generals and colonizers, merchants, consuls and archaeologists, all essayed to portray the Land, and indeed they lit up many of its dark corners. But the mystery is still profound. The Jewish scholars who engaged in this research did not fill the gap.

For only a people that dwells in its own land, and is master of it, can know it perfectly. Foreign wayfarers and students, sojourning a while in the Land, gave much to a partial understanding of it; none but a Yishuv planted on its own soil, clinging to every nook and cranny of the Land, inseparable from its plains and hills, its valleys and seas, working and embracing it, can probe the depths of its nature, its happenings and its secrets, none but a sovereign Yishuv can unveil the true splendor of the Book, and bring forth the full benediction of our Land.

Most has been penned concerning the Book. For over 2,200 years the flow of translations, commentaries and exegeses, of studies and interpretations by Jews and by Gentiles has not ceased. Yet we are still distant from full comprehension of the Bible's meaning, its teaching, history and evolution. Like the Land, the Book is open only to those who are themselves of the soil where it first took root and who own its living speech. Rarely did the commentators, of our faith or another, meet either test.

The Book is our whole language. No commentator unravelled the chapters of Joshua as did our Army's epic deeds. Already in our settlements on the banks of Jordan, in the Vale of Esdraelon and the Negev, sprout seeds which will be the living revelation of many words of Hosea, Micah and Isaiah. Only to a people home again in the setting which shines forth from every page of the Book, only to a people speaking as speaks the Book and thinking and dreaming in Bible tongue, will the Book yield up its innermost soul, and the souls of Book and nation become one and Israel's wisdom reign in Israel's land.

Youngest State in the world Israel may be, but its architect is a nation with an unbroken existence of 4,000 years. Its face is turned to the hereafter, it bears a great legacy of the past, it must see clearly Whither and Whence. Its effectiveness in the realms of economics and security will depend on scientific and technological skills; but its independence and fulfillment turn upon fealty to the moral values eternally enshrined in the Book.

* * *

Jewish research into Land and Book, then, is still in its infancy. It requires the help of all branches of learning, the natural sciences and the humanities, history and philology, botany and mineralogy, hydrology, the sciences of ocean and air and all the rest. The unearthing of antiquities takes an especial place.

Although it was not always the purest scientific motives that prompted their excavations, we are grateful to archaeologists the world over, who began antiquarian research in our Land: the British and French, the Americans and Germans, who uncovered ancient remains of Jerusalem and Gezer, of Samaria, Lachish and Megiddo, and enriched our vocabulary with the inscriptions of Mesha, king of Moab, and the tables of Gezer, Siloam and Lachish, Jewish archaeology is a cadet branch and worked in narrow bounds while our Land endured alien domination. Independence and military victories have opened new horizons. Much of our ancient territory is now in Jewish hands, and its many mounds await a Jewish spade to disclose the riddle of their past and brighten dim chronicles. Till then the Book of Books will be cryptic and dark in many a verse and the history of our Land unfinished.

Like other sciences, archaeology can achieve its whole purpose only if it be a pursuit of the Yishuv entire, in Negev or Shephelah, or Galilee or Samaria, not the closed province of eclectic specialists. Every farmer, every man of trade, can and must contribute to the enrichment of those branches of science nearest his craft; and he will, if our scientists and statesmen impart to the masses a knowledge of what science has done, if experts and Government alike develop popular appraisal of our antiquities, and our youth are taught to know and to treasure the precious relics strewn above and below ground everywhere.

During the last hundred and fifty years the wisdom of Israel had a special and limited purpose: enquiry into the history of Judaism and its literature. It is hard to forgive Jewish thinkers and writers, from the days of Chibbath Zion onwards, who shunned this budding branch of Jewish scholarship. Its few champions were eminent German Jews: Zunz, Geiger, Steinschneider, Graetz and Kaufmann, among others. That most of them leant toward assimilation does not lessen the worth of their outstanding work. Not only the monumental research of Graetz, first compiler of a Jewish History, his every page alive with national genius and faith in the immortality of Israel, but the works as well of other men, great in Israel's wisdom but lacking that faith, are assets beyond price. They should be rendered into Hebrew, every one to become a deathless part of our culture.

But it is upon a different wisdom that we now in Israel direct our gaze. Israel in exile rode wisdom's chariot: its own history, its literature and art were the theme. Its 'wisdom' was cribbed research into the past of a people and a creed. In the State, Israel is the very chariot, and can survey the world. Of a certainty embracing now the rounded wisdom of nature, universe and history, new Israel will not forsake study of our past cult and clan; in the freedom-breathing Homeland, that study will be re-united at last with its source, and ancient roots will nourish it again.

We must penetrate most secret nature and control its elements; we must possess all the wealth of man's spirit, and faithfully echo all the creations of science, religious and literary, artistic and philosophical. A scientific revolution is in process: its scope and results we dared not guess at ten years ago, and its end who may perceive? Man is near to discovery of the riddle of the atom and the darkest mysteries of our universe. Let us not be misled if these inventions have been put to warlike uses. The splitting of the atom need not bring ruin in its wake; rather it promises comfort and new creation on a scale once unthinkable.

A kilogram of coal burned in the usual way generates an energy of 8½ kw; converted into energy by atomic fission, it will yield 25 thousand million. Such is the upheaval which exploitation of atomic power implies: imagination boggles at the thought how fabulously conditions of life will change if we can harness that power to the positive needs of mankind. Jewish scientists in Italy and Scandinavia, in Great Britain and America, with Einstein at their head, had much to do with this mighty achievement. But, as always with Jewish scientists in the Diaspora, what they did only fertilized alien furrows. Why should we not be equal, independent partners in the scientific revolution of the day? Jewish genius overseas affirms the identity of matter and energy. Cannot it then, on its own hearth, set this identity to everyday work, put nature's marvellous constants, their power to add to man's creative capacity, at the service of our culture and economy?

We will want all the consummate virtues of our education, organization and economics to surmount the stumbling-blocks with which history and geography have made our path so formidable. Servitors of science, pure and applied science, we must storm the highest pinnacles of efficiency and output. We cannot rival others in numbers, wealth or battalions. But, in the supremacy of the spirit we can, in standards of culture, science and technique, so that they be not the privy domain of a handful of experts, but the common property of every worker in field and forge, office and school, airport and harbor, on land and at sea, on terra firma or in the stratosphere. Without that supremacy the desert will not bloom again or our security stay; we shall not keep our place in the world nor our historic trust.

The Hebrew University of Jerusalem is perhaps the first a people ever founded while yet its State was unborn. It was no accident, for with the earliest dawn of sovereignty restored, there dawned the vision too.

Many see in the re-establishment of the State only a victory of Jewish over Arab arms. To over-praise the Army's part would be difficult, but a judgment marking only the outward consequences, forgetful of hidden source and roots, is shallow. It was the Jewish spirit that triumphed, the moral and spiritual excellence of the nation, the vision and mission of Patriarch Israel.

The dualism of matter and spirit, much favored among the nations, from the Greeks and Persians down to Descartes and his disciples, was always repugnant to Jewish thought, in the Prophets, in Einstein, and in all between. Our intuition, religious or scientific, ever acclaims the unity of being and the universe, despite their manifold diversity. Thus it was that the Jewish people saw in renewal of the territorial and political basis of its statehood more than the stipulation of a normal, healthy existence as a nation: without that renewal its messianic purpose would be defeated. For there is no soul without body, no learning without bread, no universal mission of man without national self-determination.

Our new life is not the narrow making of parochial ordinances for ourselves alone. It will find its full and finest expression when it reveals its eternal spirit and shows itself the bespoken savior of mankind. So it is no chance thing that Israel's University was real, with the State still a dream, twenty-five years ago.

Today, as we renew our independence, our first concern must be to build up the Land, to foster its economy, its security and international status. But these are the whereby not the end. The end is a State fulfilling prophecy, bringing salvation, to be guide and exemplar to all men. In the words of the Prophet is for us a truth perpetual: 'I will give thee for a light to the Gentiles, that thou mayest be my salvation unto the end of the earth.'

In all our ways and deeds and measures we shall cultivate this leadership of the spirit, of quality, and in the healing art not least.

This, I think, is the most ancient art of Israel, perhaps in the world. There were times, throughout the Middle Ages, when few but Jews professed it. It was indeed linked once with magic everywhere, and can we say the link is broken yet? Israel, at any rate, distinguished sharply between unhallowed witchcraft and the craft of a physician, who worked with nature's aid, with knowledge of the cause and character of ailments, and of soothing nostrums. The historians of the Book of Chronicles remind us of this in their tale of the illness of Asa, the king, in the thirty-ninth year of his reign, saying that 'in his sickness he sought not to the Lord, but to the physicians.' And an eloquent sage of the Second Temple, Simon ben Sira, thus extols the physician and apothecary, who in those days and for many centuries to follow were one in their calling:

> 'Honor a physician with the honor due unto him for the uses which ye may have of him: for the Lord hath created him ... The skill of the physician shall lift up his head: and in the sight of great men he shall be in admiration. The Lord hath created medicines out of the earth; and he that is wise will not abhor them ... Of such doth the apothecary make a confection; and of his works there is no end; and from him is peace over all the earth.'

And the cry of Jeremiah, great Prophet of lamentations, grieving for the hurt of the daughter of his people: 'Is there no balm in Gilead; is there no physician there? Why then is not the health of the daughter of my people recovered?'

In such high esteem was the physician held, so utter the faith in his remedies then, hundreds of years before Hippocrates. The view finds splendid expression in the laws of Israel, as Rabbi Joseph Karo phrased them in the Shulhan Aruch:

> 'The Torah has given unto the physician the right to heal, and it is a holy command and, most wise, it is the saving of life; and if he shall hold himself back, then it is the shedding of blood, even if there be someone to heal the

sick person, for not of every sickness is man fortunate to be healed. No man shall practice healing save he be skilled, and there be none more renowned than he, for if it be not so, then he sheddeth blood . . . The physician may not take a wage for wisdom and learning, but a wage for his labor and time he may take.'

These words are not less remarkable than the celebrated Oath of Hippocrates; they show how great a value Jews always gave to health, to the boon of life, and their guardian doctors.

In exile we were made wretched by political and material ignominy, our rights taken away and the Jewish countenance disfigured; and, as much, our manliness sapped and enfeebled.

Israel, new and clamant, demands of its repatriates health and bodily strength above all. It is not only our security that may collapse, if we do not breed a generation sound and sturdy in wind and limb—and in spirit. None that are wanting in soul or body can bring back fruitfulness to the desert; War against the vast, reluctant wilderness exacts the selfless enthusiasm of pioneers, as well as a giant's strength.

Therefore the art of medicine and its practitioners in Israel must not be confined to cure of the sick, but by prophylaxis find ways of fortifying the health of our youth and grown, nativeborn and newcomer, of invigorating their muscles and mind. Only if, at the lowest, we are not in stamina less than others we shall prosper.

Nowadays, it is difficult to mark one science from the next; each wisdom is fed by the other. The chemical and bacteriological findings of such a man as Pasteur, who was not a physician, had in all likelihood greater consequences for medicine than all the inventions and discoveries of specialists in medicine before his time or after it. All, then, in Israel who labor in the field of science and education, and Civil Servants and Army commanders, likewise—let them see to the rehabilitation of the people and its physical immunity. That is their simple duty; but our physicians must direct the campaign, and our Government give them all the encouragement and help they need.

Yet another thing they must do: they must rescue Jewish medical literature of all ages from the dusty shelves of alien museums and libraries, even if it may not vie in antiquity with the Egyptian. Yet assuredly medical lore was widespread in Israel of the First Temple and here, perhaps, Judea, not Greece, took pride of place. An old commentary tells how Hezekiah, the king, hid away the book of healing and the wise men thanked him, for that the people trusted overmuch on such books. And there are hundreds of Jewish manuscripts in all branches of medicine, medication and pharmacy, manuscripts indited as long as 1,300 or 1,400 years ago, of which only a fragment has yet been published.

No one today, I grant you, will study the art of medicine from the writings of Asaph the physician, Shabetai Donnolo, Isaac ben Shlomo the Israelite or Maimonides, to mention only four of the first and greatest names, any more than from the works of Hippocrates and Galenus; or biology from the writings of Aristotle and Theophrastus. But no Jewish doctor or intellectual can eschew knowledge of the evolution of medicine in Israel, or of what learned Jews did throughout the ages to spread and elevate the art.

With the founding of our State, the hour strikes for Israel's wisdom, of all its generations, to be redeemed, with Israel's people, from Galuth. First Government will photograph minutely every Jewish manuscript in the great collections, for keeping in Jerusalem, to be viewed by scholars now in the Land. To gather this wealth of material and give it to the world is for scientists and colleges, and it is a debt of honor for our physicians to recover and publish Hebrew texts in all departments of medicine, from Asaph onwards.

* * *

REBIRTH AND DESTINY OF ISRAEL

Were I asked to sum up the age-long trend of Jewish history, I should answer in three words: Quality against Quantity. All down the years, from Joshua to the War of Independence, we have been the few withstanding the many. Even if we succeed, as succeed we shall, in bringing Jews in their millions to this Land, it will not be otherwise. Only being true to mission and vision shall we live on. Small but in ethics and intellect marvellous, Israel walks with the greatest among the nations. Except by the merit of those qualities, ever magnified, there is for us no survival in a world of rivalry, hatred and despoiling. Only by their merit, fostered tirelessly in our schools, shall we be endowed to point a new way to the world, the way of peace and justice, liberty and brotherhood of man. And this not by homily and preaching, but by the living example of our Government and ourselves, in the Land where pioneers of labor and men of spirit will join Jewish hands and forces to make our State ideal.

ISRAEL AMONG THE NATIONS
From the Government Year-book, October, 1952

> And who is like Thy people Israel, a nation one in the earth . . .
> (I CHRONICLES 17, 21)
>
> If thou shalt say in thine heart, These nations are more numerous than I . . . Thou shalt not be afraid of them.
> (DEUTERONOMY 7, 17-18)

Assuredly, on the 14th day of May, 1948, almost every Jew in the world celebrated the Proclamation of Israel's State—but few at that wonderful moment gave thought to the weighty problem which declaration of independence called up, or the tremendous difficulties which the young republic had to overcome. Yet, while the cheering of exultant crowds still echoed in our streets, the thunder of enemy guns shook the length and breadth of the Land and our sleep, that very night, was shattered by the bombs of an invading Air Force. And when, after eight long months, the War had ended, our racking cares were not dispelled. War was over but peace had not come. There began an exodus out of all the wretched exiles of Europe, Asia and Africa: hundreds of thousands of hapless, penniless men and women poured in; within three years the population had doubled itself, and we were faced with the gigantic tasks of absorption and housing, the fusion of divergent origins, the laying of foundations for an orderly State life. Many, dumbfounded, saw that the State was not come to make their lives easier; rather, it laid new burdens upon them. But little by little they began to understand the great responsibility that goes with independence, the heavy yoke which a nation that had won liberation was now placing on its own shoulders.

To be a nation answerable for its own destiny is a precious ideal, and the Jewish people has bided for that ideal with messianic longing through jubilee upon jubilee. But one must pay very dearly for it, with endless effort and grim sacrifices. A State is not manufactured by declaration; it is set up anew day after day, by toil incessant and the labor of years. A people unfit and unready to sustain the duty of sufficing unto itself will not preserve freedom even after it is won. This is so for every State, and for ours pre-eminently so. From the start, Israel's conditions of survival, its internal and its external aims, its place in the world, its security and its relations with its neighbors, were coiled in difficulties no other country knows.

Not many countries enjoy a spontaneous, a geographical, security. For long England figured among the lucky few: her island place, disjoined from Europe, made the task of any enemy supremely arduous, and, for the last thousand years, she suffered neither invasion nor foreign occupation. But immunity did not last forever. With the coming of fighter aircraft as a major instrument of warfare, even before the atomic bomb was invented, it became as feasible to strike at the towns of England as at those on the near-by continent; and that is what happened in the second World War. The sea, of itself, is a bulwark of the Isles no longer.

Almost from their first day the United States were safe from hostile attack. Two oceans watched over them, on the East and on the West; their neighbors to the North and to the South were weak by comparison, and there was no fear there of military provocation. But, in our time, this once unquestioned invulnerability has been challenged, Japan was not afraid to assault the American Navy in Pearl Harbor, and America today is assured no more against atom bombing from any sky.

Never, not in the days of the First Temple nor the Second, was the Land of Israel blessed by such conditions as kept long vigil over the safety of England and America. Israel was always a little people; it had neighbors, large and small, weak and powerful, and the powerful ones always outdid it in size, in strength, in wealth and military might. Its geography, where three continents touch, lent much importance to the Land and made it, in a sense, the lodestone of empires. But, from the viewpoint of security, it added nothing to Israel's ability to defend itself. On the contrary, it diminished it, in fact and measure. The boundaries of Israel were not fixed and set, but were shifted time and again, from the days of the Judges to the days of Bar Kochba. Even in the heyday of its expansion and growth, those boundaries were in themselves no safeguard of existence. The situation of Israel reborn is no better than in that distant past. Its geographico-physical definition is practically unaltered, although vast and vital changes have taken place in its geopolitical surroundings.

The Bible is still a closed book so far as concerns knowledge of the country and its history—political, social, cultural, military and international, yet in so far as comprehension of modern conditions, if it is to be full, needs to be illumined by the lamp of the past—and it needs that sorely—nothing can surpass the Bible as lighting up the manifold problems of our life and their recondite causes. There can be no worthwhile political or military education about Israel without profound knowledge of the Bible.

On the other hand, we must not seek in bygone days a complete and ready-made guide to the present. Geography varies little or not at all, but history varies ever, and no historical situation is like the next. The experience of history, research into the circumstances and vicissitudes of the past, are a substantial and indispensable help when we try to master our new conditions.

But experience is likely to turn into a canker and a mortal hazard if we pursue it blindfold, and mechanically pronounce our judgments according to past events, instead of sorting out the perpetual changes and mutations of history and discerning plainly the new reality wherein we have to act. It is essential to dwell on the individual character of every historical situation, and from every special circumstance to draw conclusions proper to it and to it alone.

* * *

There is no least likeness between the conquest by Joshua, or the Return from Babylon, and the modern resurrection of Israel. In Joshua's time, the tribes in the Land and on its borders were plunged in internal anarchy; and the Jews had to struggle with their neighbors for hundreds of years until a unified kingdom of Israel was established under Saul and David. But even that kingdom endured only the brief space of two generations; it was split up at the death of Solomon, whereafter the existence of the two halves was always menaced by Aram to the north and by Edom and Moab to the east, and by Egypt and Babylon above all. The never-ending rivalry between the two great empires did much, and for a fair length of time, to help Israel keep its independence. Thus domestic faction between vying orientations towards Egypt, Assyria and Babylon made up the political history of the reigns of the kings of Judah and Israel, until at last the Assyrian invader was victorious and, one after the other, Israel fell and Judah. Egypt, wherein many in Judah had trusted to save them from the hosts of Assyria and Babylon, was revealed as in truth 'the staff of this bruised reed ... on which if a man lean, it will go into his hand and pierce it; so is Pharaoh king of Egypt unto all that trust on him.'

In the days of the Second Temple, we were not independent or sovereign, unless for the short dynasty of the first Hasmonaeans up to the death of King Alexander Jannaeus and his queen, Shlom Zion. In the first two centuries after the Return from Babylon, the Land was one of the 'one hundred and twenty seven provinces' of the kings of Persia, and enjoyed only an internal, religious autonomy. Again, in the days of Alexander of Macedon and the first Diadochi, it was subject to the new Hellenistic empire.

In the upshot of the splendid wars of the Maccabees, Judea was not decisively freed until the days of Simon. 'In the one hundred and seventieth year the yoke of the heathen was lifted from Israel. The people of Israel began to write in their documents and contracts in the first year of Simon, the great High Priest and General and Ruler of the Jews.' (I Maccabees, 13, 41-42. The year 170 for the reckoning of contracts corresponded to the year 142 BCE). Only then was the political liberty of Judea gained, to last for seventy years in all and through three generations: Simon; his son John, also styled John Hyrcanus; his grandson Judah Aristobulus, first to restore the royal title to Israel; his brother Alexander Jannaeus and Queen Shlom Zion. When the great queen died, fratricidal strife broke out between her two sons and led inexorably to that Roman conquest which, many years before the physical disappearance of the Second Temple, brought the political independence of Israel to an end. The Hasmonaean period, in its beginning, lay in the shadow of the Hellenistic world, and, at its close, under the power of Rome. It was 133 years before the actual destruction of the Second Temple that Roman Pompey entered Jerusalem at the head of his legions. From then on Rome effectually ruled over Judea, and internecine quarrels throughout the days of the Second Temple speeded the open overthrow of Jewish freedom.

These two ancient epochs of Israel were alike in this, that the center of gravity of the world in which the Jewish people lived and had its being was the Mediterranean region: Egypt, Babylon, Persia, Greece and Rome. China and India, the two oldest cradles of civilization in the ancient world—and the most significant, as indeed they still are—were far away from Israel and its neighbors. Egypt, and Babylon which is Assyria, Persia, Greece and Rome were the civilizations which influenced the peoples of the Mediterranean and those contiguous to them, for thousands of years. All affected the Jewish people directly and in roundabout ways, and Israel was engaged in everlasting conflict with them, military or cultural.

Both epochs were alike in this as well, that Israel was surrounded by different peoples, whose mutual antipathies did not abate until Rome conquered most of them; and for a long time Israel was able to exploit the discord for its own protection and form alliances now with one side and now with the other. That is what David and Solomon did, and the later kings, and so, too, the Hasmonaeans essayed to do until their pact with the Romans was twisted into a noose of alien lordship.

In both epochs, the Jews had entered the Land from the east, and were nearly estopped from reaching the sea. Their principal contact was with the peoples which dwelt around them on the mainland to the south, to the north and to the east. Until the Roman era, Israel had practically no touch with the peoples of the west and the Mediterranean islands, and indeed, apart from Greece, these peoples were unimportant then in the annals of nations.

With the downfall of the Second Temple, Israel was scattered to the four winds, and it is hard to find a single corner of the earth where no remnant lingers. The return to Israel's own Land began out of the countries of the west, out of Europe and the midst of the great civilized nations of the new age. The center of the world had moved from the Mediterranean to the shores of the Atlantic Ocean. Most of Jewry were now on the continent of Europe, and especially in its eastern parts, among the Slavs and Teutons; few lived among the Latin and northern races. But nearly all had preserved the heirloom of a Jewish culture broadly based upon the Bible, though steeped as well in the new culture of the west, which in its turn was drawn from modern science and the cultural legacy of the Graeco-Roman world.

The vision of Return to Zion lived on in the hearts of all the Jewries in dispersion. Ever and anon, the messianic spark was lit and they strove to make the vision come true: now it was by natural means, by going up to the Land and building habitations in it; again, it was not thus but by miraculous power and mystic faith. All these ventures, of this kind or of that, ended in setback, yet we should not belittle their historic import or deny their share in the resurrection today. They kept whole the testament of hope in the heart of the Jewish people; else our eyes would not have seen the climax of this great hour.

From Bar Kochba to the new Jewish State, 1813 years went by. For most of that dreary wait the Jews were cut off from their Homeland and sprinkled in foreign parts among foreign peoples. In the infinite history of mankind there is nothing to equal it—a people sundered from its native heath for near two thousand years, which should yet return to it and on it stand sovereign once more. Had not that people in all its wanderings, despite the bodily wrench, hugged tightly this vision of revival, and inward kept a living link with the land of its birth, the unique thing which came to pass in our days would never have been. Nor, indeed, did it come to pass as long as the vision was fed on passive yearning and little besides. The will actively to make the vision real only leaped at the dawn of pioneer Aliyah, seventy-five years ago, which laid the foundation for agricultural settlement. That Aliyah marked a revolutionary swing in the people's spirit, from idle longing and a mystic expectancy of redemption in the dim future to the practical action and persevering effort that would hew a natural path to present salvation.

For hundreds of years the people had bowed to its lot, the lot of a folk dispersed and dependent on alien charity. Faith in its own strength and possibilities was almost lost. In the pioneer

Aliyah, there found expression a resurgence of that creative faith of the Jew, faith to become master of his destiny and to change the destiny of his people. This rekindling of belief in Jewish power and will, after centuries of sojourn in strange lands, is one of the greatest wonders in the wonderful history of our people. This renewal of trust in the resources of the Jew and Jewry, in their creative and fighting quality, drew its nourishment from three sources: the renascent influence of the Bible, the national and social revolutions in Europe, and a teeming contact with the soil of Israel.

Enlightenment in the nineteenth century brought the Bible back to Jewish youth in all its former glory. The beat of the nation's beginnings quivered again in the depths of that youth as it thirsted for light and redemption. The love of Zion, made young again, sent forth its impulse and awakened slumbering desires. To foster-children in foreign climes, the erstwhile Homeland suddenly revealed itself in all its magic. To the mind's eye of Hebrew writers and intellectuals it was as though scenes of long ago, crowded with good tidings, had been unveiled: the wanderings of the tribes of Israel in the desert, the travails of their settlement in the Promised Land, the struggles with their neighbors and among themselves, the valiant deeds of their judges and their kings, the mighty manifestations of Hebrew prophecy bearing a momentous and eternal message to nation and individual alike, glowing with the flame of faith in the great mission of the Jews and heralding a vision of the last days. The hearts of the finest youngsters of the time were one again with the sources of their race, and resolve was born to renew our days as of old.

National and social revolutions led the pick of Jewry to honor the worth of a people that fights for its freedom, typified for them the gallantry of the wretched and the under-dog, and fired their hearts with rebellious zeal for national revival. The force and value of worker and cultivator were made patent, and a new path was traced to the redemption so long awaited—the return to toil and tilth, and at home.

And so began pioneer Aliyah, forerunner and sculptor of faith in the strength and will of Jews and Jewry to create. Once more, bold and self-confident Jews gave themselves to the soil, and Jewish villages went up in swamps, on dunes, on rocky hillsides and wastes. The speech of the Prophet, which had seemed mute and silent forever, was heard again in the fields of Judea and Galilee out of the mouths of babes and sucklings. A new page was turned in the history of Land and people, a page whereon Jews would shape the course of their own lives and their people's by their own vigor and labor, by physical and spiritual exertion, not in field and workshop only but under arms as well, and if attacked, would thrust the foeman back to his borders.

The seeds of the State were sown when we founded Petah Tiqvah and Rishon, Zichron Ya'aqov, Rosh Pina and Gedera, and the settlements that came after them. The founders knew the bitter taste of the tribulations that befall the early builders of any State: a hard struggle with the afflictions of nature and beasts of the field, unfriendly neighbors, the curse of malaria and water-famine, shortages and wants of every kind, and perennial hazards of life and property.

* * *

Yes, the pillars of Jewish independence were cast in the Jewish villages and towns built by the pioneers of this Third Return to Zion, but, until the State arose, these pilgrim fathers of ours were unburdened by that highest form of responsibility which sovereignty entails. A foreign government was in control; it veered from good to bad, from friendly to inimical, but it always bore final responsibility for all that was done in Zion. In the Turkish regime, the Land of Israel was not even a political entity in itself, nor again was it encircled by independent countries; it was only one of the divisions of an Ottoman Empire which embraced all the Arab countries, and Arab and Jew alike were subject to the supreme authority of the Sublime Porte.

Under the British Administration, the frontiers were guarded by British soldiers. The Jewish community did organize itself as a State within a State, but its autonomy was confined to internal affairs. Security and defense were in the hands of the Mandatory, and, although England governed in the name of the League of Nations, yet from the point of view of economics and finance the country was a part of the British empire, and indeed invisible investments of British capital, in the maintenance of a large garrison, were an abundant source of income to the expanding Jewish economy. The scale of immigration and the growth of the Yishuv were dependent upon the policy of the Mandatory. With the end of the Mandate and the establishment of the State, all these 'heirlooms' passed to independent Israel.

On the 14th day of May, 1948, the young people of Israel, lacking all suzerain experience, took upon itself the full responsibility for the security, the existence and the upbuilding of the new State, responsibility for the fate of the scattered remnants of Israel which did not wish or were not able to stay in exile, responsibility for determining the relations of the people of Israel with the surrounding world, near and distant. And more. The State of Israel became accountable for the honor and status and, to no small degree, for the protection of the rights and very existence of all the Jews in the world.

Never before has a new and tiny State had to assume a liability so burdensome and so large, in circumstances so grievous and so difficult. And those circumstances are neither accidental nor ephemeral. There are inherent in the geography of the Land and its place in human history, in the conjunctures of the historical period in which the State of Israel had birth, in the condition of the Jewish people and its recent story, in the environment of peoples within which the State exists and acts, and lastly in the special purposes that have been laid upon it, purposes which are both its privilege and the surety of its being.

Our Land is distinguished in three respects: in topography, in geography and in history. Its appearance has no parallel on the face of the globe. Down the whole length of it, from North to South, from the heights of Lebanon and Hermon to the Red Sea, there stretches the abyss we call the Jordan Valley and the 'Arabah, at its middle point the Dead Sea, sunken 400 meters below sea-level, the lowest spot on the earth's surface. This rift, the mountains and hills on its either side, and the Mediterranean coast along the western frontier have endowed our little land with a diversity of climates, landscapes and other characteristics which are not repeated in any other country in so narrow a space. It was not without cause that one of our sages said: 'This little universe, this Land of Israel, is spiced with all things that are in the world. In all other lands, what one has the other lacks: but the Land of Israel is lacking in naught.'

The position of the land at the meeting-place of three continents has made it, small though it is, a bridge and battlefield for the conquerors of the world. From the time when man first spread over the earth and began to trek from place to place, it became a vital bivouac and strategic base for all the great phalanxes, from the interior of western and eastern Asia, or from the European mainland. It was invaded by hosts from south and north, from east and west, hosts of all tribes of mankind and in all periods of history, beginning with Elam, Egypt and Assyria at the dawn of civilization and down to Napoleon and Allenby. Great new continents have been discovered betweenwhiles, and the pendulum of man's politics and culture has swung over to other regions, but who can say with certainty that the march of foreign conquest through our Land is yet over and done with? Geographical facts are stubborn, and it is the breach in the wall that beckons, seeming to say—Enter!

Furthermore, our country holds a special place in the records of the human mind. Save Greece, no other country so small has filled so important a role in the history of mankind or left a mark so abiding on the culture of its greater part.

The Book of Books, written by the hand of the people of Israel in this Land, is the most widely read in the world, and more than any other has influenced human thought. Most religions have their origin in this Land, and many a nation owns an attachment of spirit and soul to it and to the events that have occurred in it during the last three thousand years. Of everything that happens here the echo resounds throughout the wide world. Not so resound happenings of much larger and more populous lands. This is the magnet of empires, for good and for ill.

* * *

The rebirth of Israel is unlike that of many States in recent days. It was not something restricted to the bounds of the people which brought it about, or of the land in which it took place. It was not by chance that the question of it was first debated in the highest forum of modern mankind—the Assembly of the United Nations. And if it be the case that it was determined and decided, in effect, by virtue of our own exploit and military strength, and our own victory in battle, yet in principle it was settled and accepted by the nations of the world and, among them, by the two outstanding Powers of our times, the United States of America and the Soviet Union.

It was an event of universal significance. Millions, I say, are spiritually linked with this Land, and with it are bound up international interests, strategic and political. That the Jewish people were so widely dispersed gave the rebirth an unusual international aspect. For all the narrow compass of the Land, it meant an important change in the balance of power throughout the

Middle East, and every such change is of especial moment now, when antagonisms and international rivalries throughout the world are becoming sharper. It came at one of the most dynamic, turbulent and confused periods. The yeast of history is ever in ferment, but the speed of change and revolution was scarcely ever as breakneck as it has been since the first World War. In the last forty years, far-reaching changes have altered the whole character of mankind: the first has become last and the last has become first; powerful nations have crumbled and been destroyed, and new forces, mighty and majestic, have taken their place. Wonders are still far from ceasing, and our generation, and the one to follow it, may still expect change and revolution on a scale, and of a political and social intensity, which it is impossible to foresee.

Two exceptional portents of our time should be mentioned.

First, the waning hegemony of Europe and the rise of Asia. Since the days of Alexander, Europe had ruled the known world. Although the center of domination after that, and till this very day, has moved from hand to hand and from State to State, nonetheless, until the first World War, Europe stayed the leading continent, and virtually governed most lands outside the New World. Even the American countries were colonies of Europe for a long while, and a part of its culture, economy and world power. After the first World War the greatness of Europe began to fade; it is a continuing process that has not yet reached its end. The decline is both political and economic, and cultural as well. As Europe sinks, so Asia ascends.

Asia is the largest continent, as well in area as in populousness. Thousands of years ago it was the birthplace of civilization. In it were born the sciences and the arts on which our new culture was founded. In it dwell the two most numerous races in the world—the races of China and India, between them making up almost one half of the entire human kind, and great not only numerically but also in ancient and original cultures which have persisted for thousands of years, without ebb or interruption, to this day. Many of the peoples of western Asia, too, in the Bible lands, brought no mean offerings to the treasure-house of the human spirit millennia ago, but most of them have been blotted out and passed away: Elam, Assyria, Babylon, Aram and Canaan. Then the Greeks came upon the scene, heirs and assimilants of the conquests of the mind which their oriental neighbors had first achieved, but by Greece sublimated to the heights by the greatness of its creative genius in every branch of science, thought, poetry and art, of craftsmanship and military skill. It was then the sun of Asia set. The succeeding civilization of Europe, built upon the spiritual and religious legacy of the Jews, on the wisdom, art and philosophy of the Greeks and on the political science and jurisprudence of the Romans, went on to vanquish the whole world. True, the influence of that successor civilization is no weaker now. It penetrates into every corner of the earth. Yet Europe, the hinge and bearer of it, is beginning to tremble at its political and economic foundations, and the limitless continent of Asia is stirring to new life, casting off the yoke of Europe and eager to take the place befitting it in the contemporary arena of policy, economy, culture. Only a minority of its inhabitants is still in thrall to a foreign Power. Peoples, large and small, of the mainland and in the islands of the Indian Ocean have been set free, and once again China and India stride into independence. Their weight grows in the scales of humanity and it is like to tip them hereafter.

Israel stands upon the western edge of Asia. For its first two thousand years, our people fastened its roots almost wholly in Asia and in next-door Egypt, in the midst of folk of the Bible lands whence the Greeks culled their first notions of science, art and craftsmanship, and the use of writing. In infancy it too was immersed in that ancient culture. But it warred with it as well, itself cherishing an original Jewish culture and that new way of life which made it a nation of eternity. In the next two thousand years, it was scattered athwart the lands of Europe, America and Australasia, and there drank in the culture of Europe and even took part somewhat in its development. It had its share in every achievement of modern science, art and technology, yet held resolutely to its own spiritual estates, timeless, intact and unspoiled.

Now, after two thousand years of wandering and dispersion, it is returning to its Homeland in western Asia, to build it up and within it itself to be built up as a free and independent nation. The marvel is staged as the limelight flickers over from Europe to Asia; it is just then that the people of Israel has become once more an autonomous power in Asia, albeit small in numbers and small in the area of its land, yet significant in quality and potential. It is as though by the providence of history it had been called upon to be a living bridge between the peoples of Asia and Europe. Less than all others may we of Israel shut our eyes to the rise of Asia and its peoples. We must not, we have no right to renounce our European heritage, or estrange ourselves from a much older spiritual legacy. But we must also prize the intellectual and cultural treasures of the Asian lands— Arabia, Persia and Japan, and, first and foremost, India and China. Seldom in books on general history, especially when literature and human thought are their themes, do Japan, China and India find mention. This lacuna is due to the pridefulness of Europe, itself a legacy of Greece and Rome, whose time had passed. The Jewish people of Israel neither asks nor has it means to emulate great nations in strength, in wealth or in arms, but in the kingdom of the spirit it dare not lag behind even the greatest. It is commanded to take unto itself all the spiritual riches of humanity, all those glittering qualities of mind which made it in Bible times a teacher of man. In its Galuth, those qualities were near death in the ghetto's narrow confines. But, though bent and bloodied, they did not die, and when we are established firmly in the land of our fathers as a free people, they will breathe deeply again.

Let us not belittle the spiritual testament of India, China and Japan: not only political and numerical importance but intrinsic character also, and an awakening of the spirit, make them pregnant with a destiny as great and fruitful as Europe once knew.

The second portent is the struggle for world leadership, between the United States of America and the Soviet Union, on which, at this moment of time, the gaze of international politics is riveted. They are not the largest tribes on earth. The United States are peopled by 155 millions, and Russia with its many races has about 200. India alone claims more than both together, and China surpasses India. Here again we see the exciting truth, that numbers alone do not decide. Historical and geographical circumstances have placed the rivals on the crest of global dominion. It is the outcome of a long growth which ripened in the white heat of the second World War, but for scores of years had been budding unseen. As long as 120 years ago the French writer Alexis de Tocqueville, an acute political observer, discerned this secret process and with remarkable clarity foretold its decisive consequences. When he wrote his brilliant and penetrating book on American democracy, America had only 15 million inhabitants and Russia was terra incognita to most of the people of Europe and America. It was in 1835 that he used these prophetic words*:

'There are at the present time two great nations in the world, which started from different points, but seem to tend towards the same end. I allude to the Russians and the Americans. Both of them have grown up unnoticed; and

* Democracy in America, by Alexis de Tocqueville, Volume 1. Alfred A. Knopf, 1945. Translation by Phillips Bradley.

while the attention of mankind was directed elsewhere, they have suddenly placed themselves in the front rank among the nations . . .

All other nations seem to have nearly reached their natural limits . . . but these are still in the act of growth. All the others have stopped, or continue to advance with extreme difficulty; these alone are proceeding with ease and celerity along a path to which no limit can be perceived. The American struggles against the obstacles that nature opposes to him; the adversaries of the Russian are men . . . The conquests of the American are therefore gained by the plowshare; those of the Russian by the sword. The . . . American relies upon personal interest to accomplish his ends and gives free scope to the unguided strength and common sense of the people; the Russian centers all the authority of society in a single arm. The principal instrument of the former is freedom; of the latter, servitude. Their starting-point is different and their courses are not the same; yet each of them seems marked out by the will of Heaven to sway the destinies of half the globe.'

It is almost unbelievable that this could have been said 120 years ago. Yet the words are as true now as when they were uttered. The giants wrestling on the stage of human history today, this collision of the divergent principles—democratic freedom and tyrannous compulsion—by which the lives of these two peoples are shaped, cast their dark shadow everywhere.

But it would be wrong to say that the world is divided into two parts, the Soviet bloc on one side and on the other the American. Only the Soviet bloc is uniform, cohesive, and subordinated to a single supreme authority which dwells in the Kremlin. Perhaps Communist China should be excluded, for its links with the Soviet Union are those rather of friendship than dependence. In this homogeneous organism, then, there is a highest power which decides affairs not only of economics, security and foreign and internal politics, but even of culture, science, art, literature and everyday thought and behavior, in an area that stretches from Eastern Germany, Czechoslovakia, Hungary, and Bulgaria in the west to the shores of the Pacific in the Far East and represents the greatest unbroken land-mass in the world.

The rest of mankind is not uniform or homogeneous in any respect, political, economic or cultural. Each country there is more or less self-determining, with its own forms of government and society, a little or a lot different from what is to be found in the others. There are primitive States still under a theocratic-monarchical regime like the Yemen and Saudi Arabia, or a feudal or semi-feudal one like most of the countries in the Middle East. There are capitalist-democratic countries in excelsis like North America and several countries of Latin America. There are countries of dictatorship, and progressive, socialistic countries as in Scandinavia.

Some are allied to one another for mutual defense—the countries of the Atlantic Pact, with the United States at their head. Others eschew alliances, and have only one thing in common: they reject the authority of the Soviet Union.

But even countries which belong to neither bloc, like Israel, cannot disregard this battle of Titans, which may precipitate itself into a third World War that would beyond all doubt transcend in gravity, in violence, and in perils all that man has ever suffered in the past.

It was in this hour of tension that Israel was born. The two great Powers in the maelstrom gave the birth their blessing, each for its own good reasons. But this unanimity in the Assembly of the United Nations, when the termination of the Mandate and Palestine partition were debated, did nothing to ease the strain between them in other political issues, not excepting those likely to arise in and around the new State. From the moment it first drew breath, Israel was confronted not only with acts and attitudes of enmity on the part of all its Arab neighbors, but with mankind's problem of problems today: the danger of a third World War and all the frightful hazards it would bring before ever a shot was fired.

* * *

This description of the background of historical fact to the period of the foundation of the State would be incomplete without a picture of the circumstantial background of world Jewry. Its tablets in the last years before the State was founded record two disasters which not even our people could cap, though long taught by torment: the isolation of Russian Jewry and the annihilation of the great part of the Jews of Europe.

In the last century, Jewry's center swung to eastern Europe. Western Jewry, particularly in Spain, which had led Jewish creativity in the Middle Ages, was uprooted and impoverished. In Russia, as it widened and spread eastward and west, there came to be concentrated the bulk of Jewry. As the lands of Islam declined, with the beggary of their political and cultural resources, so their source of Jewish creativeness ran dry, and Russian Jewry became leader of the Jewish people and its inspiration. It was in Russian Jewry, and to some extent in Galician, that Jewish enlightenment began and the movement of Chibbath Zion burgeoned. It was there that the keel of pioneer Aliyah was laid, and young Jewish revolutionaries showed their heroism in a fiery crusade against tyranny and oppression. The whole Jewish renaissance from the nineteenth century onward is paramountly the doing of Russian Jewry. Out of its strength came forth the great Jewish concentration of our times in America. It was the Jews of Russia outstandingly who built the new Yishuv in this Land, that made possible the revival of the State. It was they who fostered the Hebrew and Yiddish literature that rescued the masses of Israel from their spiritual tomb. From out of them arose the Jewish workers' movement that raised the dignity of so many thousands of our people. The prop and stay of the Zionist Movement—that too was Russian Jewry.

And all this when it was persecuted by the governments of the Czars, mulcted of all rights and penned within a Pale. How noble and how great was the generative force in it, if under oppression and humiliation it yet could yield such blessing of fertility!

In February 1917, when Czardom was smitten and a democratic revolution took place, it seemed the hour had struck, too, for the liberation of Russian Jewry, and it girt up its loins for the task awaiting it in the new era opening for the Jewish people. But the high hopes were short-lived. In October 1917 came the Bolshevist revolution, and Russian Jewry was amputated savagely from the Jewish body. The Zionist Movement was outlawed and its leaders were exiled or imprisoned; the teaching of Hebrew, the reading of Hebrew books, was forbidden; all communal life was extinguished. Little by little Yiddish literature as well was silenced, all free contact with world Jewry was proscribed and the gateway to the Land was barred. The greatest and grandest Jewish commmunity was doomed to be dumb and atrophied, torn from the mother-stock.

Then, after the lapse of twenty-five years, a second hideous calamity overtook European Jewry, beside which the most awful horrors chronicled pale into nothingness. The Nazi hangmen and their collaborators slaughtered six million Jews, all but a third of European Jewry was wiped out. The congregations were maimed forever, and only here and there did a tiny remnant find sanctuary. The tale of mankind has never known genocide so terrible.

The Jewry of Europe had enshrined the hope of Jewish resurrection. From it went forth the rebuilders of the Homeland, its pioneers and champions. It had hoped and longed and waited for a Jewish State: it had made itself ready, it was worthy and was fitted out, to build it, dedicating body and soul, strength and wealth, leaders and masses. The State was born indeed, but Europe's Jewry had been scorched from the earth, and left behind only a few sorry cinders snatched from the burning . . . The people of Israel had its State, but the State had its people no longer . . . The people had been massacred that wanted a State and that the State wanted, and of those who escaped by flight within Europe most are still in gyves, and there is no knowing until when.

When the State was established, there were some 650,000 Jews in it, which was about six percent of the Jews then left in the world. This little handful had to stand up to all the Arab peoples around it: Egypt, Trans-Jordan, Iraq, Syria, the Lebanon, Saudi Arabia, drummed up one and all to war upon Israel. The victories of the Israel Defense Forces are already history, but prodigious though they were, they did not solve the problem of the State's security, nor will that problem be solved easily or soon. It is one of incalculable difficulty, and we must look plainly and soberly upon its ugly visage.

In the days of the First Temple, and the Second too, it was not simple either. Then, as now, the Land was small, although its bounds varied from time to time. Then, as now, the people was a small one, and on all sides were great nations, avid of conquest. But they differed one from the other in language, culture and religion, and their differences allowed small and weaker neighbors to retain independent being. In those days Israel was never enveloped in every direction by one single nation.

Many conquerors, one on the heels of the other, have since governed the Land: Romans, Byzantines, Persians, Arabs, Mamelukes, Crusaders, Mongols, Egyptians, Turks and British. All through that length of political metamorphosis, it was never a separate and independent State; it was a province within a larger unit. Only with the disintegration of the Ottoman empire, at the end of the first World War, was it divided off again as a separate political entity, but still not independent, under the British Mandate which promised us a National Home. When the Mandate was confirmed by the Council of the League of Nations in July 1922, the country, both in principle and in practice, was cut into two parts: the west remained as the area of the National Home, and the east, on the other bank of the Jordan, was handed over under Mandatory control to the Hashemite Emir Abdullah. The State of Israel has been restored in the western part. In area it is no smaller than was the Jewish State during most of the period of the First or Second Temple, and the gravity of the current problem of security is not a matter of differing boundaries. It stems from far-reaching changes that took place near the Land about 500 years after Bar Kochba; from the spiritual convulsion which altered the face of the Middle East, of Central Asia and all the countries of North Africa.

It came about in the wide and desolate wastes of the Arabian peninsula. For thousands of years, there had wandered in that expanse a number of primitive Arab tribes, of whom the outside world knew virtually nothing. Their voice was unheard in history until the seventh century of the Christian era. They were not united, they were subject to no one overlord. But the coming of Mohammed in the first quarter of that century ushered in a new epoch. The Prophet of Islam joined together the dissident clans and made them into a nation. He gave them a new religion and breathed into them a spirit of valor and a zest for spoils, and soon after his death in the year 632 his successors broke from their peninsula on a march of world conquest, rapidly to set up a powerful Arab empire. The founding of great empires by victorious peoples is not new in history. In that adventure the Persians, the Greeks, the Romans and the Mongols forestalled the Arabs, but the Arabs were not content merely to rule, they imposed their new faith on many of the conquered. Yet even that was not a new thing; it had its precedents: the Buddhists in eastern Asia and Christianity in western Asia, and the Holy Roman Empire. The Arabs, however, carried through a transfiguration for which there is no parallel before their times, or since; they expunged the languages of the lands they overran in Asia and Africa and gave them Arabic instead. Not that all who accepted the faith of Islam accepted its Prophet's tongue as well. The Persians, the Turks and the Mongols, and so too the peoples of India and Indonesia, received the faith but kept their national speech. But Arabic supplanted all other speech in the Middle East, in the Land, in the Lebanon, Syria and Mesopotamia, North Africa from Egypt to Morocco. Today it is spoken universally from the north of Turkey along the eastern and southern shores of the Mediterranean as far as the Atlantic Ocean, by peoples which number 70 million souls; yet among them there is no partnership of blood or race or past history, it is only community of religion and language that has made them a cultural whole and may yet weld them into a solid political bloc.

Of this enormous region, in which Arabic and Islam are supreme, part is in the Middle East, and within that part are six independent States: the Lebanon, Syria, Trans-Jordan, Iraq, Saudi Arabia and the Yemen. The superficial area they occupy extends to 1,356,000 square miles, and the number of their inhabitants is nearly 20 million. In other words, an area 170 times as large as Israel's and a population 13 times as large by statistics at the outset of 1952, and 28 times as large when the State was established.

The other part is North Africa, which comprises Egypt, the Sudan, Libya, Tunis, Algeria and Morocco; it covers 3,064,123 square miles and has 45,500,000 inhabitants. Only two of these countries are independent: Egypt and Libya. Sudan is in effect under British rule, although in theory a condominium of Egypt and Great Britain and in practice a bone of contention between the theoretical co-rulers. Libya was declared independent just a year ago; Tunis and Algeria are still under French control but in a mood of revolt; Morocco is, in the main, subject to France but partly to Spain, and here, too, there is a strong insurgent trend.

If we add Egypt, let alone the Sudan, the area of the Arab countries in the Middle East will come to 1,719,000 square miles, which is 215 times that of Israel, and their population to almost 40 millions, which is 57 times that of Israel five years ago, or 27 times what it was at the beginning of 1952.

Six Arab States are now members of the United Nations: Syria, the Lebanon, Saudi Arabia, Iraq, the Yemen and Egypt, and if they are divided in opinion among themselves on many vital and less vital issues, nevertheless they represent externally a single front, and their six votes are negotiable currency, in every sense of the term.

Never once in the past was Israel girdled at every point by a tight ring of that kind. And it is a ring that is likely to expand, for we may assume that Tunis, Algeria and Morocco will become autonomous sooner or later, and be admitted, with Libya also, to the Organization of the United Nations.

The Christian States do not form a united front on any question. But that is not the case with the Moslem, where the feeling of national unity is quite strong, if not equally strong in all. Turkey, for example, looks upon itself as associate and partner of the countries of western Europe. Most of the countries of Islam, however, join forces in various political fields. The principal ones which are not Arabic-speaking are Pakistan, Persia, Afghanistan and Indonesia, and, not taking Turkey into account, they occupy an area of more than 1,800,000 square miles and have a total population exceeding 185 millions. They give co-operation to the Arab League States in the United Nations and support them as a matter of course in issues which are not crucial for themselves; their attitude towards Israel usually included.

This, then, is the sweep of the problem of security and of politics which the Arab world presents to the young State of Israel.

But to depict the position of our State vis-a-vis its neighbors and the rest of the world is not to expound fully the special troubles of Israel.

* * *

Every State consists of a land and a people. Israel is no exception, but it is a State identical neither with its land nor with its people. I have already said that when it was established it held only six percent of the Jewish people remaining alive after the Nazi cataclysm. I add now that it has been established in only a portion of the Land of Israel. Some are hesitant as to the restoration of our historical frontiers, fixed and set from the beginning of time, but even they will hardly deny the anomaly of the new lines. To them Israel is committed by armistice agreements so long as it is not again attacked; and it is honoring the commitment. But even within those lines, State and Land do not coincide. When the State was established only seven percent of its area was cultivated, and of that small fraction half was in Jewish and half in Arab hands. The War of Independence left Israel a legacy of new deserts made by the hands of men, as well as the old desert which the heavens had wrought. More than one half of the Land in the west, its southern half, was empty and barren under the British Mandate and had been so for thousands of years. But the war brought havoc on many a settlement, and when the State came into being there stood only the villages established by us in the last seventy years and a few which were not Jewish. The truth is that the State inherited a derelict and desert land which must be rebuilt almost in entirety, yet it has not the means for it, either financial or technical—materials, tools, instruments, machinery—or in manpower. Capital, materials and equipment, and manpower, must come from elsewhere. It is self-evident that they cannot come in a day or a year or a generation, and that the resources wherefrom the State must be constructed are not to be had within itself but only beyond, and depend upon the national and international makeup of that 'beyond.'

Of all the things which determine the existence, the upbuilding, the security and the future of the State, things which we can get abroad and only abroad, the most vital, of course, is the people. No one for a moment imagined that 600,000 or so Jews by themselves could set up a State, build it and watch its peace and security. The State was set up for Jewry in exile, which shall return to it. Aliyah laid the State's foundations and raised it up. Only by Aliyah will the State be built. Only by the strength of Aliyah will it triumph over its difficulties.

But Aliyah itself is beset by difficulties which call for desperate remedies.

Until 1914 every Jew was free to leave the land in which he lived. Throughout the years of Galuth, and in all the Galuth lands, the Jewish people lived on alien sufferance, although its status was not alike in all periods and places. Sometimes it had a grain of comfort and its rights were upheld, sometimes it was victim of oppression and discrimination. Its sole inviolate prerogative, at all times and everywhere, was freedom to go, yet in this very hour of the State's establishment even that has been taken away in many lands.

I have referred to Russian Jewry and its violent fission from every contact with the rest of Jewry and with Israel. An implacable blockade hems it around. The successes of the Soviet Union in the second World War and afterwards have but enlarged the area of blockade. The Jewries of Lithuania, Latvia, eastern Galicia and Bessarabia, and now Hungary as well, have been cut off and shut in. Freedom to go is denied no less to the Jews of Poland, Rumania, Czechoslovakia and Bulgaria, although these countries, after binding themselves to the Soviet regime, did allow Jews to depart to Israel even after they had generally banned the exit of their citizens.

But this is not the only change in the conditions of Jewish immigration into Israel.

During the Mandate immigration brought with it not only manpower, but also financial means and the technical and scientific skills, the vigor and wealth, needed for national reconstruction. In the countries from which it came, Jews had opportunities of education and enlightenment, in both Jewish and general subjects, and they also had material and monetary resources. The stream carried along with it a flow of capital and of liberal and intellectual talent. Only in slight degree did immigration then require the financial help of the Jewish people as a whole.

The second World War, and the political and social upheavals in its wake, transformed things entirely.

In the countries of eastern Europe within the Soviet bloc, even where Jews were permitted to emigrate, their property was nationalized and confiscated in common with that of all citizens, and immigration thence was of necessity an immigration without funds.

The obliteration of two-thirds of European Jewry, the sealing up of the Jews in the Soviet Union and many of its satellites, meant that the lands of Islam became the principal centers of Aliyah. Those lands are marked by poverty of means and mind, and most of the exiles now returning are both materially impoverished and orphaned of all education, Jewish and ordinary.

To this must be added the common factor that, except in a few instances, the transfer of capital has been prohibited even by the free democracies, and the money to pay for immigration and for the upbuilding of the State can be secured in practically only one country, the United States of America. It is there that the largest Jewish assembly is to be found today, largest in numbers, towering in financial, professional and scientific capacity, tremendous influence in the political sphere. It does not, however, regard itself as an entrant for Aliyah, although the pioneer will lives on among the best of its youth, in a limited circle.

If we consider the prospects of immigration of men, capital and professions, the lands of the Diaspora can be divided into the following categories:

(a) The Soviet Union, which has forbidden Jews to go, and has nationalized their assets as part of the general nationalization of property. Here dwells the great majority of the remnant of European Jewry, some two million souls. At this moment no emigration to Israel is possible, whether of men or money.

(b) The countries whose social structure resembles that of the Soviet Union but which allow a certain measure of emigration, such as Hungary, Rumania, Poland, Czechoslovakia and Bulgaria. Here the number of Jews at the time of the establishment of the State was 729,000, and of them, up to the beginning of 1952, 217,026 had entered Israel. It may be that there will be a further influx of immigrants but there can be none of capital. Jewish capital is no more.

(c) The countries of Islam: Iraq, Syria, the Lebanon, the Yemen, Egypt, Tripoli, Morocco, Tunis, Turkey, Persia, Afghanistan, which are the main sources of Aliyah for the time being. They bless us with immigrants, but in overwhelming number the immigrants are wanting in capital and culture, so that to integrate them productively demands financial resources and professional know-how from the centers of free and affluent Jewry. When the State began there were 889,700 Jews in those Moslem lands; up to the beginning of 1952, 329,561 had settled here.

(d) The countries of western Europe, South America and South Africa. Their Jews have both the cash and the education, and the practical ability, which are needed. At the moment the Aliyah from among them is disappointing; there are legal difficulties in the way of transferring money. The right of emigration, however, is absolutely untrammelled, if only few avail themselves of it. In 1951 the total Jewish population there was 1,746,230, including 953,200 in Europe, 627,030 in South America, and 110,000 in South Africa. In Australia and New Zealand there were

56,000. The number of immigrants up to the beginning of 1952 was 39,805.

(e) The United States of America. Here the movement of capital and of men is entirely free, and here almost one-half of world Jewry lives. Hence has come and hence will come to the State most of the capital invested and to be invested in its upbuilding: public capital through the Appeals and the Independence Loan, private capital, and the capital of the United States Government in the form of loans from the Export-Import Bank and the American Grants-in-Aid.

Counting Canada as well, there are in this sector 5,201,000 Jews. From the birth of the State to the beginning of 1952, only 1,682 have come from it to Israel as immigrants.

* * *

Even after all the horror and ruination of Nazism, it lies within the united power of the Jewish people to build up the State, and develop and fortify it so that it may succeed in its historic mission and be equal to all its difficulties. But that power just now is fragmented and dissipated, and in many countries padlocked as well, while the three things of which the State is in dire need—men, money and skill, are no longer in combination as they were in the time of the Mandate. The centers of Aliyah are distinct, the centers of capital and capacity are distinct.

At all times Aliyah has been a product of Jewish anguish, even with the men of Bilu and the Second Aliyah and the immigration that followed it. Yet with anguish there goes vision. Without vision no anguish could have become a force of freedom and redemption such as Aliyah proved to be. But vision, of and by itself, had never the power to engender mass immigration. Even in the birthplace of Jewish renaissance, in a Russian Jewry still at liberty to emigrate to the Land of Israel and bring its possessions with it, immigration was confined to the elect circles of pioneers. The leaders of Zionism in Czarist Russia, some of them men of amplest means, did not stir from their hearths or bring their wealth to the Land. And the Jews of America are no better. Nor did the Jews in Babylon hearken unto the word of Cyrus and they went not back with Zerubbabel, Ezra and Nehemiah but for forty thousand of them; only when the Government of Iraq, in our days, lifted its cordon did the forgotten congregation re-enter at the close of 2,500 years.

In the time of Cyrus it was given to the Jews to return from Babylon 'with vessels of silver, with gold, with goods, and with beasts, and with precious things.' And Cyrus made his proclamation, saying: 'Who is there among you of all His people? . . . and let him go up to Jerusalem, which is in Judah, and build the house of the Lord . . . And whosoever remaineth in any place where he sojourneth, let the men of his place help him with silver, and with gold, and with goods, and with beasts.' Nehemiah has handed down to us the exact tally of manservants and maidservants, singing men and singing women, the horses and mules, the camels and the asses, and the drams of gold and the pounds of silver which the homing exiles brought with them. But the Jews of modern Iraq were not suffered to take away their possessions, and came to us in utter penury and want. That too is the fate of the Jews of the Yemen, of Morocco, Tunis and Algeria, of Egypt and Tripolitania, of Turkey, Rumania and Poland, and so on and on.

* * *

But not only to absorption of immigration and to economic development must the State devote its energies. It must bend its stoutest efforts and apply immense resources to maintaining military and political security, safeguarding its sovereignty in the eyes of the world and armoring democratic freedom and spiritual independence at home.

These paramount missions are arbiters of Israel's external and domestic politics, they determine the trend of its international relations and its links with Jews throughout the world.

It is in three different spheres that the State has to act. First the global, embracing the whole civilized world. Israel cannot confine itself to the ambit of the Organization of the United Nations, for many countries are not members, and there is no country, remote or at hand, in which Israel has not some interest, and not just because of the fragment of Galuth it may contain.

Next there is the Middle East, where is Israel itself, and which includes the States of the Arab League and Turkey and Persia. Out of it Israel's future is likely to be faced with grave dangers, yet with chances also of deep purport.

And the third is Jewry throughout the Diaspora. It is on this, more than on any other sphere, that the future of Israel depends. The attachment between the State and the Jewish people is not one of needs and benefits; it is one of mission and destiny.

At the very base of the international politics of Israel there rests a three-fold concern: for peace among the nations, for the rights of man as such, and for freedom of contact with the Diaspora. Therefore, its most earnest wish is to establish normal relations with all countries, their Governments and their peoples, without enquiring meticulously into their internal forms, and to lend a hand in every experiment and every step designed to lessen tension between the great Powers and to keep a tranquil world.

Israel is not indifferent to the ideological conflict which is being waged simultaneously with the political and military rivalry of nations. Its devotion to the values of human freedom, freedom of thought and spirit, freedom of choice and criticism, freedom of creation and work, is ingrained in its character and spiritual heredity. It is this devotion that gave Jews the moral courage to defy every oppression and coercion, even when essayed by the lords of mighty physical forces. We are the one nation without entourage of partners in race, religion or language, that has stood for thousands of years in its splendid but tragic isolation, and, as if that were not enough, was dispersed among all peoples and in all lands. That is why, more than any other people, we long for a government of freedom, wherein every man may live, work and behave according to his own way and conscience, without hurt to the freedom of his fellow-man. Totalitarian government, of whatever brand, is deadly poison to the survival of Jews in their dispersion. International totalitarian ambitions endanger the survival of the Jewish State. Of both, Israel is implacable foe.

A universal attachment to social and international justice is engraved deep upon the nation's soul. Our Prophets inveighed passionately against violence, usurpation, oppression and lawlessness in human and in international affairs. The Prophet Isaiah was among the first to foretell the social revolution: 'For he bringeth down them that dwell on high; the lofty city, he layeth it low; he layeth it low, even to the ground; he bringeth it even to the dust. The foot shall tread it down, even the feet of the poor, and the steps of the needy . . . for when thy judgments are in the earth, the inhabitants of the world will learn righteousness.' And the minstrel of Israel sings praises of the hero and his qualities: 'Gird thy sword upon thy thigh, O most mighty . . . ride prosperously because of truth and meekness and righteousness . . . Thou lovest righteousness and hatest wickedness: therefore God . . . hath anointed thee. . .'

The State will not be true to its prophetic testament, or to the vision of salvation in the last days, unless, gratefully and respecting verity, it follows every venture that has in it to advance righteous and merciful relations between men and peoples and to build human society on foundations of equality and mutual help, not rivalry and exploitation. And who like the Jews have endured the sins of the wicked and the presumption of tyrants?

Our long acquaintance with history has taught us that not in wrongdoing can righteousness abide, that the salvation of peoples will not be brought about by alien compulsion but from within. Israel does not believe that any powerful State has the right to impose its will on a weaker, even under the cloak of reforms. The crying need of mankind is peace among the nations, and peace will not come unless powerful States cease to meddle in domestic affairs of the small and weak ones. Those who strive for peace will be adjudged earnest only if they establish truly peaceful relations even with countries whose regime is different from their own, which is so lovely in their eyes.

Therefore the Government of Israel considers it a duty to promote relations of friendship and reciprocity with every peace-loving country, without prying into its internal constitution, and to support every step which makes for peace, which guarantees the rights of man and the equality of nations, and enhances the authority and effectiveness of the United Nations.

Our Government is neither able nor entitled to vaunt that its weight in the scales of international politics is decisive or even particularly impressive. But its wishes and its capacity are not a negligible element, nor is its practical value to be measured only by the number of its inhabitants and its area. In international politics, too, there are imponderable forces, and there is no doubt that, in a fair degree, Israel is one of them. But still it dare not preen itself.

* * *

In charting its political course, the duty of any Government, large or little, is to see international facts as they are, which does not necessarily mean accepting them. The Government of Israel cannot help realizing that these facts are not precisely as it would have liked. But be it easy or not, it must adjust its politics to the conditions of reality, yet not be turned aside from the outside world and its own Land.

In its brief appearance upon the world's stage, Israel has encountered three different kinds of States. First are those which still refuse to form any liaison with us, whether because they have not yet reconciled themselves to the existence of the State or for other reasons. Here belong all the countries of the Arab

League, certain Moslem countries, like Pakistan and Afghanistan, and Ethiopia and others. In the second place are countries which permit relations only with their Governments, and not with their peoples, such as the Soviet Union, and the countries of the 'People's' Democracy. The limitation of contacts to the official channels does not apply to Israel only, but to all countries, for it derives from the Soviet form of government. Lastly, there are countries with which Israel has touch through both governmental channels and free public opinion.

The difference between the third and the second group is hardly less signal than that between the second and the first.

For every nation the freedom of its contacts with other nations, with their elected representatives, their Press, their public institutions, their apparatus of enlightenment, science and education, their workers' movement and economic circles, is of primary, even critical, importance. With Israel these contacts have a very special and vital purpose. Although the State is in being, by far the largest proportion of the Jewish people, a proportion decisive in numbers and resources, is still in the Diaspora, and the connection between Israel and the dispersed communities, the freedom of action of those communities, are crucial for the State. Only in lands of civic liberty, where there is no totalitarian enforcement by a dictatorship, is this freedom of action left. Israel does not underrate the limited contacts it keeps up through exclusively governmental channels with the countries of the 'people's' democracy and the Soviet Union; for the sake of world peace and for the sake, too, of its special needs, our Government has been sedulous to foster friendly relations with those Governments as much as possible. But there is no mistaking the portentousness of the fact that only in countries of democratic freedom and freedom of the Press is Israel able to be in reciprocal rapport with both Government and people. Only there have we uninhibited access to the Jews, and only there can we explain to public opinion at large the position of Israel, its needs, its enterprises and its aspirations; these two things together are incomparably meaningful for the basic needs of Israel—immigration, development and security.

I have told how the State was set up in a desert land and only six percent of the Jewish people then dwelt in it, and that everything which its existence, security and growth required—men, money, materials and equipment—had to be brought in. Whoever keeps this 'import' from us denies the State survival. We have seen that the 'import' of immigrants from the 'people's' democracy was of no slight dimensions between the establishment of the State and the beginning of 1952. It amounted to 214,026 out of a Jewish population there of 729,000, which means to say that in that period more than 29% of the total Jewish community of Bulgaria, Hungary, Czechoslovakia, Poland and Rumania came to Israel. Within the same period, 684,275 Jews in all came from the entire Diaspora. Thus, the share of the countries of the 'people's' democracy in that Aliyah exceeded 31%, and the State has known how to be thankful. This, and more. On December 8, 1951, it addressed the Soviet Government officially as follows:

> 'As the Government of the Soviet Union is aware, the return of Jews to their historic homeland is the pivotal mission of the State of Israel. The Government of Israel is aware that only by the preservation of world peace and the maintenance of normal relations between the various States shall we succeed in developing our country and absorbing all those Jews who wish to return. In this connection the Government of Israel appeals to the Soviet Union to enable those Jews in the Soviet Union who wish to immigrate to Israel, to do so. The Government of Israel believes that this request is in complete accord with the policy of the Soviet Union, which is based on national equality and the right of self-determination for every nation.'

So far, there has been no reply to this appeal, but the door is not closed and we must not give up hopes of seeing Russian Jewry sharing again with the other tribes of Israel in our revival.

* * *

We have no higher or advanced schools for military training as yet, and the best of our men and officers have to be sent to the right institutions overseas to gain the necessary experience, knowledge and specialization. Our Defense Forces need equipment, and this poor little country is not yet capable itself of furnishing all of it. It cannot yet make four-engined planes or warships or tanks or many another of the weapons that are indispensable; again, they must all be imported. Army and civilians alike must have food. And not enough of that can yet be produced from our own soil. Development demands raw materials: timber, iron, pipes, yarns. Machines for farm and factory. Vehicles, ships, wagons and engines. And where else are we to get them but abroad? And abroad we have to buy them. It is not only a question of foreign exchange. Of course, without that we can get nothing, and we cannot get it from the countries of the 'people's' democracy. But even when we have it, procurement of the goods we lack depends upon the goodwill of Governments, especially when it is a matter of 'goods' that are needed for defense. We have turned for help, and we are turning now, to all Governments which are in relations with us. Not from a single one of them has Israel got all that it asked for, but there is no ground for indiscriminate complaint. Every country has its particular arguments and we should distinguish between one and the next. Some are not ready to supply our needs, or even to acknowledge our approaches. They do not as much as answer: No. And when that happens with a country of the 'people's' democracy, there is nothing more to be said or done. Every negation, every absence of reply, is effectively a final rejoinder, because there is only one channel of communications, the governing officialdom.

It is otherwise with the countries of democratic freedom, although even there the Government of Israel does not invariably get each and every thing it asks for, but at least we can build up an atmosphere of friendly and mutually trustful relations with public opinion, and a No—not that we always get one—is never the last word. It is always open to us to expound, elucidate and appeal, both to the Government and to the people's representatives, and there is a free and influential Jewry there whose views, wishes and claims have to be reckoned with. Free access to public opinion, and to Jewry, in the countries of democratic freedom is, therefore, one of the main factors conditioning the security of our State and its capacity to absorb immigrants and construct the Land.

Not to recognize this factor is to ignore the vital requirements of the State. Its concern for world peace, and its anxiety for unhindered immigration out of all countries, compel the Government to give perennial heed to friendship with all States whatever their mode of domestic rule. Israel does not forget the stand taken by the Soviet Union in the Assembly of the United Nations on the historic 29th day of November, 1947, nor has it forgotten how the United States of America took its side. It remembers as vividly the aid received from Czechoslovakia during the War of Independence, and the attitude of Poland towards Jewish emigration to Israel, manifestations which without doubt bespoke sincere sympathy with our enterprise.

Yet from one adamantine and infinitely important fact there is no escaping, that only in the countries of democratic freedom, where America is in the van, has our State found or is it likely to find succor from the peoples themselves and the Jewish communities among them.

* * *

In the realm of aid to Israel, the Government has had major

success, of manifold consequence, in the United States and in a number of other democratic countries, and it should be stressed that this aid has come not from American Jewry only, but from the American people and its Government as well. It would, however, be wrong to infer from this that America, so to speak, identifies itself with Israel, or Israel with the United States. No State identifies itself with the next. There is no identity of interests between any two States, and certainly none between a rich and magnificent universal Power in the New World and a small embryo State in a distant corner of the Middle East. America has not undertaken, nor will it undertake, to back Israel in all it does or asks. America has its own considerations and they differ from Israel's, or even run counter to them. Israel, too, has its own considerations and, if they need not run counter to America's, equally they have not to be identical with them.

No external force, be it the strongest, most vehement and wealthy imaginable, is going to decide Israel's needs and values. The foreign policy of Israel is settled according to the fundamental values and the fundamental needs of the Jewish nation, and by no other determinant. But the young State must be careful to avoid the least show of arrogance or pride. There is nothing more ridiculous than a poor man's pretensions. Not only the individual but the people as a whole must learn the secret of 'walking humbly.' But that is not to say that Israel has any cause to cry itself down before others.

There are peoples immensely greater and stronger than Israel, but by standards of ethics and culture there is no call for Israel to admit the superiority of any people whatsoever, and it behooves it to guard its freedom of decision and judgment as the apple of its eye.

But if there is, and can be, no identity between two States, there is and can be partnership, not only political and economic but also in outlook towards the values of freedom, democracy and peace. From that vantage-point, Israel must draw tighter its links with all those countries which also stand upon it. Young Israel has had its victories in the international arena no doubt, but it has also had its meed of bitter disappointments; and it will have more. There are forces unfriendly to Israel even outside the membership of the Arab League, and there is a tendency to appease where it is right to appease and also where it is not. Israel has to make an international effort, considered, fully thought out, with a clear sight of current facts and of what portends. It has to show a large measure of fellow-feeling. We have to know and esteem our fellow's needs and values, even if they do not square with our own. But so long as there are people open to free propaganda, to argument and frank and public explanation, there is still a chance that Israel's utterance will be heard and understood: for it is a righteous word and true, and holds no hurt for others.

Every nation today is beset by cares. Every country is nervous about peace. All feel that the sword of war, sharper than ever it was, is hanging over the heads of mankind. The tragic part is that the nations all want peace, and those who most earnestly pursue it—not necessarily those who proclaim it night and day—must willy-nilly arm themselves to the utmost of their resources and beyond. World War need not be, but no one can guarantee that it will not be. Hence, universal fear. Yet this fear is but one among the grave concerns of Israel, threatened not only with the danger of World War, but faced also by the hostile designs of its neighbors. Effective military preparedness, and at the same time preparedness in all sincerity for sincere peace and cooperation with its Arab borderers—these are the directives of the day which shape Israel's politics in the Middle East, once for all.

No one can positively foresee how the future will turn out. In nature as in history nothing happens by chance; there are laws that govern all things and which none may break, although it is not easy to prove it incontrovertibly. There can be no creation out of nothing, no event is repeated out of the void. Today is the child of yesterday, and the sire of tomorrow. History, like nature, is an unbroken chain of events dovetailed and interdependent. Yet we cannot see ahead, with assurance, what the future may hold. We do not know in their full scope the happenings of yesterday, and much that is taking place today is concealed from us. There are unseen causes, and so the unexpected may befall. It is not enough, then, to rely upon what is known and perceptible, for we neither know nor perceive everything. In man's thinking and in his cognition of what is to come, he must be mindful to walk humbly. Reason bids us be modest.

Yet tomorrow is not altogether a blank slate. In reality, as we know it, there are many points of departure for the reckoning of things to come, and it is not entirely beyond us to predict coming events, though our prediction is neither complete, certain, nor exact. We must be content to foresee probabilities.

The intricate relations between Israel and its neighbors are further vexed by world tension. The disunity among the leading Powers prevents the Organization of the United Nations from decreeing peace between Israel and the Arab States, for all that most of its members in east and west desire it. There is no question that even in the Arab States there are responsible elements which want it too, though their voice is but seldom heard. With all its heart Israel is ready for peace, and yet there is none.

Some of the ruling juntas in the Arab countries are still not resigned to our existence, and see in us an interloper, an irritant, for whom there is no real place in this corner of the world. They cling to the wish and hope to be rid of us somehow or other, sooner or later. So they are preparing for a second round and ceaselessly strengthen their armies. Many of them find it hard to stomach the defeat they suffered in their war against us; they were many and we few; they are persuaded there was some mistake, that our victory was an accident and that in a second round they will rectify the error.

Not all pin their hopes on that. Some hug the fond delusion

that they can dispose of us otherwise: that collapse and economic disintegration await us, that we will sink beneath the press of immigration and security. And not a few are genuinely fearful, although without cause, of our growth and expansion, as though, forsooth, we were making ready to inherit Syria, Iraq and the rest of Arabia. On all these counts the Arab States are arming, enlarging their soldiery, preparing.

Is the danger of war upon us? We cannot, as I say, speak surely of the morrow, but we may utter a word of warning against undue alarm. Satanic hatred of us may be common to the Arab States, but they are far from harmonious inside or out themselves. There are antagonisms between one group and the other, and sharp dissensions within each, so that the power to act is blunted and cannot quickly be tempered. Still we must not therefore suppose that the Arabs are not capable of reforms and domestic progress. It may be that, somewhere, some adventurer will try to set at naught armistice agreements guaranteed by the United Nations and, to a certain extent also, by declaration of the United States, Great Britain and France, and thus possessing a value we will be wise not to discount.

For a long time we shall be in a state which is neither peace nor war. The Arab refugees are undoubtedly the factor which may provoke excesses, mild or major. Here are more than 600,000 despairing and disappointed people who have lost their all and had nothing in return, deceived by their leaders and 'liberators,' and left to fend for themselves in poverty and distress. Yet their wrath and rancor are not turned against the authors of their calamity—the Mufti's men and the Arab potentates, but against the Jews. They indulge in theft, robbery and murder; they engage in smuggling and the black traffic in narcotics; and they are ready for any desperate or crazy errand. Any Arab swashbuckler might employ and exploit them for the vexation of Israel.

Until they are re-settled in the Arab countries, and peace is made between us and our neighbors, they will be a nuisance, an entanglement and the mother of mischief.

* * *

Two of those neighbors, Egypt and the Lebanon, have no objective reason to quarrel with us. Their part in the invasion was largely fortuitous. As to one half of it, the Lebanon is Christian, and most of the Maronites look benevolently upon the establishment of the State of Israel, while the Moslem section is neither anxious nor interested to antagonize its Christian fellow-citizens unduly. If it were not for its fear of the Arab League, the Lebanon would be quick to make peace with us, for there are important political and economic causes which impel it towards friendship and good-neighborliness.

There is no valid ground either for Egypt to persist in its feud and involvement. Between our two countries extends the great desert of Sinai, and there is no room for border clashes. Politically and economically we are not at odds. The reverse is true. In view of the political and social difficulties in which Egypt is laboring, Israel could help it considerably, and peace with Israel would improve its position. Its cultural and economic development, its international standing, could only profit from such cooperation. The relations between us are as old as the hills. Egypt was the first country we met in our journey across the stage of history, that has now lasted four thousand years. The first encounter, in the days of Joseph, was to mutual advantage, though not all the Pharaohs knew Joseph. Egypt's invasion of new Israel was surely one of the rashest, most ill-advised and irresponsible blunders ever perpetrated by those who, four years ago, ruled Egypt.

Our relations with the Lebanon in bygone days were also friendly and mutually helpful. That State now occupies most of the cities of the Canaanites or Phoenicians: Tyre, Sidon, Arvad, Gebal, Beirut and many more. The central city, the one nearest to Israel, was Tyre 'situate at the entry of the sea, . . . a merchant of the people for many isles . . . of perfect beauty.' We have seen how David, and Solomon his son, nursed friendship with the king of Tyre, 'for Hiram was ever a lover of David.' And after the death of David: '. . . there was peace between Hiram and Solomon; and they two made a league together.' Why should not these ties be renewed today?

But the politics of the Arabs are irrational. Certain personalities and their confederate cabals, the fear of a competitor—all these play an important, sometimes a decisive, part, and there is no warranty that Egypt or the Lebanon will act according to its real political requirements and world status. We must, therefore, be prepared for a protracted spell of peacelessness, and strengthen ourselves meanwhile. Time in many things is on our side. Severance from the Arab countries vexes our economic state somewhat but, on the other hand, it enables us to develop our economy without being beholden to our neighbors or dependent on them. In the period of transition, as it were, from war to peace, it is our business to put all our energy into our reinforcement, our growth, and the consolidation of our internal resources. Every year, every month, validates our positive achievements: our wider bounds, the advance of Jewish Jerusalem and its embodiment into the State, are far more convincing than any formal recommendation of the United Nations that is still-born. Even in the question of the Arab refugees, time is not working against us. Two years ago views were still seriously voiced advocating the return of all or some refugees, but now, in the course of time, in all responsible circles of the United Nations, the conviction is gaining ground that the only practical solution of the problem is their resettlement in the Arab countries. Let us not deceive ourselves, however. This solution is not

* * *

yet near to actuality; what is important to us is only what is now internationally admitted.

On the global front and in the Middle East alike, we cannot rely solely on our own means. Without added strength we shall be trampled upon in our independent State, just as we were through all the years of exile.

We should prize the Charter of the United Nations and respect the pronouncement of the United States, Great Britain and France on the preservation of the status quo between Israel and its neighbors. These have their worth. But our whole existence will become a dangerous and vain illusion if it is to rest solely on extraneous foundations. Israel stood upright by its own strength, and will stand firm only if it trusts first and foremost in itself as a Power of growing greatness. There are still men in our midst, with Galuth ways of thought, who lack faith in the moral and practical meaning of our rise nor believe in Jewish strength. They are wont to cite the simple verse which says: 'Not by might, nor by power, but by My spirit . . .,' and they forget that even Moses believed that God brought the people of Israel out of Egypt 'with a mighty hand and with an outstretched arm, and with great terribleness.' Until the vision of the Prophets is fulfilled—and fulfilled it will be!—when nation shall not lift up sword against nation, neither shall they learn war any more, and every folk shall dwell within the family of peoples united throughout the world, until then Israel must unrelieved build up its forces, and watch jealously over its well-being with its own means. For us it is life or death; but they too are misled, and they mislead us, who see everything in power alone. In the balance of power, and of power only, we shall never tip the scales.

With us self-reliance means two things: reliance on our strength and on our righteous cause, and only one of these, of itself, can fail us. All our lives we have believed in the conscience of mankind and in justice. Times without number Galuth shook this belief, when we depended absolutely on alien charity and on the sense of fairness of those who ruled our destiny. Now we depend upon ourselves, yet let us not precipitately give up our faith in the moral forces that are behind us, now that we have become no insignificant Power. Our strength today is greater than in the War of Independence, and it is growing. We must tend it untiringly. But we must not for one second forget that there are even greater Powers, and unfriendly ones, and not in the Middle East only. What happened in our eternal city some two thousand years ago lives on in the memories and hearts of millions, and to this day they do not forgive us for spurning their Messiah, but believe that we have been condemned to wander among the nations evermore. They cannot reconcile themselves to the knowledge that after hundreds of years of wandering we have returned to our Land and have made new our sovereignty and that Jerusalem is again the capital of Israel. There are other Powers in the world which view with disfavor our autonomy of spirit and will not grant the right of any nation to decide its own fate by its own verdict, and arrange its life according to its own needs and desires. They demand one supreme authority, an authority unchallengeable in matters of economy, society and State, and in matters also of spirit, thought and science. Like none other, Israel is, and ever was, a 'stubborn and rebellious' people.

However, in international relations not only material forces and influences are at work. If it be true that conscience and equity are not yet dominant, that does not mean that they do not exist. They operate and are felt in every period of history, today no less than in the past, in spite of universal tension. Our progress during the last seventy-five years, from the founding of the first Jewish village on the banks of the Yarkon to the establishment of the State and after it, owes much to the interest and goodwill which our aims evoked from the finer nations. Nor do we deny the moral and material help, and, since the State, the financial help, that we have had. And remember that this sympathy and aid were accorded us because the nations saw the righteousness of our cause and its balm for mankind. We gain friends because they know that Israel in the Middle East is a stronghold of social advancement, political freedom and the will to peace. This international comfort we shall need hereafter as hitherto, and perhaps even more. Our strength attracts friends too, as it restrains foes, but always we must recall that we are 'the fewest of all people,' we are lonely and separate, not as the English-speaking peoples or the Spanish, or the Slavs or Scandinavia, or the Catholic Church or Islam. No other people couples us in language, religion or race. We are 'a nation one in the earth,' we are not a great nation. Only if we build on the twin bases of strength and justice shall we be delivered. And the two must at all costs be mortised and interlocked in our lives, as the sweet singer of Israel joined them, saying: 'Thou hast a mighty arm: strong is thy hand, and high is thy right hand,' and again: 'Justice and judgment are the habitation of thy throne: mercy and truth shall go before thy face.' This ancient conjunction binds us even today, and perhaps today more forcibly than ever yet. Only because we learned to foster both did we attain statehood, and only if we foster them henceforth will the State be made strong and withstand its enemies, so long as such there be.

* * *

Israel's fate turns much on its external relations and its position in the Middle East. In the forefront of its policies, in both respects, Israel sets the end of maintaining peace. Where peace is concerned, it will not distinguish between countries whose form of government resembles its own, or is agreeable, and those where the form pleases not or awakens doubts. The hostility of Arab rulers will not weaken its will to genuine peace with its neighbors. Israel cannot blink facts that stare it in the face but we have had a long and varied career, and know that circumstances can change, and it is not only the fleeting moment that one reckons. If the Arab States cannot bring themselves yet to accept the existence of Israel, there is no reason why Israel should accept the state of affairs in the Middle East. There are basic motives in history, which sooner or later reveal their force and set it going. The advent of peace between Israel and the Arab States will be hastened if, on the one hand, Israel fortifies itself economically and politically and thwarts any expectation of our enemies that it will stoop under its burdens, and if thus are removed the stumbling-blocks that stand between its neighbors and itself; and if, on the other hand, liberal and democratic processes make headway among the Arabs. And this is bound to happen eventually. The stalemate is not eternal.

These two Semitic peoples, Jews and Arab, share one mission in this corner of the world. The Jew will not budge hence, nor will the Arab change his place. History has pronounced us neighbors; and it is not merely a geographical proximity. There is much nearness in language, culture and history. Cooperation between the Jewish people in its Land and independent Arabia is an historical necessity, and it will come about, for the Arab peoples need it no less than does Israel. It is feasible only on a basis of equality, mutual respect and reciprocal aid. It will convert the Middle East into one of the cultural centers of the world, as in Bible time it was. Each of the two peoples has something to offer the other, without giving up anything of its own. This fertilizing exchange will be a boon to both, to the Middle East and the whole world.

Israel must detect the needs of the hour in all their cruel clarity, but not, on that account, overlook the needs of generations yet to come. The present situation, with all its grievous dangers from which we draw inescapable conclusions, ought not to limit our visual horizons. History makes necessary a Jewish-Arab league, and when conditions are ripe for it, it will come.

But not of itself. We must be ready for it with will and resolution. For all the seeming contradiction, Israel must prepare itself by both military efficiency and spiritual readiness for real peace and cooperation with the Arab people.

On the world scene and in the Middle East, Israel's endeavors must be the same—military and moral, but its destiny depends wholly upon the third domain, the Jewish people in all its dispersion. The State of Israel is a part of the Middle East only in geography, which is, in the main, a static element. From the decisive aspects of dynamism, creation and growth, Israel is a part of world Jewry. From that Jewry it will draw all the strength and the means for the forging of the nation in Israel and the development of the Land; through the might of world Jewry it will be built and built again. A community of destiny and destination joins together indissolubly the State of Israel and the Jewish people. There is an indestructible bond, a bond of life and death, between them.

Israel is like all States: sovereign within its confines and to those confines limited. Its governing authority reaches out to all its inhabitants, and to them only. Only its citizens determine its course and elect its Government; the laws of the Land are binding only on those who dwell in it, and all who dwell in it, be they Jews or not, have equal rights. The Jews who live in other countries are their citizens, subject to their laws and policies: the State of Israel has no authority to speak in the name of those Jews or to direct their actions. Touching the relation and link between Jews overseas and the countries where they live, Jewish citizens are no different from non-Jewish, any more than Jew differs from non-Jew in Israel. But the framework of government, at any rate outside the totalitarian countries, does not hold all of human context and relations. A totalitarian State will not recognize man's independent worth, and its dominion over its citizens is unbounded: it dictates thought, faith, appreciation, art, all human behavior, private and public. In those countries, like the rest of the population, Jews are denied all opportunity of free self-expression and, against their will, are riven from the Jewish people, its past and its future.

In countries based upon freedom of man and his free choice, loyalty to the State is not in conflict with the citizen's loyalty to values, relations and institutions over which his State has no control, but which are in the right of the individual. There, Jews may be citizens, enjoying rights and assuming obligations on a par with other citizens, and of their own volition may define their Judaism, and their Jewish connexions, not merely with the Jewish community where they are but with world Jewry also. A Jew's attachment to his people does not lessen his attachment to his country nor is lessened by it. Jews who deny their people, as there have been in all countries in every generation, do so not because they are more loyal citizens, but because they are less honorable men and have neither the self-respect nor the inner strength to throw off the complex of inferiority which clings to inferior men belonging to a small nation.

The State sees itself as the creation of the Jewish people and as designed for its redemption. It sees Jews throughout the world as one nation, now and always. The roots of the unity and continuity of the Jewish people, despite its scattering among the nations, are set not only in the all-embracing inheritance of its past, but in an historical partnership of destiny. This unity and continuity make no discord with the civic allegiance of Israel's people overseas to the countries of their residence, while that residence lasts.

* * *

Israel is the outcome of the timeless vision of redemption of the Jewish people. It is not the only State to arise to freedom as a national dream come true, after the struggles of a national movement. In the nineteenth and twentieth century many countries were restored to independence in Europe and Asia by the momentum of revivalist ecstasy which remade and emancipated subject peoples. But the State of Israel was uniquely reborn. For behind the veil of dreams elsewhere was the solid fact of a people living in its own land, even if under alien rule. By that the national movement was sustained and to accomplish its aim had only to break the foreign yoke. That done, its aspiration to nationhood was achieved in full. Not so with Israel. With us the vision lived only within and on itself, out of the people's soul; and all the hard facts were arrayed against it. The people was strewn and scattered far and wide; the land was ruled by strangers. And not only that. It was occupied by strangers, and ravaged and made desolate. Other than spiritual strength, nothing could have kept the vision alive.

Nor does the State mean its fulfillment. For by far the greater part of the people is still divided among the nations, and so the State is not yet the consummation but only the instrument of redemption, and its principal means. But by its establishment the State gave the vision body and basis of realism, and surpassing all else became a force to weld together and unify the Diaspora.

Theodor Herzl, creator of the Zionist Organization, found the perfect definition of Zionism, as he understood it, though it has been forgotten and forsaken by most of the workers in the Movement. He said: 'Zionism is the Jewish nation on the way,' and he meant the Jewish people on its way back to its Land. This profound truth was garbled soon and turned into the meaningless dictum that the Zionist Organization was a State on the way. There is no such thing as a State on the way. A State either is or it is not. When Napoleon said of his army that it was France on the march, that meant something, for everywhere the army went, there France was. But the Jewish State could not come from within 'the Jewish nation on the way.' It could not be created out of zero. Its embryo and its evolution over the years came not out of the Zionist Organization but out of the flowering of the Yishuv, its growth and its fruition. It has been built by the immigrants of all the generations of Aliyah and it will be rebuilt hereafter and made strong and firm by immigrant hands. Only Aliyah, 'the Jewish nation on the way,' as Herzl described it, is the constructive and corporeal essence of the Zionist dream. This is the truth, and the whole truth, of Zionism, that without Aliyah the Yishuv would not have been, without it the State would not have been, and without it the State will not endure.

The Zionist Organization never was and can never be an organization of immigrants; it did not oblige its members to take part in Aliyah, and does not oblige them now. Of course, a Zionist might settle in the Land, and not a few exercised the privilege. But it was not because they belonged to the Organization and it was not only members of it that came. Immigration is older than the Organization, and indeed gave birth to it. It was immigrants of many decades and sons of the Land who laid the real foundations of the State. The men who came out of walled Jerusalem over seventy years ago, Salomon and his comrades; the early pioneers from Hungary, Stampper, Raab and theirs, who built the first Jewish village of Petah Tiqvah; the members of Bilu from Russia, and the original pioneers of Rumania, who built Rishon, Gedera, Zichron, Rosh Pina, Hedera and Metullah eighty years ago—these were the founders of the new Yishuv and the founding fathers of the State. The 700,000 and more immigrants who have come since the State's beginning —it is they, hand in hand with the old Yishuv, that have built up the State during these last four years, and transfigured Israel.

This is sure and certain but it is not all. Alone, without the help of the whole people, the immigrants could not have come, or built up the Yishuv, or established the State: they could not have maintained it in the past nor will they be able to maintain it from now on. Aliyah to Israel is not like migration to America or any other immigrant country. Without that help, economic, political and moral, Jewish immigration would have been impossible for a long time to come. For this was no empty land, though its soil was neglected and in decay. It had a population too, not one of yesterday, but of hundreds of years. Those who were not Jews did not welcome Jewish immigrants and often resisted them by force. Nor was the land a political void; it was under foreign rule, of Turkey, and had been for four hundred years, and after that it was under British rule for thirty. Neither Turks nor British hated the Jewish people, but the Administration did not always smile upon Jewish immigration, and each at times forbade it.

But not only the alien population and Government stood in the way. The country itself was waste and wild. No Jewish immigrant, whether formerly or now, could by his own exertions overcome the factual, physical obstacles and hindrances, not merely those set by the Administration or mirroring the country's indigence. Constant aid was required, economic, political and moral as well, in the first phase from the Chovevei Zion and the great philanthropist,* and from the Zionist Movement and the Jewish people as a whole in the last fifty years.

The help extended before the Zionist Organization was formed was sporadic and casual; it lacked any concrete basis of ideology or policy until that Organization was created by Herzl, the prophet of State Zionism. His claim and object were to organize and muster all Jewry for the fulfillment of the dream. But even powerful enough to marshal the whole people. Instead of 'the Jewish nation on the way,' there appeared the Zionist Organization. It was, I repeat, not an Organization of immigrants or of with the great personality of Herzl, the abstract idea was not acolytes for immigration, and that was at once its moral weakness and its material strength. It was an Organization designed to spur on the Diaspora to accomplish Zionism, to mobilise the people for the educational, political and economic work without which immigration would have failed, as failed all efforts in

* Baron Edmond de Rothschild.

earlier generations to return to the Land and build it up again. The fusion and partnership developed in the last fifty years between the pioneers of Aliyah and fulfillment and the Zionist Movement made possible the Yishuv and encouraged its steady growth, its crystallization cultural and political, its economic advancement and its fitness to stand up to interference and onslaught, to tackle the difficulties inherent in a beggared land and in the ways of Galuth Jews, townsfolk speaking diverse tongues, and without sovereign, national background.

The Zionist Movement cherished an ambition which had no seeming basis in fact of Land or people. And so it was strenuously opposed by influential Jews: the ultra-pious who did believe in redemption but not by human agency; the organized workers who saw no improvement in the lot of Jewry save through world revolution; assimilationists who denied the very existence of a Jewish nation; and, above all, the multitudes of the indifferent, those without faith that the redeemer vision was real and could be fact. The greatest victory of the idea of Zionism over the Jewish people was the State's establishment, and in that the Movement had no small share. Without its work in education, administration, politics and finance, the Yishuv could not have existed nor the immigrants who joined the Yishuv have reached their mark. Precisely because the Organization was not one of immigrants or would-be immigrants it could attract large sections of Jewry, and at times most of it; and in many countries all their Jews. With complete moral right, it could count the State a fair reward for all it had striven and struggled to do, an undying testimony that its conception was utterly true. But it will make a fatal error, it will fly in the face of ideal truth, if it looks upon the State as chattel of party or Movement and not as belonging to the whole nation. Because the creation of the State was a triumph not for Zionism only. It is a tremendous turning-point in Jewish history: from the instant the State was born, except for a wretched few to the Left and to the Right who damn the

Covenant, the entire Jewish people has rallied round the State in prayer for its peace, security and grandeur, and stretches forth faithful, helping hands for its reconstruction and progress. A Zionist Organization that now becomes a screen between itself and the Jewish people is repudiating its own source and soul.

Immigration now is not limited to the ranks of the Organization nor does our political and financial aid come only thence. The State has succeeded in unifying the Jewish people compactly as no other agency did in its past. The people's love and succor to the State can be given to the State only, and they are a precious and irreplaceable asset which we must guard closely. But the Zionist Movement must be their first guardian.

We have come not to the end of the highway to redemption, but only to its commencement. Even after the gigantic total of immigration and settlement in the first four years of the State, outdoing all done in the previous seventy, we have rebuilt only one-fifth of the Land and brought together less than fifteen percent of the people.

* * *

The immigrants yet to come will be the forthright masons of the State, and complete that highest purpose. But then too, even though the State now exists, ingathering and edifice are not to be accomplished unless the whole people takes part.

Lets and hindrances that balked the newcomers in the years before the State, still block the way, although in different shape; some of them verily are more sinister and dangerous than formerly we knew. There is no strange lord now, we are sovereign in our own Land. But there are world forces which do not like us and have yet to accept Israel and its independence. The struggle we have yet to make calls for array of all the political forces of Jewry.

The non-Jewish population is no longer check or brake upon our colonization and growth. The Declaration of Independence and the war that came after changed demography in a fashion radical and revolutionary. Within our own confines we are independent, confident and free, and no element will be our enemy. But across our borders glower strong States which hold themselves still at war with us, and make no secret of their intent to fall upon us again and wipe us off the earth. For many a long day we shall need the moral and material help of all Jewry.

There is no comparing our capacity today with the Yishuv's before autonomy came. Now every acre of the State is in our hands; its budget in a single year exceeds the sum of all the budgets of the Zionist Organization in a jubilee, and yet with its own resources it cannot gather strength to swallow mass immigration at the pace and on the scale which have now become not possible only but imperative.

No one yet can tell whether the ingathering is to mean the bringing together of the whole Jewish people in Israel, or most of it, or only some parts of it. Only a few nations are wholly or nearly concentrated in their own countries, the fortunate ones that were at no time parted from them. The dispersion of Jewry has no replica in any history except its own; there was a dispersion before the Galuth of today, and not only one before this second Galuth but even one before that again.

Earlier than Babylon Jews were dispersed in Egypt, and 2,500 years ago in the sixth century BCE there was a Jewish garrison in the south of Egypt. Before the Second Temple lay in ruins, from three to five million Jews dwelt in the Roman empire. In Alexandria alone there were about a million, more than were then in Jerusalem. But never was dispersion as widespread and as fretted as in recent centuries.

Murderous Hitler drove the center of Jewish gravity from the Old World to the New. In spite of the New World's cultural and political legacy from the Old, in science, literature and art and in Christian tradition, it was a new society of nations that came to life on the American continent and in Australasia, unlike in many basic attributes to that in Europe and Asia, and it did not necessarily follow, so far as Jews were concerned, that all conditions and circumstances of the Old World would be reproduced in the New.

Zionist ideology—I mean not the vision as old as Jewry itself, but the political ideology of the Movement—crystallized among the Jews of Europe in the nineteenth century, and was nourished not a little by demonstrations of anti-semitism, and by the nationalist movements and politics of the European peoples. Every attempt automatically to transplant European inter-relations to America by a formal ukase of mutatis mutandis is likely to stultify itself. The New World has been built up, in the last few hundred years, by immigrants from many countries who have to a large extent merged with one another. The position of the Jews in America differs from that of English or French Jewry, although these too enjoy equality of rights. All political relations and conditions in America diverge from those of European countries. You cannot graft a political ideology born in the circumstances of nineteenth century Europe on to the circumstances of twentieth century America. What happened in Europe can, of course, happen in America, but it need not, and Zionism must not rest upon so doubtful and unpleasant a conjecture.

As before the State, so now too, the motors of Aliyah are anguish and vision, but the coming of the State has created a third, which in the course of time may replace the first, and that is the magnetism of the State. If only the State is made strong and durable, if only it creates a full and noble way of life equal to that of any other country, materially, morally or spiritually—and it can be done—then perhaps the Jews in lands of no distress or pressure will also find in Israel all the comfort and freedom they now enjoy. They will find here, besides, rare values and assets which Jews have nowhere else: Jewish independence and all its rich expressions in economy, politics, culture, science and art and in international status. But for that, for the ingathering, for realization in full of the material, political and cultural autarchy of the State, we need, as always, the creative pact between State and people.

* * *

Israel is become an inseparable part of the being and experience of the Diaspora. It has enriched the life of the nation and of every Jew as such. A Diaspora without the State, and moreover a State that has sloughed typical poverty and contentiousness, is conceivable no longer.

Equally we cannot conceive the growth or missionary fulfillment of the State without the whole of Israel's people in partnership. Between the two is an interaction, obligatory, organic, historical and vital, that is without like or precedent in the relations between nations and States. For the two in essence differ.

The Jewish people is not an abstract notion, or just a collective name for myriads of isolated and scattered individuals in various countries. It is a conglomerate whose actuality, will and common destiny are not open to question. But in the nature of things it has no fixed or rigid framework of uniform, planned effect; in each point of dispersion the conditions differ and conflict. The territorial groups are not fitted into a single pattern, for every Jew, like every non-Jew, is subject to the laws and policy of his country, although his ties with his brethren depend upon his free-will and personal inclinations. It was this difficulty that Herzl met when he wished to draw up the Jewish people and gather it together anew and independent in its own Homeland. That is why he brought the Zionist Organization into being, founding it upon voluntary association and voluntary effort, with no hint of coercion or imperial duty. It voices the combined historic will of the Jewish people in its longing to be redeemed. For fifty years it led the people back home and bore, at times alone, the main responsibility for establishing the State.

Now that we have a State, it is inevitable that the Zionist

Movement should be changed in cardinal ways: the content of its activity is not the same, internally or without.

What was this former content? It was first a struggle of ideas inside the Jewish people, for it proclaimed an end not to the liking of most of the Jews, even though the beginnings lay deep in their past, their literature and faith. Let us recall how they responded. Many saw it as something harmful, a blemish, imperilling Jewish existence, profaning Judaism, an ineffectual and impracticable fancy, over-sanguine and reactionary. To pietists, it was a bitter blow to religion and a repudiation of belief in the Messiah; perversely, they believed in redemption, but in a heavenly and not a prosaic one as the Zionists preached it. The assimilationists felt that it was a danger to Jewish rights, to the recognition of their civic equality and the status they had won, or aspired to win, in their countries of adoption; for them, to aspire to a Jewish Homeland was proof that Jews are not loyal citizens of their own countries. Socialists considered it a reactionary movement which diverted the minds of the masses from the political or class war which was to improve their lot and give them equal rights. Jewish socialists too believed in the redemption, but by their creed it must come through a world socialist revolution, and when the world was mended by the kingdom of socialism, so would the Jewish weal be mended without further ado. The enlightened, the men of affairs, took issue with it as a vain dream and a bleak Utopia: would the Jews return to an archaic land, wild and in ruins, inhabited by Arabs, under Turkish rule? Would townsfolk turn into tillers of the soil and Europeans settle in an Asiatic country? The traders will not allow it, the Arabs will not agree, they said, and so forth.

Our generation finds it hard to visualize the Jewish reality of forty or fifty years ago, to measure the spiritual inertia, the inertia of ideas, with which Zionism had to contend, and how diametrically it was opposed to the outlook of the Judengasse of those times. It fought against cultural forces and habits of thought which swayed the Jewish people, liberal and reactionary, orthodox and dissenter, rich and poor. It had its own internal differences of view, serious and trivial, profound and superficial, but, on the outside, the Movement in all its divisions, factions and trends has had to thrust against an Iron Curtain of prejudices and of spiritual and intellectual resistance. This struggle of ideas, fruitful and fertilizing at least within the Jewish people, engaged the Movement all its days.

There was a second struggle, the political one, outward-turning. We need not go back to Turkish times, when congressional Zionism first saw the light. For my present purpose, it will be enough to deal with Mandatory times. Zionism was not only a weltanschauung, a philosophical or religious conception, independent of time and place and circumstance; indeed for many Zionists it was in essence a Jewish philosophy combating assimilation. It had also a territorial and practical object, the Land of Israel. That Land was in turn conditioned by certain circumstances, political, demographic, economic and cultural. The Movement worked to undo these circumstances or so transform them that it might accomplish its desires. It embarked upon colonization, and had to skirmish on the political front as well, for the Land was no vacuum where a man could do what he wished, as he would beneath his own roof. It was under a Mandatory administration, uniquely devised, like all Mandates after the first World War, but enveloped in conditions not duplicated in any other Mandate. Great Britain did not govern here, as it did in Rhodesia or Ceylon, without responsibility toward an international body and with no obligations toward the inhabitants. The Mandate recognized the status of the Zionist Organization, and included specific undertakings in respect of a National Home and Jewish immigration and settlement, and the Arabs. Within this quadrilateral—Jew, Arab, Great Britain and the League of Nations, the Zionist Organization had its clearly defined place. Its task was to wage unending war, both when Great Britain was reasonably inclined to fulfill her promises to the Jews as the Jews understood them, and also, and particularly, when she strayed from them, wittingly or not. This contest, under changing conditions and in varying forms, kept the Zionist Movement at stretch for thirty years, and to a great extent the internal differences and arguments, the party strife within the Movement, turned on how the contest was fought, its substance and its form. Congresses, meetings of the Executive Committee, the Zionist Press, all found their principal topic in debating relations with the Mandatory, cooperation with it or opposition to much that it did, and how to show resistance. All the time, the Movement was sharing vigorously in the tasks of colonization and education in the Land, yet that did not bother Zionist thinking so much as did political disputation and argument. The struggle of ideas within the people, the political struggle with the Mandatory and the League of Nations, these were the core of Zionism until the State emerged. Then everything was revolutionized, although by force of habit and stagnation many Zionists still project a mentality that is altogether purposeless.

The State is. Perhaps this seismic and fateful fact has not yet entered deeply enough into Zionist consciousness, and it may be that the Movement has not drawn all the inferences from it that it should with respect to Zionist acts and ideas. Veteran public workers, so long used to tilting in the Movement's twin lists—inner and outer, keep on at their tourney even now, all unaware that the Government now under attack is not the Government they once fought; that the Jewish people which so many would-be conquerors harried in vain, is no longer the same; that the ways of the Movement before the State do not go with the new reality.

What has changed?

Jews, we saw, opposed a Jewish State for many and various

reasons, of religion, progress, socialism, feasibility, comfort, concern for rights in the Diaspora and the like. There were even Zionists, as in the Young Hashomer, and other personages, to whom the idea was anathema, because of belief in the 'forces of the morrow,' or on grounds of political realism, or owing to pacifist principles. But as soon as the State became a fact, this opposition melted away and vanished, and not only in the Zionist ranks; the people far and wide, save for negligible splinters of rejection and apostasy, greeted the State with pride and enthusiasm. Other than the Judaic faith, there has not been these thousands of years a force for uniting and solidifying all strata of the people throughout the Diaspora like the State. I cannot too often declare that the State is the greatest conquest of the idea of Zionism over the Jewish people. Every Zionist has right and reason to laud himself upon it and rejoice in it, and with deep and willing satisfaction to accept the consequence. Zionists are no longer a militant missionary sect within the nation, but the whole nation is solidly united around that central and historic undertaking of the Movement which the State is. That which Herzl with his amazing personality could not do half a century ago, the State has done: the people of Israel entire is at one and bound together in love and care for the State. That which the idea could not do, action has done. And now it is clear that Jewish hostility was mistaken from the start, and that only impatience and littleness of vision, and want of faith, made it seem as though the people sought not a State. Worse was the people's impotency to believe in its coming. We have had false messiahs, though the slur is not apt to all who at different times boldly trumpeted redemption. But we have had hopes and yearnings whereof frustration brought us grievous pain. So the people dreaded new failures and new disappointments, yet always, in its heart of hearts, longed and pined and burned for restoration, independence and sovereignty in Israel. The fearful of disappointment and failure were not only those styled anti-Zionists or non-Zionists, but also unquestioned and veteran Zionists, whether they shrank from advocating a State or their whole Zionism was that advocacy. With the birth of the State, all doubts and fears, all objections and hesitations disappeared; the inner flame, dimmed for thousands of years in the bosom of the nation, shot up, and the State became at once the focus, the center and cincture of the life of the Jewish people.

It is essential for the Movement to take in these changes and comprehend that it, the Jewish people and the State now form together a close-knit and indivisible unity. Each of them, State, nation and Organization, is still a separate organism. The State is a State. The people is still scattered and lives on in Galuth, and is not identical with the State, any more than the State is in practise identical with it. The Organization is neither State nor people, and can never take the place of either, but between the three there exists a mutual bond, necessary and welcome, an historic nexus. That one should exist without the others is fantastic, and there is no setting one over against the other or the twain. What we can and must do is strengthen the association by love, by trust and rewarding toil.

* * *

For long the builders of the Yishuv were alone, a handful, almost forlorn. Years were to pass before a new Yishuv would arise. We had not then even the Balfour Declaration, we lived and labored under a corrupt and unruly Turkish Government, the Land was given up to internal disorder, we were a tiny oasis in a wilderness of strangers. Even in our own villages Arab labor outnumbered Jewish. Every little acquisition of land involved endless trouble and took years. Every attempt to expand collided with internal difficulties, interference from our neighbors, animosity from the government. Immigration came in driblets. The gates were closed, the land belonged to others, and a foreign Power, whether Turkish or British, reined back our progress in settlement.

Then the great upheaval. Every inch of the State is now in our gift. At the gates stand Jewish officers. Hundreds of thousands of men and women, out of all the sick and subject exiles, are returning to their Land, with heads high. Hundreds of new settlements are being founded in a fever of making. The ways of the Land are changing, its needs growing with a tempo and in dimensions unheard of, all our previous concepts and manners outdated and challenged. If we do not cultivate new manners to suit the demands, the needs, the difficulties and the prospects of our new life, we shall miss the mark.

For decades we collected pennies to buy a scrap of earth. Now we have millions of dunams to dispose of, but bare and waste. The unforeseen happened: we had to fight for our independence, for our very breath, and, when the fighting began, the Arabs fled the country and it was virtually emptied of its former owners. Pre-State Zionism could not have conceived of such a thing, much less been able to tackle its consequences.

Then we affirmed: this is not the State of the 600,000 or so Jews who live in it, but a State destined for the whole people, and its doors are open wide to every Jew. The number added to us since that day, only four years ago, is greater than of those resident before the State or at the moment of its birth.

The Zionist Movement has a rich and glorious record in its struggle of ideas within the people, in its political campaigns on the international level against the Mandatory, the League of Nations, even the United Nations, in caring beneficently for the Yishuv and developing it. For fifty years the Movement has been working in these three dimensions, not unrewarded. Now comes the whirlwind of history, and sweeps the State of Israel into existence. The whole 'order of creation' in the Movement and in the Jewish people is upset. No longer internal, national clashes, no longer battles of politics with the Mandatory, no longer Aliyah by certificate and the buying of land by dunams, but an ingathering such as the chronicles of Jewry never before recounted, liberation of all the territory of the State, upbuilding of the Land faster and further than any other folk has ever ventured, and a problem of security to daunt the lionhearted.

Habits of mind, ways of work, methods and measures of yesterday's Zionism are antiquated now. You cannot cover the nakedness of grown men with swaddling clothes.

We have done great things, tomorrow we must do greater. We have triumphed over horrific dangers, we must yet face worse. But our strength is waxing and the Movement now rests on the pillars of State and people. The State has become the main and keenest instrument to fulfill the vision of Zionism and to forge the Jewish people into unity. No father is jealous of his son, no teacher of his pupil; so too there is no cause for the Movement to envy the State. Nay, the worth, the strength and potential of the State are, I say it again, the mightiest victory of Zionist thought and perception. The Movement must bring itself freely and in affection to recognize the State as prime and supreme among the bringers of redemption. But in this very superiority of the State is also the source of its limitations and contraction. Its sovereign authority is confined to its own borders and its writ runs only among its own citizens. More than four-fifths of the Jewish people are still—and who knows till when?—beyond those borders. The State cannot interfere in the domestic affairs of the Jewish communities in the Diaspora, cannot give them instructions or make demands of them. For all the dedication that marks the State on its path to resurrection, and in the tasks laid upon it, it still must behave as does every State, and its power outside its frontiers is scant. It is just there that the Zionist Organization, founded upon free-will association and voluntary effort, has the occasion and ability to do what the State neither can nor may. That is the advantage the Organization has over the State, and that is why the State, being set up, did not bring the reign of the Organization to a close, but rather has infinitely enhanced its responsibility and mission. The State and the Movement complement each other, need each other, and it is by joint endeavors that they can and must spur the Jewish people to realization of its dream.

The Movement draws its vigor and authority not from the State but from the great historical truth whereon it stands, and in which it believes, the truth of the age-long mission and dedication of the Jewish people and its Prophets' foresight of national and universal salvation. The duty of the Movement now is to take its rightful place within the scattered remnants of Israel with all the strength of its vision, its fealty and its performance.

* * *

The link with the Diaspora does not signify that its Jews will shape the State in a Galuth likeness. There would be no State, unless the builders and pioneers of the Yishuv had taken heed to change from top to bottom the structure of life and the economic, social and cultural foundations of the Jews in the Land. In most walks of life the people in the Galuth had been weaned from nature, from the soil and labor. Perforce, nearly all had become townspeople, their earning drawn from those poor callings which for some reason were unpopular among the ruling caste, or from the typical sources of livelihood of the middle class. An independent nation must take root in the paternal soil, cultivate it with its own fingers, and engage in every vocation that a free existence requires.

Amid the 155 millions who inhabit America, the majority of them tillers of the soil or workers in industry, there is space for five million Jews as well to make a living, principally in commerce, as office-workers and in the free professions, or in certain branches of tailoring. But we in Israel cannot exist on that kind of economic or social basis. In the creation of the new Yishuv, a social revolution was seething from the outset: the Jews were now returning to be, in great majority, a people of workers as every autonomous people is. It is for the State to widen and deepen this metamorphosis. The nation must get its food from its own farms, must develop basic industry and establish a network of communications on land, at sea and in the air, that will make it economically self-sufficient.

Man in Israel is being transformed, with enhancement of the values and dignity of labor, economy and society, of culture, morals and the spirit, which are foreign or failing in the Galuth. And there is a transformation of nature too, which we are commanded to carry out in our Land, changing its landscape, uncovering its hidden secrets and treasures and restoring its desolation: we shall augment its yield and fruitfulness, we shall make its desert bloom and shew forth its magnificence and glory.

The loss of independence, our expulsion from the Land and the wars that endlessly visited it since we went forth, wasted Israel, impoverished its inhabitants and spoiled every good part of it. The rich coastal plains were buried under mountains of sand that drifted in from the sea. Rain and wind tore the earth from the hills and bared the bleak rocks, when once woodland and vineyard were uprooted and destroyed by brutish men and their beasts. Bounteous valleys, renowned for plentiful harvests in bygone days, declined into malignant swamps, and the steppes of the Negev, barren for the most part ever since Creation, lost even the last little blessing which an industrious folk had conferred upon them ages ago.

For hundreds of years this process of ruin and neglect went on, until there came the sons and builders of the Land. Then, still, a foreign government and alien landlords could hamper those who sought to reprieve and rebuild the Land. Not till the State was established were the chains snapped and upon the generation of Aliyah and halutziuth dawned rarest vistas of creativeness.

The profound changes in Israel before the State, the deeper changes since, are not restricted to economy, society or nature. They leap to the eye everywhere and extend day after day. The State has brought about a spiritual and cultural change of tremendous consequence, still partly hidden from view. Its story will be unfolded in the course of time; but already, because of it, the self-discernment of Israel is completely altered, its discernment of the world and the world's discernment of Israel.

Millennial wandering and dispersion could not destroy the Jewish people or blot out its peculiar likeness. But they could and did deface and distort it: Dependence took away our freedom of thought and spirit, stamped upon us an inner vassalage, whether we knew it or not, and narrowed our perceptions. A nation surrendered to alien charity finds it hard to see itself, and others, as it should.

Revival of sovereignty is forming anew our personal character and our outward lineaments. We are drawing near and nearer to the national root and source, that legacy of the spirit which Bible times bequeathed. And we are becoming more and more free citizens of the great world, and heirs to the universal human estate of all generations and peoples.

The hand of time has dealt with us, as with other nations. No people today can or should be what it was a thousand, or two or even three thousand, years ago. Israel's restoration to autonomy is not aimed to bring back an ancient splendor. The State sets its face resolutely toward the future, but a future sustained still out of the nation's fountainhead and bathed in the light of the past. The past belongs to us, not we to the past; the past dwells within us, not we in it. The past lights up the present, and history explains today's event by yesterday's. But it may also be that the present lights up the past, and the State's establishment is such an illumination.

No man of sense can doubt further that we were a nation all through the long years of the Galuth, but a nation sui generis, unlike other nations. Nor are we like them now, nor will be hereafter. Because of our individuality we were granted to prevail and we shall be again. But perhaps only the Jews believed that all the rest of the nations were like one unto the other, and so with naive simplicity divided the world into two: Jews and Gentiles. I doubt there is a single nation in the world but regards itself as different from all others, and rightly so. The difference is all-pervading and everlasting; the only variation is in the quantity of the differential, and its strength.

The otherness of the Jewish people, the peculiar virtues of its goodly spirit and its cultural, religious and ethical creativeness from Moses to Ezra, made it an eternal folk and gave birth to one of the most vital facts in the evolution of man's spirit, that is imprinted clearly yet upon the lives of a large segment of the human race.

Springing from a unique spiritual and moral quality, this otherness persisted even when independence was lost. But in the Land it was not as it was after the people went into exile. Galuth changed the character and standing of the people from the aspect not only of politics and territory, but of spirit and culture too. Exile contracted the horizon of the nation, and shackled its spirit. The fount of creativeness did not cease to flow, nor did it flow less, but its waters were dammed within Ghetto walls.

Even when we trod our soil of old, the Jewish genius was one-sided and limited. We did not engage in science or metaphysics. We did not develop the art of painting or sculpture, and our prowess in technology, administration and the art of war was not great, though we were never counted with those who deny the life that is and condemn the world as it is, as did the wise men of India and the first Christians. Galuth made our spiritual and cultural world even smaller, and the understanding of our past was warped.

Rabbi Johanan ben Zakkai, who pleaded with the Roman conqueror for Yavneh and its scholars, may well have saved the life of Israel by his plea and made strong its spirit to withstand the troubles and misfortunes which were to dog its steps in a long and weary vagabondage. But the greatest of his disciples, Akiva ben Joseph, the most remarkable figure in Jewry after the destruction of the Second Temple, was not content with Yavneh and its scholars; he espoused the uprising of Bar Kochba for independent statehood. It was only when that last despairing effort failed that the Jewish people became the People of the Book. The great void left by freedom's forfeit, the ruin of the Homeland and of the rounded life of independence, it tried to fill with interpretations upon interpretations of interpretations of the Bible, that Bible born in a cradle of sovereignty and Homeland and in an especial periphery of nations. It could no longer view the Bible, or comprehend it, as first it was handed down.

The fate of the Book was as the fate of the people. This immortal scripture, telling with wondrous art the story of a young nation, a nation extraordinary in upbringing, in inner conflict and spiritual wrestling, in painful collision with external forces and alien influence; this Book that reflects the longings, the thoughts and vision of our people in a mirror of its great Prophets and poets; that brings to mankind an evangel of religious and ethical truths whereof the light will never dim; that has in it words of wisdom and logic, outpourings of the soul, with which little in universal literature can compare for profundity of expression, forcefulness of phrase, echoes of the deepest vibration of the heart—even it, too, was torn from the soil where it was planted and had thrived, and, with its people, was consigned to the material and spiritual dungeon of the Ghetto.

The Song of Songs, a bold and nobly eloquent hymn to nature

and to love, was diminished to an allegorical disputation between Knesseth Israel and the Almighty. David, unrivalled knight and victor among the kings of Judah, was portrayed by the homilists as a magistrate busy day and dusk adjudicating secondary questions of ritual. And not only the homilists and scriptural commentators, but even Philo of Alexandria, pupil of Greek philosophy and culture, composed a midrashic homily in exquisite Greek, giving to the Torah allegorical meanings of which the ancients never dreamt.

When freedom went, the Jews found themselves under two conflicting authorities: one, their own Jewish legacy; the other, the rule of an alien people, with all the administration, economy, culture and laws peculiar to it, and its special power to repel and attract.

This dual subjection, and the mental, spiritual and material agitation it caused—there you have, in a sentence, the whole of Jewish history in exile. Not always, not everywhere and not at all times must there needs be antagonism between the two authorities. There were periods in the Middle Ages, and there are countries today, where neither the State nor the nation of Jewish domicile sought or seeks now to hinder the Jews from living as they wish, from cultivating their own special values. But at no time or place has the basis of Galuth life undergone change: the immutable law is that the Jew, so long as somehow he stays one, is under this dyarchy, and his life and soul will surely be rent asunder in his distraction between the two parts of it.

The Jewish part is pent in a little nook of the spirit, and lives mostly on the past. The other, well-nigh illimitable, lives on the present and gazes forward; deliberately or not, it encircles the life of the Jew completely and determines his status and education, his culture, livelihood and every-day conduct. This contrast gives Galuth Jews their character in their own eyes and the Gentiles.' The Jew who wanders between ghetto and assimilation, between extinction and self-extinction, between escape from the world and escape from himself, at times retreats altogether into himself and feeds his soul on crumbs from a Jewish legacy that is in dead banishment. We must marvel at the astounding vitality and constructive power dormant in this immortal people, when even in such travail its creativeness does not cease, albeit far divorced from fact and fluttering in space without solid grasp of the demands and needs of a life ever renewing itself. At other times, the Jew flies from his lonely and outcast habitation and beats upon the portals of an alien people, beseeching to be taken into its culture and therein remade. In the first case, he renounces the world and all that is in it, and finds solace in the feeling of superiority of a Chosen People; in the present, and in this world, things are bitter and bad for his people, but it is destined in recompense to enjoy all good things in the world to come. In the second case, he is undone in the sight of others, corrupts his special character, elbows his way into a realm which is not his, accustoms himself to it and finally becomes someone else. At best, if he succeeds, he is absorbed and assimilated. If he fails, he is disgorged and humiliated, and has lost all his world.

This tug-of-war of authorities has never ended in Israel's exilic history, nor will it end, so long as Jews live in foreign lands and cannot or will not be wholly assimilated within them, or cannot or will not return to independent Israel. It has confounded Jewish outlook upon the world, and the world's verdict upon Jews.

* * *

The indictment of the Jews throughout the ages has striven to show that they were different, for ill and not for good, from all the nations, and that 'it profiteth not . . . to suffer them'; if there is aught good in them, it was taken from others. It was levelled first not in the nineteenth century or in the Middle Ages, but already when the Second Temple stood. It is found in the writings of Egypt, Greece and Rome of two thousand years ago and more. Nor did Jewish apologetics begin today or a generation ago: it is discernible in Second Temple days in the letter of Aristeas, in the Jewish Sibyls, in the works of Philo, of Josephus Flavius and the other Jewish authors of the Hellenistic period. And all who came after them tried to prove that all that was good sprang from Judaism, and that the wisdom of Greece was not the fruit but the flower.

In our exile we saw the world with eyes of fear, strangeness or envy, disparagement or self-decrial, for we had no equal share or parity in it. Perhaps we could not understand other peoples, garbed as we were either in gloomy feelings of inferiority or an unblushing sense of superiority. At best, again, we used to copy others out of deference, or sneered at their behavior and their ways, just because we had not come as far. Little, however, as we understood them, they understood us less, for their experience of nations had no satisfactory rod with which to measure us; for them we were not different only but deformed.

Now that we are independent and in our Land once more, full member in the family of free peoples, we need be sensitive no longer to the charge, we are under no compulsion to indulge in excuses. Unbound, we can and must see ourselves, in the past and in the present, as we really are with all our blemishes, our faults and shortcomings, and mend what there is to mend. Let us not show off to others the wealth and beauty we have, or have not. Let us cherish our own opulent inheritance and take to ourselves as well the finer values and assets of humanity, for we are part of humanity and nothing human is alien to us. Let us fashion our lives, our culture and our character ourselves, loyal to the great enlightenment of our past and, having done so much to create and expand them, let us share wholeheartedly in the universal truths clasped by the great thinkers and teachers of our times.

Two parallel concepts of civilization, prevailing in the world at large and in our special corner of it, exemplify and render patent the anomaly in our cultural thought in Galuth. I mean the concepts of 'the wisdom of Greece' and 'the wisdom of Israel.' But I do not speak of the pronounced and serious contrasts of character and talent between the two small peoples which, in their day, played so large a part in civilizing the world. I speak of discords of connotation, deep and essential.

When we talk of the 'wisdom of Greece' we think of the all-embracing philosophy of the great Greek sages. We think of the theories of Thales and his disciples on the principles of nature; of the philosophy of Heracleitus, Pythagoras and Parmenides on cosmic being and its evolution; of the laws of Hippocrates on the effect of climatic factors upon man's health; of the Dialogues of Plato on justice, sanctity, courage, love, education, the State, the laws, the government, and those highest axioms we call ideas; of the treatises of Aristotle on logic, science, metaphysics, poetry and ethics; of the works of Theophrastus on plants and the natural sciences; of the mathematical essays of Euclid, Archimedes, Aristarchus of Samos and others.

When, however, we speak in the Galuth of the 'wisdom of Israel,' we think of the literature and research that treat of Israel's past, its faith and writings. Writers on Jewish philosophy only bethought themselves of the theological metaphysics of Israel's scholars in relation to Judaism, and to this very day have found no room for Baruch Spinoza, our greatest philosopher in the seventeenth century and among the profoundest thinkers of mankind, although he too dwelt on the past and problems of Judaism and, three hundred years ago, foresaw the coming of the State.

* * *

Again we are under one authority, our own. This 'our own' is no fence confining us and dividing us from the rest of the world, but behind it, in freedom and equality, we are become citizens of the world in the political and economic sense, and in the spiritual and cultural as much. In Galuth we were stepcitizens, refugees without a land, needing a 'Nansen' passport which makes no distinction between one nation or State and the next. Own children now of an independent Homeland, autonomy restores to us the crown of inner identity and unity, and our link with the world and its culture is a link of equal partners.

Research and education, all intellectual endeavor in Israel are in vain if they do not take in the total world—research into atom and stars, the realm of plant and animal, the secrets of earth and seas, the winds and weather and all that nature stores in the heavens above and on the earth beneath; man's exploits from his first appearance on life's scene, his struggles, his ups and downs, his wrestlings with himself and his fellow-men, interminable and ubiquitous, as individual and as member of society. Our literature will be in vain no less if it does not compass all the inventions of human thought—scientific, artistic, philosophical, religious and poetical, all ever written in Hebrew or by Jews, and about Jewry, in a foreign language.

The study of Homeland and nation will occupy a special place. The antiquities of Israel, its geology and topography, its natural resources, its waters and climates, its seas and shores, its plant and animal-life, its prehistory; the shifts and changes in all these in the aftermath of the movement of peoples, of conquerors and wars—students from all civilized peoples have busied themselves with these subjects for generations. The abundant and polyglot literature on the Land is second almost to none in richness among countries of comparable size. Let us give full credit to scholars, of other nations and our own, who have thrown much light upon the beginnings and character of our Land. But not until the War of Independence and the dawn of sovereignty was opportunity amply given to spy out the Land which now belongs to us, and to us alone.

Only a people that lives in its own land, independent, endowed with modern cultural and scientific means, challenged to unveil the Homeland's secrets for its present and its future's sake, can decipher the hieroglyphs that are entombed yet in the depths of its soil, its many tells, the crevices of its rocks and its desert caves, and lay bare the wealth hidden in the bosom of our earth, and in our rivers, our lakes and seas. For thousands of years we have read in the Bible of 'a land whose stones are iron, and out of whose hills thou mayest dig brass.' But not before the Negev was liberated by the Israel Defense Forces did we indeed come upon the mines of copper and iron, or approach the rich deposits of phosphates and other minerals whereof we have not yet traced mention in that Book of Books which, saving the Land itself, is the most trustworthy source of knowledge of the Land. And we are only on the threshold of discovery.

Study of the Homeland is bound up inextricably with pioneer Aliyah for the peopling and progress of Israel. It helps to expand colonization and is helped by it. A nation's every scientific endeavor is an integral part of the economic, political and social course of its life.

It is not otherwise with study of nations, especially of a nation, and its cultural and spiritual creativeness, in the land of its birth. For centuries men of letters, Jewish and non-Jewish, have engaged in it. With the non-Jewish, it was often twisted because of Christian and anti-Jewish motives, influences and impediments which have no concern with enquiry into the truth. Understanding of the basic and determining phase in Jewish history, when the character of an eternal people was formed and there came about all but a few of the undying glories the Bible tells of, that period from Egypt to Babylon, from Moses to Ezra, demands of us a spiritual nearness and historical intuition, freedom of thought and intellectual self-assertion. It is not easy to find such qualities as these in the learned of other races, or even in Jewish savants who serve two masters and have not felt what it is to be a Jew free in his free Land.

Commentary upon commentary has been written on the Book of Joshua. They had their value; they gave clarity and a name to many obscure things and dark places. But the commentary given by the battles of the War of Independence, the great light that new sovereignty shed upon our past, will outshine them all.

Only a generation upright again in its Homeland will with clear vision and instinct read the Book of Books and understand the spirit and soul of its progenitors, who toiled and fought and conquered, wrought, suffered, sang and loved and prophesied within that Homeland's bounds.

Enquiry into the truth admits no bonds nor limits, and in exile the spirit of our people is still constrained. In independence regained it will cast off all species of servitude, outward and inward, that have narrowed, confined and gnarled its actions.

* * *

The giant undertaking of cultural development by Israel in its Land, no less than the ingathering and the rebuilding —again and again I must say it, cannot be carried out with the internal resources of this young and straitened State. Like the absorption of immigration, like expansion of agriculture, industry and communications, so the cultivation of the new wisdom of Israel, in its general as in its limited meaning, is impossible without the devoted and constant cooperation of the whole Jewish people. Again I say, the State was made not for its citizenry, but for all the nation of Israel, for those, too, who do not purpose to dwell in it. Free Israel has enhanced the prestige of Jews in those lands as well where there is neither will nor inclination to Aliyah in numbers. The victories of our Army, the conquests in agriculture, industry and developmental enterprises, stand to the credit of every Jew in the world, and the fair breeze of statehood blowing from Israel has in it refreshment for every Jewish soul wherever it be.

DAVID BEN GURION

In scientific research, physics, biology, sociology, politics and history, in all branches of art, literature, religion and ethics, we must develop a dependable partnership between the scholars and creative forces of the Land and those same Jewish elements in the Diaspora. Only by this common effort can we accomplish the mission of culture and education which history has set upon us.

We cannot, we may not, do without the cooperation of any Jewish group whatsoever, in the Old World or the New. And if that be so in the material and political spheres, how much more is it in the spiritual! Strength and greatness of spirit are not conditioned by number, and Moses our leader was worth sixty thousand of ordinary men. But sometimes number changes at a certain point into quality. Outside Israel, there is not at this moment a single Jewish community to equal the Jewry of America in material, political and financial power, in cultural and spiritual power. The whole future of the Jewish people, the destiny of this State, rests on close and faithful collaboration between Israel in its Land and Jewry in America. But the interdependence will not last if it represents only a partnership of money and politics. There must also be a partnership of pioneering and intellect, a partnership of body and soul, joined by the choicest youth and scholarship of American Jewry, to build, together with us, the State and the civilization of Israel.

Pioneers coming to Israel from over the sea, hand in hand with its sons, will make its deserts verdant. Among them the place of young American Jewry will not be wanting. Above all, we shall need the scholars and intellectuals, so as to magnify the new 'wisdom of Israel' whereon all our economic, military and educational undertaking will be founded.

'Is a land born in one day? Is a nation brought forth at once?', asked the Prophet Isaiah. Not many asked themselves the question on the 14th day of May, 1948.

Since that day, in these brief years, the young State has performed breath-taking feats and launched superlative ventures, at a speed and in proportions to which our history offers no parallel. But—let there be no delusion! There is still work for the State to do in the Land, amidst the people, in the east, in the world; and the work is still in its very beginnings. Not behind us, but ahead of us, are the difficulties and the exertions, the trials and the dangers. Ahead of us, too, are the campaigns and the conquests, the splendors and the portents still to come. Long and hard is the way—'and it shall be called the way of holiness.'

STATESIDE

AMERICA AND WORLD FUTURE
Published in 'Palestine and Middle East.'
October 1942

Returning from a prolonged visit to combatant America, I bring with me a redoubled conviction of that great country's historic mission for the future of mankind, for the liberty of all men and all nations. Immense natural resources and wealth, a genius in organization and action, productive and technical capacity unsurpassed, the military potential of 300,000,000 free souls possessed of the highest ideals of citizenship and civilization, the prerogatives which geography bestows on a vast continent set between two boundless oceans, and, above all, the invincible resolve of their leaders, echoed by an overwhelming mass of public opinion, to fight to the end and to total victory—all these elements have combined to make the United States the central force in this planetary civil war in which the freedom of humanity is the stake—or its enslavement.

But for all its ever-growing strength and influence, America does not underrate the importance of the part of other nations. There is especial esteem of the two main forces, Great Britain and Russia. America knows how, isolated by the collapse of France, the major share of her arms and fighting men forfeited, Britain yet displayed an epic and immortal heroism and by an unwavering stand saved the world. If the Battle of Britain had not been won, neither Russia nor the United States would have had respite to attain the stage of defense and attack, and by now Hitler and his satellites might have been masters of the earth. America knows, as surely, that since Hitler's treacherous invasion in June 1941, the Russian people and its army have shown an example of desperate and gallant resistance that counts no sacrifice too great. America also knows what it must itself do and the preparations are on a scale far beyond imagination's grasp.

This is still the phase of mobilization, America's actual and potential might is not yet felt sufficiently on the many fronts. But every day its giant war production swells and with it the military power on land, at sea and in the air which will ensure victory final and utter, if neither easy nor early. President Roosevelt's tremendous program for 125,000 aeroplanes in two years, and scores of thousands of tanks, ships and guns, is well on the way to achievement and in many respects the outcome already betters the plan. Millions of men are being called to arms, trained and equipped with the most modern weapons, and will soon be ready for battle. In Detroit I came to see for myself the meaning of Roosevelt's words 'the arsenal of democracy' and how they are becoming an immense fact. Flying from the United States back to Palestine, I saw evidence of this amazing build-up in the huge stockpiles and storehouses of war that have arisen so swiftly upon the sands of Africa within the short time since I crossed that continent last year on my way to England. And this is only a sample and a start.

Moreover, America is making ready not alone to help win the war but to settle the peace. To all men and nations there is come the noble tidings of its determination to ensure a new kind of security, a political and social order to prevent recurrence of catastrophic warfare, to remove dangerous causes and factors of human tensions and conflict. The awareness grows that all this terrific effort, bloodshed and sacrifice will be to no avail unless politics and society are rebuilt from their foundations. It is an awareness that grips not only the American labor movement, whose influence has been increasing steadily, but also liberal and progressive thought in all classes. This hardly means that reactionaries and isolationists have altogether vanished. The nation as a whole, however, in its overwhelming majority recognizes that the holocaust that blazes today was not kindled only by the selfish and shortsighted policies of those who ruled Europe after the first World War, but that America itself bears a large measure of responsibility for withdrawing into the shell of its hemisphere after the victory of 1918 and stultifying the fine effort of President Wilson to create a new world that would ensure international peace.

We must be chary of predicting the political future of a great nation with many complex problems, differences and divergent tendencies. Yet there seems to be every ground for confidence that America will not revert to a majestic aloofness but rather take an active determining, even decisive, part in shaping a new and democratic world of all the nations of five continents and the seven seas. This time America will not shun that great charge which history and current circumstance have placed in its hands, for the sake of humankind and its own vital interests.

It is providential that at this fateful hour for freedom's survival throughout the world, and for the survival of Jewry, there is in America a community of five million Jews, beyond the clutches of tyranny and free to fight against the arch-enemy of man. Already they have made a brilliant answer to democracy's roll-call: the part they have yet to play should be incomparable in devotion, intensity of purpose and self-denial.

In America itself, this community is the product of the gathering of immigrants from all parts of the world and of all social strata, and, like the general population, it exhibits a variety of divisions by origin, position and so forth. But it can be as solidly united in its fundamental issues and ideals as is the great American nation. The existence of minority groups does not make it less generally conscious of its bond with the Land that is being remade to so large an extent with its own support and share. It looks to the National Home to protect the future of the Jewish people, to redeem its exiles and give it, in the free world, a place where distinctively to enrich civilization. Organized Zionists and the myriads outside the Movement are virtually one in this, that they know that the free world of tomorrow will be but a sham if it does not restore civic equality to Jews everywhere and salvage our uncounted flotsam of the war.

From these origins developed the program of Jewish action in war-time and the peace to follow which was adopted with no dissent by the Biltmore Convention, held in New York last spring, of all Zionist parties and organizations and individuals. Underlying it is the conviction that what was once termed the Zionist maximum has now become the essential minimum. This program may well offer a rallying point for the concerted endeavors of all American Jewry. My consultations and contacts with leaders of the American Jewish Committee, the Jewish Labor Committee, B'nai Brith and other bodies encourage the belief that we shall see a unified and concentrated effort on behalf of Zion.

The war effort of Jewish Palestine, the quota it has already given in production and man-power, have inspired feelings of pride and respect in American Jewry, and won appreciation, too, from American leaders who regard the National Home as a stronghold of democracy. In his most recent message to the American Zionist Convention President Roosevelt said 'When the United Nations are at war, it is fitting to note the substantial contribution from Palestine to the United Nations war effort. This contribution is due greatly to the work of your organization in the past and present.' We find equal recognition in the unanimous declaration of the Convention of the American Federation of Labor just ended: 'The Federation traditionally affirms its sympathy with one of the most tragically persecuted of all minorities, the Jewish people, assuring them of its warm support for their just claims and declaring its complete sympathy with their national aspirations towards collective security after the present war. Since the start for such security has been made in the establishment of the National Homeland in Palestine, we reaffirm our belief that the United Nations owe the Jewish people the continuance and maintenance of this Homeland as a relief from inhuman persecution, as a guarantee of their cultural unity and continuity, as an instrument of their legal and international standing in the Court of Nations, as restitution of their national dignity, honor and creative energies. We urge the United Nations to remember in the postwar period the claims of the suffering Jewish people. We extend fraternal greetings to Labor Palestine and to the Histadruth. We look with pride upon the Jewish National Home as the pillar of democratic strength in the Middle East.'

TO AMERICA'S JEWRY
An Address delivered to American Zionists in Jerusalem, September 3, 1950

My friends, we are in the vortex of a great revolution, Jewish history is at the flood of its making. We have fought a war, we have established a State, and are building it up, but peace still eludes us; still, with security unsure and the future naked, our main purpose is unachieved. For long we must defend our freedom and frontiers against an enemy forty times as numerous in an area 220 times as large. For centuries the land had been neglected by foreign lords; the Jewish-Arab war almost led to its utter ruination, and at the end of it only one dunam in twenty was tilled. We must absorb hundreds of thousands of immigrants who can find salvation only in Israel, and in the same breath erect a new culture and society of which no Jew shall be ashamed. On us depend the prestige, the self-respect and dignity of all Jewries.

We need time to do all this. We hope that what the United Nations has done under the aegis of the United States to stop aggression in Korea may strengthen world peace. My personal belief is that there will be peace for the next three or four years at least. But we live in troubled times, and it would be sinful not to use that tranquil interlude to affirm and fortify the security of Israel and bring home every Jew in the lands of Islam and Eastern Europe, for whom the choice is death imminent where he is or independence in his own free country. It means the reception and integration of six hundred thousand in the next three years, and it will cost not less than a billion and a half dollars. The State is ready to find a third of this staggering sum, the rest must be mobilized by the Diaspora, especially in the United States. If I summarize the history of the State during the last three years, at the risk of repeating much that you already know, it may help to explain the difficulties of what we have to perform during the next three and yet how possible performance is.

The three years have been perhaps the most remarkable in Jewish history. When they began, the land was still under a Mandatory Administration, but one near to dissolution. The attitude of Jews and Arabs alike, and the pressure of world opinion, put prolongation of the Mandate out of court, morally and politically. The Assembly of the United Nations decided on partition into a Jewish and an Arab State. The Arab leaders in Palestine and the spokesmen of the Arab States in the United Nations made it clear, however, that they would resist the decision. It meant war, and it was. We were then six hundred thousand. The Arabs here were twice as many. We had 300 settlements, they 700. They occupied a continuous tract from north to south; of our settlements most were islanded, especially Jerusalem, that is the very heart of us. Their villages on every side of it, they could approach it from Nablus or Jericho, from Hebron or Jaffa; our solitary ingress was from the west. Yet worse, landwards Israel was beset by forty million sworn enemies; it had but one link with the world, the seaway, and that was blockaded by the British Navy in considerable strength to intercept Jewish manpower and arms. Before the Arab war broke out we had 10,000 rifles, 2,530 machine-guns, 766 mortars. That was all.

Against us was a population where almost every man carried a gun. There was the Arab Legion of Trans-Jordan, financed and trained by the British and officered by them, which was actually in Palestine. Arabs from Palestine and Iraq were training in Syria and the Lebanon with fellow-Arabs from those two

States. On November 30, 1947, the morrow of the decision on partition, seven Jews were murdered on the highways. Two days later the Jewish commercial center in Jerusalem was set on fire under the eyes of British policemen who prevented the Haganah from defending it. Yes, the British were still here then: the High Commissioner himself told me they had not less than 75,000 troops, but when I protested against the invasion of armed bands from Trans-Jordan and Syria, he said he had not the power or means to check it. At best the British were neutral. They did sometimes help the Haganah, but more often the Arabs. To be fair, it was on the whole a fight between Jews and Arabs. We tried our utmost to localize it but it spread. Our outlying settlements did not escape attack, but mainly the roads were our vulnerable front because not one was entirely fringed by Jews. We were, of course, outnumbered; and the British Services denied us arms. Yet we had to get arms, and it was a terrible job.

You can buy arms anywhere, but only for dollars, and only Governments may buy, but there was no Jewish Government. Our friends throughout the world, notably some of those present today—to whom the Jewish people is inexpressibly beholden—helped to find the dollars. Certain Latin American States were willing to buy on our account. But it was hard to run the blockade, and up to the withdrawal of the British on May 15, 1948, we only managed to land one shipload of 4,500 rifles, 200 machine-guns, and twenty anti-aircraft guns.

The opposing force was thrice the size of ours. But we were superior in this: we knew we were fighting for our lives and for the Jewish future. Until the British left, no Jewish settlement, however remote, was entered or seized by the Arabs, while the Haganah, under severe and frequent attack, captured many Arab positions and liberated Tiberias and Haifa, Jaffa and Safad. The first town to fall to the Haganah was Tiberias. That was on April 18. We told the Arabs there they might stay, if they gave up their arms and fought no more. They chose to go, encouraged by the British, who took them away in trucks to Syria. The same thing happened elsewhere. So, on the day of destiny, that part of Palestine where the Haganah could operate was almost clear of Arabs. Our rejoicing had its concern. In the streets of Tel Aviv jubilant choruses greeted the proclamation of the State, while in a secret place the Haganah's improvised General Staff was receiving news of Arab columns advancing into Israel from south, north and east. As the British Mandate ended at midnight, Tel Aviv was bombed by Egyptian aircraft. We were invaded by seven Arab States—Egypt, Trans-Jordan, Syria, the Lebanon, Iraq, Saudi Arabia, the Yemen.

There were thus two stages. The first with the British still here: it was principally war between the Palestine Jews and the Palestine Arabs, although the Arabs had much aid from neighboring irregulars. We had ourselves, nothing else, and by and large the Haganah did splendidly. The second stage, a seven-fold irruption, and its defeat, fell into two periods over 61 days, divided by a month's truce. The Arabs would not prolong that truce. Then our new-born Defense Army scored a signal victory in the central region, occupying Lydda and Ramleh, which meant that Jerusalem was free and could be supplied. For the first time in eighteen centuries, Jewish Jerusalem was again territorially one with the Jewish hinterland, its long Arab encirclement over.

The second truce was laid down by the United Nations to be observed until peace is made.

At that juncture the Egyptians had been holding much of the South and the Negev, and Lebanese troops a slice of Galilee. The Security Council had given us right of free passage in the Negev to our settlements and our columns. But the Egyptians flouted the decision and barred the way. We waited for three months. Time and again we applied to the United Nations Commission to enforce its will. But it was as powerless as was the Assembly to implement partition. There was no option: in mid-October our Army went forward. The campaign lasted no more than seven days: the whole of the South and most of the Negev, including Beersheba, was re-occupied, and an Egyptian flotilla sunk off Gaza, in perhaps the first naval engagement in Jewish history, without loss of a single Jewish life. A brigade commanded by a Canadian Jew cleared Galilee in two days of the notorious Kaukji's last guerrillas. Then again trouble started in the Negev, the Egyptians still recalcitrant, and our Army driven to perform what the Security Council could only preach. By the end of December, though British planes intervened on their side, the Egyptians were ousted and constrained to sign an armistice. The Lebanon, Trans-Jordan and Syria quickly followed suit, our new frontiers were guaranteed, and, by the Trans-Jordan agreement, a great central area was gained without a shot being fired, and so, too, the corridor to Jerusalem.

This has changed the face of Israel utterly. In March 1947, the population of Palestine was 1,850,000—614,000 or 33% Jews, 1,200,000 or 64% Arabs, and 36,000 Greeks, English and others. We took the first Israel census in November 1948, not reckoning all the Arabs, since Galilee was still embattled: the population then was 782,000—713,000 or 90% Jews and the rest Arabs. At the end of 1948, hostilities over, it was estimated at 867,000—760,000 or 87% Jews and 107,000 or 12% Arabs.

The Arab flight from Palestine began as soon as fighting broke out, and, as the Haganah went forward, it became a rout. The State fell heir to an almost empty territory which the Mandatory wilfully left in chaos, cut off from the world, without even telegraphs or posts. There was no handing over of authority, such as the United Nations wished. In the trenches, almost, we had to create public services anew, and welcome the forerunners of the ingathering. And now began what counts more, I hold, than victory and State.

At the end of the first World War Palestine held less than 60,000 Jews. During three decades of British Administration

464,000 entered, say a yearly average of 15,000. The bulk — 300,000 or 65% — came from East Europe; West Europe sent 78,000 or 16%; Asia, 40,000 or 8%, the New World 8,500, and Africa 4,000.

Statistics may be boring, but these I give now express the very meaning and mission of the State, the task of world Jewry, how the Yishuv was made and all our recent wars were fought and won. From May 15, 1948, till the end of last June, more than 415,000 Jews joined us here. Again Eastern Europe led, with 207,000 or 50%. Asia is next, with 100,703 or 24%, then 64,800 or 16% from Africa, and 2,700 from the New World. That is to say, ten times as many each year from Eastern Europe as before, not 10,000 but 100,000 annually, from Western Europe four times as many, from the New World five times, from Asia 34 times, and, most remarkably, from North Africa 233 times. To every three Jews of 1948 a fourth and then a fifth were added. Tremendous as the change in numbers is, the change in quality was hardly less significant. Previous immigration had brought its own means of establishment: only ten or twenty percent of the capital necessary to settle the newcomers had to be collected by national funds. Labor immigrants, as you know, were strictly regulated under the Mandate and the White Paper—though any Jew with at least £1,000 might enter. Now, with a few exceptions, our immigrant has neither cash, profession nor trade.

Manifestly, immigration hereafter will come more and more from Moslem Africa and Asia and from countries behind the Iron Curtain that will permit departure: in simple fact, from where the Jews are being, or are doomed to be, destroyed physically or spiritually, or both, unless they can escape. In North Africa, from Egypt to Morocco, through Libya, Tunisia and Algiers, there are about 620,000 Jews in that miserable plight.

Persia, second to the Yemen, has the most wretched Jews. Hearing of the State, they left their villages and flocked to

Tehran. There they had no place to lay their heads but the graveyard, and in the Jewish cemetery they are still living today, after months of waiting for a plane or a ship to take them to Israel.

There are hundreds of thousands of other Jews without a choice, and so, therefore, are we in Israel. You, my friends, will have your own say, but we in this little country still engirt by enmity, still the target of superior forces, are threatened on radio, in the newspaper, and by public utterance that soon the second round will come; from England and America they are getting planes and guns and tanks and instruction in their use. We have to spend millions—I am sorry I cannot tell you how many—on defense, but it is proportionately more than the United States, incredible though you may think it. Yet no Jew can be turned away.

It may be politically irrational, it may be economically impossible, but what are politics and economics when you want to save your son? So long as one more Jew may be rescued out of Rumania—and it must be soon, as we all know only too well—how, on moral grounds, dare we shut our doors?

I am not guillotining discussion on our immigration policy. You are entirely free to challenge its wisdom and continuance. We, too, differ about its details but are unanimous on the principle and see no alternative to it. The risks are patent, and they are not only economic: many fear that this influx from poor, undeveloped, uncultured and uneducated sources will lower the intellectual and spiritual level of the Yishuv. It is very serious, particularly from the defense angle. That we could stand up to seven Arab armies, better armed and trained, was because of our moral and spiritual advantage. If we lose that, we lose all.

Already we sense an acute need and shortage of skilled labor, of engineers, chemists and architects, physicians and nurses, and hope that the western Jewries will send such specialists to help us, for a time or always. But already the new immigrants have revealed positive features of great value. Jews from Morocco, Turkey and elsewhere in the Orient have proved our finest material. Some 14,000 young recruits, in the main Orientals, underwent an intelligence test of the American type. 31% were graded of high intelligence, 38% medium, and 31% low. Of the 3,000 sabras among them 49% passed high, 28% medium and 23% low. Of eastern Europeans 37% were high, 32% medium and 31% low; of Orientals 39% were high, 30% medium, 30.5% low. The longer one is in Israel the higher the intelligence. Two thousand five hundred men were tested after six months' stay: the result was 21% high, 30% medium, and 42% low. After a year: 34% high, 30% medium, and 36% low. After two years: 35% high, 32% medium and 33% low. After five: 36% high; from six to ten years: 51% high and only 24% low. So we can be sure our immigrants will ascend intellectually as time goes on.

One more experiment. Only men graded high are admitted to examination for commissioned rank. In the second such examination, more than 52% of the total entry failed, but only 42% of the sabras.

Just now, however, as I say, our economy, our Army and educational system are in trouble, and badly in need of western skills.

To disabuse you, nevertheless, of any lingering notion that Oriental Jews are no builders of a new country and its life, you will see tomorrow a little of what is being done by them on the land.

Our agricultural work began some seventy years before the State. The grandest pioneers of eastern Jewry, then intact, made it possible. Thousands of American Jews were among them. And perhaps not all of you know that the first Aliyah in mass after the Balfour Declaration came not from Russia or Poland or Galicia, from nowhere in Europe, but from America. I was in America during part of the first World War, after the Turks had expelled me. I came back to Palestine with 4,000 Jews in uniform to fight for it, to help to free and rebuild it. They were of the first pioneers. The first Halutz organization, to train young people for the land, was established in America in 1915, and by it the Jewish Legion was formed.

For seventy years they came, these pioneers, from Hungary, from the Old City of Jerusalem, from the Western Hemisphere, discerning truly that in a return to the soil lay national revival. To the same end all the resources of the Chovevei Zion and afterwards the Zionist Organization, all the millions of Baron Edmond de Rothschild, were devoted. In seventy years we founded 290 farm settlements, we cultivated 700,000 dunams or 10,000 every year, and settled, all told, 100,000 Jews on the land.

In the two years since the State, we have founded 240 new settlements, settled 82,000 on the land, brought 2,100,000 new dunams under the plow. Just think! Thirty times as many settlements, seventy times as much cultivation, thirty times as many settlers, all this, almost incomparably creative as it is, done by Jews from the Yemen, Morocco, Turkey and eastern Europe, at it on the land and in the factories, building villages and towns, planting forests, making roads, repeopling the Negev, restoring Jaffa, Lydda and Ramleh, Beersheba and Beisan. Many cannot read or write, but they learn quickly. Those of military age receive their Jewish and general education in the Army; the others in evening classes or from their children. Good soldiers these, and fine workers. Even in a day's journey you will see how land and people are changing: the land re-clad after centuries of nakedness, the men and women—after centuries of misery, serfdom and degradation—now free citizens proudly making their own lives, rebuilding their own country.

In your dossiers is a summary of our development plan for the next four years, envisaging, among other things, a farming community of between a fifth and a quarter of the whole. The plan is designed, in the first place, to guarantee full employment for both a domestic demand and a larger export that will reduce dependence on foreign currency, and so balance our foreign trade to the utmost. We are not wedded to total planning, believers in a wholly regimented economy and society. We see vast opportunities here for private initiative and private capital—throughout industry, in a large sector of agriculture, in communications and building. But in our still retarded circumstances, the pace and size of immigration require some broad pattern of employment, housing, and the husbandry which is cardinal both for absorption and defense. Our communications by land are, as you can see, virtually non-existent; by air and sea they are precarious. To survive, we must grow all our food from a soil we can defend: the Negev, more than half of our land area, is still bare wilderness. Without a chain of border settlements to fend off attack, we shall not be safe.

Thus was Jerusalem saved not by the Army alone, but by the settlements about the city, that for months defied the enemy to reach its gates.

And now to something of equal urgency—immigrant housing. If you had asked us three years ago to solve the problem, I doubt we could have answered. Today I can say what was done and how, and what remains.

During 1946 and the first few months of 1949 we put right 65,000 houses that had been wrecked in the fighting, and abandoned: in Jaffa, Ramleh and Lydda, in Beisan and Migdal, Acco and Haifa. That sufficed for the first inflow, but for the second wave we had to build, and by the end of last June 40,000 new houses were built. It had to be done and, incredulously, we did it.

Assume another 600,000 immigrants in the next two or three years, with some 80,000 immigrants yet not housed and 20,000 in unsafe buildings. To construct housing for this 700,000 will cost about 150 million Israel pounds; over the same period, the outlay on settling 50,000 more families on the land will be close on 250 millions.

Details need not concern us here, but astronomic though they may sound, my figures—and my confidence—are not mere wishful thinking. I speak of facts and compulsions. In two years we have absorbed more than 430,000 souls, all but a third by now integrated and in permanent employ. It had to be done and it was. Where once four settlements were founded, two hundred now rise. In twenty-four months we have placed 40,000 families on the land.

These are unvarnished facts. And the Jews of Iraq and Persia must come to Israel unless you take them in America: that, too, is the plain fact.

We are embarked upon our greatest adventure. I know only of a single precedent, and it was on a grander scale: the building of America, the conquest of the Wild West, by pioneers who found, to their great good fortune, more riches, greater expanses, fewer political dangers than are our lot. But we have initiative, the enduring spirit and a practical idealism as strong. Our high enterprise must be speedily concluded, for neither history nor our unhappy brethren can tarry, and who foresees what may happen next year or the year after anywhere on earth, or more specifically, to the Jews of Rumania or Morocco?

The task is beyond the 650,000 of the State. Already, to bring 400,000 others home, we have spent half a billion of our own, and I pledge as much again towards the sum of one and a half billion which the next three years will call for; the billion must come from the Diaspora, through appeals or loans, or both. How best to tackle the job, whether it can be done, even whether it should be tackled at all—that is what we are met together to discuss.

Affluent Jewry throughout the world, in the past decade, has lavished hundreds of millions to help the stricken. We chose the constructive way, and proved that the best way to help the Jews is to teach them to help themselves, that generations of oppression, death of material and intellectual resources, do not disfranchise them from partnership in the great auto-emancipation—to become a free and sovereign people, a moral factor for mankind, enhancing the honor of Jewry among the nations. We were driven to prove it by the dynamos of necessity, and a vision of self-help. Misery, want and ignominy can only breed their like; vision alone is ineffectual, divorced from reality it dissolves into a chimera—idle fantasy—empty phrases. But suffering and vision together can alter the very looks of this planet. That is the secret of our success in Israel before the State, of our victory in the world at large. Choice we had not, but we had vision. We fought with our backs to the wall, but for a tremendous stake, and we had to win.

That was the secret of America's greatness. The oppressed of the Old World fled there, but they brought a vision with them, as do our immigrants today—a vision of a new life in freedom. They did wonderful things, and so can we. We have begun, you must aid us to complete, the seemingly impossible. Gentlemen, I say to you, in this supreme moment of our history, when we are wreathed in victory and yet our sternest trial is to come, we must not fail.